MORE Somerset MURDERS

NICOLA SLY & JOHN VAN DER KISTE

The History Press

First published 2011

The History Press
The Mill, Brimscombe Port
Stroud, Gloucestershire, GL5 2QG
www.thehistorypress.co.uk

British Library Cataloguing in Publication Data.
A catalogue record for this book is available from the British Library.

ISBN 978 0 7524 5742 0

Typesetting and origination by The History Press
Manufacturing managed by Jellyfish Print Solutions Ltd.
Printed in India

CONTENTS

INTRODUCTION & ACKNOWLEDGEMENTS

When we collaborated on *Somerset Murders* (published in 2008), we were faced with an embarrassment of riches in finding we had far too many cases for one volume. Ongoing research since then has added to the list of those which we would have liked to cover, hence this second collection.

The majority of murders fall into a few particular categories, being motivated either by domestic incidents which have gone out of control, sheer greed, drunkenness, or perpetrated by killers who were mentally unbalanced and not completely responsible for their actions. These chapters, covering a selection of violent deaths between 1832 and 1934, include a cross-section of all. There is Eliza Pain, a maidservant little more than a child, stabbed by fellow employee Charles Wakeley at Worle in 1839; William Wilkins, an elderly shopkeeper fatally assaulted during a robbery on his premises at Nempnett Thrubwell in 1851; Ann Parker, who fell victim to her weak-minded husband Josiah at Wells in 1857; Albert Miles, stabbed in a drunken frenzy in a Bath public house in 1884; and Violet Woolmington, a young wife of only three months when she was shot dead by her husband Reginald at Milborne Port in 1934.

As always, there are numerous people to be thanked for their assistance. Our spouses, Kim Van der Kiste and Richard Sly, proved invaluable as proof readers and in offering their usual moral support. (We owe a particular debt of gratitude to Richard, who went on a two-day sortie to Somerset and took most of the photographs.) We must also thank the two barristers, who wished to remain anonymous, for guiding us through the chapter on Woolmington (1934) and ensuring that we fully understood the complex legal ramifications behind the case. Last but not least, we must thank our editors at The History Press, Matilda Richards, Beth Amphlett and Jennifer Briancourt, for their help in bringing this collection to print.

Every effort has been made to clear copyright; however, our apologies to anyone we may have inadvertently missed. We can assure you it was not deliberate but an oversight on our part.

Nicola Sly & John Van der Kiste, 2011

ALSO BY JOHN VAN DER KISTE

ALSO BY NICOLA SLY

1

'MY POOR WIFE IS CRAZY'

Churchill, 1832

George and Maria Spurlock had lived happily together in a cottage in the village of Churchill for several years. In 1828 she gave birth to twins, the last of their seven children. She had recovered quickly from her previous confinements, but this time she was very ill, and never appeared quite the same again. She suffered from increasingly severe depression, and when the twins were about a year old she cut her wrist in the first of several attempts at suicide. After a surgeon had visited her and warned George of the danger that it could easily happen again, he took care to try and keep all knives in the cottage out of her reach. However, no matter how vigilant he was, he could not stop her from obtaining further weapons elsewhere and over the next two years she repeatedly tried to kill herself. Although she had previously been a good mother to the large family, now she began to attack the children for no apparent reason, hitting them hard on the head with a brush or anything else which came to hand, when they irritated her.

Churchill village. (Authors' collection)

By the summer of 1832, her mental condition was deteriorating even further. She took to harming herself regularly with a knife, attempting to cut her throat, and repeatedly complaining of 'confusion in her head'. On one occasion she tried to drown herself. 'My poor wife is crazy,' George sadly told the children.

Matters came to a head on the morning of Friday, 10 August 1832. George asked her if she would bring his clothes downstairs. When she did so, he examined them and then told her that she had not mended his breeches, as he had asked her to do, and she admitted she had not.

'You are so lazy, you'll do nothing for me,' he snapped. In view of her recent behaviour, it was an unwise remark to make, but his patience had obviously worn thin by this time. She said nothing, but got up and went out of the room. A few minutes later she returned, brandishing a knife. Her alarmed daughter, Elizabeth, asked her what she was going to do with it, and her mother immediately struck her across the forehead with it.

George leapt to the defence of their small daughter and put his arms around her. Maria then set about him with the knife, as Elizabeth ran to the door, shouting, 'Murder!' This attracted the attention of Frederick Rowe, their neighbour, who came running to the room. He managed to take the knife out of Maria's hand without suffering any injury in the process, and pulled them apart, but she took hold of George again, and they were clinging on to each other as they went out into the garden, struggling together as George called out to Rowe that she was trying to kill him. They had only gone outside for a moment when George managed to break free, tottered back to the front door, and collapsed on the floor.

Rowe helped him into a chair, and only then did he notice that George was bleeding heavily from a wound in his right side.

'Am I not to stand in my own defence?' asked Maria, who must have realised the horror of what she had done.

About three minutes later, George was dead. Maria knelt down beside him as he sat lifeless in the chair. 'Have I murdered my dear George Spurlock?' she cried hysterically.

Thomas James, a surgeon from Rington, was called to examine the body. He found a six-inch wound, which had passed between the first and second ribs into the chest and lungs, and divided one of the large arteries and veins. There were also wounds on the left breast, about an inch deep, and on the left side lower down, six inches deep. The dead man's widow, he said, 'was in a very distracted state'.

She was charged with murder at Wells Crown Court on 17 August before Mr Justice Taunton, and pleaded not guilty. Her daughters Elizabeth and Mary appeared as witnesses for the prosecution. The former described the events of that fatal day, and the latter corroborated her sister's evidence. Frederick Rowe then related everything he had seen, and spoke of his attempts to separate husband and wife, adding that the latter 'seemed quite frantic'.

Mr James testified to the extent of George Spurlock's wounds, to the state of his widow afterwards, and to her history of apparent mental derangement over the last four years. Two other surgeons who had been in charge of her had evidence to offer. Mr Nichols had been visiting her since her last confinement, and said her mind was 'affected', while Mr Hurditch, who had been asked by the parish officers to visit her two years previously, said that she was definitely insane, and should have been admitted to an asylum.

There was no doubt that the unfortunate woman had committed the act, the judge remarked in his concluding comments, but it was clear that she was of unsound mind at the time. She was acquitted, and an order was made for her to be detained at His Majesty's pleasure.

2

'YOU RASCAL, YOU'LL BE HUNG FOR IT'

Brockley, 1835

Twenty-five-year-old John Plumley was employed as gamekeeper to the Pigott family at Brockley Hall, a position that had previously been held by his father, grandfather and great-grandfather before him. By 1834, Plumley had been promoted to head keeper and his future looked set – until another keeper was appointed in the spring of that year.

Initially, the new keeper, Joseph Dunford, shared the management of the estate with Plumley but, by the end of the year, he had been promoted over Plumley, who consequently found himself unexpectedly demoted to under keeper. With the loss of his status came the loss of his right to carry his gun about the estate, a concession only afforded to the head keeper.

Plumley saw his position as head keeper as his birthright and was most unhappy about his demotion, for which he seemed to hold Dunford personally responsible. Rightly or wrongly, Plumley believed that Dunford was plotting to get him dismissed from Pigott's service altogether and that the head keeper was constantly running to his master with complaints about his underling. Plumley's antagonistic attitude led to an uneasy working relationship between the two keepers and Dunford quickly became exasperated with his subordinate.

On the evening of 11 May 1835, arrangements had been made to dig out a fox at the edge of a wood on the estate and Dunford, along with another under keeper, Charles Coleman, and the estate gardener, William Blackwood, were impatiently waiting for Plumley to arrive to help. Blackwood told Dunford that he had seen Plumley earlier that evening when the keeper had shot a fox and that Plumley had given no indication of when he would be coming to the woods.

Eventually, the group saw Plumley sauntering casually through the woods towards them. Coleman called out a greeting and asked to see the fox that he had shot, which Plumley promptly pulled from his pocket. At the sight of the animal, Dunford remarked that it was so small that shooting it had been unnecessary – Plumley could easily have caught the animal. His comments inflamed Plumley, who cursed him and told him that he would shoot any animal he wanted to.

Brockley Hall. (Author's collection)

Recognising that Plumley appeared to have been drinking, Dunford asked him where he had been all day, receiving the surly reply that Plumley had been 'down in the Coomb'. Dunford didn't believe him. He again asked him where he had been and remonstrated with him about his lateness that evening and the fact that he had been drinking. Plumley's response was to call Dunford a 'damned liar'.

Dunford's patience finally ran out. He marched angrily towards Plumley and raged 'If you call me a liar, I'll knock your head off!'

'You are a damned liar!' repeated Plumley, shouldering his gun and taking aim at the head keeper, who stood well over 6ft tall.

'You don't mean that,' Dunford said soothingly and, for a moment, Plumley lowered his gun before defiantly raising it again and pulling the trigger. In his agitation, he had omitted to cock it and it failed to fire. Undaunted, Plumley cocked the gun and took aim again. This time, the gun discharged and the shot ripped into the left side of Dunford's chest. 'Lord have mercy on my wife and family. Plumley, thou hast done it at last,' said Dunford, as he fell to the ground mortally wounded.

Coleman and Blackwood stood frozen in shock for a few moments, before Coleman leaped into action. He vaulted the fence that enclosed the wood, threw himself at Plumley and began to belabour him with his walking stick. 'You rascal, you'll be hung for it,' he told Plumley between blows. Coleman then jumped back over the fence to pick up Dunford's gun, pointing it at Plumley and saying that it would serve him right if he shot him. Luckily, Blackwood was able to seize the weapon before Coleman could use it and, between them, the two men restrained Plumley, whose anger had now deserted him and who made no attempt to escape their clutches.

At Dunford's inquest, the coroner's jury returned a verdict of manslaughter and Plumley was committed to Shepton Mallet Gaol to await an appearance at the Somerset Lammas Assizes. Yet, when Plumley's trial opened in Bridgwater on 13 August 1835, the charge had been amended by the Grand Jury to that of wilful murder.

The first witness to testify was Charles Coleman, who stated that he could remember very little about the events of 11 May. He had no recollection of hitting Plumley with his stick, or of picking up the gun and threatening to shoot him. William Blackwood had a much clearer memory of the evening. He recalled that, after the shooting, Coleman had become almost deranged and had to be forcibly disarmed to prevent him from shooting Plumley. Blackwood testified that Plumley had previously complained about Dunford being promoted over him, a claim that was backed by estate labourer Thomas Jenkin.

A carpenter from Brockley village, John Bush, also spoke of Plumley's dislike of his victim. According to Bush, Plumley had told him that Dunford was reporting every mistake he made directly to Mr Pigott. Plumley had also alleged that Dunford was spying on him and threatened that, if he caught him watching him again, he would '… charge his rifle for him'.

Mr Pigott was called to give evidence and testified that he had always found the defendant to be a very humane man. He told the jury of the division of responsibility between the two men after he had engaged Dunford's services, which had meant that Plumley was forbidden to carry his gun about the estate. He had consented to Plumley carrying a gun on this occasion after the defendant had approached him and asked for permission to shoot some rabbits.

John Plumley's defence was presented in a written statement. On the evening of the murder, Plumley was apparently afraid that Dunford was about to attack him and had raised his gun in self-defence. He could not remember actually shooting the head gamekeeper and his first memory after raising the gun to his shoulder was of Dunford falling to the ground. Plumley swore that he bore no ill will towards his victim and had not intended to shoot him. After his defence was presented to the court, several character witnesses appeared for Plumley, pronouncing him without exception to be a man of good standing and even temperament.

Judge Baron Gurney summed up the case for the jury, advising them that they must decide between a verdict of guilty or not guilty to the charges of both murder and manslaughter. He went on to say that there was no doubt that Plumley had actually killed Dunford before leaving the jury to deliberate on the two charges.

The jury retired to discuss the evidence, returning after about thirty minutes to deliver a verdict of 'Guilty of Murder' against John Plumley, who stood in the dock with his head bowed as the judge put on his black cap to pronounce the mandatory death sentence. Describing Plumley as '... a melancholy instance of the danger resulting from the indulgence of the passion of hatred', Baron Gurney told Plumley 'He who wilfully sheds man's blood, by man must his blood be shed', before sentencing him to death.

Plumley was taken to Ilchester Gaol, where he was allowed visits from his wife and child, his mother and his five siblings. He insisted that he had been drunk when he shot Dunford, blaming the murder on his frequentation of beer houses and expressing concern for his wife and family, saying that he hoped that they would be taken care of after his death. On the morning of 17 August 1835, a very penitent Plumley was taken to the prison chapel where he received the Sacrament. From there he progressed to the scaffold where, watched by a crowd of around 500 people, he was sent to his death. His remains were buried within the prison grounds.

3

'SHE WILL BE BETTER PRESENTLY'

Worle, 1839

As Samuel Norman, the relieving officer for the Worle district, rode along Snatch Lane on 17 July 1839, he spotted a man scrambling out of a roadside ditch. Immediately afterwards, a young girl climbed out of the same ditch and began to walk towards Worle. She took only a few staggering steps before changing direction and, when she turned to face Norman, he saw that she was covered in blood, her clothes in disarray and her bonnet hanging down her back.

Norman had lost sight of the man by then, but all of a sudden he appeared next to him and said calmly, 'I must die'.

'What have you been doing? You have cut her throat.' Norman said, at which the man protested that the girl had stabbed him first.

Norman shouted to a woman passer-by, 'Run, there's a woman in distress', indicating the young lady who was now staggering about unsteadily in the lane. As Sarah Bowden rushed to assist the girl, Norman decided to take her assailant into custody. 'You must come with me' he ordered and the man willingly agreed. Norman got him to hold onto on his horse's mane so that he wouldn't lose sight of him again and they set off towards Worle, Norman alerting another passer-by to the woman's plight as he went. They had not gone far when the young man insisted that they should go back and check on the young woman.

When they got back to the victim, Norman could see that she was little more than a child.

The girl had by now collapsed face down on the road, half in and half out of the ditch, with blood gushing from her throat. Sarah Bowden and Sydney Tripp were bending over her but were able to do little more for her than preserve her modesty by pulling her skirts down over her bare legs. As Norman and his captive approached her, the man gazed dispassionately at his victim. 'She will be better presently,' he assured Norman.

Sarah Bowden immediately recognised the young man as Charles Wakeley, a servant employed by Josiah Reeves of Wick St Lawrence.

The New Inn, Worle. (© R. Sly)

'Charles, what have you done?' asked Sarah, to which Charles replied sullenly, 'She stabbed me first.'

'Who is she?' Sarah wanted to know.

'Our maid,' Wakeley replied.

Sydney Tripp rushed to the home of Josiah Reeves to inform him that his maidservant was dead. Reeves and his wife immediately ran to where Eliza Pain lay on the road and carried her body to the New Inn, to where Worle surgeon Mr J. Hardwick was summoned and pronounced life extinct. When he later conducted a post-mortem examination, Hardwick found that Eliza had five stab wounds around her left eye. There were some superficial wounds on the right-hand side of her neck and a large bruise on her left temple. However, the fatal wound was a two-inch deep, three-inch long stab wound on the left side of her neck, which had severed her jugular vein and caused her to bleed to death.

Meanwhile, Samuel Norman escorted her murderer to Worle, where he handed him over to the constable. Although Wakeley had gone quietly and apparently willingly with Norman, as soon as he saw the policeman he began to fight like a man possessed, pulling Norman off his horse and forcing the constable to hit him several times with his staff before he could securely handcuff him. Once in custody, it was obvious that Wakeley's allegations that Eliza Pain had stabbed him were completely false.

An inquest was opened the next day at the New Inn by coroner Daniel Ashford. Wakeley was brought to the proceedings and told that he would be permitted to ask questions of any of the witnesses. 'I have nothing at all to ask,' he said sullenly. Before the commencement of the inquest, he was permitted a brief meeting with his parents, to whom he handed over eight sovereigns and a few silver coins from his pocket. 'You see, I did not want for money,' he told his weeping mother.

The inquest heard from farmer Josiah Reeves, who stated that the deceased was an orphan, who was about fourteen years old. Eliza was a parish apprentice, having been sent from the workhouse to work as a maid for the Reeves family, and was, by all accounts, a pleasant, hard-working girl of excellent character. Charles Wakeley had worked for Reeves for two and a half years and was also a highly-regarded servant. Nobody in the family had noticed any particular intimacy between twenty-nine-year-old Wakeley and Eliza Pain, nor had they noticed any animosity between them.

Wakeley and Pain had been milking the cows together when Reeves called Eliza and asked her to go and do some shopping at Worle. Eliza fetched her coat and bonnet and set off straight away.

Fellow servant Henry Howell told the inquest that Eliza and Wakeley were friendly and that, on the day of Eliza's murder, there had been no quarrel between them. When Eliza was sent to Worle, Wakeley asked her to collect his boots from the cobbler, something which Eliza apparently refused to do. Howell recalled that Wakeley had not seemed in the slightest bit annoyed at her refusal, telling Howell that he supposed he would have to collect his boots himself and leaving the farm a few minutes after Eliza. A bloody clasp knife had been found in the ditch near to where Eliza's body lay and Howell positively identified it as belonging to Charles Wakeley.

The inquest heard from Sarah Bowden, Sydney Tripp, Samuel Norman and surgeon Mr Hardwick, after which the coroner invited Wakeley to make a statement, if he wanted to.

'I have nothing to say,' replied Wakeley, who had spent most of the inquest with his face buried in a handkerchief.

The jury needed no time for deliberation, immediately returning a verdict of wilful murder against Charles Wakeley, who was committed for trial at the next Somerset Assizes on the coroner's warrant.

He appeared before Mr Justice Coleridge at Bridgwater on 8 August 1839, where he shocked everyone by resolutely pleading guilty to the charge of wilful murder of Eliza Pain. Coleridge begged him to reconsider his plea, saying that it was better for him to be convicted on evidence rather than on his own confession but Wakeley refused to budge, determinedly sticking to his guns when Coleridge asked him again how he pleaded.

He was removed from court while the judge heard other cases and brought back to the dock later in the morning, by which time Wakeley had been counselled by the governor of Ilchester Gaol, who also urged him to plead not guilty and face his trial. For the third time, Mr Justice Coleridge asked Wakeley how he pleaded and, for the third time, Wakeley resignedly said, 'Guilty.'

Nevertheless, Coleridge insisted on hearing all the evidence against the prisoner before sentencing him but, in the face of Wakeley's plea, the judge had no option other than to pass the mandatory death sentence. The only person in court who seemed unmoved was the defendant. Coleridge himself fought back sobs, at one stage covering his face with his handkerchief while he composed himself sufficiently to speak. His voice cracking with emotion, he finally managed to sentence Wakeley to death, advising him to hold out no hopes of mercy.

Wakeley's execution on 4 September had the distinction of being the last public execution to be held at Ilchester Gaol. He went to the gallows without ever revealing his motives for the brutal murder of his fellow servant, although it was speculated that he had killed Eliza Pain in temper, after she spurned his sexual advances.

Note: There are several variations in the spelling of the murderer's name in the contemporary newspaper reports of the case. He is variously referred to as Wakly, Wakeley and, in the official court records, as Charles Weakly.

4

'THE FEARFUL CRIMES OF INFANTICIDE, FRATRICIDE AND MATRICIDE'

Shapwick, 1843-4

'If the suspicions at present entertained should turn out to be well-founded, we doubt whether the criminal annals of this country can present a case of parallel atrocity' wrote the *Bristol Mercury* reporter on 10 January 1845, continuing:

> Not only have several human beings been prematurely hurried out of existence by the hands of one hardened woman but the ties of relationship between the murderess and her victims are of so near a character that the unhappy wretch has perpetrated with her own hands the fearful crimes of infanticide, fratricide and matricide.

The 'unhappy wretch' referred to in the article was twenty-eight-year-old Sarah Freeman, a native of Shapwick, near Bridgwater. Sarah came from a poor, yet respectable family and was an intelligent child, attending the village school until she was fourteen. However, she had a fearsome temper and after leaving school she fell into a dissolute lifestyle, giving birth to two, possibly even three, illegitimate children while still in her teens. Her scandalous behaviour was deemed even more shocking as it was widely believed that the father of at least one of the children was a Church of England clergyman. When she was hounded out of the village as an undesirable, the clergyman apparently made a generous monetary gift to Henry Freeman, a labourer from Shapwick, on the condition that he married the errant Sarah. However, the marriage proved far from happy as Henry seemed unable to forget Sarah's past transgressions, which caused constant friction between the couple.

Sarah and Henry settled in the village of Pedwell, where they lived with James Dimont, Sarah's illegitimate son. (Her other two children both died in infancy.) In addition, the Freemans had a lodger, John Wake, who shared a room and a bed

Shapwick High Street. (Authors' collection)

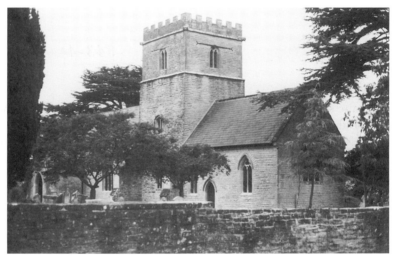

Shapwick parish church. (© R. Sly)

Shapwick today. (© R. Sly)

with little James. To all intents and purposes, Henry accepted the boy as his own child and James was well-treated by his 'parents', who both seemed very fond of him.

Seven-year-old James was a healthy little boy until 12 November 1843. On that day he attended Sunday school in Pedwell, returning home in time for his tea. Having eaten a meal of bread and butter and drunk a cup of tea, James complained of having stomach ache and, within minutes of eating, he began vomiting. Sarah put him to bed, where he was shortly joined by John Wake.

Wake was later to say that the child vomited throughout the night and continually complained of being thirsty. At that time, Henry Freeman was also unwell and, while he was aware that James was ill, he had little to do with the boy's care, being confined to his own sick bed. Thus, Sarah was initially the only person to nurse James through his illness and, according to John Wake, she did so almost reluctantly. Although Wake claimed to have called Sarah to come and attend to her son several times during the night, she refused to do so, repeatedly assuring him that the child was '… often took like that'.

Eventually, in response to Wake's insistence that the child was getting worse, Sarah came to the bedroom carrying a candle and took the boy downstairs for a drink of tea. When he returned to bed fifteen minutes later, his condition seemed to have improved and when Wake got up the following morning, James told him that he felt much better. Wake went off to work, leaving James in bed but by the time he got home again, the child had died.

An inquest was opened into his death, at which the chief witnesses were John Wake, a surgeon who had examined the child's body and the Freemans' next-door neighbour, Mrs Chapple, who had been called in by Sarah on the Monday morning to help care for James and who had also assisted in laying out his body.

Wake gave his account of the boy's brief illness and Mrs Chapple spoke of seeing the child in his final hours. She insisted that, at the time, James did not look 'unhealthy', although she stated that she had been convinced that the boy was about to die and had therefore sent for Sarah's mother to support her when his death occurred. Mrs Chapple told the inquest that she had seen no marks of violence on the boy and that, as far as she was concerned, he had died a natural death.

The surgeon who examined the boy after his death took the same view. There was nothing to suggest that anything unlawful had occurred and, apart from the fact that the inside of James's mouth appeared very dry, his symptoms, as related by his mother, were consistent with those of English cholera. The surgeon offered to perform a full post-mortem examination should the coroner order it but, anxious to avoid expense, the coroner declined his offer. The inquest jury returned a verdict of 'death from natural causes' and James was laid to rest in Shapwick churchyard.

A few days before Christmas 1843, twenty-four-year-old Henry Freeman returned home from work and ate his evening meal of potatoes, cooked for him by his wife. Soon afterwards, he began to complain of feeling ill and surgeon Mr Edward England Phillips was summoned to attend him. Phillips found Henry sitting by the fire, complaining of stomach ache, vomiting and heart palpitations.

Having examined the sick man, Phillips left some medicine for him, giving Sarah strict instructions that he was to be sent for immediately if her husband's illness worsened. When the surgeon returned the following day, there had been a marked deterioration in Henry's condition and Phillips suspected that he hadn't been given his medicine. Sarah told him that her husband was constipated and Phillips repeated his instructions that he was to be summoned should Henry not improve. However, when he called back on the following day, it was to find that his patient had died several hours earlier.

Henry Freeman belonged to a 'Death Club', which met regularly at the Masons' Arms public house in Bridgwater. For some months before his death, he had paid a small but regular premium and, within hours of his demise, Sarah Freeman contacted the club secretary, William Manning, to tell him that Henry had died from 'inflammation of the bowels' and to ask him for an advance on the payment she believed was due to her. Sarah was given £5 and was eventually to receive a total payout of more than £20 from the club as settlement for Henry's death, although she was evidently dissatisfied with the sum and obviously expected it to be greater.

Henry was buried in Shapwick churchyard on 2 January 1844, the cause of his death having been recorded as 'English cholera'. His widow almost immediately left the area and, after a brief visit to her parents in Shapwick, it is believed that she went to London, where she stayed until December 1844, before going back to Bridgwater. Once in Somerset, she asked some friends to write to her family to see if she might return to live with them in Shapwick but she received a strongly worded reply from her brother telling her in no uncertain terms that she would not be welcome.

As soon as Sarah received the letter, she visited Bridgwater chemist Mr Varder and tried to purchase three-pennyworth of arsenic. Since she was not personally known to Mr Varder's apprentice, William Hare, he quite properly refused to sell it to her, but she told him that she was the sister of the local postman and carrier, Edmund Durstin, and that he had sent her to buy the arsenic on his behalf to deal with an infestation of rats and mice. Since Durstin was well known in the shop, Sarah's subterfuge worked and she was allowed to purchase the poison, although she was warned that it was a lethal substance and cautioned about its use.

With her small package suitably wrapped and clearly labelled 'Poison', Sarah left the shop, having also purchased a bottle of hair oil. She then approached Mr Durstin and, seemingly undeterred by the tone of her brother's letter, she persuaded Durstin to give her a lift to Shapwick in his cart. She mentioned at the time that she had just passed herself off as his sister in the chemist's shop, adding that she had purchased some hair oil but saying nothing about any arsenic. Perhaps surprisingly, Durstin seems to have accepted Sarah's actions without feeling any need to ask her why she had pretended to be a relation of his.

Sarah arrived at her family home in Shapwick on 9 December 1844 to a less than enthusiastic welcome. Her brother Charles was at work when she arrived and her mother and her other brother, John, were extremely reluctant to allow her to stay, while her elderly father was so deaf that he was able to take little part in the heated discussion that followed her arrival. Sarah turned on the tears and eventually a bed was made up for her to stay. However, when Charles arrived home from work, he was absolutely furious to find his sister there.

Charles worked for farmer William Thomsey, who had been one of the main protagonists in hounding Sarah from the village because of her unacceptable lifestyle and loose morals. As soon as Thomsey heard that Sarah was back, he confronted Charles, telling him that he was not happy for the wages that he was paying to be used to support Sarah and therefore, if she stayed at the family home, he would be forced to sack Charles. Unhappy about losing a job that he had held for three years, Charles issued Sarah with an ultimatum – she could stay until the weekend, then she must return to Bridgwater and turn herself in at the workhouse.

Although Sarah's mother Mary was seventy-two years old, she was generally in good health, apart from a persistent cough. However, on 12 December she ate some pea soup prepared for her by her daughter and almost immediately began to complain of feeling unwell. After suffering from severe stomach cramps and vomiting, Mary died on 14 December.

Sarah successfully argued that she should remain at the house until after her mother's funeral. However, once Mary was buried on 22 December, Charles renewed his efforts to evict his sister from the family home, saying that he would rather see her on the streets than lose his job. The fact that Charles wanted to marry and bring his bride, Joan, to the house added impetus to his campaign and the arguments and disputes continued over Christmas. By now, John and his father were beginning to lean towards allowing Sarah to stay but Charles was adamant that she had to leave. Sarah was equally determined to stay and, in the presence of witnesses, made several veiled threats. 'Charles do want to have his glee over me but there will be something turn up for him,' she told neighbour Maria Hucker and she informed another neighbour, Henry Woodland, 'Charles do want to turn me out of doors and take home his Joanie – I'll take care of that.' She raged to Reuben Walker that she would be damned if she would allow her brother to turn her out in favour of his wife and that '... if he didn't look damned sharp, she would take damned good care he should not be there himself very long.'

In the past, Charles had suffered from a bowel complaint, for which he had frequently consulted surgeon Mr Phillips. The doctor normally prescribed pills, which quickly relieved Charles's symptoms. However, on Boxing Day 1844, Charles ate a lunch of salt herring and potatoes prepared for him by Sarah and soon afterwards he began to feel ill. Although he returned to his work after lunch, he spent much of the afternoon clutching his stomach and vomiting, telling his workmates that he was very sick. Fearing that his bowel problem had returned, when he got home from work that evening, Charles sent for Phillips, who arrived to find his patient huddled close to the fire, complaining of feeling bitterly cold and suffering from bouts of vomiting. Phillips observed that his patient's heartbeat was weak and that his pulse was racing at between 140 and 150 beats per minute. He prescribed the usual pills but on this occasion, they proved completely ineffective.

Charles spent the next few days in bed, with such severe pain in his stomach that he could barely tolerate the weight of the bedclothes on his body. His condition gradually improved, only to suddenly worsen again, mainly after he had eaten the gruel or drank the peppermint tea that Sarah prepared for him. In the early hours of the morning of 31 December, Charles finally succumbed to his illness and died.

Finding himself baffled by the death of his patient, surgeon Mr Phillips immediately suspected foul play. Accordingly, when he performed the necessary post-mortem examination, he removed several organs from Charles's body, which he personally delivered to analytical chemist William Herapath at his home in Bristol, along with several carefully labelled bottles of liquid.

Herapath immediately began a series of tests for the presence of poison in the viscera and fluids supplied to him by Mr Phillips. He found no traces of poison in the bottles labelled 'gruel', 'rejected stomach contents', 'contents of the stomach' or 'contents of the thorax' but the viscera told an entirely different story. When Herapath and Phillips together examined the body parts more closely, they observed an unnatural inflammation of the interior of the stomach, along with a couple of small patches of gangrene. The inflammation continued into the duodenum and small intestines and, while Herapath was not able to isolate any noxious substances in the stomach itself, the intestinal canal and liver both tested positive for the presence of arsenic. 'I never saw a stomach more inflamed in my life,' commented Herapath. 'Whoever it was, they must have suffered horribly.'

With Herapath prepared to state that the cause of Charles Dimont's death was poisoning by arsenic, it was decided to exhume the recently buried remains of Mary Dimont. Once again, Herapath was called upon and found arsenic to be present in the dead woman's stomach.

At the inquest into the death of Charles Dimont, held at Shapwick by county coroner Mr Caines, the jury returned a verdict of wilful murder against Sarah Freeman, who was immediately arrested by Constable James Eardley and taken into custody, charged with her brother's murder. The coroner then proceeded with an inquest into the death of Sarah's mother and this time the jury reached a verdict that Mary Dimont had died due to the administration of arsenic by person or persons unknown. However, at a later hearing before magistrates, held at Bridgwater Town Hall, Sarah was additionally charged with the wilful murder of her mother, at which she vehemently protested her innocence, as indeed she had continually done since her arrest on the charge of murdering her brother.

In view of the two sudden deaths in the Dimont family and the resulting suspicion cast on Sarah Freeman, the coroner issued an order for the exhumation of the bodies of Henry Freeman and James Dimont. Both exhumations were carried out on 11 January 1845, in the presence of Mr Herapath, who removed samples from each for further testing. Once the results of the tests were known, the coroner opened two new inquests into the deaths at which Herapath was the chief witness.

He described James's body as being decomposed, stating that there was sufficient water in the coffin to almost entirely cover his remains. However, the boy's internal organs were remarkably well preserved and Herapath was able to remove them for closer examination. He recovered three tamarind stones from James's stomach, which he noted was severely inflamed, as was the duodenum. Herapath was able to isolate a significant quantity of arsenic from James's organs and, although the excessive water in the coffin prevented him from estimating precisely how much poison the boy had consumed, he was able to state unequivocally that James had died from the ingestion of arsenic. Herapath obtained similar results from his analysis of the remains of Henry Freeman and was again prepared to attribute his death to arsenic poisoning.

At the conclusion of the two inquests, the jury returned two more verdicts of wilful murder against Sarah Freeman – one for her husband and one for her son. In concluding the proceedings, the coroner thanked Mr Herapath for his efforts, adding, 'I am afraid I shall have further occasion for your services.' Mr Caines went on to explain that he had received a letter from 'a highly respectable person', informing him of the suspicious deaths of five members of one family in the Shapwick area. The writer alleged that Sarah Freeman was a frequent visitor to the family's home.

Although Sarah Freeman was charged with four murders, she was actually tried only for the murder of her brother, Charles, appearing before Mr Justice Coleridge at the Somerset Assizes on 5 April 1845. Since she had no legal representation, Coleridge asked Mr Stock to act in her defence and he was pitted against Mr Sergeant Kinglake and Mr Rawlinson for the prosecution. Described as a small-featured woman with rather prominent eyes, Sarah's face betrayed little emotion as the proceedings unfolded, although she spent much of the trial nervously rocking backwards and forwards in her seat.

Opening for the prosecution, Mr Kinglake told the jury that they were there to determine whether a fellow human being had come to his death by poison and, if so, whether the prisoner's hand had administered that poison. He urged the jury to disregard anything they might have previously read or heard about the case and to focus their attention solely on the evidence that would be presented to them in court. With that, the prosecution called their first witness.

Chemist's apprentice William Hare was followed into the witness box by Edmund Durstin, who had transported Sarah Freeman home to Shapwick. The court then heard from Sarah's surviving brother, John, her father and several neighbours, all of whom related the progress of Charles's illness towards his ultimate demise. Many detailed the arguments between Sarah and Charles and testified to the fact that Sarah had hinted that their disagreement would soon come to an end. One of the most important witnesses was PC James Eardley, who told the court that he had searched Sarah after her arrest and that he had also thoroughly searched her family home. Eardley stated that he had found no arsenic whatsoever, either on Sarah's person or at the cottage in Shapwick.

This was one of the points emphasised by defence counsel Mr Stock, who addressed the jury after the appearance of the medical witnesses, Mr Phillips and Mr Herapath. After bemoaning the fact that he had barely had sufficient time to fully acquaint himself with the details of the case, Stock pointed out to the jury that, in arriving at

Mr Justice Coleridge.
(Authors' collection)

their verdict, they must remember that it was for the prosecution to prove his client guilty, rather than for him to prove her innocent. And, if the prosecution succeeded in that task, it must be proven beyond any reasonable doubt. Stock contended that the evidence against Sarah Freeman was largely circumstantial. The jury must first determine whether or not Charles Dimont died from poisoning rather than from a reoccurrence of the bowel problems that he was known to suffer from. Only if they were sure of the cause of death beyond reasonable doubt should they consider whether or not Sarah Freeman was responsible. Nobody had seen Sarah Freeman administering arsenic to her brother and the medical witnesses were unable to pinpoint with any accuracy any time or times at which she may have done so, nor were they able to quantify the dose or doses given. Besides, where was Sarah Freeman's motive, asked Stock. Reminding the jury that they should not allow anything but the 'most conclusive and satisfactory evidence' to influence their verdict, he stressed that their decision could ultimately have 'awful and fatal consequences to a fellow creature'.

Once Mr Justice Coleridge had summed up the evidence for the jury at length, they retired to consider their verdict, returning in fifteen minutes to pronounce Sarah Freeman 'guilty' of the wilful murder of her brother. Coleridge passed the mandatory sentence of death, at which Sarah Freeman turned to him and said, 'Justice has not been done me; my life has been unfairly taken away.'

In the condemned cell at Taunton Gaol, Sarah brooded sullenly on her situation for a few days, determinedly resisting the pleas from the warders and the prison chaplain to prepare herself spiritually for her execution by confessing her sins and so cleansing her soul. However, on 10 April, she surprised everyone by asking to make a statement. Yet rather than the expected confession, she now accused her brother, John, of poisoning both Charles and their mother. Sarah insisted that she had purchased the arsenic with the intention of committing suicide and that John had subsequently found it in her basket and used it to poison the family.

Sarah made a very detailed statement, accusing John of framing her for the murders and the prison governor took it upon himself to interview several people, all of whom were quick to refute Sarah's allegations. Once her statement had been dismissed as entirely false, Sarah adopted a 'couldn't care less' attitude to her predicament, treating everyone with equal disdain and contempt. Of her father, she stated, 'I wish he had crumbled to dust before he was allowed to appear on my trial' and a visit from her brother, John, prompted a violent outburst.

She spent the weekend before her scheduled execution making herself a cap, telling the prison matron, 'I am not going up there a perfect fright.' On the day before she was due to die, she asked permission to distribute her clothes among her fellow prisoners and, when this request was granted, she busied herself making a list of who was to be given her belongings after her death.

Sarah Freeman kept her appointment with the executioner without ever having confessed to committing murder. As she mounted the gallows on 23 April 1845, before an estimated crowd of more than 10,000 spectators, her last words were, 'I am as innocent as a lamb'.

Tried only for the murder of her brother, there seems little doubt that Sarah Freeman claimed yet more victims. Before her trial, the Grand Jury deemed that there was insufficient evidence to proceed with the charges of murder against her in respect of her husband, Henry, and son, James, and, sentenced to death for the murder of Charles Dimont, there was little point in also trying her for the murder of her mother, Mary. As far as can be established, she was never charged in connection with the five suspicious deaths alluded to by the coroner at the inquest into the deaths of her husband and son. Nor were any charges brought against her in connection with the deaths of her other two children, even though both were deemed 'suspicious and mysterious'.

Note: There is considerable confusion in the contemporary press on the subject of Sarah's illegitimate children. While most newspapers agree that the child that was poisoned was seven years old and the alleged offspring of the Church of England clergyman, some newspapers name the child as James Dimond, (aka James Strong or James Freeman) others as Sarah. (In one newspaper article, the dead child's gender changes from 'he' to 'she' and back several times.) Other newspapers name both children separately as victims, stating that James died in November 1843 and Sarah in March 1844. I have been unable to find any official records of Sarah, although the search is not helped by frequent variations in the spelling of the surname (Dimond, Dymen, Dimont, Diment etc). There are also variations in the spelling of numerous other names connected with the case – for example, farmer William Thomsey is also named Tomsey and neighbour Maria Hucker is alternatively named Maria Utter.

5

'YOU'VE GOT ENOUGH OF IT'

Little Elm, Frome, 1846

On the evening of 16 June 1846, after a satisfactory day at Little Elm Fair, near Frome, William Glindell of Bristol and his servant, Thomas Wiggins, went to a public house. After enjoying a drink together, they made their way into a small tent at the fair. It was about ten o'clock when thirty-year-old Robert Williams came and joined them. Wiggins had helped Williams to sell a horse earlier that day, and had been promised his cut, but Williams had so far failed to pay up as agreed and was showing no signs of being prepared to honour his part of the deal. Both men began to quarrel, with a good deal of profane language being used. Glindell told Wiggins sharply that he ought to know better. Wiggins apologised, sat down and lit his pipe.

Williams walked out of the booth but returned about a minute later, intent on further verbal abuse of Wiggins. After a while Wiggins said he could not put up with any more, and, as Williams obviously wanted to fight, he would have two rounds with him for 6*d*. Williams proceeded to insult him all the more, and stood up as if ready to fight. Wiggins took off his coat and muttered something which evidently nobody heard properly but Williams, who said, 'I can bear it no longer.'

Both men immediately began to lay into each other. They fell to the floor, Williams lying on top of his opponent, who was evidently getting the worst of it. One of the men standing nearby then noticed that Williams had a knife in his hand.

Then Wiggins put his hand to his neck, and called out feebly, 'Oh dear! I am stabbed – I'm a dead man!'

'You've had enough of it,' muttered Williams.

The men standing around went and helped Wiggins to his feet, and removed his neckerchief. Blood was pouring from a deep wound in his neck. Williams tried to leave, but Glindell ran after him, seized him by the arm and brought him back, telling him he had killed Wiggins.

'No, I have not killed the bastard,' he insisted.

However, Wiggins had clearly breathed his last. The police were called, and a junior officer, Michael Reed, came to take charge of the situation until the arrival of his superior, Constable Hurst, who took Williams into custody. When asked if he had anything to say, he declared that he would not have stabbed his opponent if he had not been drunk.

At a post-mortem, Wiggins' body was examined by surgeon Joseph Springfield. He found that the carotid artery had been divided by a punctured wound which would have immediately caused death. There were eleven wounds altogether, three about the ear, all punctured wounds which had been inflicted by the point of a penknife. Another six were stabs over the chest, and there were two on the arms.

Williams was charged with wilful murder, taken into custody, and appeared at the Western Assizes, Wells, before Mr Justice Erle on 8 August. Mr Phinn conducted the case for the prosecution and Mr Stone defended the prisoner.

The first witness for the prosecution was Glindell, who described what he had seen on the night his servant was killed. Under cross-examination, he said that he did not think that either man was any the worse for drink. Such a statement was at variance with the evidence of Mr Hurst, who repeated Williams' remark that he would not have killed the man if only he had been sober. He said he showed the prisoner a knife. 'Ah, I was eating bread and cheese with that knife,' was the response, 'and that's how the man came to be stabbed.' When they fought, Williams had the knife in his hand, and when he saw Wiggins bleeding, he ran away. When cross-examined, he said that Wiggins must have fallen upon the knife. The inference was that, despite the men coming to blows, it must have been a tragic accident.

Next to address the court was Mr Reed, who confirmed Williams' statement that 'It is a very bad job, and I am very sorry for it; if I had not been drunk, I should not have done it; but he began the row.' Williams had appeared to him the worse for liquor, but not to the extent that he did not know what he was doing. When cross-examined, he said the prisoner 'did not do it wilfully'.

Two more witnesses were then called. Samuel Organ, landlord of the public house, the George Inn, said that after hearing a noise in the booth, he went and looked in. There he saw both men fighting, 'striking blows very fast', and noticed Williams striking Wiggins on the neck. Finally, Mr Springfield confirmed the findings he had made at the post-mortem.

Summing up for the defence, Mr Stone contended that the offence merely amounted to manslaughter, even supposing the wounds had not been inflicted by accident, which he firmly believed they were.

Mr Justice Erle then addressed the jury, saying there was no doubt that the death of Wiggins had been caused by the prisoner, and he did not see any reasonable doubt that his inflicting the wounds on his victim had been a wilful act. Was he guilty of murder, or was the crime reduced by circumstances to that of manslaughter? If two persons engaged in a sudden fight and one happened to be carrying a deadly weapon, that amounted to the crime of manslaughter only. However, if two persons entered into some angry contest, and in a pause one of them prepared a deadly weapon for the purpose of using it, and did use it, and occasioned death, that person was guilty of the crime of murder. They had to consider whether, after the angry words had first passed, the evidence satisfied them that the prisoner prepared the knife in question for the contest, and used it in pursuance of that intention. If he did, their verdict must be one of murder; but if the knife was there for a lawful purpose, and the prisoner used it without premeditation, the verdict should be one of manslaughter.

As the jury prepared to retire, the judge was evidently quite moved by Williams' ordeal. It was if he had a presentiment that the crime fell short of premeditated murder, but that the prisoner was nonetheless destined for the gallows. If so, he was proved correct, for the jury returned to court after half an hour with a verdict of guilty of murder.

Whatever his personal feelings, Erle did not flinch from his legal obligation. In donning the black cap and addressing Williams, he told him sternly that there had been no statement of regret from him to any of those who had 'witnessed this horrid transaction'. It was the duty of those who administered the law of the land, he went on, 'to endeavour to repress the pernicious practice of resorting to deadly weapons, and I feel bound upon this occasion, by the awful example of your ignominious death, to give a warning of the dreadful consequences that will follow those who incur guilt like that which you stand to answer for.' He had allowed no time to his victim to prepare for eternity, but had 'hurried him in one moment before his Creator'.

Williams was removed from the dock crying bitterly. It appeared that there could be only one possible conclusion, and that was the death sentence. However, there were those who thought differently. The Revd Robert Montgomery, a preacher from London, was so horrified by what he believed was an unduly harsh judgment, that he accordingly drew up a petition in which he emphasised what he saw as the extenuating circumstances, and his fervent belief that the killing of Wiggins did not amount to murder. He obtained the signatures of all the clergymen and ministers in the district and took it to London, where he placed it before Mr Justice Erle and the Home Secretary. In the third week of August, it was announced that Her Majesty had been pleased to commute the sentence on Robert Williams to one of transportation for life.

6

A SERIOUS CASE
OF MELANCHOLIA

Bath, 1847

William and Jane Ridout lived in Bath close to the Kennet and Avon canal towpath. They had three sons, William John, aged seven, George, aged two and a half and Mark, aged eight months, and a daughter, Fanny, aged four. Their home was a tiny one-floor cottage with two rooms, a kitchen and sitting-room combined, and a communal bedroom. William was a jobbing brewer, who often worked some distance from home, and early in December 1847 he found employment at the Beefsteak Tavern.

Jane had long a history of severe depression, doubtless exacerbated by the fact that their eldest child was a deaf-mute, and also by her husband's regular absences from home because of his employment. On one occasion in the autumn she had taken their children for a walk to the river, intending to do away with the five of them, but they cried loudly and begged her to spare them. She freely admitted it to her husband afterwards, and he was sufficiently concerned by her behaviour to try and avoid such a thing happening again by asking Jane's mother, Elizabeth Lintran, to move in with them so she could keep an eye on her when he was away. With three adults and four children, the cottage must have been extremely crowded, but under the circumstances there was no real alternative. He also spoke to John Woodward, a surgeon, who advised him that in view of her 'melancholia', he should keep all sharp instruments beyond her reach and should really have her 'placed under restraint' – in other words, probably in a lunatic asylum.

Sadly, all this did not prove enough to avert the horror which befell the community on the afternoon of Monday, 6 December 1847. Sarah Seer, who lived nearby, had long been a close friend of Jane Ridout and both women would meet, usually once a day, for company and conversation. That morning, Mrs Seer had not seen anything of her, and thought this unusual. After going to the pump for some water, she decided to call on her neighbour and make sure she was well. When she tried the door of the cottage she found it was locked.

Looking in through the window, she could hardly believe her eyes. Jane Ridout was lying on the kitchen floor, covered in blood.

Bath from Beecham Cliff. (Authors' collection)

Mrs Seer immediately went and fetched the next neighbour she could find, a labourer. After looking at the dreadful sight as well, he went for the police. An inspector and another officer were despatched to the premises. They broke the door open, to find a most distressing sight. Jane Ridout's throat had been cut, and a bloodstained razor was by her side. In the bedroom were the bodies of all four children, all of whom had been killed in the same manner. Beside them was a large tub almost full of blood and water. It appeared that the mother had cut their throats and then held their heads over tub as their wounds bled. One of the victims was found with his legs partly hanging over the step leading to the bedroom, as if he had struggled and made an abortive effort to escape.

It was obvious that nobody else would be sought in connection with the deaths. An inquest was held at the Crown Tavern, Bathwick, on the afternoon of Thursday 9 December. The coroner, Mr A.H. English, presided over the sad formality.

Elizabeth Lintran, mother of Jane Ridout, was the first witness to be examined. She spoke of having been living with her daughter for the previous five weeks, at her son-in-law's request. Jane, she said, 'had been in a low state of mind,' and told him about having gone out with the intention of drowning them and herself. On the morning of

Tuesday 30 November, Mrs Lintran had returned to her home town of Trowbridge where she intended to make arrangements to give up the cottage she was renting there, the arrange to find another place close to her daughter. She was still away on the evening of Sunday 5 December, when William left home for his current work.

Still deeply affected, William was the next to give evidence. He confirmed everything that his mother-in-law had said and spoke of his consultations with Mr Woodward. Mrs Seer described her discovery of the bodies in the cottage, and Inspector Evans, from the local police force, spoke of having to break the door down. Mr Woodward testified to his recommendation that removal to an asylum might have been the only remedy to the unhappy problem.

It was a foregone conclusion when the jury returned a verdict of four charges of wilful murder against Mrs Ridout, and that in her case, she had 'destroyed herself during temporary insanity.'

7

'WHAT A GOOD THING IF SHE WERE A WIDOW'

Bath, 1849

Henry Marchant, who lived at Angel Buildings, Bath, worked in the local quarries. After completing his regular shift at around midday on Saturday, 31 March 1849, he stopped to enjoy a drink with some of his colleagues at the local inn, where he stayed for an hour or so. When he arrived home, his wife Charlotte made him a cup of tea. That night he felt unwell, but thought nothing of it and went to work as usual the following day. However after a few hours at the quarry he felt worse than ever, and he was sent home early with terrible stomach pains and violent nausea. He had always been fit and healthy, and at first Charlotte was reluctant to send for a surgeon, on the grounds that he was one of those tough men who would strongly object to the presence of having a medical person in the house. But he was obviously very sick indeed and after a while she realised that she had no alternative. She accordingly sent for Mr Lloyd from Bath to come and attend to him.

On examining the patient, Lloyd considered it to be no more than a severe case of gastric trouble, and prescribed the standard treatment. Yet Henry did not respond, but became rapidly worse and after lingering in increasing agony for several days, he died on 7 April. Although he was only twenty-eight years old, four years younger than his wife, and had previously been well, nobody had good reason to suspect anything out of the ordinary. He was buried on 13 April.

Three days later, the apparently merry widow married again. Her second husband, Mr Harris, described as 'a man of property', was aged seventy. As well as their disparity in ages, it was said that he had buried two, perhaps even three, wives, within the previous thirteen months. The last of these had passed away only a few weeks before this latest marriage. Mr Marchant's death had surely happened at too convenient a time to be the result of natural causes.

Tongues soon wagged, the authorities were alerted, and the dead man's body was disinterred for examination. An inquest was held later that week, and the jury unanimously decided that samples from his stomach should be taken and sent for analysis by Professor William Herapath at Bristol Medical School. When he found traces of arsenic in the body, he notified the police and Charlotte was arrested and taken into custody on a charge of murder.

The case came to trial at the Western Assizes, Bridgwater, before Mr Justice Cresswell, on 2 August. The prosecution brought forward a witness, who lived near the Marchants. She told the court that about six or seven weeks before the deceased was taken ill and died, his wife had told two people in the area that Mr Harris had offered her his hand in marriage, 'observing what a good thing it would be if she were a widow'. On the day that her husband's sufferings began, she had been to visit Harris's house. She was in his room with him for some time, and they had tea together. As she was leaving, she told a Mrs Shayler, who lived under the same roof, that she was about to be married to Mr Harris. On the day after the death of her husband she and her septuagenarian suitor were again seen in each others company, and it was not long after that that the marriage took place. If anybody present at the ceremony had known of any just cause or impediment to their matrimonial union, they remained silent.

Evidence was also produced to show that at just before Henry Marchant became ill, his wife had purchased some poison from Mr Bright, a chemist in Bath.

After two days in court, all the evidence had been heard, and the jury retired. It took them only one hour to reach a verdict that Mrs Harris was guilty of murder, and the judge passed sentence of death on her.

At this, Mr Saunders, on behalf of the defence, put in a plea of arrest on the grounds that the prisoner was pregnant. 'Pleading the belly' was a common excuse in the eighteenth and nineteenth century by women who were convicted of capital crimes. If they were considered to be 'quick with child', it would be down to the judge's discretion as to whether he would grant a stay of execution, commute a death sentence to transportation, or even reprieve her altogether. Mr Justice Cresswell then ordered the doors of the court to be closed, and asked the High Sheriff to empanel a jury of matrons from women within the court for the purpose of trying the prisoner's plea.

Twelve ladies who had entered the court as spectators were then asked to enter a box as a 'jury of matrons', some doing so with a great show of reluctance, and were sworn in by the crier. His lordship said that they had just heard from the oath administered to them the nature of the duties upon which they had been empanelled. They would at once retire and perform those duties, with suitable assistance from a member of the medical profession. They were then escorted by the High Sheriff to the rear of the court, and returned in a few minutes. The clerk of assize then asked them if they were agreed on their verdict. Did they think the prisoner was expecting a child?

Several ladies confirmed that in their opinion she was. This was good enough for the judge, who asked for the sentence to be respited. Women who were convicted of murder by poison were very rarely given a reprieve, on the grounds that anyone found guilty of administering poison had demonstrated clear proof of premeditated killing. Few, if any, of those present in court doubted that Charlotte Harris, formerly Marchant, was responsible for the death of her late husband. Assuming that the jury of matrons was correct, she was very fortunate in that impending motherhood had saved her from the gallows.

8

'I SHALL NEVER SEE YOUR FACE ANY MORE'

Walcot, 1850

Edmund Francis Hunt, a plasterer, lived at Cornwall Terrace, Walcot. Aged about thirty-five, he was known as a hard and conscientious worker, as well as a good and faithful husband and father to his wife and their five children. Sadly, his wife Mary was not of the same impeachable character. She drank too much, and when he could not or would not provide her with money to spend at the local inns, she took to shoplifting. Several times she was caught, and went to prison. In the autumn of 1849 she was several months pregnant, but this did not stop the authorities from passing the usual custodial sentence after her latest offence and conviction, and she gave birth to their youngest child while she was still in prison.

Edmund was increasingly distressed by her refusal to mend her ways, and eventually he had had enough. This time, he warned her that if she committed another theft, he would put an end to himself.

On 2 February 1850, at about midday, Edmund went out to work. He had had to postpone his departure from the house because the weather had been so wet and windy. He returned about six hours later, washed and put some clean clothes on, then went out again to collect his wages.

An hour later his eldest son, also called Edmund, aged about thirteen, was walking back from his grandmother's house, and met his mother, who told him she was going to look for his father and asked him to stay at home with the younger children. He stayed there all evening, and eventually there was a knock at the door. A policeman had come to look for Mrs Hunt. On being told she was not there, he went away but returned a little later, insisting that he would wait for her. When she appeared, the policeman accompanied her into the house, saying that they had to look for a cloak. It was not found, but her previous record was enough for her to be asked to accompany him to the police station where she was arrested on two charges of shoplifting.

Her husband returned to the house shortly after midnight. Normally the most sober of citizens, this time he had been drinking. He was holding some beer in a pewter pot, and seemed a little the worse for wear. Mr Heath, a neighbour, had stopped him on his way and told him the unhappy, if hardly unexpected, news.

'Where's mother?' he asked young Edmund. The latter wisely, if perhaps not truthfully, said he did not know, but as the game had already been given away, it seemed a pointless question. Then he heard the voice of his daughter Sally, aged two and a half, calling him. He asked Edmund to go upstairs and bring her down. Whether the boy had any idea of what was going to happen, one can only guess, but he did not dare disobey. Taking the little child in his arms, the father ordered his son to go to bed. When the latter begged his father to do likewise, Edmund replied sharply, 'Go on; I shall never see your face any more.'

With fear in his heart, the younger Edmund did once again as he was told. A little later he heard his father go outside, walking down the steps nearby that led to the river Avon flowing past their road, murmuring something to Sally.

In the morning, young Edmund got up and searched the house for his father, but without success. When Mr Heath came to enquire if everything was all right, it became clear that the worst had probably happened. People from the neighbouring houses were alerted and the river was searched. Later on that day, about forty yards from the house, Edmund's body was found in the river, his arms in a folded position, as if he had been clasping his youngest child. As for his beloved Sally, her body in a high dress, with a small silk necklace, was taken out of the river about eighteen miles away early next morning.

An inquest was held on Monday evening by Mr A.H. English, the coroner for Bath. To Edmund Hunt the younger fell the sorrowful duty of recounting the tragic events of that night, and a verdict of 'temporary insanity' was recorded. Earlier that same day, Mary Hunt was charged again with shoplifting and committed by the city magistrates to take her trial at the next sessions.

Note: There is some question about the name of Edmund Hunt's daughter. She is rarely named in contemporary newspaper reports of the murder but the majority of the reports that do name her refer to her as Sarah 'Sally' Hunt. However, she is occasionally named Dora and official records tend to support this version. We have used 'Sally' as this is the most frequently reported.

9

'YOU HAVE BEEN DOING SOMETHING'

Nempnett Thrubwell, 1851

William Wilkins had spent most of his life working as a farm labourer. Now aged seventy-four, he and his seventy-year-old wife, Sarah, kept a small shop in the front room of their cottage in the village of Nempnett Thrubwell, about eight miles from Bristol.

On the morning of 8 February 1851, they were peacefully going about their normal daily business when two men, John Wiles and John Smith, entered the shop and asked for a loaf of bread. Sarah obviously found something disturbing about the two men as she asked to see their money before handing over the bread. At this, Wiles turned to his companion and asked him for 6d. When Smith admitted that he had no money, Wiles asked angrily, 'What did you send me on such a fool's errand for, then?' and the two men left the shop empty handed.

However, they were not gone long, returning within the hour and repeating their request. Wiles assured Sarah, 'Now, mistress, I have got some money for the bread'. Sarah turned to reach for a loaf and, as she did, Wiles dealt her a fearsome blow on the head with an iron-banded stick.

The force of the attack sent Sarah flying to the ground. Badly injured, she managed to scramble to her knees, all the while begging for mercy. Before she could get up, she was hit on the head again, this time with a spade, which had been standing by the shop door. As Sarah lay dazed and bleeding on the floor, she heard someone entering the kitchen, where she knew that they would find her husband, William, sitting in the chimney corner by the fire eating his breakfast. She recalled hearing the sounds of a violent scuffle punctuated by dreadful cries of 'murder' from her husband, then briefly lost consciousness.

It was not long before the little shop had another customer, a seven-year-old girl sent on an errand. The child was understandably horrified by what she saw and ran the twenty yards back to her home to fetch her mother, Elizabeth Derring, who rushed straight to the Wilkins' shop to find both William and Sarah lying on the floor in pools of blood. Surgeon Thomas Jackman was summoned and, on examining William, found him to be suffering from a fractured skull and a severed artery on

Taunton Castle, former site of the assizes. (Authors' collection)

the left-hand side of his head, from which blood was still pumping. The surgeon immediately administered stimulants, managing first to stem the flow of blood and eventually to completely stop the bleeding, but William's head injuries proved so serious that he died at ten o'clock that evening. At his post-mortem examination, conducted by surgeons E.J.L. Whitmore and Mr Jackman, he was found to have seven wounds on the back and left-hand side of his head and four more on the right, along with injuries to his chin, cheek and temple. Several of his head wounds had corresponding skull fractures and his hands, shoulders and arms were also badly cut and bruised. Sarah's wounds, while severe, were not judged to be life threatening and, once they had been dressed, she was put to bed. Nevertheless, in the opinion of the surgeon, she was lucky to be alive – her skull was depressed from the violent blows she had received and, had she not put up her hands to protect herself, she might not have survived the terrible onslaught that left her with gashes over both eyes, a split scalp and cuts and bruising to her arms and shoulders.

Meanwhile, a neighbour, Thomas Radford, had heard the commotion and, noticing Smith and Wiles leaving the shop, he surreptitiously followed them as they walked across fields to nearby Blagdon. Having tracked them to the George Inn, he notified the local constable, James Clarke, who apprehended the pair as they were enjoying a meal of bread and cheese and a drink. When searched, both men were found to have objects from the shop in their possession, including a loaf of bread, a pair of spectacles, some silver coins, several two-ounce packets of tobacco, and a small, ivory-handled penknife that had been in the pocket of Sarah's apron before the attack. She later identified the penknife as one she had owned for more than twenty years.

Once in custody, Smith made a statement exonerating himself from all blame. He alleged that Wiles had planned to rob the elderly couple at their first visit to the shop, but had caught a glimpse of Mr Wilkins sitting in the back kitchen. Thinking that Wilkins would probably go to work shortly, the men had returned to the shop later, expecting to find Sarah on her own. According to Smith, he had not been in the shop while Sarah was being beaten but had entered only when he heard William's desperate cries of 'murder'. He had grabbed the spade with which his companion was belaying the old man, at which Wiles had picked up an iron and continued to beat Wilkins into unconsciousness. Wiles then returned to the shop where he found Sarah struggling to get to her feet. He hit her with the iron, then, once she too was unconscious, he searched her clothes, ripping off her apron pocket to get at the coins within. Smith then left the house and began walking towards Ubley. Wiles caught up with him shortly afterwards and offered him *5s 6d* – a half share of the proceeds of the robbery – which he took.

Not surprisingly, Wiles's statement was in direct contrast to that of his accomplice. According to Wiles, it was he who had waited outside the shop, while Smith had gone inside. When he returned, Wiles noticed that Smith had a considerable amount of blood on his trousers and challenged him, saying, 'You have been doing something.' Smith assured Wiles that he had done nothing and then attempted to hide the bloodstains on his clothes by rubbing them with dirt.

An inquest was held before coroner Mr Uphill, the two prisoners being taken to Sarah's sickbed, where she was able to positively identify them as the men who had attacked her. The coroner's jury deemed that William Wilkins had died as a direct result of his injuries and Wiles and Smith were indicted by magistrates for his wilful murder and sent to Shepton Mallett Gaol to await their trial at the Spring Assizes.

The trial opened at Taunton on 4 April 1851, with Lord Chief Justice Baron presiding. The prosecuting counsels were Mr Phinn and Mr Tring and, while Mr Edwards represented Smith, Wiles was not defended. Both men were charged with the murder of William Wilkins and Smith was additionally charged with aiding and abetting Wiles. Before the court, Smith admitted to having committed the robbery but denied any involvement in the violent attack on the elderly couple and maintained that he did not know in what state the couple were left. His judge, he added, would be in Heaven.

The chief witness was Sarah Wilkins, who was carried into court on a chair and was obviously still very much affected by her injuries. She begged not to be seated near to the two defendants and, several times during her testimony, appeared on the verge of fainting and had to be assisted by the surgeons attending as witnesses.

Once all the evidence had been heard, Mr Edwards stood up to address the court in Smith's defence. He told the jury that one of the prisoners must have committed the murder but that there was insufficient evidence to suggest that Smith was the killer, or even that he had any inkling of his companion's intentions on entering the shop.

The judge then summed up the case. The evidence against the two men, he observed, was overwhelming. They had been seen together in the vicinity of the shop shortly before the murder and were discovered together after it. They had been followed from the scene of the crime and, on being apprehended, both men were found to have items stolen from the shop on their persons. The judge then clarified the law regarding joint culpability for the jury. If two parties were together jointly concerned in a felony, he told them, and in the commission of this felony, one of them committed a murder in the presence of the other, then both were equally guilty. In this case, Smith had admitted to being present and had accepted a share of the spoils, even though he had denied any responsibility for the death of the old man. It was up to the jury to decide whether there was any doubt in their minds that, even if he had not actively participated in the killing, he had consented to the death. He reminded the jury that, although they owed a duty to the two accused men, they also held a duty to society and to the protection of the lives of her Majesty's subjects. They must give their verdict according to the evidence they had heard and the oaths they had taken.

The jury returned shortly afterwards to deliver their verdict that Smith and Wiles were equally guilty of wilful murder, leaving the judge to pass sentence of death on both men.

While awaiting their fate, both Smith and Wiles made a full confession, both admitting to an equal part in the crime and expressing remorse for their actions. Smith was, at the time of the murder, thirty-two years old and apparently, the name 'Smith' was an alias that he had adopted to protect his respectable and well-to-do family from the notoriety of any association with his crimes. To the last, he refused to divulge his real name. A vagabond, he had met fifty-six-year-old Wiles only a week before the murder. Wiles, who was a blacksmith by trade, was a married man with several children. He was known to be a drunkard and had recently deserted his wife and family and taken to wandering about the country. After his incarceration, his wife visited him in prison and the couple appeared to reconcile their differences.

The double execution took place at Taunton Gaol on 23 April 1851. It was originally scheduled to take place at eleven o'clock in the morning but the businessmen of Taunton protested about the disruption that this would cause to their trade and the authorities agreed to bring the time forward to nine o'clock. Both men walked firmly to the gallows and joined with the prison chaplain, Revd Joseph Gatley, in final prayers. Then executioner William Calcraft released the drop and both men fell, Wiles dying instantly, Smith kicking and convulsing for a few moments before his life ended. After hanging for the customary period of one hour, the two men were buried within the grounds of the gaol.

Note: In various contemporary accounts of the murder, Wiles is alternatively named as Wills. However, official records indicate that Wiles is the correct name. The surgeon, Thomas Jackman, is also referred to as Thomas Jackman Howkins or Hawkins and John Hawkes Jackman.

10

'WHAT A PRETTY LITTLE WOMAN YOU WILL MAKE'

Cutcombe, 1853

Twelve-year-old Eliza Coles lived with her mother and older brother Richard at Lype Cottage, an isolated dwelling at Cutcombe, near Dunster. On the morning of 8 November 1853, Richard left for work at a nearby quarry and, soon afterwards, his mother also went to work, leaving Eliza alone at home. However, eighty-two-year-old Mary Norman lodged in an adjoining part of the house and was always at home should Eliza need her.

That day, Eliza wasn't alone for long. When Mary Norman checked on her at about ten o'clock, Eliza was sitting on one side of the fireplace and James Bailey on the other. Bailey, a nineteen-year-old labourer, lived with his parents about half a mile from the Coles family and had been very friendly with Eliza's father, who had died just a month earlier. Whenever Bailey visited Mr Coles, he would gently tease Eliza, who looked far older than her years, telling her, 'What a pretty little woman you will make. I should like to have you for my wife.'

Mary Norman asked Eliza what she was doing and the little girl innocently replied that she was making a dress for her doll. Mary then went about her housework, keeping half an ear on Eliza and James Bailey. She heard them talking for about an hour, although she was unable to hear what was being said. Mary didn't hear Bailey leave but, later that afternoon, he called on her and told her that there was nobody at home next door and the front door was wide open. Mary assumed that Eliza had gone out and carelessly left the door open, so she shut it.

When Richard came home from work at about six o'clock he found the cottage deserted. He spoke to Mary and learned that she hadn't seen Eliza since that morning, so went out to look for her. When he couldn't find her, he set out to meet his mother, thinking that Eliza might have done the same.

Elizabeth had not seen her daughter. Together, she and Richard searched for the little girl, a fruitless exercise until they reached a dilapidated old barn, just a stone's throw from the cottage. Richard opened the barn door and peered into the gloom. 'Mother, what is that?' he asked, pointing into the darkness. 'I see something white.'

Elizabeth made her way to the spot and reached towards the whiteness. To her horror, she touched a dead body, which was stiff and cold.

Although Elizabeth could tell that it was the body of a small woman, whose skirts had been pulled up over her head, in the dim light of her lamp she was unable to recognise it as her daughter's body. She picked up the corpse, noticing as she did that the head flopped backwards and made her way to the barn door, all the while shouting for help. When more lamps were brought, it finally dawned on Elizabeth that the body was Eliza's. Her throat was cut through to her backbone, severing her jugular vein and carotid artery and she had two puncture wounds close to the gash in her throat and a cut over her left eye. When surgeon Robert Holmes conducted a post-mortem examination, he found that Eliza had been hit twice on the head, with sufficient force to stun her. Holmes was able to state categorically that Eliza had not been raped before her murder.

Constable William Langdon was summoned and, after speaking to Mary Norman and finding out that Eliza had last been seen alive in the company of James Bailey, he went straight to Bailey's home.

Bailey was in bed and when Langdon told him that he was arresting him on suspicion of the wilful murder of Eliza Coles, he showed no surprise on hearing that Eliza was dead. 'I didn't murder her,' he told Langdon, adding that he had visited Eliza that morning and that she walked a little way with him, as far as the house of a man named George Pope. There, she left him to return home, saying that she was going to gather some sticks for the fire, and he continued on his journey. Bailey willingly handed over his knife to the constable and also the clothes that he had been wearing that day.

At daybreak the next morning, the scene of the murder yielded several clues. The barn floor was covered with ashes, in which there were numerous bloodstains and footprints, along with parts of a broken belt and buckle. More footprints were found close to a small stream near the barn.

When Bailey's clothes were examined, daylight revealed spots of blood that had hitherto been invisible by candlelight. These included a line of blood, which had been partially washed out. Challenged about the stains, Bailey stated that they were his own blood, claiming to suffer from frequent nosebleeds and to have cut himself a few weeks ago, at harvest time. Bailey's boots were compared to the footprints in the barn and by the stream and found to be a perfect match. Shown the pieces of belt, Bailey denied that the broken belt was his but admitted that he had a very similar one, which he told PC Langdon was at his home.

Bailey was taken before magistrates at Dunster, where he remained sullenly mute, refusing to answer any questions. On the same day, coroner William Munckton opened an inquest at the Rest and Be Thankful Inn at Cutcombe, although finding that all of the witnesses were at the magistrates' court in Dunster, he was forced to adjourn the proceedings until the following day. Eventually, the magistrates and inquest jury arrived at the same conclusion and James Bailey was committed for trial at the Somerset Assizes charged with the wilful murder of Eliza Coles.

Cutcombe. (© R. Sly)

The Rest and Be Thankful Inn, Cutcombe. (© R. Sly)

The trial took place at Taunton on 25 March 1854 and was presided over by Mr Justice Erle and prosecuted by Mr Stone and Mr Phinn, while Mr Collier and Mr Karslake conducted Bailey's defence. Stone opened the proceedings by describing the events of the day of the murder to the court, calling Elizabeth and Richard Coles, Mary Norman and surgeon Robert Holmes as witnesses.

The court heard that Bailey was seen with Eliza at eleven o'clock on the morning of 8 November, the last time that anyone had seen her alive. Shortly afterwards, labourer William Sedgemore saw Bailey coming from the direction of Eliza's home. Sedgemore described Bailey as looking frightened and very red in the face, as if he had been running. Mary Pope told the court that Bailey had visited her at about half-past eleven and told her that he was going to Stowey Quarry, which was where Richard Coles worked. He reached the quarry at about midday and spent four hours there, before returning to Lype Cottage and telling Mary Norman that the door was open but there was nobody at home.

The prosecution then called Anne Howe, who had found the broken belt in the barn, and Richard Norman, who was present when she found it. They were followed into the witness box by PC Langdon and gamekeeper George Hole, who had looked after Bailey after his arrest. Bailey told the same story to both Langdon and Hole – he visited Eliza, she walked a little way with him and then left him to go and gather some sticks.

The prosecution then tried to establish ownership of the broken belt. William Yandall, a workmate of Bailey's, stated that he had borrowed a belt from him several times in the past and that he recognised the broken pieces found at the murder scene as belonging to Bailey. The defence immediately tried to discredit Yandall as a witness, forcing him to admit under cross-examination that he had previously been tried and convicted for stealing a watchcase. Yandall denied that he had bullied Bailey at work and that Bailey had once accused him of stealing mutton fat from him.

Another workmate, John Kane, also recognised the belt as belonging to Bailey, pointing out some distinctive splicing, which he believed made the belt very identifiable. Again, the defence tried to discredit Kane, suggesting that he was only testifying for the prosecution because he owed Bailey 4d and didn't want to pay it back. Both Sedgemore and Kane were adamant that they had never seen Bailey suffering from nosebleeds.

The prosecution then called George Green, a shoemaker and part-time constable from Dunster. Green related comparing Bailey's boots to the footprints found near Eliza's body, saying that they were a perfect match. There were fragments of ash in the prints near the stream, suggesting that whoever had made them had previously been into the barn and picked up ashes from the floor in the tread of his boots.

Coroner William Munckton testified to taking Bailey's clothes and boots and handing them to analytical chemist William Herapath of Bristol. Herapath then took the witness stand and described his examination of the garments and the conclusions he had reached.

Inside the right-hand pocket of Bailey's jacket were two bloody finger marks and a small spot of blood. In Herapath's opinion, the two finger marks were made by blood on the backs of the fingers and knuckles. There was a line of fifteen blood spots on the right-hand side of the jacket and another spot on the outside of the right-hand pocket, all of which had been partially washed out. Herapath believed that this blood had projected onto the coat with force, possibly when the wearer's right arm was thrown violently outwards in a slashing motion, while holding a bloody knife or similar weapon in the right hand. Although Herapath could not be positive that the stains were of human rather than animal origin, he described the tests that he had carried out, the results of which indicated that the stains were blood rather than any other fluid. Herapath also stated that the stains were not consistent with blood dropping onto the garments during a nosebleed.

Defence counsel Mr Collier immediately challenged Herapath's conclusions, asking him a series of hypothetical questions that eventually became so far-fetched that the judge intervened. Herapath was strongly criticised by Collier for smiling at his questions. 'Remember, Mr Herapath, this is not the first occasion on which you have been rebuked for flippancy.'

Herapath indignantly denied any such occurrence, at which Collier countered, 'Well, sir, answer my questions properly, without smiling.'

'I will if you put them properly,' Herapath retaliated, bringing the spat to a close.

Mr Justice Erle then asked Herapath a few questions about the type of bleeding that could be expected from such a wound as the one to Eliza's throat.

'When the carotid artery is cut, there is a continuous stream of blood in alternations and not a succession of spurts unless the opening was compressed or divided by any resisting medium' [sic] explained Herapath. 'If a man's hand so compressed a cut carotid artery, it would be almost immersed in blood from the stream forced against it.' In response to the judge's questions, Herapath further stated that the blood found on Bailey's clothes could have been there for up to six months.

The prosecution then rested, leaving Mr Collier to open his defence of Bailey. Collier's first action was to recall William Yandall to the witness box and Yandall now stated that he had seen Bailey have at least two nosebleeds while they were working together.

Collier then addressed the jury. He pointed out that there was no apparent motive for Eliza's murder – no hope of gain, no desire for revenge and no 'promptings of animosity.' Collier maintained that his client was a man of weak intellect, something that had made him the butt of countless jokes, taunting and teasing from those around him. Not once in the face of this torment had Bailey ever reacted violently, neither had he shown any temper, nor any desire for revenge.

According to Herapath, said Collier, if Bailey had committed the murder, he would have been wet with the blood of his victim. Why, then, would he choose to visit Mary Pope? And why would he even consider going to the workplace of his victim's brother or going back to the scene of the crime and speaking to Mary Norman? Was it possible that a man who had so brutally murdered an innocent child would actively seek to place himself in the society of other people, when a more logical reaction would be to hide away or flee?

Collier asked the jury to look beyond science and look at the evidence in their hearts rather than relying on the imperfect recollection of a constable or the spurious similarities of belts and buckles or even the microscopic examination of globules of blood. If the blood on Bailey's jacket had been projected there by force, surely it could have been blown from his nose during a nosebleed, rather than just having dripped onto the garments. Reminding the jury that a young man's life depended on their decision, Collier told them that his client's conduct from beginning to end was more consistent with innocence than with guilt and that, unless the jury disregarded everything they had ever known or read about murder and murderers, it was impossible to come to the conclusion that Bailey was guilty.

After Mr Justice Erle had summed up the case, the jury retired to consider their verdict. 'The learned judge summed up with great perspicuity and impartiality' wrote the contemporary newspapers. Yet, considering that the members of the jury were all Somerset men, most would have read details of the case in the *Somerset County Gazette*, which were printed after Bailey appeared before magistrates. Then the newspapers reported, 'It is said that the prisoner has often taken liberties with females and that, on their resistance, he has evinced great anger and on one occasion he even went so far as to pursue a young woman whom he had thus treated with a pick-axe, threatening to take her life because she refused to submit to his brutal desire.'

After deliberating the case for almost two hours, the jury returned with a verdict of guilty, which they tempered with a strong recommendation for mercy on account of Bailey's weak intellect. Bailey, who seemed indifferent to his fate, refused to answer when Mr Justice Erle asked if he had anything to say, so Erle donned his square of black silk and, after promising to forward the jury's recommendations to the relevant authorities, pronounced the death sentence on James Bailey.

The date of Bailey's execution was provisionally set for 15 April 1854 and, shortly before he was due to die, Bailey confessed to the murder. According to Bailey, he went to the barn in search of a piece of chain and Eliza followed him and began making fun of him and calling him names. In a rage, he first tried to strangle her with his belt, cutting her throat with his knife when the belt broke. 'This is all I have to say,' he concluded, taciturn to the last.

Probably because of his acknowledged 'weakness of intellect', Bailey was not executed. His death sentence commuted to one of transportation for life and he apparently set sail for Australia aboard the *Lord Dalhousie* on 19 September 1863. His whereabouts in the intervening years between his trial and his departure for Australia are not known.

Note: Eliza's age at the time of her murder is variously given as eleven and twelve years old. The surgeon who conducted the post-mortem examination is named in contemporary newspaper reports as Robert Holmes and Robert Hole.

11

'YOU DON'T MEAN IT!'

Wiveliscombe, 1856

On the afternoon on Tuesday, 23 December 1856, John Aplin was in the mood for going out to celebrate. Aged about twenty-two, and planning to be married the following year to the young woman who was already bearing his child, he was an agricultural labourer employed by Mr Corner at Kings Brompton. After being given a £5 banknote by his generous employer as a gesture of seasonal goodwill, he went to Wiveliscombe Christmas market, where he exchanged the note for cash. Thomas Nation, a fellow labourer who lived at Upton, was also going into town, and he too was planning to enjoy the benefits of a festive thank-you from his employer, in this case a half-sovereign. According to various witnesses who would be called upon to give their recollections in court a few weeks later, Nation and Aplin were seen riding in a cart together towards Wiveliscombe spent much of the day in each others' company at several different inns in or near the town, including the Wheatsheaf and the White Hart. For part of the time they were joined by Aplin's brothers, George and Thomas.

After having been drinking for several hours, by early evening John Aplin was naturally a little the worse for wear and in a very open-handed frame of mind, as he freely treated the others to similar refreshment. Rather foolishly, he chose to reveal to them how much money he was carrying around, by emptying his pockets in full view as he counted out his remaining money – about £5 – and placed it in a purse. Keen to ingratiate himself with this incautious benefactor, Nation produced a carpetbag containing some tobacco, and invited them all to share it.

At about nine o'clock, Nation and Aplin left the Wheatsheaf together. Nation had decided that it would be as well to attach himself to this new-found friend, who had now evidently come to his senses and was equally certain he would rather go on his own. However, any effort he may have made to persuade the other man to leave him alone proved unsuccessful, and both men climbed into a horse-drawn cart together, Aplin planning to return the vehicle and animal to his employer and then go home. His brothers had left some time previously. If only they had stayed longer, the course of subsequent events might have been very different.

They were seen to go through the gate at Langley turnpike near Wiveliscombe, but shortly afterwards they turned back and went some distance in the opposite direction

Wiveliscombe High Street. (Authors' collection)

before turning round again. It was thought that Nation had seen George Aplin a little way ahead of them, and persuaded John to hang back. Perhaps the latter realised that it would not be wise to do anything that might provoke his passenger.

Later that evening Mr and Mrs Slocombe were walking along Grant's Lane, towards their home at Langley. Suddenly they heard a horse and cart coming rather quickly down the lane, and they moved into the hedge to let it pass. The horse went past them at a full gallop, and they were surprised to notice that the cart seemed to be empty. Vehicle and animal continued down the lane, and Mr Slocombe heard the cart stop near the house.

Mr Hayes, who lived there and was upstairs at the time, was equally startled that it should be outside his front door. He went to his window and called outside. Receiving no reply, he got a light and went out to the cart. On looking inside, he was horrified to see the body of a man whose throat had been cut from ear to ear. His heels were hanging over the front of the trap, his head was lying on a bag covered with blood, and a gurgling in the throat indicated that he was dying. He immediately called a doctor, but by the time the latter arrived, the injured man was beyond salvation. His body was searched, and no money was found in his pockets.

The matter was reported to Mr Lacy Collard at the county constabulary at Wiveliscombe. George and Thomas Aplin were found in an inn at about eleven o'clock and searched, but no money or blood was found on them, and they were able to account satisfactorily for their movements during the last few hours. Enquiries immediately led them to Thomas Nation, who had long had a reputation as a petty crook and thief. The parish constable and Mr Collard went to the house of Nation's father at Upton. As he was not there, they returned to a roadside inn at Loter's

The Square and White Hart, Wiveliscombe. (© R. Sly)

Cross, to keep watch. Nobody appeared, so they returned to Upton, but Nation had still not returned.

On Wednesday morning, Christmas Eve, shortly before seven o'clock, Officer Tout saw a man walking towards Upton. He called to Collard, and they followed the man, who turned out to be Nation. They took him into custody just as he was within a few yards of his father's house. 'You don't mean it!' was his sole response on being apprehended and charged.

Denying he had any money on him, Nation was taken to the White Hart, Wiveliscombe, where Collard proceeded to make a thorough search of his clothing, which revealed some money and a bloodstained knife. There was also blood on his trouser pocket and his hands, which he said he could explain as he had just been cutting some beef. He was then taken to Wiveliscombe police station, searched further, and three sovereigns were found on him. As soon as he was apprehended, his shoes were taken off. One of them was compared with the marks of footsteps on the road leading from the spot where the body of Alpin had been found dead in the cart, and the shoe corresponded exactly with one of those marks in every way.

That afternoon Nation appeared before the county magistrates at Milverton. Formal evidence was produced, and he was remanded in gaol at Taunton for further examination on Wednesday 31 December.

Meanwhile, an inquest on Aplin was held at Wiveliscombe Town Hall on Saturday 27 December. The jury returned a verdict of wilful murder, and Nation was committed for trial. A few days later it was reported by the local papers that John Aplin's betrothed, who also lived at Kings Brompton, was for some time said to be 'prostrate in violent hysterics'.

Nation appeared on trial for murder at Taunton on 2 and 3 April before Lord Chief Justice Cockburn. Mr Slade and Mr Prideaux were the counsel for the prosecution, while Mr Coleridge and Mr Kingdon appeared for the defence.

After the main sequence of events from 23 December onwards was outlined, Professor Herapath stated that on 31 December he had been sent the knife and some badly bloodstained clothes for examination. When he tested the blood on the knife, he found it had been immersed in 'living blood' up to the hilt. The blood had not coagulated until it was on the knife. Blood from a human body would coagulate in about twelve minutes. The globules were the same size as those of his own blood and of other men. He had compared them with blood from oxen, sheep and pigs, and the globules were larger than those of either of the three animals. Thus they were clearly from human blood, and the blood of a man who had consumed alcohol would have made no difference to his findings. There were also some cotton fibres in the nail notch of the knife, plainly visible through the microscope, giving every appearance of the knife having passed through the fabric twice.

Dr Edwards stated that the cut in the throat was nine inches long, from one ear to the other; it was a clean incision, and must have been made with a sharp instrument. There had been repeated cuts, four on the right side, first superficially and then sinking deep into the throat, making one deep cut, passing through the windpipe, dividing the whole of the blood vessels on the left side of the throat and the muscles that protected them, terminating one inch beyond the left ear and one inch below it. That in itself would have been sufficient to cause death, and the wound could certainly not have been self-inflicted. There were marks on the left cheek which looked to have been done by fingernails, as if the cheek had been held while the throat was being cut. The neckerchief was cut through for about five inches, tallying with the wound in the throat. It must have been inflicted while Aplin was in the cart, as the blood had run out at the bottom of the cart on to the ground, and there was blood outside the cart as well as inside.

Nation explained that he had fallen down, knocked some skin from his knuckles, cut off the loose skin with his knife, and then put the knife in his pocket. At the time, he was on his way home and, as it was cold, he had put his hand in his pocket. All the blood to be found there had resulted from this wound. As he had just had two teeth drawn, there was some blood from his mouth as well.

Altogether thirty-five witnesses were called to give evidence. The first to be called by the defence was Mr Hill, a dentist at Wiveliscombe, who said that Nation had come to his premises on 23 December at about three o'clock in the afternoon where he purchased some tobacco, snuff and hair cream. When the elder Mr Nation entered, his son told him that he had come in to have two or three teeth extracted. Hill asked if he should draw them, and the prisoner said he might. Hill removed two stumps and a large grinder, and then advised the patient to wash his mouth out. Saying he did not mind a drop of blood, Nation paid 2s in silver for extracting the teeth, 2s 5½d for the items purchased, and then left.

James Nation, the prisoner's father, confirmed that his son lived with him. Some years ago the son had saved some money, his father added to it, and put £50 into the

Taunton Savings Bank for him. About three years earlier he had bought four acres of ground, and his son lent him £50 towards it, and the father drew it out of the bank. With regard to events on the day in question, he had been at Wiveliscombe and bought 60lb of meat there. He then drove down to the White Hart. Thomas came to him there, and showed him three teeth. He was scraping one with the knife. His mouth was full of blood, and he wiped it with his hand and his sleeve as he had no handkerchief. When he asked for some meat from his father's cart, the latter cut some off and handed it to him. He then asked if he could have some money, and his father gave him three and a half sovereigns and left him at the White Hart. There was no shortage of work at the time, as Mr Nation Senior was a contractor for the repair of the local highways, and was currently employed on a route about twelve miles long.

When cross-examined, he said his son had had breakfast with him on the morning of 23 December. He did not ask for any money then, and he assumed the younger man was going out to work. When questioned as to the matter of cutting the meat, he said they often ate it raw at market, as it was generally so busy. Other witnesses for the defence included Mr Hill, an Upton farmer, and William Palfry, an innkeeper, who used to live near the prisoner. Both said he had worked for them and had always been reliable, the latter adding that he had always found him 'a very honest, sober character'.

The first witness called by the prosecution was Mr Collard, who said that when he went to Mr Nation's house on the night of the murder, the father wanted to know what was the matter. 'Your father has given some person in charge,' said Mr Tout, one of the other officers, 'has he got much money about him?' He may have a few shillings,' said the father, 'but I don't know whether he has so much.' Tout and Rocket, another officer, corroborated this evidence, but all three varied slightly in recalling the conversation which had taken place.

Mr Slade summed up for the prosecution, reminding the jury that it was not upon the speeches of counsel, but on the evidence, that they were to decide. They had to consider whether they had been given them a satisfactory explanation of the knife, the blood, the footsteps, and the carpetbag.

The Lord Chief Justice summed up in an address lasting three and a half hours, then the jury retired at eight o'clock, and returned twenty minutes later with a verdict of 'Guilty'.

In addressing the prisoner, the judge told him that what he had done was 'no crime done upon sudden provocation or in the heat of blood, or under the influence of those passions which sometimes lead men to commit acts against God and man's law'. He had killed for the mere motive of plunder, knowing that his victim had a few pieces of gold in his possession, and 'though he was your companion and your friend, you took advantage of the opportunity afforded by the darkness of the night, and you sprung upon him in the loneliness of his helplessness'. Donning the black cap, he sentenced Nation to death.

On Sunday 5 April, the condemned man spent some time in conversation with his father and brother, but still refrained from confessing that he was guilty of killing

Thomas Aplin. To his family, and to the clergymen who visited him during the remaining few days of his life, he refused to admit being the murderer. He admitted having been responsible for other crimes 'as numerous as the hairs of his head', but insisted that he was not guilty of the one for which he had been convicted.

At daybreak on 21 April, the scaffold was erected at Somerset County Gaol, Taunton. Not wishing to make the event too much of a spectacle, the authorities kept the hour of execution secret, and told some representatives of the local press that it would not take place until midday. It was therefore a smaller crowd than usual, numbering no more than 8,000, who gathered to see Thomas Nation pay for his crime with the full penalty of the law. Few people from Taunton were present, and 'the crowd for the most part was composed of rustics, among whom were many of the gipsy tribe'.

At seven o'clock divine service was performed in the gaol chapel by the chaplain, Revd R. Mant, and alone of the prisoners who attended, Nation stayed behind afterwards to receive the Sacrament. He was then escorted to the scaffold where William Calcraft was waiting to perform his duty. As he pinioned the prisoner, the latter begged, 'Don't hurt me; I can hardly breathe'. After he was launched into eternity with a few convulsive struggles, the crowd dispersed.

12

'TAKE ME AWAY AND HANG ME AT ONCE'

Bath, 1856 and 1864

Known to all as 'Ferret', costermonger James Howell peddled oysters, nuts and other items around the streets of Bath, where he lived in Avon Street with his wife, Eliza. The marriage had produced four children, all of whom had died at birth or in infancy but in January 1856, Eliza was close to giving birth to another baby.

On the evening of 19 January, James and Eliza were drinking together in The Seven Dials public house in Bath. As they frequently did, the couple were quarrelling and, when Eliza called James a profane name, he took a swing at her, hitting her mouth and making it bleed. Eliza burst into tears and James stormed out of the pub, leaving her sitting sobbing, her head in her hands.

However, this particular domestic fight was to be short lived, as James soon returned and tried to make amends, offering to buy Eliza a drink. At first she refused but James managed to talk her round and by the time the pub closed, the couple seemed to be on the best of terms.

The Howells left the pub together but somehow got separated on the short walk home. James arrived at Avon Street first and was furious to find that his wife was not already there. Neighbours John and Mary Brown heard him ranting and raving, threatening to 'kill the ******* cow' and vowing 'God strike me dead, I'll do some mischief and I'll go and drown myself.'

Eliza arrived back before too long, having stopped at a shop to buy some potatoes, and the Browns heard her telling James that she had been looking for him but couldn't find him. Moments later, they heard the sound of two blows, immediately followed by something or someone falling heavily and Eliza's voice saying, 'Jim, you have killed your child and you have killed me. Look about you and see what you have done.'

Immediately afterwards, the Browns heard Howell's footsteps pounding downstairs and out of the house. As soon as he was gone, Eliza called out desperately to Mary Brown, 'Missus, for mercy's sake come in to me.' Mary went to the Howells' rooms, where she found Eliza lying on her side on the floor, which was awash with blood. 'Jim has killed me,' she moaned.

Avon Street, Bath. (© R. Sly,)

Meanwhile, James Howell had run to Abbey Street to fetch midwife Mrs Webb, who was asleep in bed. As she struggled to get dressed, Howell paced up and down on the landing outside her room, drunkenly urging her to hurry up. 'Bring the bitch out or she will be dead before the bitch gets there,' he yelled at Mrs Webb's neighbour, James Box. So aggressive was Howell's demeanour that a terrified Mrs Webb eventually went off with him half-dressed.

When she arrived at Howell's home, Mrs Webb quickly realised that she needed urgent medical assistance and sent for a surgeon. Eliza was lying on the floor covered in blood and gasping for breath. While waiting for the doctor, Mrs Webb checked her pulse, which was barely perceptible, and felt beneath her bodice for a heartbeat, fearing that her patient was very near death.

Surgeon Mr W.A. Cox arrived within minutes, accompanied by another surgeon, John Barrett, who happened to be visiting him when he received the request to attend Eliza. The surgeons found that the lower half of Eliza's dress was drenched in blood and, when they investigated the source of the bleeding, they found a deep cut on her genitals. Cox barely had time to try and staunch the bleeding with a wet cloth before Eliza gasped feebly and died. The surgeons immediately attempted to deliver her baby by Caesarean section but the baby boy was dead. When Cox later conducted a post-mortem examination, there was scarcely a drop of blood left in Eliza's body. He and Barrett were both of the opinion that the wound was caused by a heavy kick from a man's boots.

An inquest was opened on Eliza Howell's death at which the jury returned a verdict of 'manslaughter' against James Howell. However, by the time the inquest concluded, Howell had already appeared before magistrates in Bath, who had determined that his offence was the more serious one of wilful murder and it was on that indictment that he stood trial before Mr Justice Crowder at the next Somerset Assizes. The case was prosecuted by Mr Lempiere and Howell was undefended, although, at the request of the judge, Mr Poulden agreed to act for him.

The court heard that Howell had seemed very distressed at his wife's death, telling the police, 'Take me away and hang me at once.' He was very drunk on his arrest and swore that he had not intended to hurt Eliza or his baby. Having heard the case for the prosecution, Mr Poulden intimated that his client was willing to plead guilty to manslaughter. In his summary of the case for the jury, Mr Justice Crowder seemed to place great emphasis on the fact that Howell had used no weapon in his brutal attack on Eliza and stated that it was impossible to arrive at the conclusion that Howell had deliberately killed his wife. Crowder told the jury that he believed that they would be of the opinion that the prisoner was guilty of manslaughter and the jury concurred, leaving Crowder to sentence Howell to six years' penal servitude.

By February 1864, Howell had been freed on a ticket of leave and was now living in an apartment on Little Corn Street, with a woman named Susan Cleverly. On the morning of 16 February, his landlord and next-door neighbour, Philip Marsh, heard cries of 'murder' coming from Howell's apartment, along with what sounded like somebody jumping heavily on something soft. Marsh went to investigate the noises and, as he opened his front door to go next door, he happened to spot a policeman on the street.

Together, Marsh and PC William James went to Howell's apartment, where they found Howell sitting calmly on the bed, dressed only in his trousers and a torn shirt while Susan Cleverly stood nearby looking frightened and distressed, a large bump over one of her eyes. Marsh protested at the noise that the couple were making, at which Susan ran to the policeman and begged him, 'For God's sake, take him into custody or he will murder me.'

PC James asked Howell what he was up to, to which Howell replied that he didn't know. 'You blackguard, you have murdered one and now you want to murder me' Susan interrupted.

'I will murder thee, for thee's been and broke my shirt,' Howell growled at her.

PC James indicated the large lump over Susan's eye, which was roughly the size of a duck egg.

'Do you mean to say you've done that?' he asked Howell.

'Yes, I have, I'll kill the bitch,' Howell replied.

PC James took Susan to one side and asked her if she wanted him to arrest Howell. Susan considered the question carefully before deciding that, if Howell was arrested, he would not be detained in custody for long and would surely murder her when he got out. She told PC James that she was too frightened to press charges against Howell and, after warning the couple to keep the noise down, James and Mr Marsh left Susan to her fate. As soon as the policeman left, Susan fled to a neighbour's room in terror, while Howell ran through the house brandishing a poker and threatening to kill her and anyone who harboured her.

Susan stayed with James Howell for another couple of days before approaching their landlord and asking him to find her alternative accommodation. She moved into another property owned by Mr Marsh, where she died on 21 February. Surgeon Mr Barrett, who had already witnessed the results of Howell's violence eight years earlier, conducted a post-mortem examination with Dr James Tunstall. Susan had two black eyes, scratches, cuts and bruises all over her body, a bloody wound on her lip and her abdomen was unusually swollen. The doctors found head injuries, with corresponding bleeding in her brain, and noted that her lungs were inflamed and filled with bloody serum. Both surgeons agreed that Susan Cleverly, a previously healthy woman, had died from injuries to her brain and lungs caused by a violent beating or kicking.

Once again, Howell was arrested and appeared before magistrates at Bath Police Court, where he was sent for trial at the next Somerset Assizes, charged with Susan Cleverly's wilful murder. His trial took place before Mr Baron Martin on 18 March 1864, with Mr T.W. Saunders and Mr Bailey prosecuting. Howell, who was undefended, pleaded 'Not Guilty'.

The court heard evidence from medical witnesses Mr Barrett and Dr Tunstall, as well as Philip Marsh and his wife Mary Ann, PC James and another neighbour, Mary Adams, who lived in the room below Howell's apartment and testified to hearing Howell violently beating Susan Cleverly on more than one occasion. All the witnesses seemed to agree that Susan Cleverly had died violently at Howell's hands, yet once again, the judge intervened and steered the jury, saying that, in his opinion, it was scarcely a case of murder but, according to the present administration of the law, it amounted only to manslaughter.

As instructed, the jury found Howell guilty of the lesser offence of manslaughter, at which Mr Baron Martin turned to address Howell. Martin described Howell's conduct as '... as scandalous and unmanly as it had been unlawful', adding that it approached as nearly as possible to murder. Commenting that Howell seemed to have learned nothing from his incarceration for the murder of his wife, Martin announced his intention of imposing the maximum penalty that the law allowed, sentencing Howell to penal servitude for life. He was later transported to Western Australia, departing on *Belgravia* on 4 April 1866.

13

'I'LL GIVE THEE VEAL CUTLETS'

Wells, 1857

In 1839 Josiah and Ann Parker were married, and they settled at Wells, where he made a living as a butcher. In due course they had a family of four children, and over the next seventeen years they led a life together which would have been happy and contented, had it not been for Joseph's occasional outbursts of distressing behaviour, which clearly called his state of mind into question. The worst was on the day when he cut his throat, arms and legs, telling Ann that he wanted to bleed to death. She called the doctor, and had him sent to an asylum. However, he soon recovered, was discharged, and came home again.

Unhappily, worse was to follow. Early in 1857 he began acting strangely again, accusing Ann of infidelity, and threatening to attack her. She was so alarmed that on the morning of 9 February she went to see Mr Nicholls, a surgeon at Wells, to consult him on her husband's state of mind. Mr Nicholls came and visited him that afternoon and thought he seemed perfectly sane. Under the impression that there was little to worry about, he left and told her that he would return the following day to make a second examination if she wished.

Yet she had seen too much of her husband's behaviour not to be seriously concerned for her safety as well as his health. Before she went to bed that night, she asked their servant girl to sit with him throughout the hours of darkness as he slept. In order that no harm would befall their employee either, she sent for a policeman to stay in the house overnight as well. At the same time, she said that she would not rest easily until he was sent back to the lunatic asylum – for good, if necessary.

The night passed without incident, and Mr Nicholls returned. This time he began to share her concerns, and formed the opinion that the patient was definitely mad. Nicholls had a discussion with him about his reasons for believing that his wife was cheating on him, and told him he was sure there were no reasons for believing it. Parker then became rational again, asked him for a draught to soothe his nerves, and promised he would go to bed. Next morning, he assured them, he would get up 'a new man and would live a new life'.

Wells. (Authors' collection)

Before they parted, Nicholls begged Parker to be kind to his wife, and the latter vowed he would not hurt a hair of her head. He had once been teetotal, and during that period had shown signs of insanity. The surgeon then went on his way, doubtless hoping all would be well. Sadly, events were about to prove otherwise.

At about five o'clock in the afternoon, Josiah and Ann were about to have tea, and planned to have veal cutlets. Ann went to the shop door and asked her husband if he had cut them ready for cooking.

Without any warning, he shouted at her, 'I'll give thee veal cutlets!' He then seized a cleaver and struck her on the head several times until she fell over. He then jumped on her, stamped on her chest, and repeatedly aimed at her head. Neighbours, alarmed by the sound of her cries, came in and tried to pull him off her as they attempted to prise the weapon from his grasp. A doctor was summoned, but it was too late for him to save her. Her head was badly gashed, and one of her hands was almost severed. She lingered in agony, followed by increasing spells of unconsciousness, for another six days before dying of her injuries.

When Parker was arrested, he walked to the station with the police quite calmly. As they went, he said that he regretted not having also killed his eldest and youngest children as well.

At the inquest a few days later, before the coroner, Mr Fry, it was established that Parker had long been a heavy drinker, and he was angry with his wife because he knew she was taking steps to try and have him moved back to the asylum. As he had been in such an establishment once if not twice before, he was determined not to go back. The inquest proceedings were adjourned briefly so he could be brought

Wells Market Place, 1920s. (Authors' collection)

into the court. As he was led in, 'pale as death, with his eyes closed', supported by two policemen, 'his appearance excited a feeling of commiseration'. The Coroner told him that he had no wish to cause him unnecessary pain, or to have him made a spectacle of, but it was only right that he should have an opportunity of hearing the evidence brought against him, so he could confront his accusers if he wished. However, he was equally free to retire.

'I know I am guilty,' he answered sadly. 'I mean to plead guilty at my trial. I don't wish to live. I've brought ruin and desolation on all my family. Let the matter be as short as you can, and have no more ceremony than is requisite. I shall plead guilty at my trial.' After a pause, he went on, stating that he had been 'urged to it. I was worked to madness by an accessory. That accessory has murdered my wife. We ought to be hung side by side. I don't want to save my life; I would not raise my finger to save it. The man who urged me to do it always heard all he could and published it. I was driven to it.'

The Coroner then asked him to name the man.

'It is of little use,' he replied. 'The whole world knows it. I have nothing more to say.'

A verdict of wilful murder was returned against him, and he was committed for trial at the next Taunton Assizes, where he appeared on 2 April before Lord Chief Justice Cockburn. Mr Kingdon was counsel for the prosecution, and Mr Prideaux acted for the prisoner. After the facts of the case were recounted, Prideaux claimed that the prisoner had not been in a sane state of mind when he committed the act. For some time he had been under the delusion that his wife was being unfaithful. He would wander around the house muttering to himself, or get up in the middle of the night and light the fire, then leave it unattended, thus running the risk of burning the cottage down.

Mr Nicholls then addressed the jury, telling them of his dealings with Mr Parker. He concluded by remarking that the prisoner had generally been very kind to his wife. Nevertheless, there had been occurrences of distressing behaviour, self-injury, and at least one short spell in the asylum. Madness ran in the family, as his father had also gone insane, an aunt had hanged herself, and a cousin had died while an inmate in St Luke's Asylum. The matter of drunkenness came up, and Nicholls said that while the prisoner had been dependent on alcohol for part of the time, there had been a period when he was teetotal, yet that corresponded with one of his phases of mental derangement. His poor health could therefore not be ascribed to heavy drinking.

Having listened to the evidence, Lord Chief Justice Cockburn realised that Josiah Parker was to be pitied rather than treated as a common evil murderer, and could not be held accountable for his actions. He said that the case should not proceed any further, then directed the jury to find him not guilty on the grounds of insanity, and made an order that he should be detained at Her Majesty's pleasure.

14

'THEE HAST DONE 'IM'

Buckland Dinham, near Frome, 1861

On 5 August 1861, Byard Greenland and his nephew, Uriah Greenland, left the village of Buckland Dinham, near Frome, in search of work, along with a third labourer, William Millgrove. They found employment on a farm near Warminster, Wiltshire, where they helped with the corn harvest before setting off to walk back home on 10 August, their scythes over their shoulders. Their journey was punctuated by visits to several public houses and, although all three remained sober, there was a slight altercation with some other drinkers, during which Uriah Greenland was knocked down three or four times. Although he subsequently complained of a pain in his hip, he suffered no apparent injury other than bruised pride.

As the three men neared Buckland Dinham, they began to argue about the division of the money they had earned for their labours of the past week. As the most senior member of the group, Byard had been entrusted with all of their pay. Now he insisted that 1s 6d should be deducted from Uriah's share of the money, on account of his having damaged a gun belonging to Byard. Uriah agreed, adding that the deduction should not prevent Millgrove from receiving his money and the men laid down their scythes on the side of the road so that Byard could 'put the reckoning to rights', calculating how much was due to each of them after deduction of their expenses for rail fares and food. However, as soon as he had put down his scythe, Byard suddenly lunged at Uriah, who immediately fell to the ground.

'Oh, Bill. He has hit his knife into I,' Uriah told the shocked Millgrove, who hastened to help his injured friend, carrying him to the roadside and propping him up against a bank.

'Thee hast done 'im,' he accused Byard, as he tried to staunch the blood pouring from Uriah's chest.

'Thee can't swear that, Bill,' retaliated Byard.

'I can,' argued Millgrove.

The three men had halted their journey near to the turnpike gate, and Millgrove ran to the gatehouse, where he told toll collector James Gane what had happened. Gane advised Millgrove to hurry into Frome for a doctor and, while he did, Gane went to the Greenlands to see if he could be of assistance.

Buckland Dinham. (© R. Sly)

Byard told Gane that Uriah had accidentally run into his scythe and injured himself, asking Gane to take possession of his scythe and check to see if there was any blood on it. While Gane tried to comfort Uriah, who was obviously near to death, Byard walked away. He went in search of his wife, Jane, finding her visiting a cottage in Buckland Dinham belonging to labourer James Bailey.

Meanwhile, William Millgrove had returned with surgeon Benjamin Mallam. By that time, Uriah had died and Mallam asked Millgrove to go back to Frome to inform the police, asking a passer by on horseback to inform the constable at Buckland of what had occurred and get him to arrest Byard. Mallam then had Uriah's body carried to a nearby pub, where a closer examination revealed that he had been stabbed once in the chest, between his second and third ribs. The knife had penetrated his heart and left lung, causing his death.

Once Police Sergeant Watts heard about the incident from Mallam's messenger, he and PC Milward went straight to Byard Greenland's house, where they found Byard in the act of changing his clothes, obviously in preparation to leave hurriedly. Watts arrested Byard, who was described in the contemporary newspapers as 'a giant in height and strength'.

Byard was taken before magistrates on 12 August where, after William Millgrove, James Gane and Benjamin Mallam had testified, Uriah's pregnant widow, Elizabeth, took the stand to describe the relationship between her husband and his uncle and alleged killer. Elizabeth stated that Uriah and Byard had once been on very friendly terms but had quarrelled twice in March and April of that year, supposedly about work. Byard had threatened his nephew with a knife at least once and, on 29 April, after the second fight Uriah had taken out a summons against his uncle. However, the summons was never signed, as both Byard and his wife pleaded with Uriah to drop the case. Eventually, Uriah agreed, on the condition that Byard pay the cost of issuing the summons. Byard handed over two shillings and the two men shook hands.

After hearing from several people who identified a bloody clasp knife found near the scene of the murder as belonging to Byard and from the arresting officers, the magistrates remanded Byard to Shepton Mallet Gaol.

On the following day, coroner Bruges Fry opened an inquest at the Globe Inn. For some reason, Byard Greenland was not there and the coroner expressed surprise on learning that Chief Constable Valentine Gould had refused him permission to attend. Having heard evidence only from Millgrove and Benjamin Hallam, Fry adjourned the inquest until the next day, in an effort to ensure that Byard was given the chance to be present.

When the inquest resumed, the jury were told that magistrates had refused to order the Chief Constable to permit Byard to attend, a situation that, according to the foreman of the jury, was both 'unfair and un-English'. Nevertheless, the inquest proceeded without Byard Greenland, with much of the same evidence being repeated as had already been heard at the magistrates' court two days earlier. The one exception was the testimony of Elizabeth Greenland, who, since the magistrates' hearing, now claimed that her husband and Byard had fought three times, not twice.

The cause of the first fight was an indecent assault on her by Byard Greenland. Elizabeth alleged that Byard had attempted to take liberties with her in her own house, forcing her against a wall, putting his knee between her legs and attempting to undress her. When she resisted, Byard assured her that 'it was no harm' because he was her uncle. Elizabeth told him that if he didn't stop, she would scream and call the police. Initially too frightened to tell Uriah what had happened, she eventually plucked up enough courage to do so. Although she didn't know what had passed between her husband and his uncle after her revelations, she believed that Uriah was angry with Byard for trying to take liberties with her and that Byard was equally angry at the fact that Uriah knew what he had tried to do.

The inquest jury returned a verdict of wilful murder against Byard Greenland, as did the magistrates when the court hearing resumed and Byard was committed for trial at the next Somerset Assizes, where he appeared before Mr Justice Williams on 19 December 1861. Mr Prideaux and Mr T.W. Saunders conducted the prosecution and Williams asked Mr Brodrick to defend Greenland.

The first witness was William Millgrove, who told the court that it had been too dark at the time of the incident for him to see whether or not Byard had a knife in his hand when he suddenly lunged at his nephew. However, Millgrove was able to discredit Byard's explanation that Uriah had accidentally fallen onto his scythe, saying that the four scythes and four reap-hooks that the men had been carrying

Portland Prison, which was later converted to a borstal. (Authors' collection)

had been lying flat on the ground when Uriah fell and that he had fallen way from the scythes.

It was revealed at court that Byard's father and uncle had both been deaf and dumb and that Byard himself was known to suffer from epileptic fits. He had also suffered a serious head injury, after a man drove a pick into his head ten or so years earlier.

After hearing evidence about the ownership of the knife found at the scene of the murder, which several witnesses swore belonged to Byard, surgeon Benjamin Mallam took the stand. He recounted his initial examination of Uriah Greenland at the roadside by candlelight, followed by a more detailed and better illuminated inspection of Uriah's body at the inn and subsequent post-mortem examination.

Mallam told the court that the cause of Uriah's death was a single stab wound to his heart, which had penetrated his chest in a downwards direction. From this, Mallam concluded that Uriah had been stabbed by a much taller man. Mallam was positive that the wound could not have been caused by the deceased accidentally falling onto a scythe. The wound was the wrong shape to have been produced by the blade of a scythe and the four scythes that the three labourers were carrying had been tied together in pairs. Thus, if Byard's explanation for Uriah's injury were correct, Hallam stated that he would have expected to see two wounds, not one, besides which there were no traces of blood on the blades of any of the implements. Hallam had examined the bloody knife found near Uriah's body and confirmed that it was the right shape to have produced the wound in his chest. He had microscopically examined the knife blade and found that the stains on it were fresh blood, although he was unable to ascertain whether it was human or animal in origin.

Mr Brodrick then addressed the court for the defence. He pointed out that, although the prosecution counsels had handled the case fairly and skilfully, they had been unable to come up with any motive for Uriah's murder, save for two trumpery quarrels, both of which were made up almost as soon as they had taken place. Brodrick then questioned the conduct of William Millgrove and James Gane on the night of the murder, asking the jury why, if the two men truly believed that Byard was a murderer, they would have left him alone with his victim and then allowed him to wander off home unchecked.

Brodrick told the jury that he was not suggesting insanity as a reason for the murder but reminded them that Byard was an epileptic and might possibly do things as a result of his medical condition that would seem abnormal. Finally, Brodrick dealt with Millgrove's account of the sequence of events leading to Uriah's death.

He told the jury that Uriah had already been involved in a fight earlier that evening and was undoubtedly 'excited' and angered. Recalling the darkness of the night, Brodrick suggested that Uriah was annoyed that Byard intended to deduct money from his wages and had consequently rushed onto Byard's knife. Byard could have stabbed him by accident or in self defence.

Mr Justice Williams summed up the evidence for the jury in a way that the contemporary newspapers described as '... on the whole, unfavourably for the prisoner.' The jury then retired, deliberating for ten minutes before returning to pronounce Byard Greenland guilty, although they recommended mercy since they didn't believe that there had been any premeditation on Byard's part.

'My Lord, I am as innocent as a child unborn,' protested Byard to the judge. 'I did not wish to hurt my poor dear nephew.' In spite of his protests, Byard was sentenced to death and Mr Justice Williams commented adversely on the fact that he had maintained to the bitter end that Uriah's death was the result of a tragic accident, even in the face of conclusive evidence to the contrary. As Williams pronounced the death sentence, the bells of St Mary's Church tolled mournfully in the background, heightening the gravity of the judge's words.

Greenland's sentence was eventually commuted to one of life imprisonment and, on 11 March 1863, he was transported from Portland Prison to Western Australia on board the convict ship *Clyde*. He left behind his wife and eight children. Byard Greenland is believed to have been released from prison in July 1867, after which he settled In Australia until his death in 1879.

Note: William Millgrove's name is alternatively spelled Milgrove in some contemporary accounts of the case. The arresting officer's name is given as PC Ward and PC Milward.

15

'UNNATURAL AND UNSKILFUL INTERFERENCE'

Yeovil, 1863 and 1880

Elizabeth Fox worked as a servant at The Rectory at Rimpton and at the end of September 1863 she announced her intentions of going to visit her parents in Dorset. However, the proposed trip home was nothing more than a ruse since twenty-year-old Elizabeth was pregnant and unmarried. Instead of heading for Dorset, she went to the home of herbalists Robert Slade Colmer and his wife, Jane, who practised their trade at Yeovil.

Elizabeth stayed with the Colmers for a week until 4 October, when she suddenly died. The Colmers shared their home with their son, a doctor who had recently qualified at the Royal College of Physicians at Edinburgh. Shortly before Elizabeth's death, Robert Colmer called his son to attend to her. Dr Colmer found the girl in bed, complaining of intense pain in her stomach and determined that she was bleeding internally. He gave Elizabeth brandy and ergot of rye and pressed on her lower abdomen, which caused a flood of blood to gush from her vagina. However, in spite of the doctor's efforts, Elizabeth died soon afterwards.

Dr Colmer notified the police of the sudden death and a post-mortem examination was carried out two days later in the presence of five doctors, of which Colmer was one. It was found that Elizabeth had been between five and six months pregnant but had lost the baby and that her death had resulted from an extensive tear in her womb, which had been made by instruments of some kind. It was deemed impossible for the injury to have been spontaneous or for Elizabeth to have caused it herself.

At the subsequent inquest into Elizabeth's death, Robert Colmer explained that Elizabeth had suffered a miscarriage, expelling a foetus the size of a pigeon's egg. Following his training as a herbalist, Colmer told the inquest that he had burned the foetus and afterbirth, in the belief that doing so would prevent Elizabeth from suffering pain or contracting an infection.

In addressing his jury, the coroner pointed out that the law expected every medical man to be competent at handling any cases he undertook, be that man a qualified

Yeovil High Street, 1959. (Authors' collection)

surgeon, a doctor or a quack. If the jury believed that Elizabeth had gone to the Colmers for the sole purpose of procuring an abortion and Colmer had undertaken to carry out this procedure, in the eyes of the law, he was guilty of wilful murder. If, on the other hand, the jury found that Elizabeth had taken something of her own accord to induce an abortion and had then died as a result of the gross ignorance of Robert Colmer, then the proper verdict would be manslaughter.

The inquest jury found a verdict of manslaughter against Robert Colmer, who was tried for the offence at the Somerset Assizes in Taunton. However, once the prosecution had presented their evidence, the judge intervened, saying that he could see nothing to connect the accused with the rupture in her womb that ultimately killed Elizabeth Fox. The only offence that he could see was concealment of the birth, resulting from the fact that Colmer had burned the miscarried child. The jury could not recognise Elizabeth's foetus as 'a child' and immediately acquitted Colmer of this offence. He walked from the dock a free man.

Some years later, thirty-six-year-old Mary Budge, the widow of a solicitor from Crewkerne, embarrassingly found herself pregnant as a result of a relationship with John Haddy Foster, her much younger lodger. Like Elizabeth Fox before her, her situation filled her with shame and dread, particularly since she already had five children to support and very little money.

On 17 March 1880, Mary Budge visited the Colmers at their practice in Yeovil. By then, Robert Colmer had established his own practice in Old Market Street, Bristol, 'The Anglo-American Institute of Eclectic and Progressive Medicine etc.' where he proclaimed himself to be 'Dr Colmer MD, United States of America'. Jane Colmer,

Market Street, Crewkerne (Authors' collection)

also claiming to be an American MD, now ran the practice in Yeovil, at which her husband attended weekly as a consultant.

Nobody knew what passed between Mary Budge and the Colmers on 17 March, but Mary wrote to Jane Colmer on the following day:

> Madam, I have made excuses to get away and will be at your house at between half-past twelve or one on Friday. I shall be glad to go back by the next train if possible. I have procured the eighteen pounds. M BUDGE

On 19 March, Mary set out alone from Crewkerne station to travel to Yeovil. Having reached the station, she then caught an omnibus, which dropped her off close to the Colmers' shop at around midday. She spent most of the afternoon in the back room of the shop with Robert Colmer and, when she returned to Crewkerne later that night, she was obviously in agony.

Mary brought a medicine bottle of powder home with her, which she asked her daughter Annie to fill with sherry, telling her that it was a remedy for worms. She then passed an uncomfortable night, suffering from severe bleeding and agonising stomach cramps, in spite of which she refused to allow a doctor to be called to attend to her. Only on the following afternoon, when Mary was clearly near to death, did Annie summon medical assistance, by which time it was too late. Mary Budge died in her blood-drenched bed within an hour of the doctor's arrival. A post-mortem examination showed the cause of her death to be blood loss resulting from an injury to her uterus, made by 'unnatural and unskilful interference'.

An inquest into Mary Budge's death, held by coroner Mr Wybrants, returned a verdict of wilful murder against both Robert and Jane Colmer, even though Jane vehemently denied that Mrs Budge had been at her premises on 19 March. Both of the Colmers appeared before magistrates at Yeovil, although Jane was in an almost comatose condition and had to be carried into the hearing and revived with brandy and smelling salts.

It was shown that Mary Budge was dropped off by the omnibus driver directly outside Jane Colmer's shop and that he had seen her entering the premises. Jane's servant, Ellen Cheney, testified that Jane had then sent her to fetch Robert from his son-in-law's house nearby and Robert had gone into the back room with Mary. Ellen continued to say that at about three o'clock, Robert had called for his wife to come in and help him because Mary Budge had fainted. The servant girl was then kept busy running errands for the rest of the afternoon but saw Mary Budge once more at seven o'clock in the evening, when she glimpsed her through an open door, sitting on a sofa looking ill and distressed and being supported by Jane Colmer.

It emerged at the magistrates' court that John Foster, the father of Mary Budge's unborn child, had not told the whole truth at the inquest, under the mistaken impression that he was protecting his lover's reputation. He now revised his statement, saying that he had known that Mary was going to Yeovil and the purpose of her visit. When the Colmers were sent for trial, Foster's conflicting statements were crucial to their defence.

Originally scheduled to be held at the next Somerset Assizes, the trial was eventually moved to the Central Criminal Court in London, since a local jury would have been aware of Robert Colmer's previous indictment for manslaughter in similar circumstances and it was thought that he would not get a fair trial. Mr Justice Hawkins presided over the proceedings, with Mr H.B. Poland, Mr Montagu Williams and Mr J.F. Norris prosecuting, while Mr E. Clarke QC MP and Mr Bullen defended. Both Jane and Robert Colmer pleaded not guilty to the charge of wilful murder against them.

Much of the prosecution's case hinged on the testimony of medical witnesses such as George Frederick Wills, who was Mary Budge's doctor and had been called in too late to save her life. The doctor described examining Mary immediately after her death and observing that, although there were no marks of violence on her body, she was '... a most peculiar yellow colour.' Wills performed a post-mortem examination the next day, finding that all her organs were healthy with the exception of her uterus, which he sent to Dr Braxton Hicks at Guy's Hospital for his opinion. Braxton Hicks in turn forwarded the uterus to another doctor, Dr Galabin. All three doctors had absolutely no doubt that Mary Budge had been between two and three months pregnant and that the foetus had been removed from her womb 'by violence'. The appearance of the uterus suggested that a hard instrument had been used to induce an abortion, resulting in a laceration.

Wills continued to say that an abortion was a highly dangerous operation and that, after undergoing such a procedure, a woman would need very careful treatment.

*The Old Bailey,
London. (Authors'
collection)*

*Mr Justice Hawkins.
(Authors' collection)*

The fact that Mary Budge had been permitted to travel home by omnibus and train had undoubtedly increased the danger to her life.

The medicine bottle that Mary had brought home with her from Yeovil was also analysed and found by county analyst Mr James W. Gatehouse to contain a mixture of quinine sulphate and sherry. At the time, quinine was falsely believed to induce abortion and Gatehouse testified that there was an unusually large amount of quinine present in Mary's medicine. Whereas he would normally have expected to find two grains per ounce of fluid, Mary's bottle contained five grains of dissolved quinine per ounce, with an additional three grains per ounce of solid quinine. All the doctors believed that such a large amount would have affected her internal organs.

The Colmers defence was simple, with both denying ever having seen Mary Budge. Jane Colmer deposed that, on 19 March, there had been nobody at her house but herself and her family and servants. Her husband had not visited her and so could not have operated on Mary Budge, even had she been there. However, the prosecution had recovered telegrams sent by Robert Colmer to his wife over the preceding few days that seemed to indicate that he was planning to be in Yeovil on 17 March – the date of Mary Budge's first visit – but was detained by other business. The last telegram, sent on 18 March, read: 'Important business detains me to-night; will come by first train in the morning arriving at Yeovil nine o'clock certain' [sic].

Mr Clarke addressed the jury in defence of the Colmers, stating that, in his opinion, the telegrams had nothing to do with the case and neither did the medical evidence regarding the contents of Mary Budge's stomach and the analysis of her medicine. Clarke reminded the jury that a search of the premises at Yeovil had revealed no surgical instruments other than a speculum and that instrument had definitely not been used to procure any abortions.

Clarke next dealt with the evidence of Mary's lover, twenty-three-year-old John Foster. At the time of Mary Budge's pregnancy, Foster had held a good job at a bank, earning an annual salary of £90 and having the security of a job for life. After the death of Mary Budge, he had been forced to resign his position. Clarke argued that, for Foster, the termination of Mrs Budge's pregnancy was of the highest possible importance. Believing that he was protecting his lover's reputation, Foster had lied at the inquest about his own complicity in procuring her abortion and, by his own admission, he was morally guilty of the same crime with which the defendants were now charged. Clarke argued that Foster was not just morally guilty but also legally guilty, since he was an accessory before the fact. In effect, Foster was not only a perjurer but he was also an accomplice in Mary Budge's murder. It was all very well for him to say 'I endeavoured to shield the reputation of the deceased woman' but this left the prosecution's case resting almost entirely on the evidence of someone who was dishonest and not only stood to profit from the crime but had even made arrangements for it to be committed.

Ellen Cheney was quite simply mistaken in her testimony about Mary Budge's presence at Mrs Colmer's house on 19 March, suggested Clarke and, apart from Ellen Cheney, nobody had actually seen Robert Colmer at or near his wife's premises on the day in question. Clarke added that 19 March was a Friday and Friday was market day in Yeovil. If the Colmers had carried out an illegal operation on Mary Budge, would they have chosen a Friday on which to do so – a day when they knew that their shop would be exceptionally busy with customers, any one of whom could have interrupted the procedure at any time?

Surprisingly, Clarke then terminated his defence of the Colmers without calling any witnesses, even though he was said to have twelve or thirteen people waiting to testify. Thus, it only remained for Mr Justice Hawkins to summarise the case for the jury. He informed the jury of the laws relating to abortion, which were:

> Whosoever, with intent to procure the miscarriage of any woman, whether she be or be not with child, shall minister to her or cause to be taken by her any poison or any other noxious thing or shall unlawfully use any instrument or any other means whatsoever with the like intent shall be guilty of felony.

In charging the defendants with murder, it was not alleged that they bore any animosity towards the victim but that they had performed a very cruel, very barbarous and very wicked unlawful operation – in itself a felony – which had resulted in her death.

The jury must determine whether either or both of the defendants had performed an illegal operation on Mary Budge. If the jury came to the conclusion that they had and that Mary Budge's death had resulted, then the defendants were guilty of wilful murder. There was no proof that anything had been done by the Colmers – nobody had seen the actual operation performed, although the evidence suggested that the deceased had left her home in perfect health and returned near to death, having spent the intervening time at the Colmers premises in Yeovil. The omnibus driver saw her entering the premises, Ellen Cheney saw her inside and numerous other customers from the shop had spoken of hearing groans coming from a back room that day. Nobody had seen Mary Budge anywhere else in Yeovil during the entire day in question.

Legally, it didn't matter whether the operation had been preformed by Robert Colmer, Jane Colmer or both of them together. By law, if two defendants were jointly engaged in an illegal act, each was equally culpable for the consequences.

Regarding the evidence of John Foster, Hawkins reminded the jury that Foster had admitted to lying at the inquest, saying that he had been trying to protect his lover's reputation. However, even though he had given contradictory evidence in court, he had sworn on oath that he was now telling the truth, saying that he hadn't fully appreciated the seriousness of the matter before.

After debating the evidence for forty-five minutes, the jury returned to court having found both Robert and Jane Colmer guilty of wilful murder. Hawkins donned his black cap and asked the defendants if they had anything to say before he passed sentence.

Both defendants seemed stunned by the verdict and, although Robert Colmer tried to speak, he was unable to. It wasn't until Hawkins began to pronounce the death sentence that he found his voice and protested not only his own innocence but that

Pentonville Prison, 1914. (Authors' collection)

of his wife. Eventually, Jane Colmer also managed to tell the judge that she too was innocent but Hawkins said that he was sadly unable to believe her.

Having received her death sentence, Jane Colmer was questioned to see if she was pregnant, which would have meant an automatic stay of execution had she answered in the affirmative. Once it was established that she was not pregnant, the judge ordered both prisoners to be removed to Newgate Prison and then sent to Somerset, where they would be executed. However, neither of the Colmers ultimately faced the official executioner.

It later emerged that the jury had specifically recommended mercy for both prisoners, since they believed that Mary Budge had hastened her own death by insisting on returning to Crewkerne immediately after her abortion. Thus, both of their sentences were commuted to life imprisonment and Robert was initially sent to Pentonville, while Jane went to Milbank Prison in London.

It is believed that Jane was eventually released and returned to Yeovil to live with her children, before dying in 1918 at the age of eighty-four. Robert is believed to have died in 1889, while still incarcerated.

16

'I'LL KISS THEE, THEN'

Hatch Beauchamp, 1864

John Allen was a labourer, who lived with Betsy, his wife of more than twenty years, in a cottage at Hatch Beauchamp. By 1864, like many other villagers, the Allens had taken advantage of the coming of the Chard and Taunton Railway to earn extra money by letting rooms to the navvies employed in its construction. Mr Strode and Mr Steele, lodged with the Allens, along with a young labourer named Billy.

John Allen was fiercely jealous and constantly accused his wife of improper associations with James Steele, something that Betsy repeatedly denied. However, the ongoing affair between Betsy and her lodger was common knowledge in the village – in fact John Allen seemed to be the only person who didn't know what was going on behind his back. Matters came to a head in early May, when John Allen and James Steele fought. Allen was soundly beaten, spending the next few days sporting a pair of black eyes that earned him jeers and taunting from other navvies working in the village and, to compound his hurt and humiliation, Betsy laughed at her husband's predicament, saying that it served him right.

On 4 May, John Allen got up early to go to work. His married daughter, Jane, was unwell, so Allen went to collect some medicine for her from North Curry, which he brought back home with him and placed on the table. Betsy Allen was busy cooking and hardly looked up as her husband came into the house.

'Give me a kiss,' Allen demanded of his wife, who made an excuse about wanting some sticks for the fire and left the room.

'I'll kiss thee, then.' Allen responded, following his wife outside to the log store.

Another daughter, ten-year-old Hannah, was in the kitchen at the time, holding the baby. She suddenly heard her mother shout 'Dear, dear, John; what are you going to do?'

'Look here; I'll serve myself the same,' replied her father.

Hannah ran outside, where her father was holding her mother down over a cider barrel and, as Hannah watched in horror, she saw her father cut her mother's throat twice and then his own. As soon as her husband released his hold on her, Betsy Allen ran back into the house, with John in pursuit. He caught up with his wife and knocked her to the floor, slashing at her throat a further three times before Betsy managed to snatch the razor from his hand, break it and throw it across the room. Undeterred,

Hatch Beauchamp. (Authors' collection)

John reached into his pocket for his knife but by that time, he was so weak through loss of blood that Hannah managed to disarm him. John then scrabbled for the broken razor and picked it up, cutting Betsy's hand as she fought to take it off him.

By that time, Hannah had seen enough and fled the house, running to fetch her sister Jane from her work. By the time Jane got to her parents' house, both John and Betsy were sitting in chairs, one on each side of the fireplace, Betsy's heavily bleeding throat bound with a towel.

A doctor was summoned but was out when the call for assistance came. Thus the first to arrive was Frederick Morgan, assistant to Dr Cordwent, who was quickly followed by Cordwent himself and a surgeon, Charles Halse. The doctors ascertained that John's wounds were not life threatening and focused their attention on Betsy, who was taken to Taunton Hospital, where doctors believed that she was unlikely to survive her injuries. John Allen was later taken by cart to the same hospital, where surgeon Mr Gibson stitched the wound in his throat. Allen persistently tried to tear out the stitches and open the wound again until eventually he was put under police guard. Even so, he continued to try and rip open his own throat and was consequently strapped to his bed to prevent him from injuring himself.

Both John and Betsy Allen gave statements while in hospital, Betsy under the impression that she was dying from her wounds. She told magistrates that she and John hadn't quarrelled at all on the morning of 4 May and there had been no anger between them. John had tried to persuade her to kiss him and, when she protested that she was too busy, had followed her into the yard and cut her throat. John told a slightly different story to PC Robert Gilson, stating that, on the night before his

The Hatch Inn, Beauchamp. (© R. Sly)

attack on Betsy, James Steele had abused and cursed her in his hearing, which had upset him greatly. John said that he had asked Betsy to come to bed with him but she refused. John then asked James Steele to go to bed to give him some privacy to talk to Betsy but Steele would not leave the couple alone. Finally, Betsy told John that she was intending to leave him and go to London with Steele. John told the police that he begged his wife not to go but she was adamant that she was going. The only way that John could think of to stop her was to kill her and commit suicide, so that they might both lie together forever in the same grave. 'That's all I can say about it and the law can't more than hang me for it,' he concluded.

Against all odds, Betsy Allen gradually recovered from her husband's attempt to kill her and, a month later, her wound had healed perfectly. Yet, just when it seemed as if she would make a full return to health, she began to experience breathing difficulties and, on 17 June 1864, she died. Doctors Halse and Cordwent performed a post-mortem examination and found that her throat was badly inflamed. Scar tissue had narrowed her windpipe to such an extent that, although she was still able to breathe, she was unable to cough up mucus and had ultimately been suffocated by an accumulation of phlegm on her chest. Coroner Mr W.W. Munckton held an inquest at the Hatch Inn, Hatch Beauchamp and the jury found a verdict of wilful murder against John Allen, who was committed for trial at the Somerset Assizes on the coroner's warrant.

The trial took place in August 1864. Mr Justice Williams was set to preside but was unfortunately unwell and his place was taken by a deputy, Mr Thomas Chambers QC, Common Serjeant. The case was prosecuted by Mr Speke and Mr Murch, while Allen was defended by Mr Bere.

The prosecution outlined the facts of the case, calling the Allen's two daughters as the chief witnesses for the prosecution. Both girls were understandably distraught at having to testify against their father and many of the female spectators (and even some of the men) were reduced to tears by their accounts of the death of their mother. The prosecution also called a plethora of medical witnesses, including Mr Morgan, Mr Cordwent, Mr Halse and the doctors from Taunton Hospital. Whereas all were agreed that the thickening of Betsy Allen's windpipe by scar tissue arising from her wound had been the cause of her death, there was some disagreement as to what had caused the build up of phlegm on her chest, which could have occurred as a result of something as simple as a common cold.

Thus it was Mr Bere's contention that Betsy Allen had not died as a direct result of the injury inflicted on her by her husband, who could not therefore be held responsible for her murder. He failed to convince the jury, who returned a verdict of 'Guilty'. John Allen, who had sobbed piteously throughout most of his trial, collapsed when the judge pronounced the death sentence and was carried from the court insensible.

Allen seemed to resign himself to his fate, taking great comfort in the ministrations of the prison chaplain. However, he was unaware that a number of people – including the trial judge – had expressed dissatisfaction at the verdict and were making strenuous efforts to overturn his sentence. The chief complaint was that the defence had failed to call a particular witness, a Mr Cannicott from Weston-super-Mare, who was present in court and fully expected to testify.

Cannicott was a former employer of John Allen, who held him in the highest regard. Cannicott had also once lived next door to the Allens for ten years and was willing to state that Allen had spoken to Betsy numerous times about her 'disgraceful conduct' and had forgiven many of her past indiscretions. In addition to the lost opportunity of hearing from Mr Cannicott, many people felt that John Allen had been sorely provoked before murdering his wife, both by her infidelities and by the taunts and jeers of the navvies about his black eyes, as he returned from collecting his daughter's medicine shortly before attacking Betsy.

A petition was raised bearing more than 500 signatures, including clergy, gentry and many prominent people from Taunton and the surrounding areas. The Bishop of Bath and Wells was one of those prepared to put his name to the petition and he also wrote privately to the Secretary of State, pleading Allen's case.

In the event, the government announced a respite for John Allen even before the petition arrived in London and it was speculated that judge Mr Chambers had intervened on his behalf. When news of his reprieve reached Allen, he was so shocked that he immediately fainted and had to be placed on the hospital wing of the prison, under the care of the gaol surgeons. He appears to have served his sentence at Knaphill Invalid Convict Prison in Surrey.

Note: Surgeon Mr Halse is also named as Mr Mules in some contemporary accounts of the case. The Allens' daughter, who witnessed the attack, is usually named Anna in reports of the murder. However, official records seem to show that her name was Hannah.

17

'SHE IS NOT DEAD, SHE IS CRYING'

Bath, 1865

Shoemaker Henry Fisher and his wife, Mary, lived in Northampton Street, Bath. They had been married for fourteen years and the marriage had produced one child, who died in infancy. The couple lived a fairly comfortable life and Henry was a particularly devoted and affectionate husband, although somewhat under Mary's thumb. She took all financial responsibility for the household and Henry meekly handed all his earnings over to her each week, asking her for any money that he needed for himself. Yet the fact that Mary was very much the dominant partner in their relationship seemed to suit Henry, who had spent some time in a lunatic asylum before meeting her, having suffered a nervous breakdown. Although he had been officially pronounced cured, he was still prone to occasional bouts of depression and was willing to go to almost any lengths to keep Mary happy and avoid any conflict within his marriage.

By January 1865, Henry was beginning to have serious concerns about his business. He was unable to get over his belief that the ever increasing use of machinery in shoemaking would lead to his eventual financial ruin and gloomily forecast that he and Mary were bound to end up destitute in the workhouse. Together he and Mary brooded about what they were beginning to see as a grim and hopeless future and, at some stage, made a decision to commit suicide together.

Nobody knew anything of this decision until Henry's stepmother, also called Mary Fisher, tried to visit the couple on the afternoon of 6 January. Receiving no response to her knocks on the door, Mrs Fisher assumed that her stepson and step daughter-in-law had gone out. She called back later that evening, peering through the keyhole when there was still no response from within. Since the key wasn't in the door, she assumed that the Fishers were still out but on her third visit at nine o'clock that evening she began to grow concerned, particularly when the couple's neighbours told her that they hadn't seen Henry and his wife leaving the house. Mrs Fisher knocked even harder and called her stepson's name and was rewarded by a faint noise from inside. Moments later, Henry opened the door, looking weak and ill.

'We couldn't help it,' he told his stepmother, when she asked what was going on.

Northampton Street, Bath. (© R. Sly, 2010)

'What couldn't you help?' asked Mrs Fisher.

'She is not dead, she is crying,' replied Henry.

Mrs Fisher demanded a light, anxious to see what on earth Henry was talking about. When he fetched a lamp, she could see his wife lying motionless in bed, dressed in a clean nightdress and her best night cap.

Mrs Fisher senior announced her intention of summoning a doctor. 'Oh, don't bring a doctor caddling round here – we want to die together,' Henry begged her, but his stepmother ignored his pleading and sent the friend who had accompanied her, Christina Scott, to fetch a doctor.

Dr Hugh Massey arrived within minutes and quickly assessed the situation. When he questioned Henry, Massey discovered that both he and his wife had each taken eleven teaspoonfuls of laudanum. 'We worked ourselves up to it,' Henry told the doctor, insisting that both he and Mary wanted to die.

A look around the room confirmed that Henry Fisher had vomited up most of the poison he had taken. The police were sent for and, thinking that a walk in the fresh air would do Henry some good, Massey sent him off to the hospital with PC James Chamberlain, while he focused on trying to revive Mrs Fisher, who had fallen into a coma. The doctor cared for Mrs Fisher for two days but, in spite of his best efforts, she died without ever regaining consciousness and a post-mortem examination confirmed opium poisoning as the cause of her death.

Meanwhile, Henry had been taken to the Bath United Hospital, where he was given a mustard emetic and vomited up even more of the poison. He was treated by

Dr William Freeman, who had absolutely no doubt in his mind that his patient had taken an overdose of opium. Henry explained that he and his wife had been secretly buying small bottles of laudanum from the local chemist's shops for several weeks, not wanting to arouse suspicions by buying too much at any one time. In total, they had bought a shilling's worth of laudanum before deciding that they had amassed sufficient to kill themselves.

Henry told Dr Freeman that he had carefully measured eleven teaspoonfuls of the drug into each of two tumblers, which he then topped up with porter. He drank his glass first, before retiring behind a screen to allow his wife privacy in which to undress and put on her nightclothes and, although he hadn't actually seen Mary drink her draught, he had heard her swallowing it. The two then lay down in bed together and waited to die.

When Mary Fisher died, her husband was arrested for her wilful murder and was eventually to appear at the Somerset Assizes before Mr Justice Crompton. Mr T.W. Saunders and Mr March were charged with prosecuting what the contemporary newspapers referred to as 'a most romantic case', while Mr Prideaux appeared in defence of Henry Fisher.

There was little doubt in anybody's mind that Henry Fisher was technically guilty of murder, for which there was a mandatory death penalty. After all, he had purchased and personally administered the poison that ultimately caused the death of his wife, a fact even his defence counsel couldn't argue. After the prosecution counsels had outlined the facts of the case and their witnesses had been heard, Mr Prideaux began a lengthy speech in Fisher's defence.

Prideaux reminded the jury that they were not being asked to consider a case in which envy, hatred, malice or any other 'uncharitableness' was a factor, nor was there any development of violent and malicious human passion. Rather, this case was hinged on one of the deepest and most sacred of all human affections – conjugal love. Henry Fisher had attempted to commit suicide and yet God, in His infinite wisdom, had spared him. Prideaux asked the jury to consider why God had not let Henry Fisher die, suggesting that perhaps it was intended that Fisher should live out his days on earth in penitence and mourning for his dead wife. He reminded the jury how ironic it would be if they found Fisher guilty, thus going against God's will by putting an end to his life. To convict Fisher, continued Prideaux, would be contrary to the will of Divine Providence, since it had pleased God to raise him 'from death unto life.'

Having literally put the fear of God into the jury, Prideaux then changed tack, claiming that, since Mary Fisher had always been the dominant partner in the marriage, it was highly likely that the suicide pact between her and her husband was her idea and that Henry was nothing more than a servant to his strong-minded wife's whims. If Mary Fisher was determined to die and felt that she and her husband should not be separated in death, then her fond, loving but weak-willed husband would have done anything to please her.

With that thought in the jury's minds, Prideaux made the point that, although Henry had confessed to both the police and doctors that he had given his wife laudanum, that confession had been made when he too was under the influence of an overdose and, in the words of Dr Massey and PC Chamberlain, 'partially conscious' and 'sleepy and sick'. It was Prideaux's contention that Henry Fisher had gallantly taken the blame for his wife's death to spare her reputation and protect her good name.

Prideaux closed his defence by again asking the jury to pause before consigning to death on the gallows the man whom God had seen fit to raise from death unto life.

It was left for Mr Justice Crompton to summarise the case for the jury. Crompton opened his summary by commenting that it was a pity that there were not more minute distinctions made in classifying charges of murder but the law was quite clearly laid down and it was the jury's duty to act upon it. Crompton then took issue with some of the statements made by the defence counsel, saying that he could not condone Prideaux's invitation to the jury to look into acts of Divine Providence and that it was more profanity than religious to suggest that the Deity had seen fit to take one life and spare the other and that it would be thwarting the Almighty to send Fisher to the gallows. The judge went as far as to say that it shocked him to think that anyone should be speculating on how the Almighty dealt with His creatures. There was no evidence to suggest any insanity in the case, added Crompton and, even though Fisher had spent time in a lunatic asylum in 1847, there was no medical evidence to say that he was anything but a reasonable being and fully accountable for his actions.

The jury retired for twenty-five minutes, returning with a verdict of 'Guilty', tempered by a strong recommendation for mercy. Mr Justice Crompton told them that he thought they had returned a just and proper verdict, adding that, had they acquitted Fisher, it would have opened the doors for anyone who might want to help another commit self murder. Crompton then turned to Henry Fisher, asking him if there was any reason why he should not be sentenced to death.

Fisher, who had sobbed bitterly throughout his trial, told the judge, 'All I have to say is that I had no feeling of envy, hatred, anger or malice or any sinister intentions or any sinister thought towards her. It was the effect of our weak minds and of not trusting in Providence. If we had trusted in Providence it would not have happened. I hope that whatever my ultimate fate it will be a warning to all and everyone to trust in God more than I and my unfortunate wife did. Whatever punishment I may be subjected to, I take it that God meant it for me, through not trusting Him.'

Crompton pronounced sentence of death on Henry Fisher but it appears that the jury's recommendation was heeded. It is believed that, by 1871, Henry Fisher was a free man, lodging in Clement Street, Bath and that he died in Bath seven years later.

18

'OH, WHAT POWER THE DEVIL MUST HAVE HAD OVER ME'

Woolverton, 1867

On 20 July 1867, George Rogers was walking to work at four o'clock in the morning when he noticed smoke issuing from the malt house at Woolverton, which belonged to George Britten and was leased by maltster Edward Francis Moger. The malt house was situated in the garden of the thatched cottage that George Britten shared with his wife and young son and, concerned that the fire would spread, Rogers hammered on the cottage door, pelting the windows with gravel when his knocks and shouts went unanswered.

After several minutes, a corner of a blind in an upstairs window was raised and Britten peered out. Even the knowledge that there was a fire on his premises did little to hurry him and he took several more minutes to dress and come downstairs, by which time, several of his neighbours had arrived and were trying to put out the fire. The malt house door was forced open and Britten anxiously insisted that it was closed, before the draught made the fire worse, but people had already noticed what appeared to be a human body lying on a board, beneath which burned a pile of coke. When the body was pointed out to Britten, he immediately went for a closer look and clumsily tipped it off the board directly onto the flames.

A message had been sent to the police station at Frome asking for assistance and Superintendent Edward Deggan had alerted the members of the Volunteer Fire Brigade, who were on their way to tackle the fire. It was quickly doused with buckets of water and a further message was sent to say that the fire engines were not required but, by then, PC Abel Chandler was already well on his way to Woolverton and, when he arrived and saw the body, he immediately sent for Deggan.

It was first thought that a tramp had broken into the malt house and started the fire but, as Deggan moved the body's charred limbs, he found remnants of garments that had not been completely consumed by the flames. There was a pair of men's trousers but there were also two pairs of women's stockings and a bonnet. Deggan therefore concluded that the body was that of a woman and, whoever she was, she had

Woolverton. (© R. Sly)

apparently been murdered before the fire started, since most of her hair had survived the flames and was covered in blood. The most notable thing was that she had two very protruding front teeth, a feature shared by Britten's wife, Martha. Several people who were at the scene of the fire commented on their resemblance to Martha's teeth but, when George Britten was brought to view the body, he was positive that it was not Martha, telling Deggan that she was away visiting friends at West Pennard. Yet Britten's neighbours were so certain that the body was that of Martha Britten that Deggan asked him to look again, paying particular attention to the hair and teeth.

Britten kneeled down by the corpse and Deggan carefully lifted the head, so that he could get a better look.

'I cannot recognise her,' he insisted but Deggan noticed that Britten was trembling violently and asked him to look once more. Finally, Britten admitted that the body was Martha, at which Deggan arrested him and charged him with her wilful murder and with setting fire to the malt house.

Britten was taken to Frome police station, where he initially made little comment other than saying, 'It's a bad job.' However, the following day, his brother-in-law, Mr Woolly came to the police station to see him. Deggan saw Britten trying to hand Woolly a note and quickly took possession of it. The document was an incomplete handwritten confession to the murder of Woolly's sister, Martha, and, later that afternoon Britten asked Deggan for a pen and the paper and, in Deggan's presence, continued his confession where he had left off:

With shame and true abhorrence and repentance of the deed I have done, I confess it was I that foully murdered my poor wife. It was done in the heat of passion and in a fit of jealousy and arose thus; I saw what I shall keep to myself, told her of it; she treated it lightly, which enraged me. I caught hold of the first thing that came to hand, struck her with it three or four times … Oh, what power the Devil must have had over me.

The statement continued to say that Britten had intended to kill himself but had not done so for two reasons. Firstly, he had not wanted his young son to find the bodies of both of his parents, saying that it would probably have caused him to lose his reason and secondly, while he believed that God might forgive a murderer, he didn't believe that he would forgive self-murder. 'Oh, God forgive me, I loved her,' Britten sobbed, telling Deggan that the weapon he had used against his wife was a large piece of lead and, indeed, a piece of lead weighing 6-7lbs was subsequently found in the cellar of Britten's house, although there was no trace of blood on it. Britten wrote that he had killed Martha on 18 July, dragging her body to the malt house in the early hours of the morning of 20 July and starting the fire in an effort to conceal his crime. His statement ended by imploring his brother-in-law, Mr Woolly, to take care of his son, directing him to a trunk in the cottage where a bank draft for £350 might be found.

A post-mortem examination was conducted on what remained of Martha Britten by father and son surgeons Joshua and Henry Franklin Parsons, who found several injuries on her head and face, including a gaping cut on her left temple, a deep contused wound on her forehead at the hairline and a large, v-shaped wound on the back of her head. The surgeons concluded that Martha had been struck at least three times with a hammer or similar blunt instrument and confirmed that she had been dead for some time before the fire started. They gave the cause of her death as concussion of the brain, which was reduced to a pulp in places and which Henry Parsons described as 'like blackcurrant jelly'. Both surgeons noted that Martha had an exceptionally thick skull, which had not been fractured by the blows to her head. This evidence, coupled with Britten's statement, was sufficient for the jury at the inquest on Martha's death to return a verdict of wilful murder against Henry Britten, who was committed for trial at the next Assizes. After the inquest, Britten wrote another lengthy statement, in which he corrected some of the statements made by witnesses. (He also urged people to avoid tobacco, which he described as 'his bane'!)

Britten appeared before Mr Justice Willes at Wells on 7 August 1867, charged with murdering his wife with malice aforethought.

When the charge was read out to Britten and Willes asked how he pleaded, Britten replied, 'Guilty of the act but not with malice aforethought.' Willes took this as a plea of 'Not Guilty' and allowed Mr T.W. Saunders to open the case for the prosecution.

Saunders began by telling the jury that there had been so much publicity about the case in the newspapers that he suspected that they had already formed an opinion as

Mr Justice Willes. (Authors' collection)

to Britten's guilt or innocence. He urged them to put aside their preconceptions and judge the case only on the evidence they were about to hear. Saunders then said that the defence would try to convince them that this was a case of manslaughter rather than murder, since Martha Britten had been killed in the heat of passion.

No one would be happier than he if the jury found Britten guilty of manslaughter, said Saunders. However, before that happened, he begged to be allowed to remind the jury that medical evidence would show that Martha Britten had been hit over the head not once, but as many as four times. Mr Edlin, who was assisting with the prosecution then called his first witness, George Rogers, who related his discovery of the fire in the malt house.

Rogers was followed into the witness box by a succession of Britten's neighbours, who had assisted in extinguishing the blaze. All stated that Britten himself had done very little to help put out the fire and that he had made every effort to ensure that the door to the malt house was kept closed.

Once Britten's statements had been admitted as evidence and the doctors had testified, the prosecution rested, leaving Mr Prideaux and Mr Folkard to open the defence. As Saunders had suspected, they argued that Martha Britten's murder was a crime of passion, committed in the heat of the moment, on an irresistible impulse, by a devoted and loving husband. Even though Prideaux spoke for almost two hours in Britten's defence, it took the jury less than three minutes to find their client guilty of wilful murder, the deciding factor apparently being the fact that George Britten had set the fire in an attempt to destroy his wife's body and all evidence of his brutal act.

Fifty-one-year-old Britten accepted his death sentence, showing far less emotion as it was pronounced than Mr Justice Willes.

In the aftermath of the trial, the contemporary newspapers revealed some hitherto unknown facts about Britten. Formerly a farmer, at the time of the murder he was living on the income from properties he owned. In 1862, Britten suddenly and unexpectedly disappeared and for a time it was assumed that he had been murdered, since his bloodstained hat and battered lantern were found on the roadside near his home. There had long been rumours in the neighbourhood that Bittern was having an affair and, after his disappearance, the woman with whom he was alleged to have formed an 'improper intimacy' was found drowned. At the time, her death was not thought to be suspicious but, in the light of the murder of Britten's wife, the rumours began anew.

Just as suddenly as he had disappeared, Britten suddenly reappeared in 1865, having spent three years in New Zealand. Martha immediately forgave him for deserting her and he picked up the threads of his marriage as if he had never been away.

Although efforts were made to secure a reprieve for George Britten, they were unsuccessful. Britten received the news with his customary lack of emotion, saying that he was ready to die for what he had done. His execution by William Calcraft on 29 August 1867 was the last ever public hanging at Taunton Gaol.

19

'I'LL KILL ALL THE DAMNED LOT OF YOU'

Charterhouse, 1872

William Lace was a miner who worked in the pits on the Mendip hills. He and his wife lived in a cottage at Charterhouse. They had four children, the two elder aged fifteen and twelve respectively, and the youngest a babe in arms.

To all outward appearances they had been a happy family for some years, and Mr Lace was said to have 'an excellent character for sobriety and good temper'. Nevertheless, some of the neighbours thought he seemed jealous of his wife, although without good reason. Whatever the cause, it all started to go wrong on Monday, 22 April 1872. He left home as usual at about seven o'clock in the morning to go to work, saying he planned to be back at about eight in the evening. In the event, he returned a little earlier, and seemed annoyed that his supper was not ready for him at once.

The next day he left his work at about five o'clock in the afternoon and went for a drink in the inn with some of his friends. One or two of them made some flippant comments about how his wife was cheating on him. If it was meant as a joke, it was in very poor taste. Two hours after leaving work, Lace was back home. While coming along the road one of his neighbours spoke to him but and not notice anything out of the ordinary. When he reached the garden gate Lace met his eldest daughter, and said rather brusquely to her, 'Go into house. Where's your mother?'

She told him that her mother was indoors. 'I'll make you both prove your words,' he muttered.

His daughter then left as she was running an errand, and he went into the house through the garden and the rear entrance. At the corner of the house he met his younger daughter. 'I'll kill all the damned lot of you,' he growled at her. Going inside, he found his wife with the two younger children, holding the baby.

'You've been out in the hundred acres with a hundred fellows a month ago,' he snapped at her.

'I don't know what you mean,' she answered.

'I'll let you know. I will kill you.'

Without giving her a chance to put the baby down, he seized her by the arm and threw her against the dresser. She dodged him, ran out of the house and into the cottage of their neighbours, Mr and Mrs Phear, the latter heavily pregnant. Mrs Lace was followed in hot pursuit by her husband and the twelve-year-old daughter, and he ordered her to go back home, promising he would not hit her again. She got up and walked into the garden, but was reluctant to trust him. Instead, she and their daughter crossed the road into another cottage, where she found their friend Mrs Herring, together with her children and a nurse. Mr Lace continued to follow them and order them back. When she asked what for, he told her angrily, 'You know.'

The nurse, who evidently knew that they were not the happy family nearly everyone thought they were, told him that he was not to beat his wife any more. He promised he would not, as long as she went back, but she was always running about 'newsing'. She then left, he followed her, and as soon as they were back in their own garden he hit her again, knocked her down, and kicked at her. The girl took the baby and went into the Phears' cottage, trying to get help.

Meanwhile, the Herrings' eighteen-year-old son George had arrived back at his parents' cottage. Mrs Lace escaped from her house and returned to the Herrings, followed by her husband – only to find the door had been locked against her. By now increasingly desperate and fearing for her life, she went back towards her own cottage, but her husband attacked her again, knocking her down, kicking her and finally dragging her round the corner of the cottage and indoors.

Astonishingly, George Herring was watching this domestic drama take place from the comfort of his home without making any effort to prevent it. He unlocked his door, saw the vicious assault on Mrs Lace, and then went up the road to fetch something. Returning about five minutes later, he saw Mr Lace fetching three pails of water. As there seemed to be no noise from the cottage, he and his father went indoors to supper.

By now, the Laces' daughter had raised the alarm. Mr Wood, a nearby farmer, came to see the situation for himself, and sent for a policeman and a surgeon. The girl returned back home, meeting her distraught sister on the way. They were greeted by the dreadful sight of their mother's dead body, covered in blood and water, with her clothes badly torn. They had only just arrived when Lace walked into the room, picked the body up and threw it against the dresser.

'Don't, father,' the elder girl cried, 'she is dead.'

'She is only dead drunk,' he snapped.

He then went to the Phears' cottage, and told the family that he had killed his wife. Some people in his position, he added, would then kill themselves, but he was ready to give himself up. When Mr Wood, the surgeon and the policeman arrived, Lace told them he had attacked his wife while 'in a passion'. He was arrested and charged with murder.

At the post-mortem, the surgeon found about a dozen jagged wounds in the victim's scalp. These, and the repeated violence to which she had been subjected, had caused her death.

Lace went on trial at the Western Circuit Assizes, Wells, on 5 August, before Mr Justice Mellor, with Mr Bailey and Mr Valpy for the prosecution, and Mr Saunders for

Mr Justice Mellor. (Author's collection)

the defence. During proceedings, it was commented on that one of the most painful aspects of the trial was that the prisoners' daughters, who had tragically witnessed their father's brutal behaviour at such close range, were the principal witnesses for the prosecution. Their evidence, and that of the neighbours, was sufficient to establish his guilt. The counsel for the defence suggested that there had been no intention on the part of the prisoner to take life, but he was unable to present a convincing argument why this should have been the case.

In summing up, the judge commented severely on the conduct of some of the neighbours. He singled out George Herring for particular blame, remarking that if the young man had only had the courage to intervene, he might well have saved Mrs Lace's life. The jury did not take long to find Lace guilty, and he was sentenced to death. He was led from the dock to spend the rest of his days at Taunton gaol.

Friends and family tried to plead for a commutation, and a petition was sent to the home secretary. Their failure was probably a relief to the prisoner, who repeatedly told his chaplain and others that he had no desire to live. 'I know I killed her,' he told Mr Oakley, the prison governor, 'and I deserve my sentence. There was some jealousy before the men spoke to me.' His drinking cronies who had suggested that his wife was carrying on behind his back may have been partly to blame, though what if any justification he had for believing such stories was a secret which he took with him to the grave. His children dutifully visited him during the last few days, but he doubtless took more comfort from their farewell than they did.

Lace kept his appointment at the gallows at Taunton at eight o'clock on the morning of Monday 26 August with William Calcraft.

20

'A CONSIDERATION FOR AN IMMORAL RETURN'

North Perrott, 1874

On Tuesday, 17 March 1874, at about a quarter past nine in the morning, herdsman Eli Symes drove some bullocks to a field in Trendlewell Lane, North Perrott after finishing the morning milking on his employer's farm. The animals suddenly became unusually restless, snorting and blowing and baulking as they passed the small pond just inside the field gate. When Symes parted the bushes that surrounded the pond to investigate the cause of their distress, he was horrified to discover the battered and very muddy body of a woman.

The woman lay on her back at the edge of the pond with her head stuck between the bank and a tree trunk and thus firmly lodged underwater. Her dress and petticoats were disturbed, she was barefoot and bare legged and there were liberal splashes of fresh blood all around the body. A bloodstained stone, weighing almost four pounds lay nearby, with numerous hairs matching those of the dead woman stuck firmly to it by dried blood.

Although the bullocks were extremely reluctant to pass the body, Symes managed to persuade them to the move to the farthest part of the field before rushing to summon help. He asked one man to go and stand by the pond to keep the beasts away from the body, then despatched another to fetch the local police constable.

The first officer to arrive, PC Joseph Williams from Crewkerne, sensibly protected the crime scene from further disturbance. A thorough search of the area revealed two places on Trendlewell Lane where a desperate struggle had evidently taken place. It appeared as though the woman had either been thrown down or had lain down of her own accord. Blood spattered the banks and hedges and a hank of hair and a hairpin lay on the lane, from where there were drag marks some seventy yards long leading to the pond. Williams noted the prints of small hobnailed boots and something resembling the imprint of a corduroy-clad knee, both in the mud and on the woman's clothes. He also saw a deep impression in the mud that looked as though it had been made by a head being forcefully pushed down into the soft ground on the edge of a ditch. Various items of clothing were scattered close by, seemingly thrown carelessly over the hedge, including a shawl and a woman's boot. Finally a woman's garden bonnet was found partially burnt.

The Manor Arms, North Perrott. (Authors' collection)

Trendlewell Lane. (Authors' collection)

Williams left three trustworthy villagers guarding the scene while he returned to Crewkerne to summon medical assistance and alert his sergeant to the terrible crime by telegraph. Accompanied by two doctors, Dr Wills and Dr Albert Cox, he then went straight back to North Perrott.

With some difficulty, the woman's body was removed from the pond and, even though her head was described in the contemporary newspapers as having been '... beaten to a jelly'; Constable Williams was able to identify her immediately as Ruth Butcher, a single mother who lived in a rented cottage in Pillhead Lane, less than a quarter of a mile as the crow flies from the scene of her murder. In her early forties, Ruth had two illegitimate children, a son and a daughter. Her daughter, Annie, aged fourteen, was no longer living with her at home, having gone into service at Halstock a few weeks earlier. Ruth supported herself and her seven-year-old son, John, by working at home as a weaver for a manufacturer of hair netting and webbing and by taking in washing. She had the reputation of being 'of light character'. Constable Williams believed that she would be likely to meet a man by appointment and he had personally seen her with a man in an outhouse. It was intimated that Ruth wasn't averse to making a little extra money by granting sexual favours to supplement her legitimate income.

Ruth's body was returned to her home on a farm wagon. There, two local women washed her before Dr Cox carried out an autopsy. He determined that she had severe head injuries; eight wounds in all, including a fractured skull, which he believed had been caused by a sharp weapon such as a hatchet or a billhook and also a heavy stone. One of her eyes had been 'beaten in' and her upper lip and one ear had been almost completely severed. However, apart from the wounds to Ruth's head and a large bruise on her left arm, caused, the doctor believed, by the pressure of a hand, there were no other signs of violence to be seen. There was no evidence of any sexual interference and, other than having some traces of scarring due to pleurisy in one lung and a heart 'loaded with fat', Cox described Ruth as having been a reasonably healthy woman. Her pockets were turned out and found to contain a piece of bacon weighing almost 1lb, which had been neatly wrapped in paper and secured with a length of jute yarn.

So appalling was the murder that the Chief Constable himself, Mr Valentine Gould, headed the police investigations. Superintendent Everitt from Ilminster, Superintendent Smith from Yeovil and Sergeant Giles of Crewkerne assisted him in his enquiries. One of their first actions was to request that an appeal for assistance be printed in the local newspaper. It mentioned that the woman had a piece of bacon in her pocket that had been wrapped in coarse brown paper, tied with a piece of jute yarn. It also asked for information about a medium-sized dark check handkerchief found at the murder site. In a subsequent edition, the newspaper followed the notice of appeal with corrections, stating that the paper in which the bacon was wrapped was in fact white, not brown and that the handkerchief was silk. By the time this notice went to print, the owner of the handkerchief had been traced and found to have no connection with the murder.

It was determined that Ruth's murder had been committed on the Monday night, possibly at around twenty minutes past ten, when a woman living nearby reported hearing screams. A search of the area where the body was discovered revealed a trail of bloodstains on gates and stiles. Police were able to follow this trail across the fields leading to Hardington, then back towards Haselbury Plucknett, until it eventually petered out close to the vicarage in Danes Field.

The coroner's inquest, presided over by J. Wybrants, opened on 19 March. One of the first witnesses to give evidence was Ruth's neighbour, Martha Pool. Martha had seen Ruth at about five-thirty on the afternoon of her murder, at which time she had complained of feeling unwell and having pains in her head and chest. She had been heard talking to her son at about a quarter past seven by another neighbour, James Marks, who had also heard the door of her cottage closing about fifteen to thirty minutes later. The inquest was then adjourned for one week, pending further investigations by the police.

On 20 March, Ruth's body was buried in a pauper's grave in the churchyard at North Perrott. The funeral was attended by some fifty villagers, including Ruth's two children. Annie sobbed loudly throughout the service, while John seemed to be in a trance. His ragged clothes reflected his poverty and he was soon to be taken into the care of the parish but the coroner's jury had kindly donated their fees to Annie Butcher, so that she might buy some decent clothes.

When the inquest reopened on 26 March, the only new evidence came from Superintendent Everitt, who announced a reward of £100 for information leading to the arrest of Ruth Butcher's killer. With so little progress made on the investigation, the inquest was adjourned for a second time until 20 April. However, when it reopened again, the police still had little news to report. Meanwhile, the *Bristol Mercury* informed their readers that, on one Sunday alone, more than 4,000 curious people had visited the site of the murder, stripping every blood-spattered leaf and blade of grass, which they took away as souvenirs.

Unsurprisingly in the light of such ghoulish behaviour, detailed searches of the area had revealed no further clues, although several leads had been followed up and discounted. A man from Crewkerne, Mr Genge, was initially suspected and, on hearing that his name was being associated with the murder, he confronted a local police officer, PC Warren and used such foul and violent language that he was promptly arrested. His home was thoroughly searched but not a shred of incriminating evidence was found. Suspicion also fell on a man who had previously lived with Ruth Butcher in her cottage. Ruth's daughter, Annie, had testified at the inquest to hearing rows between him and her mother but the man had left Ruth's house several weeks before the murder and, since there was already a warrant for his arrest for the desertion of his own children, he was assumed to have moved away from the area to avoid detention.

It was thought that the killer was a local man, since only someone who was very familiar with the location would have known of the existence of the pond on Trendlewell Lane where the body was left. Given that the murder took place in a small village, with only a few hundred inhabitants, it seems inconceivable that the killer was never brought to justice, but despite an extensive search of the area, which included draining the pond, no trace was ever found of the murder weapon. It was theorised that the partially burned bonnet found at the scene might have been lit and then used as a torch by the killer to find and retrieve it. With no real new evidence, the Coroner's jury returned the verdict of wilful murder against some person or persons unknown and in fact the identity of Ruth Butcher's killer was never discovered.

It was reported that, only a couple of days before her death, Ruth had been heard to say that she would like a piece of bacon but had no money to buy one. Her extreme poverty was widely known throughout the village and thus seemed to rule out robbery as a motive for her murder. It was surmised that Ruth Butcher had slipped out of her cottage that night with the intention of meeting a man, possibly receiving the bacon as what was described by the local newspaper as 'a consideration for an immoral return'. She would not have dared to entertain a gentleman at home, as her landlord would have disapproved of such unseemly behaviour and turned her out on the streets had he discovered it.

If this were the case, then Ruth's choice of companion – and her craving for a piece of bacon – may well have been her undoing.

Note: In various sources, Butcher's neighbour is named as Martha Pool or Poole. The murder site is variously referred to as Trinarvel Lane, Trendlewell Lane or Trundlewell Lane, but is now known as Trindlewell Lane.

21

'I'VE SHOT 'EE AND NOW I'M GOING TO SHOOT THEE'

Beckington, near Frome, 1882

Samuel Silas Phippen was a staunch, almost fanatical teetotaller until he reached his mid-twenties when something made him turn to drink. By 1882, when Phippen was twenty-five years old, he was drinking heavily, so much so that in May of that year he had a severe attack of *delirium tremens* and became very violent. He was forced to seek medical treatment and, although he recovered within a few days, he continued to drink against the advice of his doctor. The excesses of alcohol led to a second bout of *delirium tremens* in late August, although this was less serious than the first and Phippen recovered without medical intervention.

Phippen was a tenant farmer and at Christmas 1881 he took over the tenancy of Whiterow Farm at Beckington, near Frome. His sister, Ada, moved in to act as his housekeeper and, in July 1882, another sister, Lucy, came on an extended visit. He also employed two labourers, Christopher Hill and George Greenland.

On 29 September, everything at Whiterow Farm seemed normal. Hill and Greenland went about their work as they usually did and Phippen left the farm at about half-past eight in the morning to visit the Crown Inn at Beckington, where he drank two pints of beer, while reading the daily newspaper. He walked back to the farm and sat down in the living room, immediately falling asleep, then woke again just after midday and went back to the Crown Inn, drinking another pint of beer, before returning to Whiterow for his lunch.

Phippen and his two sisters ate together and then Phippen rested his head on the table and went to sleep again. Ada went off into nearby Rudge to do some shopping, while Lucy busied herself with housework. Shortly afterwards, she heard the front door of the farmhouse open and close, swiftly followed by the sound of a gunshot. Lucy ran upstairs and looked out of a bedroom window, from where she saw her brother crouching down behind a wall in the farmyard, clutching his shotgun. Assuming that he had shot at a rat or a starling, she carried on with her chores.

Beckington. (© R. Sly)

Beckington. (© R. Sly)

Southwick. (© R. Sly)

Meanwhile, fourteen-year-old George Greenland had also heard the sound of a shot and went to the farmyard to investigate. He saw a puff of smoke coming through the open door of the meal house and, when he went to check, he found Christopher Hill lying dead, killed by a single gunshot to his head. Greenland rushed off to find Phippen and soon spotted him crossing a ploughed field, coming from the direction of the woods behind the farm.

'Christopher is in there dead,' Greenland told Phippen, pointing towards the meal house.

The news came as no surprise to Phippen, who replied, 'I know he is. I've shot 'ee and now I'm going to shoot thee.' He then deliberately raised his gun to his shoulder and pulled the trigger.

The shot caught Greenland on the shoulder and upper arm, knocking him off his feet. As he lay on the ground waiting to be shot again, Greenland saw his employer walking away, so scrambled to his feet and ran as fast as he could towards his home. He got as far as the lane outside the farm before collapsing again but fortunately carter Henry Gunstone happened to drive past just minutes later and took Greenland home, where a doctor was called to attend him. Dr Evans bandaged Greenland's wounds and then, having heard how the boy got them, went straight to Whiterow Farm. He saw Hill lying dead in the outbuilding but could find no trace of Phippen.

By now, other people had heard about the shooting and rushed to Phippen's farm to see if they could be of assistance. Headley Moon, Charles Bourne and Charles Hillman actually spoke to Phippen in the farmyard, asking him if there was anything the matter. Phippen replied that there wasn't and then walked off. The three men watched him walking across a field then, moments later, they heard another gunshot and, when they headed towards the spot where they had last seen Phippen in the distance, they found the body of Charles Sheppard, who had also been shot in the head. Sixty-four-year-old Sheppard, who worked for a neighbouring farmer, was a stranger to Phippen, who had apparently shot him through the hedge.

After shooting Sheppard, Phippen strolled into Rudge and bought a bottle of ginger beer from baker Mrs Sainsbury. From there, he walked to the New Inn at Southwick, where he propped his gun up against the wall and ordered a pint of beer and a cigar. As he sat calmly drinking and smoking, landlord Samuel Lusty spotted the gun and asked conversationally if he had been shooting and if he had bagged much game.

'No, not much particularly,' Phippen replied.

The news of the shootings in the neighbouring village had reached Southwick and, realising that he had the perpetrator in his bar, Lusty sent his wife for a policeman, while keeping a close eye on Phippen, who sat quietly and seemed perfectly sober and composed, although a little pale. When PC George King arrived, Phippen readily surrendered his weapon and, when King charged him with the two murders, Phippen replied, 'That's got to be proved. Nobody saw me do it.'

On the journey to the police station at Frome, Phippen seemed happy to talk about anything but the murders. He commented to King that he had recently attended Frome fair and hadn't expected to be back in the town again so soon 'on this job'. At the police station, he suddenly seemed very tired and, after asking for a drop of small beer, he went to sleep, spending much of the next day either dozing or pacing about in his cell.

In November 1882, Phippen appeared before Mr Justice Bowen at the Bristol and Somerset Assizes, held at the Guildhall, Bristol, where he faced two charges of wilful murder and a further charge of shooting at George Greenland with intent to murder him. The contemporary newspapers reported that the court was packed with spectators, many of whom were women and, even when the court room was filled to capacity, people queued outside for hours in the vain hope of gaining admittance.

Initially, Phippen was tried only for the murder of Christopher Hill and Mr Bompas QC opened the case for the prosecution by describing the events of 29 September. Fully expecting an insanity defence, Bompas assured the court that they would find no trace whatsoever of any insanity, apart from the severity of the crime and the apparent lack of motive. Phippen was not insane before 29 September, he was not insane on 29 September and he was not insane now stated Bompas, virtually challenging defence counsels Mr Collins QC and Mr Poole to prove otherwise.

The prosecution's first witness was Harriet Wingrove, the landlady of the Crown Inn where Phippen had spent the morning of the murder. Phippen was known as a quiet, even morose man and Mrs Wingrove testified that his behaviour before the murders appeared completely normal to her. She stressed that he seemed sober and couldn't agree when Mr Collins asked if Phippen had perhaps been a little quieter than normal.

Ada Phippen was next to take the witness stand, describing what was a very normal day at Whiterow Farm until the shootings occurred. As she was returning from her shopping trip, Ada told the court that she had seen her brother heading across the fields towards Rudge with his gun. She momentarily lost sight of him, and then heard a gunshot, obviously the shot that killed Sheppard.

Ada was much keener to help Mr Collins to establish an insanity defence. She stated that her brother had always been a very quiet man and that, up until recently he had totally abstained from drinking alcohol. He had only started drinking six or seven months before the murders and had since experienced two bouts of *delirium tremens*, the first of which had made him behave very violently. Prior to the murders, Samuel seemed to sleep an awful lot, said Ada, adding that he often complained about pains in his head. His behaviour was strange, especially in the month before the killings, when he looked very pale and almost didn't seem to know what he was doing. Lucy Phippen followed her sister into the witness box and confirmed Ada's impressions that their brother had been behaving very strangely.

George Greenland described finding Christopher Hill's body, the odd remarks made by his employer and being shot by Phippen, while Henry Gunstone, Headley Moon, Charles Bourne and Charles Hillman recalled their parts in the aftermath of the shooting.

Then it was the turn of the medical witnesses. The first of these was Dr Evans, who treated George Greenland's wounds before going to Whiterow Farm to see what he could do to help. Dr Evans was also Phippen's regular doctor and it was he who had cared for Phippen during his first attack of *delirium tremens* in May 1882.

Evans stated that the fact that Phippen seemed unusually sleepy in the run up to the murders precluded another attack of *delirium tremens* as an explanation for the shootings. He denied that Phippen had been violent during his illness in May, stating that he seemed morose and somewhat weak-willed. However, Evans did concede that he personally believed that Phippen was insane at the time of the murders and therefore totally incapable of differentiating between right and wrong.

At this, Mr Justice Bowen interrupted, seeking some clarification on how exactly Evans had arrived at these conclusions and needing the doctor's confirmation that Phippen didn't know right from wrong when he shot Hill and Sheppard. Mr Collins asked Evans again, 'taking all things into consideration, do you think he [Phippen] was capable of knowing right from wrong?'

'No, I do not,' replied Evans, who was then to face a gruelling cross-examination from prosecuting counsel, Mr Bompas.

Bompas maintained that Phippen's heavy drinking had produced his sleepiness and apparent stupor, asking the doctor if he would have expected Phippen's mind to be so clouded that he didn't know what he was doing once he had slept off his excesses.

Evans answered that he would have expected quite the opposite, saying that Phippen should be sober and rational after a sound sleep. Bompas forced an admission from Evans that, in his opinion, the shootings had nothing to do with Phippen's ability to differentiate between right and wrong but were the result of an impulse to commit an act that he was powerless to resist.

Mr and Mrs Lusty, baker Mrs Sainsbury and several police officers all testified that Phippen was quiet and pale after the shootings but, at the same time, seemed both

The Assize Courts, Bristol. (Authors' collection)

sober and sane. Custody officer Superintendent Deggan added that Phippen had been alternately quiet and restless for his first couple of days in gaol, after which '... his manner was quite that of a man in his ordinary senses.'

The next four witnesses testified about Phippen's demeanour immediately before 29 September. James Porch said that he had often been in Phippen's company in the days leading up to the murder and had noticed nothing strange in either his manner or his talk. Porch revealed that Christopher Hill had handed his notice in to Phippen shortly before his death but had been persuaded to retract it on the promise that Phippen would pay off a small debt that Hill owed.

Mr Franks had been playing cards with Phippen on the night before the murders and he believed that Phippen had not played as well as he usually did and was having difficulty concentrating. Franks stated that, in his opinion, Phippen's behaviour had been a little strange and he believed it was because Phippen was drunk. The Beckington village constable, PC Brunt, and the owner of Whiterow Farm, Mr Pargeter, also said that Phippen had occasionally behaved a little strangely, both adding that he was normally a quiet, almost sullen man.

The next witnesses were the surgeon and warder of Shepton Mallet Prison, where Phippen had been incarcerated while awaiting his trial. The surgeon, Dr J.T. Hyatt, examined Phippen on his arrival at the prison and had not found any evidence that he was of unsound mind. Hyatt admitted that Phippen had been quiet, morose and reluctant to answer questions, which he attributed to the effects of the prisoner's heavy drinking. Hyatt insisted that Phippen's demeanour was much better by the next day and that his physical and mental health had greatly improved since he had been in prison and was unable to drink. Warder Joseph Lough told much the same story, stating that Phippen had been agitated and delusional on his arrival at the prison but had gradually improved while he was incarcerated.

It was then left to Mr Collins to take the floor in Phippen's defence. Collins did not deny the fact that two men had been killed and one maimed by his client. However, he believed that he could prove to the jury's satisfaction that his client was insane at the time and that he deserved to be acquitted on the grounds of his insanity and be detained during her Majesty's pleasure rather than forfeiting his life.

Collins called Phippen's mother, Lucy Phippen senior. Mrs Phippen referred to her son as 'a very good boy', whose health had always been somewhat delicate. She reiterated her daughter's testimony, that Samuel had been a total abstainer from drink until recently, explaining that Samuel's father had been very much addicted to drink and had consequently been committed to Dorchester Lunatic Asylum, dying five weeks after his release. Samuel's maternal aunt had died while a patient in Wells Asylum and his uncle had suffered from epilepsy. His paternal grandfather was notoriously crazy and 'not right in his mind', although he had never been in an asylum and other more distant relatives had committed suicide or been in-patients at asylums.

The defence then called their own medical witnesses. Surgeon and coroner Jonathan Wybrants had conducted the inquest on the victims and had then accompanied Phippen on his journey from the inquest to prison. He believed that, at that time, Phippen was of unsound mind, adding that he had not seemed to understand what was going on at the inquest and had appeared in a low and desponding state.

The medical superintendent at Laverstock Asylum in Salisbury concurred. Having examined Phippen on 23 October, Dr W.J. Manning found him to be a man of low intellect, who had very little recollection of the murders. Manning believed that the sleepiness and pains in the head that Phippen complained of were indicative of a diseased brain and that the likelihood was that, on 29 September, Phippen was suffering from a homicidal mania and was utterly incapable of distinguishing between right and wrong. Under cross-examination by Mr Bompas, Manning stated that the mania could last minutes, hours or days but, once it had passed, the sufferer could give every appearance of rational thoughts and deeds.

Once again, Mr Justice Bowen sought further explanation, asking if such a mania would be accompanied by violent speech or demeanour. Manning replied that he was uncertain of the answer to the judge's question but explained that it was perfectly possible for Phippen to know that he was killing someone without actually appreciating that he was doing wrong.

Dr Wade, the medical superintendent of the Wells Asylum, agreed with Dr Manning and Mr Collins rested his case, stating that he believed that he had proved beyond all reasonable doubt that Phippen was not in his right mind when he killed Hill and Sheppard and was therefore not legally responsible for his actions.

It was left for Mr Justice Bowen to summarise the evidence for the jury. He reminded them that two innocent and peaceable men had lost their lives and that it was up to the jury to see justice done. Yet, at the same time, a man's life depended on their verdict.

In one sense, it was possible to surmise that anyone who committed murder had a diseased mind and in this case, he was sure that the jury would find that the defendant's mind was somewhat 'off its balance'. However, the question they must answer was whether or not it was sufficiently off balance to render him incapable of knowing the difference between what was right and what was wrong. There was a difference between acting in a drunken frenzy and having a brain that was adversely affected by previous intemperance – a person could choose whether or not to get drunk but could not choose whether or not to have a damaged brain. If the jury felt that Phippen had murdered through bloodthirstiness, in a drunken fit or through an impulse that he knew was wrong, they should find him guilty. If, on the other hand, they believed that the defendant's brain was affected by his previous intemperate habits or by insanity, they should find accordingly.

The jury deliberated for thirty minutes before returning with a verdict of 'not guilty by reason of insanity'. Mr Justice Bowen ordered Phippen to be detained during her Majesty's pleasure, placing the cases for the murder of Sheppard and the shooting of George Greenland on file.

Phippen was sent to Broadmoor Criminal Lunatic Asylum, where he was still a patient in 1891. He is believed to have died in 1934, aged seventy-six, but interestingly, he also appears to have married in 1901.

22

'I SHALL DO FOR HIM'

Wincanton, 1883

The odds seemed to be stacked against Albion Wadman from the word go. He was a tiny baby, who, according to Elizabeth Hannam who nursed his mother throughout her confinement, would have fitted comfortably into a quart jug. Soon after his birth, doctors told his parents that he was suffering from water on the brain. Albion grew into a sickly, delicate child, who began to be afflicted by fits at the age of about six or seven years yet, despite this, his father, Henry, remembered little difference between Albion and his more robust siblings in childhood.

When he grew up, Albion followed his brothers into the shoemaking trade, often finding employment in the factories around Wincanton. He married and, fathered three sons of his own. Yet, by the time he reached his mid-thirties, Albion's life was gradually falling apart.

His wife had shown disturbing signs of mental illness and, as a result, was committed to a lunatic asylum, leaving Albion as the sole parent to their three young boys. The youngest two boys had fallen ill and were admitted to the hospital wing of Wincanton Workhouse. Left with only seven-year-old James to care for, Albion struggled to cope as his own failing health and eyesight made it more and more difficult for him to work and earn sufficient money to support himself and his son.

Albion was extremely fond of his eldest son and, as he became increasingly less capable of working, the boy became his constant companion. However, there was no doubt that Wadman found single parenthood difficult. Having repaired a pair of boots for a neighbour, Emma Steele, Albion confided his frustrations to her that the boy wouldn't listen to him, telling her, 'I shall do for him'. Emma suggested that Wadman should take the boy to the workhouse, but he refused.

Doubtless many harassed parents have made similar remarks over the years and, although Emma was sufficiently disturbed by the conversation to relate it to one of Albion's brothers, it is unlikely that either she, or anyone else, could have predicted the tragic events that followed just a few months later – the first murder to occur in Wincanton in living memory.

At ten minutes to ten o'clock, on the morning of Tuesday, 17 April 1883, Wadman presented himself at the police station in Wincanton, demanding to be arrested. Sergeant David Smith listened incredulously as the heavily bloodstained man told

Wincanton. (Authors' collection)

Church Street, Wincanton. (Authors' collection)

him, 'I have killed my little boy. He is up at the top of the lane and you will find him in the field with a razor by his side.'

Smith went straight to his superior, Superintendent Joseph Williams, who was working in the police station office and related Wadman's story to him. Williams instructed Smith to call out another officer, Constable Scadding and, on his arrival, to escort Wadman to the site of the alleged crime.

The officers removed Wadman's boots to prevent him from making an escape, although this precaution was hardly necessary, since he was trembling so much that he could barely walk. Then, the two constables set out with Wadman along Congyar Lane towards Spring Close, where he had indicated that they would find the boy. They had barely left the police station when Superintendent Williams caught up with them. As the party approached Spring Close, Wadman pointed to a field and Williams climbed over the stile, while the other two officers stood guard over Wadman at the field entrance.

In a ditch, close to the entrance of the field, Williams spotted a young boy, lying on his back with his legs drawn up. As he approached more closely, he noticed that the child's throat had been cut from ear to ear with such force that his head was almost severed from his body. Nearby, stuck in a bank, was an open and bloodstained razor, which was obviously the murder weapon. (Its sheath was later found in Wadman's pocket.)

Superintendent Williams was disturbed in his contemplation of the horrific scene by a sudden commotion from the gateway. A sobbing Wadman shouted, 'Let me come up! Let me come up!' and, on being permitted to enter the field, looked tearfully at his son's body and asked pathetically, 'Is he dead?' Williams confirmed that the boy was indeed dead then proceeded to caution Wadman and charge him with the wilful murder of his son. He was escorted the 200 yards back to the police station and placed in custody, while Sergeant Smith waited with the body for the arrival of the doctor, James Colthurst.

Having examined the boy at the scene of the crime, Dr Colthurst arranged for the body to be transported to the dead house at Wincanton Work House for inspection by the coroner Mr W. Muller and his jury. Meanwhile, in the holding cell at Wincanton police station, Wadman was stricken with remorse. Prostrate with grief, between sobs, he told Constable John Bailey that the idea of killing his son had been on his mind for about three weeks. Every morning, he had woken up and chided himself for not having committed the crime – today had been his first real chance and he had taken it.

On the following afternoon, thirty-four-year-old Wadman appeared before magistrates at Taunton. He was a sorry sight, his eyes red from crying and his worn handkerchief drenched with tears. After the police and Dr Colthurst had given their evidence, the magistrates next called upon two witnesses who had met Wadman and his son on the morning of the murder.

The first of these was Frederick Tucker, who had briefly discussed the weather with Wadman as he made his way towards Spring Close. As usual, James had been closely

Shepton Mallet Prison. (Authors' collection)

following his father and Tucker had noticed nothing unusual about the pair. Tucker was followed into the witness box by Eliza Day, a neighbour of Wadman, who had been standing at her garden gate at eight thirty in the morning when he and James had passed. Having exchanged greetings, Day asked Wadman how he was that morning, to which he had replied 'Middling.' Eliza recalled that her neighbour seemed in particularly low spirits as he told her that he was going to pick some flowers for his son. The boy did not speak at all, but had quietly followed behind Wadman as they continued on their last walk together.

Once Emma Steele had repeated her conversation with Wadman, during which she maintained that Wadman had said either, 'I shall do for him' or 'I shall have to do for him', the accused was committed to Shepton Mallet Prison to await his trial at the Spring Assizes.

The trial opened on 28 April at Taunton, presided over by Baron Huddleston. Wadman was not defended. In the dock, he initially pleaded guilty to the murder of his son, but was immediately taken aside by Mr Kitley, the Governor of the County Gaol. After a quiet discussion with Kitley, Wadman tearfully revised his plea to one of not guilty.

Having listened to the witnesses from the magistrates court repeating their testimony, the next witness called was Dr Wybrants, who had attended Wadman for some three years prior to the murder. He testified that the defendant was suffering from 'cerebral irritation'. This had caused the deterioration of Wadman's eyesight, which prevented him from working. In addition, Wybrants had also treated him

Broadmoor Criminal Lunatic Asylum. (Authors' collection)

for anaemia, which, he maintained, would have prevented adequate nourishment from reaching Wadman's brain. Although Wybrants stated that he had never known Wadman to suffer from insanity, he conceded that his brain might be so affected as to prevent him knowing right from wrong on occasions.

Doctor James Taylor Hyatt, the medical officer for Shepton Mallet Prison, supported Wybrants's testimony. Having observed Wadman closely for a week while he had been in custody, he believed that the prisoner had a weak mind. In addition, a peculiarity of his gait suggested the presence of a disease of the brain. In Hyatt's opinion, Wadman, who was known as a quiet, steady man and a teetotaller, could be thrown off balance by the smallest incident or provocation and so be unable to distinguish between right and wrong.

The prosecuting counsel, Mr Hooper, was scrupulously fair and objective in summing up the case for the jury. Hooper pointed out that there was absolutely no doubt that Albion Wadman was guilty of the wilful murder of James, but that the law allowed for humanity as well as justice. If the jury felt that Wadman was not accountable for his actions at the time of his murder, then they should find him not guilty on the grounds of insanity.

Judge Huddleston affirmed that there was no question that Wadman had caused the death of his son and that, in the eyes of the law, this was wilful murder. There was also no doubt that the murder was premeditated, given Wadman's confession to

PC Bailey in the holding cell at Wincanton. However, the medical witnesses had testified that Wadman was suffering from a mental illness that might, at certain times, prevent him from differentiating between right and wrong. If the jury accepted the medical evidence, then they should find the defendant not guilty.

The jury took only a short time to put forward the expected verdict of 'Not Guilty on the ground of insanity', leaving the judge to order the sobbing defendant to be detained at her Majesty's pleasure. Wadman was sent to Broadmoor Criminal Lunatic Asylum and is believed to have died there in 1893.

Note: In various accounts of the murder, both Albion Wadman and his son James are referred to as John and Albion's name is alternatively spelled either Albin or Albon. James's age is variously given as six and seven years old.

23

'A DELIBERATE AND VERY TREACHEROUS MURDER'

Bath, 1884

Over the years, many a Temperance activist has railed against the effects and consequences of too much alcohol. One sorry example occurred in Bath in the first week of the new year 1884.

Charles Kite was a hawker of wood, and Albert Miles carried on a similar trade in fish around the city streets. Both men, aged twenty-one, lived close to each other, Kite in a cottage forming part of the block of the Lamb and Lion Yard, and Miles at Bolwell Court, Corn Street. The Malt and Hope Inn in Corn Street was their favourite pub and Kite spent much of 2 January drinking there. Between four and five in the afternoon Miles, generally known to his friends as Jack, also came in for refreshment, joined Kite in conversation, and both seemed quite friendly at first. However, other customers nearby soon became aware that friction was developing. They seemed to be 'twitting' each other, or suggesting that the other had committed some offence which would probably result in a prison sentence if he was caught. All this might have started off as a joke, but it gradually became more bad-tempered, and Miles threatened Kite that he would 'give him in charge' before he went to bed that night.

Matters were escalating when one of the other customers, Henry Parsons, saw Kite take a knife from his pocket, and asked him what he wanted it for.

'I mean doing for somebody,' he retorted. Parsons told him to put it away and to 'think no more about it'.

Kite put the knife back in his pocket, but tempers were rising, and they began swearing at each other. Frederick Smith, the landlord, told them he could no longer tolerate such language on his premises, and asked them to leave. Kite was the first to go, and as he walked out Smith saw him take the knife from his pocket. A little later, Miles followed him. Within a few minutes they returned and went to the bar, asking for a pint of ale each. Mr Smith refused to serve them, particularly Kite, after what he had seen. In any case, their conduct had 'disturbed his company' and caused considerable annoyance to others.

Corn Street, Bath. (Authors' collection)

Meanwhile, both men were carrying on a conversation, and Kite said to Miles, 'If I were as good a man as you, Jack, you should not talk to me like that.'

Miles was eating a hot potato which he held in his right hand. He proffered his left, suggesting that if they shook hands, 'perhaps the governor will let us have something, and we'll drink together.' Kite took his left hand and gave it a half-hearted shake. Ever since they had left the inn, he had been holding his right hand in the pocket of his trousers. Now he whipped it out, and lunged at Miles, swearing as he slashed at his neck.

Crying out that he had been stabbed, Miles reeled to the wall at the other end of the bar and collapsed on the floor. Several people tried to save him, while Smith ran for help from the Royal United Hospital just along the road. The house surgeon, Mr Pagon Lowe, rushed back with him to the bar, but Miles had died of his injuries within two or three minutes. There was a downward wound inside the collarbone, which had been delivered with considerable force, passing between the ribs where they joined the breastbone and into the aorta. Mr Lowe gave orders for the body to be removed on a stretcher to the hospital. Parsons struck at Kite with his stick and tried to stop him from getting away, but the latter still escaped and walked home.

Constable Berry was on duty at the Central police station. He and Detective Singer went in search of Kite, who had handed the bloodstained weapon, a garden pruning knife, to his father. Two of the policemen guarded the entrance to Bolwell Court while the third went into the house and apprehended Kite. He was taken to

High Street and the Guildhall, Bath. (Authors' collections)

the central police station, placed in the dock and charged with having slain Albert Miles, but denied knowing anything about it. Early reports of the murder in the local press described Kite as 'a thin, ill-fed looking man, of rather diminutive stature', and asserted that although Miles had been sober, his assailant 'is said to have been rather the worse for liquor.'

Next morning he was brought up at Bath Police Court, with Mr J.F. Tuttell appearing on his behalf. The main witness was Frederick Smith, who described what had happened. After he had finished speaking, the clerk told Kite that he had the right to cross-examine Smith, but his solicitor had deferred that. When the chairman of the magistrates asked him if he was content with that, Kite agreed he was, and he was then remanded in custody.

That evening, an inquest on Miles was opened at the Guildhall. As they were about to start, Mr W.J. English, the coroner, asked the jury to be guided solely by evidence and not to allow previous conclusions to influence them.

The first to speak was Miles's mother, Mary Ann. Between four and five o'clock the previous afternoon he asked her for sixpence, which she gave him, saying she hoped he would not spend it on drink, and he promised her he would not. That was the last time she saw him, until six o'clock when she was called to identify his body at the hospital. She had not been aware of any ill-feeling between him and the prisoner.

Smith then repeated the evidence given earlier at the police court, and the foreman asked him why he did nothing to check the prisoner when he saw the knife in his hand the first time he left the Malt and Hope Inn. 'My duty was over when he left my premises,' was the reply. 'I did not think it my duty to act as constable in the public streets.' He admitted that he had warned Miles after seeing the knife in Kite's hand. The surgeon, Dr Lowe, gave details of the wounds inflicted on the deceased, and said that in his view the latter had had very little to drink. Three others, cab driver John Cruce, William Organ, and Henry Parsons, who had been drinking in the inn at the same time all said that they had heard Kite threaten Miles, as well as seen him strike him and inflict the fatal wound.

The inquest was adjourned until the following day. After the police officers present had given their evidence, Mr English summed up. He said the case was 'free from complexity', and that it was not necessary that the jury should be satisfied as to premeditation, as 'the law implied premeditation as well as malice from the act'. One point they needed to consider was the drunkenness or sobriety of the prisoner, but drunkenness was no excuse for the crime, and even if the jury were of opinion that he was intoxicated at the time he committed the offence, it would not affect their verdict. If they believed substantially that the witnesses had spoken the truth and that the prisoner, not in a paroxysm of fury, but with set purpose, stabbed the deceased, and that act caused his death, it would be their duty to bring in a verdict of wilful murder against Charles Kite.

They retired for quarter of an hour, and returned with a unanimous verdict of guilty of wilful murder. When the coroner asked Kite if he had anything to say, he answered that, 'I cannot remember anything about it whatever.' He was then committed for trial at the next county assize at Taunton.

On 6 February he appeared before Mr Justice Cave. Mr Murch and Mr Douglas Metcalfe were counsel for the prosecution, while Mr Blake Odgers was retained for the defence, instructed by Mr Tuttell. Looking pale, Kite pleaded not guilty in 'a tolerably firm voice'.

Mr Murch gave a summary of the events of 2 January in the Malt and Hope. He concluded his statement by saying that if a man without adequate provocation struck a man with a deadly weapon and thus caused his death, even if there was no express malice, he was presumed to have malice aforethought, and that was wilful murder. There could, he feared, be only one conclusion.

Mrs Miles and Mr Smith were the first witnesses for the prosecution. They were followed by William Morgan, John Cruce, Henry Parsons, Thomas Pagon Lowe, and finally the police officers involved. Morgan had known Kite and Miles, and said he had overheard the latter threatening to give the other in charge, though he did not hear any explanation why. Parsons had heard Kite telling Miles that he would be 'a dead man before tonight,' inviting Miles's question, 'What have I done to you?' After they had finished speaking Murch reviewed the evidence, and reaffirmed that he could not do much other than characterise the act as 'a deliberate and very treacherous murder'.

On behalf of the defence, Mr Odgers said he would not attempt to make out that this was an accident. He could not deny that the killing had been committed by the prisoner with the knife produced. It was also impossible to suggest that the prisoner was out of his senses, and he could not say that the prisoner was drunk in the sense that it would be a defence, but drunkenness was one of the facts necessary for them to consider as to intent and the state of his mind.

He had to admit that the prisoner was guilty of manslaughter, and that turned upon the question whether the prisoner did it with malice aforethought or not. Both men had been friends together, drinking in a public house, and 'using loose expressions'. When a man was in a drunken state, the jury ought not to regard the words which he used and the expressions which fell from him as showing deliberate intention as if he were in his sober senses. There was no concealment of the weapon, an ordinary knife which was not particularly sharp. (That its owner found it sharp enough to inflict a wound which immediately proved fatal might have detracted somewhat from his argument.) A degree of provocation could be cited, as the man whose own mother admitted was known in the neighbourhood as 'Rough Jack' was a large, powerfully-built man, who certainly looked and probably was easily the physical superior of the rather diminutive, smallpox-marked man now on trial for his life, and he kept on charging the prisoner with committing crimes, as saying he ought to be locked up, telling him that two or three times that before going to bed that night he would give him in charge and have him sent to prison. The landlord, he said, apparently attached no great importance to the prisoner having his knife out again. If Kite followed Miles to inflict a blow, he had ample opportunity of doing so outside. Would any man in his sober senses come back to the public house where he was well known by the other customers, and in the presence of the prisoners commit such a crime? At the time the prisoner had no intention of doing any injury to his friend.

In summing up, the judge said the law of England was that if one man stabbed another in a part of the body likely to occasion death, and death ensued, then that was murder, unless circumstances existed which might reduce it to manslaughter. If the jury believed the evidence of the landlord, Mr Smith, there was surely no provocation which would justify them in reducing the offence. The jury retired for half an hour, and returned with a verdict of guilty, adding a recommendation to mercy. The clerk of assize asked Kite if he had anything to say.

'I never had any malice against the young man,' he said. 'I know nothing about it. I had been drinking a fortnight. I had no malice against him. If I had been in my right, sober senses I should not have done it. I knew nothing about it until I woke up in the morning. When I woke up I had a black eye. We were always very good friends. I am very sorry; I cannot rest for it.'

This was not enough to save him from the ultimate sentence. The judge told him that upon the evidence that had been laid before the jury; he did not see how they could have arrived at any other conclusion. While the recommendation to mercy would be passed to the proper quarter, but duty required him to sentence him to hang. Looking somewhat dazed, Kite was led away to the cells to spend much of the next few weeks reading the scriptures and in prayer with the prison chaplain.

On 18 February a meeting was held at the Guildhall in the Sessions Court, to consider the advisability of sending a petition to the Home Secretary in favour of a reprieve for Kite. Several civic dignitaries and clergymen attended, and the Chairman read a letter from the Clerk to the Justices, expressing every sympathy with the object of the meeting. They unanimously agreed to get up a memorial which would be signed by as many citizens as convenient and sent to the Home Secretary. A petition attracted nearly two thousand signatures, asking Her Majesty to reprieve Kite on the grounds that he was intoxicated at the time of the offence.

When his parents and friends visited him in gaol on 20 February, everybody was hopeful that he would still be spared. Three days later, at least one regional newspaper carried the news with a brief paragraph to the effect that the Home Secretary had issued a reprieve. A reporter had either spoken too soon or got his facts wrong. On the morning of 25 February Kite made his walk to the gallows at Taunton Gaol to be hanged by Bartholomew Binns and his assistant Albert Archery.

24

'RESERVED AND QUIET IN MANNER'

East Lambrook, 1888

In 1888 Frederick George Lye was a thirty-year-old bachelor, and regarded in the East Lambrook area as rather an eccentric by some, or less charitably by others as a ne'er-do-well if not an idiot. His parents had died when he was about eighteen, leaving their four or five children quite well off. He did not get on with his siblings; one by one they left home, some of the younger ones to an orphanage in Bristol, and within nine years he was alone in their old-fashioned house in the centre of the village. It became increasingly dilapidated as he took to the bottle.

Almost immediately opposite him in the village was the cottage where Mr and Mrs Charles lived. At fifty-four, Martha Charles was considerably younger than her bedridden elderly, partially blind and slightly senile husband, a former mason by trade. As he was no longer fit to work, she supported him and Caroline Priddle, her fifteen-year-old daughter by a previous marriage, by doing housework and washing for Lye and several others who lived in the farmhouses nearby.

At about half-past ten on the evening of Friday, 23 March 1888, Mrs Charles was getting ready for bed, when Lye appeared at her cottage door and asked her if she would bring his washing over. He needed his clothes at once so he could leave the house early next morning. Tired but as obliging as ever, she told him they were not yet completely dry, but she would do her best to make sure they would be ready as soon as possible. She rekindled the fire, and with Caroline's help she ironed the items he needed, a coloured shirt, collar, pair of stockings and a towel. He had returned to his house, and within about half an hour she was able to take them over to him.

When she went out she left the door open, and Caroline sat by the fire reading, waiting for her mother to return. After an hour she felt she had waited long enough, so she put her slippers on and went over to Lye's house herself to find out what was keeping her. His front door was open, and he was at the back door, apparently going out and shutting the door after him. When Lye saw her, he moved quickly towards the front door as if to prevent her from coming in, and she asked him where her mother was.

'How the devil should I know?' he asked.

'Who ought to know but you?' was her reply.

East Lambrook. (© R. Sly)

He then told her that her mother had probably gone to visit Sally Trott, who lived at the end of the street. When Caroline said she did not believe him, he admitted that her mother was inside the house, doing some sewing for him, but would be back at her house in about half an hour. Still feeling uneasy, but trying to reassure herself that her mother often stayed for quite a long time whenever she was at Lye's house, Caroline went back to her parents' cottage and lay dozing on her bed.

When dawn broke and she realised that her mother was still not back, she was increasingly alarmed, and went to try again. Unable to rouse Lye, she knocked on the door of a neighbour, Mr Millard. She had told him of her fears and he called two of his friends, Charles Porter and Richard Scott. They went round to the back of Lye's place and, finding a door open, walked through the kitchen. As they opened the door leading into an inner sitting room, they were horrified to discover the body of Martha Charles, stretched out on the floor, in a pool of blood. The clean linen was hanging on a chair in the corner of the room. A large axe, which Lye's father had used in his trade as a butcher, was by the woman's side, also covered with blood. It was apparent that she had been struck first in the centre of the skull by the chopping side of the axe, must have fallen to the ground stunned, and then been hacked about by her assailant. There were five wounds in the skull, one of them very deep, and in the doctor's opinion, sufficient on its own to have caused death.

East Lambrook was a closely-knit community and by the time Superintendent Self of Ilminster had been telegraphed, news of the horrific discovery had spread far and wide. Lye had lost no time in running away. Shortly before Mrs Charles had come to his house, a neighbour had heard him playing his violin, and there were two empty gin bottles on the table in the kitchen where his victim lay. Most people assumed he had committed the deed while in a drunken frenzy and that he had probably since killed himself.

Nevertheless, an announcement was circulated to all police stations in the county, describing the wanted George Lye as 'about 5ft 7ins in height, light whiskers and moustache, brown hair, near sighted, large Roman nose; dressed in speckled suit, nearly new.' It mentioned that he was known to have relatives at Taunton, Sheerness, Pinsford, and East Harptree, 'and is addicted to drink'.

Far from having committed suicide, George Lye was very much alive and well. Early next morning he was at the Cross Keys Inn, East Lydford, about fifteen miles away, asking for a pint of beer. However, the net was closing in on him. He spent the night at the home of a Mr Dyer, which could have either been a boarding-house or the home of a friend, at Charlton Adam, near Somerton. It was there that the police caught up with him, arrested him on the morning of Sunday 25 March, and remanded him in custody.

Three days later, Martha Charles was buried at Kingsbury. That same day Lye was brought before the magistrates at Ilminster and formally charged with her murder. Superintendent Self asked for a remand until Saturday 31 March, when he would be prepared with witnesses to proceed with the case.

The trial was at Wells Assizes on 13 July before Mr Justice Day. Mr Kinglake and Mr Wilson Cox appeared for the prosecution and Charles Mathews for the defence.

Among witnesses called for the prosecution were Caroline Priddle and the neighbours who had helped by entering Lye's house on the morning after her mother was killed, and William Walker of South Petherton, the surgeon who conducted the post-mortem. He said that from the position of the wounds, he thought that Mrs Charles had been struck first on the top of the head and that the other blows were delivered while she lay on the floor, but the first blow had probably proved fatal. John Best, a carpenter who had known the prisoner all his life and had been acquainted with the family, said that his maternal grandfather had been mentally unstable, and eventually hanged himself, while another member of the family had died in an asylum at Wells the previous year after suffering from sunstroke. Lye himself was very peculiar in his behaviour, and sometimes wandered around at night after staying in his house all day. He was 'reserved and quiet in manner', and often seemed rather depressed.

Rosina Munckton, who lived near Lye's house, had been working at a sewing machine near her window on the evening of 23 March. She recalled that at about ten minutes past eleven, she had heard a noise from his parlour which sounded as if he was chopping wood.

For the defence, Mathews admitted that he was not attempting to challenge the basic facts that the unhappy woman had indeed been the victim of the prisoner's

Exeter Prison, 1905. (Authors' collection)

violence. The main issue to be addressed was whether the prisoner was a responsible human being, or whether there was sufficient evidence to satisfy them that 'for a long time past he had been one of those unhappy creatures who had fallen under the hand of nature, whether his mind had not been overthrown, and by means of that overthrown mind he had been completely unable to gauge what it was that he did, or to control the doing of it, and blind to its terrible nature'.

He then called several witnesses who were able to testify to Lye's state of mind. The first was his sister Clara, who produced a long, rambling letter written to her by her brother twelve months previously. It referred to various 'conspiracies and combinations' which he believed existed against him. Lye's second cousin, Henry, who lived at Clevedon, confirmed that the prisoner was in the habit of going absent at night. On one occasion after they had spoken together when he had been out all night, he said he had been out counting the stars. His mother had also been very odd.

Edward Satherley said he had known the prisoner for several years, and always found him rather strange in his manner. Once he went to Lye's house, and found him talking loudly to himself. He asked him if he was going crazy, and Lye said he had terrible pains in his head. Satherley had known his grandfather, who was decidedly odd, he was often teased by the local boys and eventually he hanged himself.

All this was corroborated by Mr T.W. Caird, a prison surgeon at Exeter, who explained that Lye had been admitted on 31 March. After observing the prisoner for a time, he thought he was weak-minded. Solitude had a bad effect on him, and so he was placed in an association cell with two other prisoners. On 4 June he was removed to Shepton Mallet Gaol. On cross-examination by Mr Kinglake, Caird said that in his opinion the prisoner knew right from wrong. Had he been an ordinary prisoner, the surgeon said he would have taken him before the magistrates and had him examined by another medical man, and had no doubt he would have been sent to an asylum.

Mathews summed up the defence to the jury, and said he thought after the evidence he had called that the jury must come to the conclusion that it had been placed beyond all controversy that on the night the terrible deed was committed, the prisoner was of unsound mind.

The judge said in his summing up that the law as to insanity had been clearly defined and ascertained by a long course of judicial decisions. Insanity, to excuse a man from responsibility for acts which were in themselves *prima facie* criminal, must amount to such a condition of mind, arising from disease, which disabled him from distinguishing him from the nature and quality of the act with which he was charged.

The jury retired at quarter to five, and took thirty-five minutes to consider their verdict. On returning to the courtroom the foreman then said they found the prisoner guilty of murder, but that he was of unsound mind at the time. Although in many a similar case of the age, a plea by the defence counsel of insanity and proof of weak-minded relatives was not enough to save a convicted killer from the hangman, Lye was more fortunate than most. The judge directed that he should be detained in prison at Her Majesty's pleasure.

25

'DON'T, HARRY, DON'T!'

Bath, 1891

Harry Dainton, a thirty-five-year-old mason, lived in Avon Street, Bath, with his wife Hannah and their five children. It was a stormy marriage, and Harry was notorious for his violent temper. On at least two occasions a terrified Hannah, who feared increasingly for her life and with good reason, went to the police and had him summoned before the local bench on charges of assault. In April 1891 they fined him 5s for one such offence, and she was granted a separation order. On 20 August he was convicted a second time, sentenced to two consecutive terms of seven days imprisonment, and bound over to keep the peace. He was released on 3 September.

There are two sides to every story, and it was apparent that her reputation as a wife was not a spotless one. In an age where women were either far more moderate drinkers than men, and if not, were very secretive about such an indulgence, she seemed quite unashamed of her tippling, and he had often remonstrated with her but to no lasting effect. On the morning of 8 September he was working at Bathwick Hill for a Mr Matthews, in the company of Richard Simmonds, a fellow labourer who lived at Peter Street. Not long after midday, he said he thought 'something was going to happen at home,' and needed to return. Shortly before two o'clock, he was seen with his wife in Kingsmead Square by Isabella Hardwick, the wife of Hannah's brother. When he saw the latter, he walked over to her and complained that he had found his wife in the Black Horse Inn. 'If I am of the same mind as I am now, she shall not walk about much longer,' he added darkly.

'If thee's threaten[ing] her,' she told him angrily, 'I shall have thee bottled.' This was due warning that if he dared to lay a finger on his wife, she would see that he was taken back into custody. As he had only just finished serving a sentence, he ran every risk of being arrested again and put away for longer. Presumably on the basis that if one cannot beat them one might as well join them, or possibly so he could keep an eye on her, he and Hannah went together into the Lord Nelson and she made her way home again not long afterwards. Then he resumed his work, telling Simmonds sadly that his wife was 'on the booze' again. In the evening he made a similar complaint to his sister-in-law, Mrs Vaughan, and repeated more or less word for word the threat he had uttered to his other sister-in-law Mrs Hardwick a few hours earlier.

At about half past seven that evening, Hannah and another woman went into the Cabinet Makers Arms and a while later her husband and Simmonds followed them there. During the evening Mr and Mrs Dainton quarrelled, and she was seen with blood streaming down her face. She said her husband had struck her, but he denied any such thing. They left the Cabinet Makers Arms shortly before ten o'clock that evening, and from then until the woman was seen in the river, nobody saw her at sufficiently close range to be able to identify her with certainty.

About half an hour later screams of 'Murder!', followed by 'Don't, Harry, don't!' and then a loud splash, were heard coming from the direction of the towing path by the side of the river.

Sergeant Townsend and Constable Millard, who were on duty at Bath Central police station, were alerted by a nearby resident, and Constables Wyatt and Smith were sent to the scene. By this time a large crowd had gathered by the river. The search came to an end when a shout came from someone who had found the body in a shallow part of the water, less than 2ft deep, near the engineering works of Messrs Stothert and Pitt. It was lying on its right side, with an arm extended out of the water, and the head close to the bank. Several people recognised it as Hannah Dainton. Wyatt tried to administer artificial respiration, but it was too late, and he took the body to the mortuary. On his way he saw Dainton coming towards him, whom he recognised, and called out to him.

'For God's sake, governor, what have you got there?' Dainton replied.

'From what they say it is your wife,' Wyatt told him. 'You had better come to the mortuary with me to identify her.' Dainton did so, and duly identified the body.

It was common knowledge that husband and wife had quarrelled on a regular basis. Dainton was well known in the area, news of what had happened spread so quickly, and the general feeling against him was so strong in the neighbourhood that he spent the rest of the night at the police station. It was rumoured that a group of people had come to look for him with the intention of attacking him, and the police feared he could be seriously hurt or even lynched if left to the full force of public vengeance.

He was taken into custody and asked to go to the police station. 'For God's sake, master, I didn't do it,' he insisted when charged with killing his wife. 'We had a few words about nine o'clock; she ran away towards the Blue Coat School, and I ran after her.'

Sergeant Newton had been to search his house, and found the bundle of wet clothing which he had been at pains to change on returning that evening. On being asked to explain his wet clothes, he said he had jumped into the water to drown himself. His boots were examined, and found to have clay on them which corresponded to traces found on his wife's body, and to footprints on the bank where she had been found.

In the morning Wyatt searched the area where the attack had taken place. There were signs of a struggle on the river bank close to where the body was recovered. Ten yards further alongside the river were marks suggesting that somebody had got out of the water and walked away with wet clothes, which had dripped on to the dust.

Dainton was brought before the magistrates and charged with murder at Bath City Police Court that same morning, 9 September. He pleaded not guilty, saying that his

Wells Town Hall and Court. (© R. Sly)

wife had threatened to commit suicide. Sergeant Flower said the prisoner entered the Central police station at 9.40 that morning with some sand in his hand. He said, 'I have brought this sand from my work in Bathwick Hill, which is the colour of that on my clothes, which they accused me of having on them from the waterside last night.' When Flower told him that he would have to charge him with the murder of his wife by drowning, Dainton said he had known nothing about his wife having died until he met the police with her body and went with them to identify her.

Frank Goodson, a stoker of Roebuck Cottages, Lower Bristol Road, on the opposite side of the river to where the body was found, said he was at home at about half-past ten on the previous night, preparing for bed, when he heard a woman's screams of 'Murder!' and 'Harry, let me get out!' He came downstairs at once, went to the wall of the river, about six yards from his house, and by electric light nearby he distinctly saw a man and woman struggling with each other on the towpath, their forms clearly visible from the electric light in Green Park. Next he heard the woman say more calmly two or three times in succession, 'Harry, what's this for?' and the next thing he was aware of was something plunging in the water, after which all was still. Although he ran round to where he thought the cries had come, he could see nobody there. It was too dark for him to be able to describe the appearance of either person, and he did not hear a man's voice at any point.

Mary Ann Vaughan, Dainton's sister-in-law, said that at a quarter to seven the previous evening, she was standing at her door, when he came up to her and said, 'She's on again.' Then he said in the course of conversation that he had had to leave his work at eleven o'clock that day because things were going wrong, and if he kept in the same mind as he was then, 'she would not walk about as she did now.' She said she had never heard Mrs Dainton threaten to take her own life.

Dainton was remanded for a week, extended several times. When his trial on 24 November opened at the Wells Assizes before Mr Justice Cave, he pleaded not guilty to murder. Mr R.A. Kinglake and Mr G.R. Askwith were the counsel for the prosecution, with Mr H.E. Duke for the defence.

Kinglake opened proceedings by outlining the previous history of Dainton's misdemeanours and brushes with the law, and events leading up to the death of Hannah Dainton that evening. The first witness he called was her sister, Mary Ann Vaughan, who said that Harry had complained to her of his wife being 'on the drink' again, whereupon she retorted that Hannah had gone to look for work, as their mother had told her so. Dainton told her he had been at work, but came back home as he was uneasy something was going to happen. After he had uttered threats against his wife, Mary told him firmly not to go about beating her, 'for you know what you are under now.' After some further conversation, he said he would go and search for her.

Ellen Morley, wife of the landlord of the Cabinet Makers Arms in Trim Street, said that at about seven o'clock on that night Hannah Dainton and some other women had entered her premises. She had a drink and shortly afterwards the other women left. While Hannah was on her own, Simmonds and Dainton came in and the former took hold of her by the arm, saying, 'Come on out of it. I'll see who you are with.' Mrs Morley intervened, telling them that she was with nobody, and her husband John told Dainton that he ought to be ashamed of himself for letting somebody else pull his wife about so roughly. Dainton said that as he was out on bail, he could not do anything himself. Hannah Dainton struck Simmonds in the face, and Dainton advised him to go and call a policeman. He asked Hannah repeatedly to leave the inn and go home, to which she retorted, 'What for? To have a good hiding when I get there?' When he accused his wife of pawning their son's clothes, she defended herself by saying that he was to blame as he never gave her enough money to feed the children. Dainton said he had little money as there had been hardly any work recently.

Soon afterwards, Mrs Morley went into another room and while she was there she heard a loud noise. Returning to the room where she had left the Daintons, she found blood streaming from the latter's face. Dainton denied having struck her, and said that she was telling lies. They then had some ginger beer and Dainton assured the Morleys that they would be all right after that. They left the house together at about quarter to ten, Mrs Morley warning Dainton as they were did so that, 'She's leaving the house all right; if you knock her about I will give evidence against you.' Although tempers had run high and blows were exchanged during the evening, there was never any suggestion that anybody had been drunk at any stage.

John Morley corroborated his wife's evidence, although he had almost nothing to add. When he saw Hannah's face streaming with blood, he turned to her husband and asked, 'Do you call yourself a man to do this?'

'I didn't do it,' was the answer. 'She came towards me, and I put out my hand. It caught her nose, which will bleed in a second.'

'Harry, you know you did it,' Hannah snapped.

Simmonds, who alone of the witnesses was Dainton's sole defender, confirmed that he had been working alongside him on the day of the murder. At about one o'clock Dainton said, 'Something is going wrong, and I shall walk down home around the town.' He went back to his work about an hour afterwards. Simmonds met him in the evening between six and seven o'clock and they walked around the town, going into the Cabinet Makers Arms at eight o'clock. He recalled that husband and wife 'had a few words', but as far as he could remember, they did not touch or strike each other, before he left a few minutes later.

One witness, William Maber, who lived in a house at Kingsmead Terrace, said that he saw the prisoner dragging a woman down the terrace steps, leading to the towing path, at about twenty past ten. He heard her say, 'You serve me too bad; you serve me too wicked. I'll go round with the old woman.' This last sentence evidently referred to one of her regular friends with whom she visited the inn. 'No you won't,' was the man's reply. He was followed by Frank Goodson, who repeated the evidence he had given at the City Police Court on the day after the murder.

Mr Duke asked him whether they fell in to the river, and if so, might it have been accidental? 'I do not say accidentally at all,' was the reply. When the judge asked him to elaborate as to which threw the other in, he said he thought that after having witnessed the struggle and heard her cries of 'murder' the man threw the woman in the water.

Another witness, Edward Stokes, who lived at Belmead Place, Lower Bristol Road, saw a man holding a woman under in the water, and was sure she was trying to resist. He went close enough to see them fall in, heard the cry of 'Murder!' three times, noticed the man climb out and up the bank, and then went to inform the police. On being cross-examined, he said it was evident that the man was forcing the woman in, while she was trying hard to get away from him. Similar evidence was offered by another Lower Bristol Road resident, Frank Jefferies. When they heard the cries of 'murder', he and another young man immediately jumped into a boat, and rowed across to the spot from where they had heard the cries. As they reached the other side, he saw a man looking over the wall, but he disappeared almost at once.

Constable Wyatt then took the stand to describe his finding of Mrs Dainton's lifeless body in the water, his unsuccessful efforts to restore life, and his seeing Dainton while going to the mortuary.

'When you told him it was his wife, did he make any exclamation?' asked Kinglake. 'No, he made no reply,' said Wyatt. He added that on their way to the mortuary Dainton admitted that they had had a few words at the bottom of Queen Street, she ran away and he pursued her. Wyatt cautioned him, to which Dainton denied having killed her. 'You know when we had a few words. She threatened to do away with herself.'

Next to speak was the prisoner's fourteen-year-old son Alfred. According to the local reporter, he was 'a bright little fellow, and gave his evidence in a most intelligent manner'. Between ten-thirty and eleven o'clock, he said, he and several other boys had been playing at the top of Avon Street when he saw his father going home, with water dripping off his clothes. He followed him home, and saw him go back into the house. As he looked through the window, he watched him change his clothes and remove his stockings. The clothes which had been produced in court were those his father had been wearing, and he then left the house wearing a pair of corduroy trousers and a black jacket.

Mrs Hardwick, of Kingsmead Square, Hannah Dainton's sister-in-law, said husband and wife had been living on very unhappy terms with each other. He was followed by several police officers in succession. The last was former Sergeant Flowers, who said that when charged with the murder Dainton said, 'I knew nothing about the drowning until I saw her with the policeman on the ambulance.' He showed Flowers some clay, which he said he had brought from the place where he worked, and it was similar in colour to that on the clothes.

The two mortuary keepers, Arthur and William White, confirmed the identity of the body. Henry Culliford Hopkins, surgeon, had made a post-mortem examination, said the body was well-nourished and developed. There was mud on the face, under the nails, and in the hair, with a recent bruise over the eye. Death was due to drowning. When he was asked whether it was likely that she had drowned herself or was drowned by somebody else, he said there was no indication, except for a blow to the nose which might have caused her to faint and fall on her face in the water. There was also a blow over the right eye, which might have caused her to faint, though he thought this unlikely.

This evidence closed the case for the prosecution. There were few witnesses for the defence, and none of them added materially to the facts already stated. Dainton's employer, George Matthews, stated that the prisoner 'bore an excellent character as to his bearing and demeanour towards those about him', but such a statement was never likely to have carried much weight against the evidence already presented as to the events of that fatal night.

Addressing the jury, Mr Duke said that if the man and woman had fallen into the water and the man, whoever he was, scrambled out forthwith, that in itself did not amount to the crime with which the prisoner was charged. Even if the jury concluded that the man was the aggressor and was to blame for the fall which resulted in the woman's death, that at most would be an offence of manslaughter, not murder. Such a course of events, he said, had been suggested by one witness. He put it to the jury 'that it would be their pleasure, as it was their solemn interest and their sworn duty,' to give the prisoner the benefit of that witness's statement, 'as well as of every doubt which existed in the chain of circumstantial evidence which had been woven against him'. The day might come when the mystery in the case had been cleared up, and then they might look back and say that they were grateful they did not find the man guilty of the murder he was alleged to have committed.

At the conclusion of his speech there was a burst of applause, and the judge ordered the public gallery to be cleared, as he could not allow such conduct in a court of justice. The order was promptly carried out.

Mr Kinglake then replied on behalf of the prosecution, remarking that all circumstances pointed to the prisoner's guilt.

The judge began summing up at half-past six. In an address lasting forty minutes, he said the jury had to consider whether the prosecution had satisfied them that the prisoner was the man struggling with the deceased woman on the bank. The prisoner had not accounted for how he had spent his time corresponding with the period at which it was alleged the murder was committed. That he should have attempted to commit suicide at the very time when another man was getting wet in trying to drown his wife suggested 'a tremendous tissue of improbabilities' which showed how difficult it was to conclude that someone other than the prisoner had committed such an offence. If the jury had any reasonable doubt on the matter, the prisoner was entitled to an acquittal, but if they were satisfied by the concurrence of testimony that had been adduced that he did commit the offence – that he, being the only person who could be suggested to have had a motive, did quarrel with the woman – then came the question as to whether the crime was one of manslaughter or murder. If he took her to the river bank for the purpose of getting her into the water, and deliberately held her down until she was drowned, that was murder. If in the struggle they fell into the water accidentally, and he scrambled out without assisting her, that would amount to manslaughter only, because however morally he might be to blame, yet still a man was not punishable for murder for not doing something that moral duty would prompt him to do.

After a further twelve minutes' consultation, the jury found Dainton guilty, but recommended him to mercy on account of his wife's provocative conduct. This was not enough to prevent the judge from donning the black cap and passing a sentence of death on the prisoner, who was led back to captivity at Shepton Mallet gaol.

On 14 December he wrote letters to all his brothers, begging them to give up drink, and when his sister visited him in prison, he implored her never to enter a public house herself. Leaving no written confession, he said he would rather confess to God, not man.

He was hanged at the gaol at eight o'clock on the morning of 15 December 1891 by James Billington. Although it was raining heavily, about 500 people gathered to see the hoisting of the black flag once the sentence had been carried out.

26

'MY DEAR BROTHER, WHAT HAVE YOU DONE?'

North Petherton, 1897

Charles Tucker Roach was always something of a drifter, described by his mother, Ann, as having been '… of an irritable, roving and unsettled disposition' even as a boy. At twelve years old Roach started work on the London & South Western Railway and, after five or six years, he moved to Swansea to live with an uncle, finding work there in the docks. Less than a year later, he returned to his home in Devon and began working as a platelayer on the Exe Valley Railway but, in a matter of months, his wanderlust had taken him to Wareham in Dorset and, shortly afterwards, he enlisted in the army. He was based at Southampton, serving as a gunner in the Field Artillery.

However, after only nine months, his military career came to a premature end when an old fracture on the bridge of his nose, sustained while working on the railways, was cited as reason for his discharge for being unfit for service. He returned to Exeter, where he was admitted to the Devon and Exeter Hospital for corrective surgery and after convalescing for about four months, he once again took up a position with the London & South Western Railway, this time working at Okehampton. While there, he suffered an accidental fall from a trolley, which rendered him unconscious and left him with several broken ribs.

He spent several weeks living at his parents' home, recuperating from his head injury, before finding work as a labourer in the Crediton area of Devon. Once again, he was unlucky, sustaining yet more head injuries in a fall from scaffolding while working for a mason. He held several different labouring jobs before returning to the railways, where he worked for about two years before being suspended for neglecting his duties.

At this, he packed a few belongings and took to the roads, becoming a tramp. He travelled all over England on foot for some time before returning unexpectedly to his parents and working as a labourer again. Then, one morning, he packed up his lunch as he did on every other normal working day, walked out of his parents' house as if going to his job and simply disappeared for three weeks, eventually turning up in Wales.

Fore Street, North Petherton. (Authors' collection)

There he secured a job as a tipper, building the new railway line running from Briton Ferry to Swansea and taking up lodgings at Briton Ferry with Mrs Margaret Thomas. Soon he began keeping company with Mrs Thomas's granddaughter, Elizabeth Williams, who was, at that time, still only fifteen or sixteen years old. Roach was almost twice her age and Elizabeth's family were universally opposed to the relationship. Hence, when Elizabeth fell pregnant, the couple ran away together, setting up home together in rented accommodation at Commercial Road, Cadoxton in South Wales. It was here that their daughter Jessy was born.

A few weeks later, Roach took his 'wife' and child to North Petherton, where his sister, Jessie Drake, lived with her husband Samuel, the village blacksmith. Roach found work at the Great Western Railway Works in Bridgwater, lodging with his sister and brother-in-law. On Boxing Day 1896, Roach moved his wife and daughter to a rented cottage in North Street.

Charles and Elizabeth deliberately kept a low profile in the village. Elizabeth had just turned eighteen (although she always gave her age as several years older) and was, by now, heavily pregnant with their second child. There was a great deal of social stigma in nineteenth-century England against children born out of wedlock and, in addition, there was always a slim chance that Elizabeth's father might somehow find out where they were living and try to force his daughter home to Wales. The villagers of North Petherton described them as quiet, sober people, who gave every appearance of enjoying a loving and happy relationship. Samuel Drake, at whose home the couple had stayed for about five months, described them as 'living together

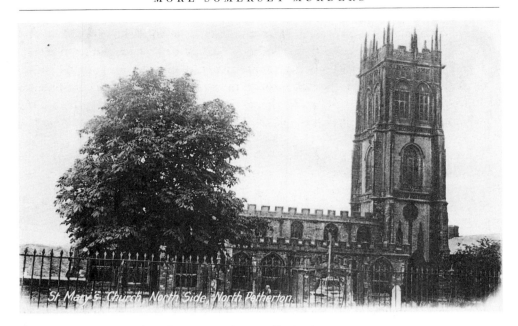

St Mary's Church, North Petherton. (Authors' collection)

on the best of terms', stating that Roach appeared to be very fond of both Elizabeth and his daughter, Jessy.

The move to a new home seemed to herald a new beginning for Roach and, on Saturday 9 January 1897, he took advantage of his employee's privilege ticket and went with Elizabeth by train to Exeter, where the couple married at the Registry Office.

Roach's sister, Jessie, visited her brother every evening in order to lend him her watch, which he used to ensure that he got to work on time each morning. On Monday 11 January she arrived as usual, finding the family sitting comfortably by the fire. Roach was nursing the child and, when his sister entered the room, he playfully made as if to toss the baby to her, saying, 'Here, you take the little one.' Jessie noticed that her brother's food was packed ready for work the following morning and that he and his new wife seemed to be behaving as normal. There were no signs of any quarrel between them, although Jessie instinctively felt that her brother was 'a little low' in spirits.

It was Elizabeth's habit to call on her sister-in-law every morning for a cup of tea. When she didn't appear on the morning of 12 January, Jessie went to see why. The window blinds were still down at the Roachs' home and the door was locked, indicating that nobody at the house was up. Jessie waited until just after nine o'clock before returning to find the house exactly as she had left it, the blinds still drawn closed. Worried, Jessie knocked at the door then tapped at the bedroom window with a clothes prop that she found in the garden, but could not rouse anyone.

By ten o'clock the house was still locked and Jessie was becoming increasingly more concerned. Seeing the milkman, Mr Joseph Jones, she told him that she had been unable to make anybody hear. Jones knocked at the door, shouting 'Milk' and he too tapped at the window with the clothes prop, but the house remained silent.

A neighbour, Mr Trott, climbed an apple tree in the front garden of the house and tried, unsuccessfully, to peer in through the window, while Jessie continued to hammer desperately on the door. Hearing no sounds of movement from within the house, she turned to leave and was halfway up the path to the garden gate when the door slowly opened.

There, on the doorstep, stood Charles Roach, his shirt drenched in blood. Jessie quickly went back towards the house, asking, 'My dear brother, what have you done?' Roach did not reply. Only then did Jessie notice that her brother's throat was cut.

She immediately ran to summon help, marshalling two neighbours, Mr Isaacs and Mrs Chick, who returned to the house with her. By the time they got back, Charles Roach had disappeared from the doorstep, leaving the front door standing open. The three went upstairs to the main bedroom, where they found that Charles had got back into bed. Lying there with him, quite dead, were Elizabeth and ten-month-old Jessy, their throats also cut.

Jessie immediately sent for the police and a doctor. First to arrive was PC Henry Coles, who was closely followed by Sergeant Blacker and Dr Hawkins. Along with several neighbours, they crowded into the bedroom where the injured man now lay in bed, cradling his dead daughter. Roach, who was unable to speak above a whisper, pointed to a bloody open razor lying on the bedroom floor, indicating that it should be passed to him, a request that was naturally refused. While the doctor bandaged his wounded throat, he managed to communicate by a mixture of whispers and sign language that he had killed his wife and child at about three o'clock that morning. Elizabeth had been the first to die and had been awake when her throat had been cut, pleading with her husband to 'Spare my life'. When asked why he had committed such a terrible deed, Roach merely pointed to his head and replied, 'I have been drinking.' It was discovered that a piece of rope had been removed from the bed frame and thrown over a beam in the kitchen. Bloodstains on the rope suggested that Roach had intended to hang himself.

Having administered what first aid he could, Dr Hawkins asked Mr Jones the milkman to procure a conveyance to transport the injured man to Bridgwater Infirmary. By the time this was done, Roach had been dressed and taken downstairs – he was loaded into a closed carriage and accompanied to the hospital by Jones and PC Coles.

The first bulletin, issued by the hospital at two o'clock that afternoon, stated that Roach's injuries were likely to prove fatal. However, his wounds stitched and a tube inserted in his throat, Roach defied all expectations by passing a peaceful night.

The funeral of Elizabeth and Jessy was held in the village on the following Monday afternoon. It attracted a huge crowd of people, many drawn from nearby Bridgwater by morbid curiosity. Elizabeth's father, a miner who spoke only Welsh, travelled from Port Talbot to attend and sobbed bitterly as his daughter – one of ten children – was laid to rest at the expense of the parish. Several of Roach's relatives were also present, but Roach himself was still under police guard at Bridgwater Infirmary, where he was apparently making slow progress towards recovery.

Meanwhile, an inquest into the deaths had been opened and adjourned until 11 February, in the hope that Roach himself might by then be sufficiently recovered to be present. Doctors at the Bridgwater Infirmary had provided a written certificate indicating that he was currently unfit to attend and, following instructions he had received in a recent circular from the Home Office, the coroner felt obliged to defer proceedings until Roach was well enough to have the opportunity of giving evidence should he choose to do so.

Roach was escorted to the resumed inquest at the George Hotel, North Petherton by Superintendent Vowles of Bridgwater Police and two other constables. Although normally clean-shaven, Roach was now bearded, having apparently vowed never to pick up another razor again. Appearing weak and ill, he sat tearfully in the meeting room of the hotel with his head bowed, his face covered by a handkerchief.

At the inquest, the district coroner, Mr Foster-Barham, heard from the numerous inhabitants of the village who had been immediately involved in the aftermath of the tragic killings. Amongst these was Mary Ann England, who lived in the adjoining cottage to the Roach family. She testified that she had spoken to Elizabeth Roach at twenty to eight on the eve of her murder. Elizabeth had asked the time and continued to say that she and Charles were planning to go to bed soon, as he had to be up early for work and wasn't feeling well. Mrs England had indeed heard footsteps going upstairs in the Roach household at about eight o'clock. Professing herself to be a very light sleeper, who had in fact slept very little on the night of the murder, Mrs England denied hearing any further sounds coming from her neighbours' house, knowing nothing of the events that had taken place within until half past ten on the following morning.

Also present at the inquest was a work colleague of Roach, Lucas Storey. Storey identified the razor produced in court as being exactly like one he had sold to Roach on 9 November 1896. Roach, he maintained, had asked him several times if he had a razor for sale saying that there was nobody in North Petherton who could shave him and thus he wanted to shave himself. Despite initially being reluctant to sell his spare razor, Storey had eventually relented and Roach had paid him the sum of 7d.

Without exception, all those appearing before the coroner maintained that the relationship between Charles and Elizabeth Roach had been a happy one and that they were looking forward to the imminent birth of their second child. Roach himself did not give evidence.

Having heard all the witnesses, the coroner proceeded to address the inquest. He first pointed out that, since baby Jessy had been born out of wedlock then she must be known by her mother's maiden name of Williams. Thus, the inquest was into the deaths of Elizabeth Roach and Jessy Williams, both of which had undoubtedly resulted from wounds to their throats. The coroner said that the evidence suggested that these wounds had been inflicted by Charles Tucker Roach and if the jury were satisfied that this was indeed the case then they must find Roach guilty of wilful murder. It was not their duty to consider the state of mind of Charles Roach, or to determine whether he was sane or insane at the time of the murders – that matter would be dealt with by a higher court. Accordingly, after a brief debate, the jury returned a verdict of wilful murder by Roach of both his wife and daughter.

In due course, Roach was brought before magistrates at Bridgwater who, having heard the evidence as presented at the inquest, committed Roach to stand trial at Somerset Assizes.

He was held in Shepton Mallet Gaol until June 1897, when the trial opened at Wells. Mr Kinglake and Mr Askwith led the prosecution, while Mr Weatherly was left with the thankless task of defending Roach. Speaking in a husky voice, Roach pleaded 'Not Guilty' to the murders of his wife and child. He then sank into his chair in the dock, slumping over, weeping and moaning quietly, a position he held for the majority of the proceedings.

Having heard from the witnesses who had testified at the inquest, much of the court sitting was devoted to trying to establish Roach's mental state at the time of the murders. While in custody, Roach had made several statements, the first from his hospital bed on the day after the murders. Proclaiming, 'I know I done it' and referring to the murders as 'a bad job'. He continuously maintained that he couldn't think what had made him do it, professing to love every hair on his wife's head and to not know what had come over him.

It was disclosed in court that Roach was an epileptic. While fitting, he was known to react violently and thus it was thought possible that the murders may have been committed either during, or in the aftermath of, an epileptic fit when he was in a state of 'reduced consciousness'. The doctors at Bridgwater Infirmary, who treated Roach for the self-inflicted wound to his throat, were surprised to find that, on arrival at hospital, he had an unusually high temperature. Dr Parker from the hospital testified that conversely he would have expected a man with such an injury to have a low temperature. Roach's behaviour in hospital was likened to being in a stupor rather than a mania, something that doctors believed may have been indicative of him having suffered a recent epileptic fit. However, Roach had suffered no fits while in hospital or while detained in gaol, neither had he shown any signs whatsoever of insanity. Doctors had, however, observed some episodes of mild twitching, immediately followed by drowsiness.

None of the medical witnesses could find any evidence to suggest that Roach had been drinking prior to the murders, despite his own whispered admission at the scene that he had. Although generally a sober man, Roach was known on occasions to binge drink, consuming large quantities of alcohol, after which he would abstain completely for months at a time. He was also noted to suffer from severe depression on occasions.

Roach's mother appeared greatly distressed in court. She testified about her son's past head injuries and about the history of mental instability in the immediate family. An aunt of her husband's was described as 'an idiot', while her mother-in-law was '… an imbecile for several years before she died'. A cousin had died in Crediton Asylum of 'softening of the brain'.

Instructing the jury, the judge pointed out that it was not their concern whether or not a motive had been established for the murders, as it clearly had not. Rather, they should focus on determining whether or not the two victims had been killed by the hand of the accused and the balance of evidence seemed to clearly indicate that they had. Thus it only remained for the jury to decide whether or not Roach was insane at the time of the murders, in which case he would be absolved of all responsibility for the deaths.

The jury debated the case for around fifty minutes before returning a verdict of 'Guilty, but insane'. Roach was sentenced to be detained during her Majesty's pleasure.

Note: In various contemporary accounts of the murder, Roach's daughter's name is given both as Jessy and Jessie. Jessy has been used for this account to avoid confusion between the baby and Roach's sister, Jessie Drake – however, it seems most likely that both names were spelled with an 'ie' at the end.

27

'HE IMAGINED EVERYONE WAS AGAINST HIM'

Butleigh, 1898

Charles Weaver, a bachelor of about forty, and his widowed father, James, lived together in a cottage at Butleigh. They ran a family butchery business between them, and both were well respected in the community as tradesmen, and Charles in his capacity as a long-serving member of the West Somerset Yeomanry. The only other person under the same roof was Annie Brownsell, a widow of forty-four with three grown-up daughters, who had been their housekeeper for about three years.

Unfortunately, there was some evidence of mental instability in the family. The elder Mr Weaver seemed mercifully free from the problem, but his wife had been insane for several years prior to her death at around Christmas 1897. Since then Charles had suffered from acute mental instability and severe depression. His father was so anxious about his condition that he sought help for him, both locally and with a specialist in Bath.

Nothing they tried seemed to have any lasting effect. Charles's behaviour became increasingly odd, and on at least one occasion he declared that Mrs Brownsell was trying to poison his food. James feared that sooner or later he could become violent, and consulted doctors about the possibility of sending him to a lunatic asylum at Wells. It was probably in connection with this that he left the house early on the morning of 15 April 1898, having asked Mr Kellen, the landlord of a local public house, to keep an eye on his son. Kellen had to leave the house for a short time, but was called back by the sound of screaming. Their neighbour Mr Cox followed him, and they ran to the house, only to find the front and back doors locked against them.

Kellen fetched a hammer, and they broke the door open. In the kitchen they found Charles Weaver sitting on the body of Mrs Brownsell, repeatedly stabbing her in the throat with a small table knife. They seized him, Kellen sustaining a cut finger as he grappled with the man.

Just then Mrs Brownsell feebly muttered the words, 'Oh my dear'. She was found to have been stabbed in several places in the throat and face, with one deep wound having severed the main artery in the neck. It was assumed that Weaver had begun assaulting her with a carving knife, as a bloodstained one was found in another part

Butleigh. (© R. Sly)

of the room. The knife box and its contents were also covered with blood. Three fingers of her left hand had nearly been severed, probably as she tried to wrest the weapon from his grip. Her throat was badly gashed and the main artery had been cut. The floor and walls were splashed with blood, suggesting that she had put up a fierce struggle before losing consciousness.

Dr Knivett was summoned from Butleigh Hospital, but by the time he arrived, Mrs Brownsell was dead. Charles Weaver was arrested, charged with murder and taken into custody at Glastonbury police station, before being held at Shepton Mallet to await trial.

Dr A. Law Wade, superintendent of the Wells asylum, was asked to come and visit him in his cell three or four occasions from the middle of May onwards. A few conversations with Weaver were enough to convince him that he was suffering from delusions; 'that he imagined everyone was against him; that he had no bones, no feeling like other men; that he was stabbed, but could not bleed, he had no inside and could not die; that he was going to be burned alive, and then buried alive'.

Under the circumstances, there was initially some doubt as to whether anything would be gained by sending him to trial. At the County Assizes, Wells, on 9 June, Wade told the Lord Chief Justice, the Rt Hon Charles Lord Russell of Killowan, that the prisoner was 'in such an insane state of mind' that he would be unable to plead, and he would not be able to understand why he was in a court of law at all. Nevertheless, the due processes of justice had to take their course, and Russell said that a jury must be empanelled whether or not he was fit to take his place in the dock and plead. Messrs Kinglake and Pugh appeared for the prosecution and Mr Hugh Neville for the defence.

The first to address the jury was Mr Kinglake. He said that if after they had heard the evidence it was their opinion that the prisoner was sane and capable of understanding the proceedings taking place against him, then they would find he was of sound mind and the trial for murder would go on as usual. If, on the other hand, it was their opinion that, after they had heard the evidence of the medical gentlemen about to be called before them, that the prisoner was of unsound mind, suffering from delusions, and unable to comprehend what was happening, under his lordship's direction they would find the prisoner was insane. He then described the facts of the case, emphasising the sad irony that a certificate was going to be granted enabling him to be sent to an asylum on the very day the killing took place.

Mr Wade then spoke, to confirm his conclusions on the prisoner's state of mind. His findings were corroborated by Mr Hyatt, Medical Officer at Shepton Mallet Gaol. He had seen Weaver almost daily since his arrival on 16 April, and was sure he was insane.

This was all the judge needed to hear. Addressing the jury, he said that when a man was called upon in a criminal court to answer a criminal charge, the law had to be satisfied that he was in a condition of mind to enable him to appreciate the character and gravity of the proceedings, to plead if called upon in answer to the conclusions made against him, and to give such reasonable assistance as a man of ordinarily sane mind would be able to give to those charged with his defence. If the jury found that he was not in that fit state, then the law had provided that he should be taken care of, and committed to a proper institution, where he might be safeguarded and remain there during the pleasure of the Crown. If at a later stage it was considered that he was found to be in a condition of mind in which he might be called upon in point of law to plead, he might be called upon to take his trial for the offence. Upon that trial the question would then arise with which at present they had nothing whatever to do, whether when he committed the offence he was in a condition in point of law to be legally responsible for what he did. They therefore had merely to consider the question whether he was then in a state of mind to be called upon to plead, whether he was capable of understanding the character of the proceedings, or whether he was by reason of insanity unable to understand those proceedings and reasonably instruct counsel for his defence. Two medical gentlemen had told them the prisoner was not in that condition of mind, but on the contrary was incapable of doing what his position called upon him to do. If they accepted that view they were bound to return a verdict that he was not then in a proper condition to be called upon.

The jury found unanimously that the prisoner was insane, and the judge ordered that he should be kept in strict custody until the pleasure of the Crown should be known. He was then transferred to the cells.

28

'IS THIS TRUE OR IS IT A HORRIBLE DREAM?'

Alcombe, Near Minehead, 1928

At about 11.15 on the morning of 28 July 1928, butcher's assistant Mr Harrison called at the home of the Banks family in Collins Road, Alcombe near Minehead. At first, there was no response to his knocks on the door, then Harrison heard somebody tapping on a window from inside the house to attract his attention. Finally, a white-haired man dressed in pyjamas and a dressing gown opened the window and urged Harrison to 'Get the police at once. I am in trouble.'

Harrison did as he was asked and immediately went to fetch PC Dredge, directing him to the Banks' house. When Dredge knocked on the door, it was answered by fifty-one-year-old Albert Spencer Banks, the newly appointed manager of the Labour Exchange at Minehead. Banks greeted the policeman with the words 'For God's sake, Constable, come in. A terrible thing has happened. I have shot my wife and daughter.'

Dredge went to check on the man's story, finding two women lying in separate bedrooms in the house, one shot in the back of her head and the other in her head and chest. Although both women were clearly beyond any medical help, Dredge sent for a doctor and within a short time Dr Harry Bertram Walker arrived from Minehead and formally declared life extinct. He then turned his attention to Mr Banks, who was laying on a couch downstairs, his eyes tightly closed.

Walker felt for the man's pulse, at which Banks opened his eyes and asked him 'Are you a doctor?' When Walker confirmed that he was, Banks wanted to know 'Is this true or is it a horrible dream?' Walker soothingly advised Banks not to worry at present and Banks said no more until he was taken to the police station at Minehead and charged with two counts of murder.

Banks professed to remember little about the murders, although, when asked about the death of his fifty-three-year-old wife, Edith, he admitted to Inspector Fry, 'I believe I did kill her but I cannot remember properly.' All Banks could recall was waking up on the sofa earlier that morning, something that came as a surprise to him as he thought that he had retired to bed on the previous night as he normally did. Expecting to find his wife and daughter up and about the house, he went to look for them, finding instead some cushions and his revolver on the floor. According to

Alcombe. (Authors' collection)

Banks, this triggered a terrifying flashback of shooting his wife and daughter during the night. Too afraid to go upstairs to check, he tried to attract the attention of a man working in his garden by knocking on the window. When that failed, he waited until the butcher's boy called, asking him to fetch a policeman. While Banks was waiting for the police to come, work men from a local furniture shop arrived to keep an appointment to lay some lino. When they rang the doorbell, Banks dismissed them, telling them that he had sent for the police as he was 'in trouble'. He then sat quietly in the dining room until the arrival of PC Dredge.

Having established that Banks could remember very little about the murder of his wife, Fry then questioned him about his daughter's killing. 'It is just the same as the other,' replied Banks tearfully.

Banks was remanded in custody in Exeter Prison and, before he left Minehead, Inspector Fry asked if he would like him to get in touch with a solicitor on his behalf. 'No,' replied Banks. 'He would only try and get me out of it and I do not want that. I want to be hanged.'

Post-mortem examinations conducted on Edith and twenty-year-old Marian Aldith Banks indicated that both women had been shot in their beds. Mrs Banks had a single wound behind her left ear, the bullet passing diagonally through her head and coming to rest in the socket of her right eye. Her daughter had been shot twice, once in the head and once in the chest, either wound being sufficiently serious to kill her. Since there were no signs that any struggle had taken place, it was surmised that both women had been shot while asleep. A revolver containing three spent cartridges and two live ones was found on the floor of the house.

After appearing before magistrates at Dunster Police Court, Banks was committed for trial at the Autumn Assizes in Wells and appeared before Mr Justice Shearman in October 1928. Although charged with two murders, his trial dealt only with the murder of his wife and it quickly became apparent that Mr Holman Gregory KC and Mr F.A. Wilshire, who appeared for Banks, were relying on an insanity defence.

Banks was a former soldier, who served as a quartermaster sergeant in India. After twenty years in the Royal Artillery, he took a job as a civilian clerk at the Somerset County Police Headquarters in Taunton, where he worked for four years before beginning a new job as the district manager of the Labour Exchange at Minehead, a position he had held for just a few weeks at the time of the murders. Banks was universally known as a man of the highest character, described on his discharge from the army as '... a steady, sober, honest, intelligent, reliable, hard-working man.' However, in previous years, he had experienced at least two periods of mental illness. In 1926, he was hospitalised for observation for thirty days and, in 1913, he spent nineteen days undergoing treatment for what was described as 'delusional insanity'. On that occasion, he had become convinced that his wife and daughter had been killed by native Indians and had spent two or three days absent from his army post while he scoured the nearby jungle looking for the culprits. On both occasions, he was deemed well enough to resume his duties on his discharge from hospital.

Banks's relationship with his wife and daughter was said to be 'loving' and 'devoted'. The family had moved to the house in Alcombe only a few weeks before the murders and had proudly named it 'Almardith' – a combination of syllables from the names Albert, Marian and Edith.

There was evidence that, immediately prior to 28 July, Banks was in the grip of some form of nervous illness. On 17 June, shortly before taking up his employment at the Labour Exchange, he bought a revolver, having been granted a licence by the police on the grounds that he would soon be handling large sums of money. Banks started his new job on 3 July and, days later, he was officially visited by Fred Hillman, the deputy manager of the Taunton Labour Exchange. Hillman found Banks to be having some difficulties, although he testified in court that he believed it nothing more serious than any man would experience having taken a job that was strange to him, saying that Banks had seemed unduly nervous and jumpy throughout the visit.

On 27 July, Banks was visited at work by Mr Frederick Western, an inspector in the insurance department of the Ministry of Health. Western believed that Banks was then on the verge of a nervous breakdown, describing him as twitching and visibly trembling and relating that Banks persistently referred to him as 'Mr Comfort', even when corrected.

Inspector Fry had known Banks personally for about a year prior to the murders and had always regarded him as a solid and upright citizen, although he was aware that Banks had '... some weakness in regard to his head'. Fry told the court that, at Minehead police station, Banks seemed perfectly rational while making his statement until he related his vague recall of having shot his wife and daughter during the night, at which he broke down and sobbed bitterly.

Dr Rutherford, who served as the medical adviser to the Brislington Private Mental Hospital, described him as having a 'constitutional weakness, which rendered him liable to break down under any undue worry or strain.' Everything about Banks's behaviour pointed to instability of his mind, testified Rutherford.

Counsel for the prosecution J.D. Casswell did little more than outline the facts of the case, leaving the floor clear for Mr Holman Gregory to present his arguments for the defence. Struggling to control his own emotions, Gregory told the court that the saddest thing about the case was that Banks's delusional insanity was transitory – as the defendant stood in court, his delusions had now passed and he was only too aware of what had happened. Gregory explained that Banks suffered from a form of melancholia and his resulting delusions robbed him of the power of 'right thinking' and of knowing the difference between right and wrong. Tragically, his delusions were always connected with those dearest to him.

Mr Justice Shearman summed up the case for the jury, helpfully pointing out to them that there was 'abundant evidence' that would permit them to reach a verdict of insanity. As soon as Shearman had completed his summary, Banks stood up in the dock and asked, 'My Lord, may I say a word?'

Shearman and Mr Gregory both tried to silence Banks but he insisted on speaking, saying that it was essential for his own peace of mind that his counsel should read out a written statement that Banks had prepared earlier. 'I have to live with this afterwards and for that reason, I must have the statement read,' argued Banks.

Eventually, the judge agreed to hear the statement, which was read out to the court by Mr Gregory. Banks now stated that, after sleeping on the statement that he had initially given to Inspector Fry at Minehead, he had felt horribly ashamed. That statement was false and I deliberately killed my wife and daughter, Banks explained, adding, 'But for the words malice and aforethought, I would gladly plead guilty. There was no malice or aforethought.'

It was left to Mr Justice Shearman to explain to the jury that they needn't be concerned by the question of malice aforethought. 'If a man intentionally kills anybody, even though he may make up his mind to do it only five seconds before, that is what the law calls 'malice aforethought,' he told the jury, who didn't even find it necessary to retire to deliberate the case. They found Banks 'Guilty', adding that he was insane at the time of murdering his wife. Mr Justice Shearman ordered Banks to be detained during his Majesty's pleasure, ruling that the murder of Marian Banks was to remain on file.

Note: Witness Frederick Western is alternatively named Weston in some accounts of the murders.

'DID YOU THINK HE WAS DANGEROUS?'

Hembridge, 1928

The First World War took a dreadful toll on farmer's son Stanley George Kingston, who served with the Devon Regiment for three years on the front lines in France. During his service, he was bombed several times and saw many of his comrades killed and mutilated in battle. He returned from the front to work on his father's farm in his home village of Hembridge a much changed man, suffering from shell shock and described by his family as '… a bundle of nerves'. He became 'wild in his ways' and developed a taste for alcohol that led to him indulging in frequent bouts of binge drinking but, in spite of this, his father, George, saw no need to keep the farm guns locked away. As far as he was concerned, Stanley had never threatened to harm anybody and his ready access to guns posed no threat to himself or to anyone else.

In 1926, Stanley became friendly with Gladys, the eldest child of farm labourer Samuel Henry Martin, who lived in a cottage near to the Kingston family farm. Although Stanley's relationship with Gladys initially seemed to have a beneficial effect on his mental health, the couple's courtship was far from smooth as Stanley, who was twenty years older than Gladys, gradually became more and more abusive towards her, particularly when he had been drinking. By 1927, Samuel felt bound to intervene to protect his daughter and, having heard that Stanley had shouted and sworn at Gladys, he confronted him and forbade him from contacting her again.

Prevented from seeing Gladys, Stanley resorted to stalking her, becoming both distraught and enraged when he believed that she was seeing another young man. Once more, Gladys complained to her father that Stanley was shouting and swearing at her and on Friday, 9 November 1928, Samuel witnessed this behaviour himself. While standing at the door of his cottage with Gladys at about 10.20 p.m., Samuel heard a man's voice, which he clearly recognised as Stanley Kingston's, shouting abuse at his daughter. On that occasion, he chose to ignore Kingston and simply shut the cottage door against him and went inside.

At about a quarter-past six on the following morning, Gladys's mother was walking down the stairs in the family's cottage, when Stanley Kingston suddenly burst in and charged up the stairs towards her, brushing aside her attempts to grab him and heading straight for the bedroom where Gladys was still asleep. To her horror, Mrs Martin saw that he had a double-barrelled shot gun in his hand. She called out a desperate warning to her daughter, telling her to jump out of the bedroom window as Stanley was going to shoot her. However, for some reason, Gladys didn't heed her mother's warning, emerging from her room and choosing instead to try and escape down the stairs.

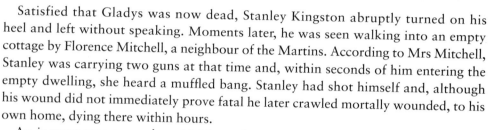

She ran past Stanley Kingston, who immediately turned, aimed the gun at her and fired. Gladys cried out as the bullet hit her but continued to run from her assailant, getting as far as the back door of the cottage before a second bullet struck her. Mrs Martin, who was trying to go for help, had already reached the back door and caught her as she fell.

Satisfied that Gladys was now dead, Stanley Kingston abruptly turned on his heel and left without speaking. Moments later, he was seen walking into an empty cottage by Florence Mitchell, a neighbour of the Martins. According to Mrs Mitchell, Stanley was carrying two guns at that time and, within seconds of him entering the empty dwelling, she heard a muffled bang. Stanley had shot himself and, although his wound did not immediately prove fatal he later crawled mortally wounded, to his own home, dying there within hours.

An inquest was opened on 12 November into both deaths, at which the main witnesses were members of the families of the victims. Mrs Martin, who was almost prostrate with grief, related her unsuccessful attempts to prevent Kingston from shooting her daughter, while Samuel Martin described the verbal abuse that seventeen-year-old Gladys had suffered from her thirty-seven-year-old admirer.

George Henry Kingston told the inquest of his son's war service and of the changes in his personality that had resulted from the terrible things he had experienced while in France. 'After Martin told him to keep away from the house, Stanley used to watch the girl to see if she had a young man,' George stated, adding in response to a question from the coroner, 'I thought he was deranged in his mind altogether. He used to watch the girl out with other chaps and that annoyed him.' Stanley's brother, Cecil, corroborated his father's account.

'I never thought he would ever use the gun,' said George Kingston, when the coroner asked him, 'Did you think he was dangerous?'

The coroner summed up the evidence for the inquest jury, telling them that it was abundantly clear that Stanley Kingston was more or less demented as a result of his wartime experiences and that he was totally incapable of accepting the rejection of his advances by Gladys Martin, spending much of his time brooding over her. The inquest jury returned the only possible verdict – that Stanley Kingston had murdered Gladys Martin then died from a self-inflicted gun shot wound.

Thus an innocent teenager unwittingly became an indirect victim of the atrocities of the First World War, which turned a young man '... deranged in his mind altogether.'

Note: Some contemporary reports of the Hembridge tragedy name Kingston as George Stanley Kingston, a variation that seems to be supported by official documents. However, in view of the fact that his father was also named George, it seems likely that Stanley was commonly used as a forename to prevent confusion between the two men.

30

'BUT O FOR THE TOUCH OF A VANISH'D HAND ...'

Bath, 1928

Twenty-three-year-old William Bartlett from Birmingham had a tragic childhood. Orphaned at an early age, Bartlett later fell in the school playground and injured his knee, which subsequently became infected with tuberculosis, the disease that had already claimed the lives of both of his parents and his sister. Surgeons battled to save his leg but, by the time Bartlett was eighteen years old and had endured three operations, it was finally decided to remove the diseased limb completely and his leg was amputated at the hip.

Although he trained as a boot and shoe repairer, Bartlett practically became a recluse, spending most of his time closeted in his room and avoiding contact with other people, to the extent that he would hide if he was ever approached on the street. However, in 1928, he was persuaded to visit some relatives in Weston-super-Mare and there he met his cousin Marjorie Aileen Hall for the first time.

Marjorie, who was also an orphan, must have seemed like a kindred spirit to the lonely Bartlett. Against the advice of Frederick Comfort, Marjorie's uncle and guardian, who urged them to wait a while, the couple married just a few weeks later after a whirlwind courtship. On her marriage, Marjorie came into an inheritance of £290 and the couple decided to use the money to buy a sweet shop. Soon they were settled in rooms above 'The Chocolate Box', which was located in Monmouth Street, Bath.

Unfortunately, neither William nor Marjorie had any business acumen whatsoever and from day one the little shop traded at a loss. Within five months of opening their dream business, the Bartletts were in grave financial trouble – their capital was long gone and, even though they had virtually no income, the bills kept coming. On 24 October 1928, Marjorie made a last ditch attempt to appease the couple's creditors by selling off some of the shop's fixtures and fittings, for which she received the sum of £11. Knowing that she could fend off the bailiffs at least temporarily was a great relief to Marjorie and a neighbour who saw her later that day noticed that she seemed much more cheerful and optimistic than she had been in previous weeks. However, her positive frame of mind was sadly short lived as, less than twelve hours later, Marjorie Bartlett was dead.

Monmouth Street, Bath. (© R. Sly)

County Building, Taunton, site of the assizes. (Authors' collection)

Her death went unnoticed until William Bartlett limped into a police station in Paddington Green, London on 26 October and told the surprised duty officer, Sergeant Ledyard, 'I have murdered my wife by hitting her over the head with an iron bar.'

Naturally, when the Bath Police were informed of this they immediately went to 'The Chocolate Box', where they found twenty-three-year-old Marjorie Bartlett lying in bed, her head beaten almost to a pulp. The bedclothes, pillows and mattress were drenched in her blood, which had spattered liberally over the walls and ceilings. Even though Marjorie was dead, blood was still oozing from her horrific wounds and, when police surgeon Maurice Harper conducted a post-mortem examination, he found that her skull was fractured, which, coupled with massive blood loss, Harper gave as the cause of her death. A 2ft-long, heavy iron bar, which was obviously the murder weapon, lay discarded on the bedroom floor.

A thorough search of the house revealed only 8d in cash in Marjorie's handbag, while, even after paying his fare to London, William Bartlett had £2 14s 1½d in his pocket on his arrest.

An inquest into Marjorie's death was opened by Bath coroner Mr F.E. Shum and almost immediately adjourned to allow the police more time to conduct their investigations. By the time it reopened on 17 December, Bartlett had already been charged with the wilful murder of his wife and committed by magistrates to stand trial at the Taunton Assizes.

The trial opened before Mr Justice MacKinnon, with Bartlett determinedly pleading 'not guilty'. Ever since his arrest, Bartlett had consistently told the same story – he had taken his wife an early morning cup of tea in bed and she had made some 'sharp remarks'. Bartlett remembered feeling very strange, as though his head was splitting apart, one side of it hot and the other cold. A mist descended before his eyes and he could recall nothing else until he heard the clang of an iron bar dropping to the floor and falling at his feet.

Seeing the bed awash with blood, he realised that he had hurt Marjorie and fled the house in a panic. He spent some time wandering aimlessly around Bristol before catching a train to London where, after walking the streets for almost twelve hours, he handed himself in at the police station.

To prosecution counsel John Lhind Pratt, the motive for the brutal and ferocious attack on Marjorie Bartlett was quite straightforward – money. Both William and Marjorie had been desperately worried by the state of their finances and Marjorie was known to have received £11 just the day before she died. Acknowledging the fact that the amount concerned was only small, Pratt pointed out to the jury that many a murder had been committed for lesser sums.

Defence counsel J.D. Casswell was less convinced. He believed that the 'hot and cold' sensations in his head experienced by Bartlett suggested that he had suffered from an epileptic fit. In spite of the fact that Bartlett was not known to be epileptic, Casswell called two eminent neurologists to support his theory, both of whom were prepared to state that tuberculous patients often suffered from epilepsy.

The prosecution countered by calling the prison doctor from Taunton Gaol, in whose charge Bartlett had been since his arrest. The doctor testified that the defendant had never shown any symptoms of either insanity or epilepsy while, but Casswell cleverly pointed out that, in view of Bartlett's story, it was remarkable that he hadn't feigned illness or insanity while in custody.

'If the prisoner were going to pretend to be unbalanced, would not one surely expect him to pursue that pretence while under the authorities' observation?' asked Casswell and the doctor was forced to concede that he would.

Even with this concession, all the evidence seemed to favour the prosecution's case. A young woman, whose only apparent transgression was making a few 'sharp remarks', had been brutally battered to death in her own bed by someone who had then taken all of her money and fled, without even calling for medical assistance. However, Casswell made an impassioned speech on behalf of his client, stressing Bartlett's unfortunate childhood and citing Marjorie as the one good thing in the troubled young defendant's life. Casswell reminded the jury that their marriage was a love match and that the newlyweds had appeared blissfully happy, in spite of their impoverishment. Dramatically, Casswell finished his speech by quoting a couple of lines from Tennyson's poem 'Break, Break, Break':

> But O for the touch of a vanish'd hand,
> And the sound of a voice that is still.

When Casswell looked up at the end of his speech, he realised that he had reduced the jury to tears. In spite of the best efforts of Mr Pratt, and a summary of the case by Justice MacKinnon, which was apparently somewhat biased towards the prosecution, the jury eventually found in Casswell's favour, pronouncing William Bartlett 'Guilty but insane'.

Sentenced to be detained during the King's pleasure, William Bartlett spent a few years in Broadmoor Criminal Lunatic Asylum before being freed. According to Casswell, who wrote about the case in his book *A Lance for Liberty*, on his release, Bartlett went on to lead '… a normal and useful life'. Meanwhile, it was reported that, while living in Calcutta, Marjorie Bartlett's late father had incurred the wrath of an Indian fakir and, as a result, the fakir had placed the curse of early death on him and his entire family. In Marjorie's case at least, the curse came true.

'ARE YOU COMING HOME OR NOT?'

Milborne Port, 1934

The marriage of farm labourer Reginald Woolmington and glove maker Violet Katherine Smith on 25 August 1934 seemed beset with potential difficulties from the moment they first left the church at Milborne Port as man and wife. Although the couple had known each other for more than two years, Violet was still only seventeen and was heavily pregnant. The newlyweds had no home of their own and so were forced to move into a cramped cottage with Reginald's parents.

However, twenty-one-year-old Reginald secured a good job with a local farmer, Albert Cheeseman, which came with a tied cottage at Castleton, near Sherborne. After six weeks of living with Reg's parents, the couple finally had a place that they could call their own. Yet, having moved in, Violet and Reginald had very little time alone together in their new home as Violet gave birth to their son only a week later.

Unfortunately, marriage and motherhood failed to live up to Violet's expectations. Confined day after day with a fractious new baby in a remote cottage, with her husband working long hours, Violet became stressed and dissatisfied, feeling lonely and trapped. Her mother, Lillian 'Lily' Smith, was a frequent visitor to the cottage and her presence seemed to exacerbate the couple's marital discord. Before her marriage, Violet and her mother had worked at home as outworkers, making gloves for a local factory. When Violet married and moved out, Lily keenly felt the loss of her daughter's income and, when she visited Violet, she often took unmade gloves with her, which she and Violet worked on together while baby Reginald was asleep.

It seemed to Reginald as though Lily was continually conspiring to persuade Violet to leave him and return to her former home in Milborne Port. Lily's perceived interference in her daughter's marriage was the cause of numerous rows between the Woolmingtons, which came to a head on 22 November 1934.

On that day, Reginald returned from work for his lunch break to find his mother-in-law at the cottage. Violet told him that she and her mother were planning to go to Sherborne that afternoon and that they would be taking the baby with them. Reginald protested that it was far too cold to take a four-week-old baby out but Violet stood her ground, telling him that they were going, whether he liked it or not.

The Cross, High Street, Milborne Port.

Milborne Port. (Authors' collection)

Mrs Smith took her daughter's side in the resulting argument and Reginald lost his temper. Telling his mother-in-law to stop interfering and go home, he stormed out of the cottage and went back to his work.

He returned that evening to find the cottage empty. Propped on the mantelpiece was a note from Violet, which read, 'I've gone home. Don't come up, I've asked my mother to have me. I've made up my mind to go to service.'

Reginald was distraught and made every possible effort to persuade Violet to come home with the baby, even asking his employer, Mr Cheeseman, to visit her and plead for her to return. However, Violet was adamant that she wanted nothing more to do with Reginald and that, as far as she was concerned, their brief marriage was over. Reginald was still desperately in love with his wife and on 9 December, a chance meeting with her brother in Sherborne proved the catalyst for events that were to eventually change the face of British justice.

Violet's brother apparently told Reginald that she had gone to the cinema with another man and hearing that someone had already replaced him in Violet's affections was the last straw for the abandoned young husband. After spending a sleepless night, Reginald went to work the next morning and milked the cows, as he normally did. He went to his parents' house for breakfast then returned to work, where he took an old shotgun belonging to his employer and, having sawn off the barrels, he attached a loop of electric flex to the gun in order to hang it over his arm. Then, with the gun concealed under his overcoat, he cycled to his mother-in-law's home at Milborne Port.

Violet's aunt, Mrs Daisy Brine, lived in the house next door and was hanging out her washing in the garden. She clearly heard a man's voice, which she recognised as that of Reginald Woolmington, asking 'Are you coming home or not?' Although she did not hear the reply, the question was almost immediately followed by a door slamming and then a loud bang and, as Mrs Brine ran to investigate the noise, she saw Reginald run out of her sister's house, mount his bicycle and pedal off. Mrs Brine found Violet lying dead on the floor of the cottage, shot through the heart. Baby Reginald slept undisturbed in his cot and there was no sign of Lily, who, perhaps fortunately, was not at home at the time of her son-in-law's visit.

Reginald Woolmington cycled to his parents' home, where he told his horrified mother, 'I've been up and shot Violet'. From there, he cycled back to his work, telling Mr Cheeseman, 'I shan't be coming in to work anymore. I've been and shot Vi.' From the farm, he rushed back to his parents' home, telling his father that he was gong to kill himself. Mr Woolmington managed to keep his son talking until the police arrived and, when Reginald was arrested and charged with the murder of his wife, he made a statement saying, 'I want to say nothing except I done it and they can do what they like to me. It was jealousy, I suppose. Her mother enticed her away from me. I done all I could to get her back. That's all'.

Searched at the police station, a note was found in Reginald's overcoat pocket:

Goodbye all. It is agonies to carry on any longer. I have kept true hoping she would return this is the only way out. They ruined me and I'll have my revenge. May God forgive me for doing this but it is the Best thing. Ask Jess to call for the money paid on motorbike (Wed.). Her mother is no good on this earth but have no more cartridges only 2 one for her and one for me. I am of a sound mind now. Forgive me for all trouble caused. I love Violet with all my heart. Good bye all, REG. [sic]

Such was Reginald Woolmington's despondency at the end of his marriage that his own life seemed to have lost all meaning and he seemed quite content to go to the gallows for killing Violet. Yet, by the time his case came to trial at the Somerset Assizes in Taunton on 23 January 1935 he had undergone a change of heart, since he now claimed that her death been a tragic accident. Reginald maintained that he had never had any intention of killing his wife when he went to her mother's home at Milborne Port but had intended only to frighten her by threatening to kill himself, in the hope that this might induce her to give their marriage another chance. When he pulled the gun from under his overcoat, it went off.

'I swear my finger never touched the trigger,' he told the court. 'I did not intend the gun to go off, nor to injure my wife in any way.'

Woolmington explained the note found in his pocket after his arrest, saying that, on realising that his wife was dead, he intended to commit suicide. Rather than writing the note before shooting his wife, it had actually been written at his parents' house after her death.

J.D. Casswell, who was acting in Woolmington's defence, called an expert gunsmith who had examined the sawn-off shotgun and found that it had an exceptionally light trigger pull and was thus liable to discharge accidentally. While counsel for the prosecution Mr J.G. Trapnell KC argued that Reginald had shot Violet in a jealous rage, Casswell insisted that there had been no intention to murder. Reginald loved Violet far too much to ever want to hurt her and all he wanted was to persuade her to return home with the baby.

The presiding judge, Mr Justice Findlay, summed up the evidence to the jury, who retired to consider their verdict. They returned to court after eighty-five minutes to inform the judge that they were unable to reach an agreement. 'We could not agree if we sat until tomorrow morning' the foreman stated, leaving Mr Justice Findlay no choice but to discharge them and order a re-trial at the next Bristol Assizes, which were due to take place on 14 February.

This time, the presiding judge was Mr Justice Swift. The second trial was an almost carbon copy of the first, until the time came for the judge to sum up the case. In the course of his summary, Swift referred to a book entitled 'Archbold's Criminal Pleading', from which he read a passage to the jurors.

'All homicide is presumed to be malicious, and murder, unless the contrary appears from circumstances of alleviation, excuse or justification. In every charge of murder, the fact of the killing being first proved, all the circumstances of accident, necessity or infirmity are to be satisfactorily proved by the prisoner, unless they arise out of evidence produced against him, for the law presumeth the fact to have been found in malice unless the contrary appeareth.'

Swift went on to clarify the meaning of the passage in layman's terms, telling the jury that it meant that it was for the guilty party to satisfy a jury that his crime was anything less than murder. 'A charge is made against Reginald Woolmington, the prisoner at the bar, of wilful murder' continued the judge.' It is said that on the morning of 10 December, about half-past nine, he murdered his wife. That she died whilst he was in that house you will, I should think, have little doubt. It is a matter entirely for you. If you accept his evidence, you will have little doubt that she died in consequence of a gun-shot wound which was inflicted by a gun which he had taken to this house, and which was in his hands, or in his possession, at the time that it exploded. If you come to the conclusion that she died in consequence of injuries from the gun which he was carrying, you are put by the law of this country into this position ... The Crown has got to satisfy you that this woman, Violet Woolmington, died at the prisoner's hands. They must satisfy you of that beyond any reasonable doubt. If they satisfy you of that, then he has to show that there are circumstances to be found in the evidence which has been given from the witness-box in this case, which alleviate the crime so that it is only manslaughter, or which excuse the homicide altogether by showing that it was a pure accident.'

It took the jury at Woolmington's second trial sixty-nine minutes of deliberation to return a verdict of 'Guilty of wilful murder' against him, at which he was sentenced to death.

His defence counsel was appalled at the verdict. To Casswell, the judge's summary seemed to go against what he believed was the basic principle of English criminal law – a man was presumed innocent until the prosecution had proved his guilt beyond reasonable doubt. Casswell immediately announced his intention of appealing the verdict and on 18 March 1935, he appeared at the Royal Courts of Justice before Mr Justice Avory, Mr Justice Lawrence and Mr Justice Greaves-Lord to put forward his application for leave to appeal.

Having listened to both Casswell and counsel for the prosecution Mr Trapnell, Mr Justice Avory voiced the court's decision – leave to appeal was denied. Casswell immediately wrote to Sir Thomas Inskip KC, the then Attorney-General, asking for his approval for the case to be heard by the House of Lords. Inskip invited Casswell to his private room at the House of Commons to brief him on the case and, less than twenty-four hours later Casswell was notified that the right to appeal had been granted.

Terence O'Connor KC was now appointed to lead Woolmington's defence and, assisted by Casswell, he presented Woolmington's case before Lord Chancellor Viscount Sankey, Lord Chief Justice Hewart and Lords Atkin, Tomlin and Wright. The main grounds for appeal were that Mr Justice Swift had misdirected the jury by telling them that the onus was on the defence to prove that the shooting was accidental and that he had failed to inform them that it was the prosecution's responsibility to satisfy the jury of Woolmington's guilt beyond reasonable doubt.

Trapnell argued that all the Crown had to prove was 'killing and malice' and, in this case, all that Swift had stated in his summary was that the malice had to be presumed from the killing. The crux of the matter was whether or not Swift was correct in giving that direction.

Lord Atkin argued that the problem was more with Swift's directions to the jury that, once it was shown that a person had died through the act of another it was presumed to be murder unless the defendant could satisfy the jury otherwise.

After two days of legal wrangling, watched from the gallery by a somewhat bemused Reginald Woolmington, the Lords retired to deliberate the matter. It took them only five minutes to announce that Woolmington's appeal had been upheld and his conviction quashed.

Less than fifteen minutes later, Woolmington was a free man. He was quickly spirited away from the House of Lords by a national newspaper and, on the following morning, was pictured on the front page with the captions 'It's great to light a pipe again', 'I knew that justice would prevail' and 'But I shall miss my wife'.

It took several weeks before the Law Lords published their reasons for their decision, stating that some of the legal principles concerned dated back as far as the time of King Canute. The main principle to which Swift referred in his summing up dated from 1762. In a famous speech, which has since become known as the 'Golden Thread Speech', Viscount Sankey stated, 'Throughout the web of the English Criminal Law one golden thread is always to be seen, that it is the duty of the prosecution to prove the prisoner's guilt. If, at the end of and on the whole of the case, there is a reasonable doubt, created by the evidence given by either the prosecution or the prisoner, as to whether the prisoner killed the deceased with a malicious intention, the prosecution has not made out the case and the prisoner is entitled to an acquittal.

No matter what the charge or where the trial, the principle that the prosecution must prove the guilt of the prisoner is part of the common law of England and no attempt to whittle it down can be entertained. When dealing with a murder case the Crown must prove (a) death as the result of a voluntary act of the accused and (b) malice of the accused.'

Thus, a cornerstone of English criminal law was established. Now, as a result of Woolmington's case, it has been clarified once and for all that all defendants are presumed innocent until the prosecution has proved all aspects of their case to the jury beyond reasonable doubt.

In the immediate aftermath of his acquittal, Reginald Woolmington became a minor celebrity and was offered a variety of jobs by numerous well-wishers, including a stint as a music hall artist. However, he soon faded into obscurity and is now largely remembered only by those in the legal profession, for whom Woolmington v DPP remains a landmark case in English law.

BIBLIOGRAPHY

Books

Casswell QC, J.D., *A Lance for Liberty* (George G. Harrap, 1961)
Clark, Richard, *Women and the Noose: A History of Female Execution* (Tempus, 2007)
Fielding, Steve, *The Hangman's Record, Vol. 1, 1868-1899; Vol. 2, 1900-1929; Vol. 3, 1930-1964* (CBD, 1994-2005)

Newspapers

Bath Herald
Bristol Mercury and Daily Post
Daily News
Dorset Chronicle
Glasgow Herald
Lloyds Weekly Newspaper
Manchester Times
Morning Chronicle
Morning Post
Northern Star and National Trades Journal
Somerset County Chronicle
The Guardian / Manchester Guardian
The Times
Weekly Dispatch
Western Mercury
Western Gazette

INDEX

THE DEATH OF KNOWLEDGE

A SCOLARIS MYSTERY, BOOK 1

LOU COLLINS

For stardust and wither ♥

Knowledge

noun

facts, information, and skills acquired through experience or education; the theoretical or practical understanding of a subject

the sum of what is known

true, justified belief; certain understanding, as opposed to opinion

awareness or familiarity gained by experience of a fact or situation [1]

Oxford Dictionaries

It was the touch of the imperfect upon the would-be perfect that gave the sweetness, because it was that which gave the humanity.

Thomas Hardy, Tess of the D'Urbervilles

Prologue

Gaia was an artisan, a collector and connoisseur of exquisite things. Living or dead, before that moment it had never mattered. The latest collectible lay frigid in the dawn air, beautiful despite its imperfections. Gaia had surpassed herself on this occasion, fascinated by the beauty before her. So much so that it consumed every waking moment. Intoxicated, she longed to explore every inch of translucent skin, clutch each strand of hair and smooth out the plain brown tunic pressed against those faint soft curves. The artiste surrendered, caressing silky bare soles, her breathless body craving the rising heat. Perfecting the technique had been far too challenging. But, at long last, they found the exact formula. It was a pity that the personal cost to produce the chemical was so high. Never mind, it was worth it.

It was all but impossible to tear herself away from those almond-shaped eyes, cut-glass-blue interspersed with minute flecks of jet black, catching a glint of her own reflection. Not a single crease or sign of age was visible, and an upturned look of transcendent joy proved beyond doubt that the serum worked. At the last second of living, the soul glimpsed its innate creative skill, and the perfect face gleamed with that epiphany.

For centuries the City of Scolaris worshipped the pursuit of knowledge, at the expense of everything else. That needed to change. They would see the reality of what was missing from their miserable existence. Her lip curled, mind recoiling, remembering the loose ends still to be tied. Gaia battled the anger and frustration, cutting them down, whimpering into submission. The plan's success demanded, more than ever, a focus on the end goal. Emotions only hindered progress, and that was unthinkable. Feeling the shape of her mouth, she stretched her ruby lips upward, forcing a smile. There was still time. It could wait a few moments more.

Like a scavenger, Gaia returned to the object at her disposal, sighing and slipping its feet inside the crimson slippers. As she caressed its auburn tresses with great care, she plaited them between nimble fingers and sang. The brooding tone echoed around the abandoned building as the universe paused and listened to the melancholy refrain. A song lost for generations.

Pleased with the work, she finished weaving the lengthy strands. And, taking a ribbon from her own neck, secured the tips of the braid and laid it flat against the creature's collar bone. Gaia lit up, stooping little by little to kiss the raised edges of the teardrop scar at the base of the décolletage. She inhaled hard, greedy to enjoy the plain soap fragrance of it, though it was becoming more difficult to ignore the hint of something rotten. Ironic how such an enchantress presented itself from such a low source. She glanced at the others; they were more typical of their class, but they had played their part.

As sunlight broke through the cracked windowpane illuminating Gaia's water-colour grey eyes, time ran out. She vowed never to return to this place unless granted an opportunity to restore it to its former glory. It would only be a matter of days or weeks before it revealed its secrets. She had required many deaths in her lifetime, but none wounded the psyche in so cruel a fashion. This first paper-cut of grief festered and might never heal.

The girl in the blood-red shoes, hair fixed in a plait, adorned with a matching ribbon, lay dead. A servant in life. Now she served Gaia, a new mistress in death.

Chapter One

Late again, Quill charged headlong through the central corridor of the library. It did not matter that she spent every day there and knew all the nooks and crannies. The place still took her breath away. The repository of knowledge at the heart of the City of Scolaris, it contained every scrap of information collected by generations of library custodians and the scholars who studied there. She pinched herself each day that she lived there.

"Knowledge is King," boomed the mechanical voice, vibrating the air around her sprinting frame, making her tremble. The six am alarm call roused the daytime shift from their slumber and sent the exhausted night workers to their beds. This was a day like any other. Scolarians received the signal to work, sure in the understanding that their purpose was to acquire knowledge. She groaned and picked up the pace. The Master would be unimpressed. He was very particular about punctuality.

At right-angles to Quill's trajectory were endless other corridors, fanning out to the building's perimeter like the tentacles of a sea monster. And lining each of these channels, shelves that passed from floor to ceiling, hundreds of feet high. Crowded onto those platforms, squashed together like reluctant, brittle lovers, were countless millions of books, pamphlets and scrolls of different shapes and sizes.

Finally, she arrived at the far end of the aisle, gasping for breath and clutching at the invisible knife stabbing her right side. She just needed a few more seconds to set-up the reading room before heading across to the Master's study. Grasping the door-knob, she pressed downward and pushed. But no matter how many times it rattled, the handle did not budge. Odd, she thought, why was the place locked? And then, remembering the hour, decided it had to wait.

Although it was early, the spring sunshine poured in through the towering stained glass windows. Spaced at regular intervals along the outer wall, they commanded a view of the entire city. Quill looked up, studying the miraculous spectacle of the sunlight refracted into rainbows through the multi-coloured glass. Since infant hood, she had loved watching the dust motes floating from the roof, imagining that they were miniature people flying in from an imaginary world. Awoken out of the reverie, an object above captured her eye.

Gossamer wings displayed a kaleidoscope of colour, every visible hue and shade. It was the most intriguing butterfly Quill had ever seen. Perhaps it had flown through the tinted glass, absorbing the colours from the panes. Caught by surprise, struck by how enchanting it was, she hung her head, at once ashamed. She needed to do better, be a stronger person. The law was unequivocal, knowledge was pure and worthy, beauty forbidden.

Her heart throbbed, keeping pace with the colourful wings which fluttered more and more insistently, and then it dawned on her—something was wrong. As Quill peered more intently, she saw it caught in the sticky tendrils of a spider web. Unable to bear the poor creature's struggle, she had to help. Her wide unblinking eyes darted in every direction, senses hyper vigilant, pulse urgent and vociferous—but no-one was there.

Stood on tiptoes, Quill's throat constricted as over and over she reached out an arm, only to find that a petite frame meant the web was out of reach. The fluttering increased. Time was running out. Scowling, she dragged the nearest stool into position, hesitating for a second, worried to leave a mark on the forest-green velvet seat. Pushing that anxious thought aside, up she climbed. And then, stretching her hand and fingers as far as possible, she pulled away hair like strands from the cobweb and finally freed the wretched creature.

The butterfly soared, flapping its wings in rhythmic appreciation, and settled itself high on the thick stone surface above her head. She smiled to herself with immense satisfaction. It was going to be another great day.

"Quill, Quill. Where have you been, child? You're late again. Help me get out of this confounded contraption."

Despite Master Wittgenstein's chastisement, which she had grown accustomed to, the crisp sound of the nickname on his lips never failed to elicit an ample smile. Her father had given her the pet name Quill early on, and the Master had adopted it at once. If only he could stop calling her 'child'. Admittedly, she was small, but at twenty-four years of age, it irritated more than it should. So far, she had resisted the urge to tell him. She reminded herself daily that she owed the venerable man everything—a job, a home, a life.

"Do you mean the bed, Master?"

"You know precisely what I mean. Don't be facetious," he replied, in a voice hoarse and husky from sleep.

The scholar was heavy, which was surprising when compared with his thin, bony frame. Deep lines criss-crossed his forehead, hair as white as the skull bones protruding from his temples extended the full length of his back. The knotted and unkempt mane, together with his mood, showed how he had slept, though suggesting brushing it was a lousy idea.

"Quit staring at me like a demented idiot and pass me my robes," he ranted. The fellow was cantankerous, worse after a dreadful night, but, underneath the bluster, a sparkle remained in those deep emerald eyes.

At eighty-six years old, he was the oldest and without doubt the wisest member of The Protectorate—the city's ruling council. As Custodian of the Great Library, the Master had spent his entire lifetime studying every pamphlet, scroll and book and adding to the vast catalogue. It was no wonder he didn't sleep. His brain overflowed with thoughts and ideas, preventing rest. For that reason, they had moved the rickety iron bedstead into the study so that he could work through the night. He was racing against time to complete his life's endeavour. Quill fiddled and fretted around him, chewing non-existent nails, doing an excellent job of getting in the way and trying in vain to banish any thoughts of mortality.

White robes thrown over the head in a single fluid motion signalled that it was time for him to work, followed by lowering himself into the customary seat. In his youth, he had carved the chair out of the stump of an ancient oak tree, and it hugged his sinewy frame, a nest in which to shelter from the world. He was tall and dignified, but it was becoming harder to overlook a hunched and rounded spine.

The desk was a jumble, as usual, documentation strewn everywhere. Befuddled, he lifted and repositioned each pile from one side to the other. "Where is that diary?" he muttered, a frown deepening the channels on his wrinkled face.

"Here, let me help you," Quill suggested, despite recognising that it was almost impossible to locate anything in the sprawling untidiness. She loved the rooms exactly as they were, comforting and homely compared to the cavernous library, but they begged to be de-cluttered. He believed in organised chaos, insisted every single thing was right where it should be, and swore that if she tidied away, he could find nothing. As a result, the hunt for missing belongings was a regular occurrence.

"Where is that damn thing? How am I supposed to see what appointments I have without it? Child, you're just making a mess," he hesitated, rubbing wiry eyebrows and added, "go to the Science District. I was at Professor Hawkin's glass monstrosity of a place yesterday. It must be there."

Tense, Quill ceased the shuffling of papers and shifted instead to obsessive-compulsive fixing and re-organising the bed covers.

"Did you hear me, child?" he asked, head cocked, waiting for a response. "Quill, are you choosing to ignore me? Fetch my diary at once."

Wrenched from the house-keeping, the fluttering stomach refused to subside. And then she touched his shoulder and mumbled, "Do I have to go?"

The Master jerked, dislodging her hand, and yelled, "I won't say it again. Get the appointment list. And hurry. We need to prepare and open the reading room."

Returned to the library, Quill paused, wishing she could come up with an alternative to the errand. But it was useless, and to make matters worse, scholars might arrive at any minute. If they found that the reading area was unavailable, they would ask tough questions. She needed to recover the diary, and sooner rather than later.

Resigned to the undertaking, Quill glanced up, yearning to see the multicoloured winged insect. But it had gone.

Confident that it had flown to safety, she smiled, thinking of the daring rescue.

The library was pentagonal, each section housing one key subject: Science, Medicine, Law, Engineering or Architecture. The layout of the city mirrored the arrangement. Five subjects served by five districts.

In a whirl, running once more, Quill sped towards the north-eastern corner, headed for the Science District. Professor Hawkin was a man of influence, the Protector in charge of the Science community and the family's apartment sat across a courtyard which surrounded the library walls.

As she pushed wide the solid timber door, the early morning sunshine had vanished, replaced by thick, grey storm clouds. Disappointed and looking downward at tan suede moccasins, she hoped that the rain would hold off, knowing from experience the slippers soaked up water like a sponge.

Quill marched across the cobbled courtyard, still fretting about the shoes. As she toyed with the idea of returning to fetch a pair of boots, something bright and colourful caught her attention on the pathway a few metres ahead. Quill blanched, unwanted images flashing through her mind. Forward she crept, breathing ragged, hoping that her eyes deceived, but they did not. It was the twisted carcass of the butterfly. Vision blurred, she turned away—it was dead.

Chapter Two

"Jim, Jim," Deputy Red shouted across the dingy office, slamming down the phone.

"That's Chief to you, sunshine, and what is it, you're disturbing my morning read," came the gruff retort.

"Sorry, Chief," he mumbled, shuffling into the man's private sanctuary, shutting the door behind him. Why did he always forget to use his title?

Jim Ross was Chief of the City Guard and his boss. It was difficult not to stare at the man's balding head, where random tufts of white hair punctuated the polished glow like lost sheep. Why he didn't shave them off was an ongoing mystery. Red imagined the top man had been muscular and toned in his youth, but aging and sitting for hours on end had taken its toll. Muscle had turned to fat, which he carried like a tool belt encircling his middle.

"It's just—there's been another one," Red continued.

The Chief didn't even look up, glued to a text which he squinted at, holding the page about two inches from his face. A well-thumbed manual on forensic science that he'd been studying all day, every day since Red had served under him—which was the best part of three years! "What do you mean, another one?" the Chief snapped.

"Another report of a missing person from the Defecto quarters. That's the sixth one this month."

"I've told you before, Defectos don't go missing. They're only servants, who cares. Lazy oafs who can't get out of bed or they've stolen a silver egg cup from their employers and are hiding out someplace. Now let me continue studying my book, sunshine. 'Knowledge is King!',," proclaimed the boss in a fake serious tone, eyes puckered at the corners, disappearing under deep-set eyelids and shoulders bobbing.

Each occasion someone called in with a missing person report, this was the response. Cold indifference. Red appreciated this was the way of the world; each citizen in their lawful place, every facet of Scolaris society governed by The Protectorate, who oversaw each districts' contribution to the accumulation of knowledge. The system of government worked efficiently. One quick glimpse around the tatty place and at his studious colleagues was all the proof needed. Serious crime, in fact any crime, was unheard of in Scolaris, and every member of the City Guard sat at a desk reading. Each mundane day identical to the next. Books on criminology, books on interviewing technique, an endless list of dry titles. Red rubbed his smooth forehead. His brain hurt just thinking of it.

To be honest, Red suspected the Chief was right, and these statements were unreliable. But doubts lingered as he stared at the ground, perplexed, reaching for answers. Could it really just be a coincidence? Six separate 'misper' reports in such a brief space of time. Red knew it was wrong, but longed for the day-to-day monotony to change. And perhaps this was it. Maybe, finally, there would be a crime to investigate.

Red paced back and forth on dusty wooden floorboards filled with knots and wormholes. Whoever the cleaners were, they needed sacking. Distracted, he rolled his shoulders, trying to oust the tension from the upper body. Fists thrust hard into pockets, hiding the emotion from his colleagues, glowering. He needn't have worried, as, without exception, every man's face appeared to be wearing a book. The six reports of missing servants replayed in a continual circle, his mind attempting to form a cohesive picture of the sparse information. Each of the five city districts had its own Defecto annex. The Defectos who served each district lived there, at their employers beck and call. Meticulous organisation meant that nothing interfered with the smooth running of the place.

In short, there had been two accounts of missing servants from the Science District. A boy from Engineering, two men from Physicians and today's report, a girl from this district, Law and Order. No obvious pattern jumped out at him. No doubt the Chief was right and a desperation for excitement of any kind was getting the better of him.

But the churning in the pit of Red's gut would not settle. The simple truth was that nobody even considered asking questions. So how could they know if the statements were true? Granted, it might get him into trouble but, the longer he speculated about the situation, the more his resolve to carry out a few basic enquiries hardened. After all, it just wasn't conceivable that all servants were thieves or layabouts. His face lit up as a memory of old Nan came to mind, the family's servant during his childhood. The woman's plump cheeks and doughy arms reached out and quelled his frustrations. To be frank, it pained him to recognise that he felt more connection to her than to his own mother. Defectos might be servants, but they were still people and deserved to be treated the same as everyone else.

Red took a last look around the office, at the faded notices peeling off the redundant cork boards like crisp, sun-burnt skin, and concluded that it was time to investigate. A plausible excuse to leave needed to present itself.

"Hey Chief, shall I grab us something for lunch?" Red asked, predicting the answer.

"Thought you'd never ask. I'll have the usual, sunshine."

Red winked and gave a thumbs-up. Perfect. An open appeal to the Chief's stomach was often the best way to get out of headquarters.

Chapter Three

Numb disbelief nibbled at Quill's frame as, hugging herself with slender arms, she shrank into the cobbled pathway. How did this happen? As she gulped in cool air, desperate to gain control, she knew there was no time for distractions. Physical beauty was fleeting, worthless. If anyone wanted any further proof, they just had to examine the tiny dead body.

Enduring the discomfort, Quill pressed on, crossing the courtyard and arriving at the entranceway to Professor Hawkin's apartment. As a minimum, ten of her bedrooms could sit in the passage, but that did not seem such a big deal at that moment. Twinges of resentment and want fed curiosity and a thirst for knowledge and were the reason for the hidden stockpile of books below her bed. In reality, Quill suspected she would only ever be a servant. Still, it didn't stop the dream that, one day, she could train to become a scholar, just like the Master.

Without warning, pebbles of water pounded her cheekbones, sending her hurtling into the walkway where ornamental trees lined glass walls. Thick with fuchsia-pink blossoms, their heady floral scent stifled and suffocated the atmosphere. But Quill just breathed it in, grateful to get out of the rain. The long expanse of corridor drew the eye to the jet-black, industrial front door of 1 Courtyard Place. The challenge now was ignoring a quivering heart and the voice ordering her to head back to the safety of the library. Quill tapped on the striking entrance and waited. After what seemed an eternity of utter silence, she knocked again, only much louder.

The woman who appeared clung to the open door frame, squinting and shading her eyes from the light. "Yes, may— I help you?" she said, stumbling over the words.

Quill registered the plummy diction, head bowing in deference and hiding the embarrassment which no doubt grew red and hot on her cheeks. This must be Mrs. Hawkin. Why was she opening the front door? Where was the servant?

"Do hurry girl, spit it out, I don't have all day." Her shrill cry sawed through the air like a bread knife, making Quill flinch. Something in her mind rang alarm bells in response to the way Mrs. Hawkin adhered to the door-jamb, as if still half asleep. To confirm this thought, Quill noticed that the middle-aged lady stood in little more than a midnight-blue silk nightdress. At least two hours must have passed since the morning alarm call, so to meet someone in this state of undress was unusual.

From the pinched expression on Mrs Hawkin's face, Quill wondered if she was staring at the important woman and looked away, fiddling with the hem of her plain brown tunic. "Sorry to bother you, madam, but Master Wittgenstein has sent me to collect his diary."

"I don't understand what you want me to do about it, girl. I have a beastly head," replied the scantily clad woman, rubbing her temples. "You can't possibly expect me to look for it. And I wish I knew where that good-for-nothing Ezra had got to."

Quill surmised from that snippet that Ezra was their servant and Mrs Hawkin was not in the best frame of mind.

"Please, it's vital that I find the Master's diary. Can I come in?"

The woman recoiled, a pained black look undisguised, "Certainly not," she declared, and slammed the door in Quills' face.

Quill chewed a lip, exposed, a flush creeping up her neck. She scanned the conversation, looking for answers to why she'd been dismissed out of hand, but didn't think she had been rude. The Master was a grump, but he never disparaged her. What to do now was the question?

Quill's muscles tensed, cringing at the idea of dealing with Mrs Hawkin again. On the other hand, dire consequences would follow reporting to the Master without the appointment book.

Contemplating the options cleared her mind. The choices were limited; the diary was essential. Determined not to let the pompous old woman win, Quill took a deep breath, straightened her clothes and knocked once more, as confidently as trembling fingers allowed.

"Will you stop knocking so loud? You'll wake the dead! I've told you once I don't know where the diary is. Now go away!"

Mrs Hawkin's aura of superiority had all but vanished as a small glob of spit pooled at the left-hand crevice of her mouth, where her lips touched. Unconcerned, she swiped it aside with the back of her hand.

Quill decided a change of approach might work. Even if it bruised her pride, grovelling might just be the key to getting into the apartment. "I can only apologise again for disturbing you, Mrs Hawkin, and I promise that I'll be as quick as possible. May I please search for the diary? As you know, Master Wit is not getting any younger. And between you and me," she confided, leaning in towards the silk-wrapped woman, "he finds it tough to keep track of all his appointments these days. I'm positive he'll be extremely indebted to you when we find it."

Mrs Hawkin was mute, pensive, as she deliberated for a few seconds. But the undeniable appeal of the Master being in her debt was too tempting to ignore. "You'd better come in," she said.

"Thank you so much, you're too kind," Quill gushed, trying to keep the woman on side. Inside the entrance, stepping up close and personal to Mrs Hawkin, it was hard not to gawk at her grey hair. The colour of steel, it stuck out at jaunty angles to the scalp. 'Bed-head', her father would have called it. Quill wondered quite how old she was. There were laughter lines around the corners of her mouth, though in all honesty it was impossible to imagine Mrs Hawkin ever laughing! It was conceivable the lady was in her late fifties, but first impressions were often misleading. Nevertheless, as the woman relinquished the security of the door frame, a rigid upright posture perfected over many years took hold. A stature symbolic of wealth and influence.

Mrs. Hawkin stabbed a slender, manicured finger, instructing Quill to head into the residence. "Wait in there, while I dress, and don't touch anything," she hissed.

As Quill stepped through the hallway into the living room, she halted, holding still, seduced by the initial glimpse of the interior. The apartment mirrored the outside passageway. Sleek lines and glass walls stretched into the distance. Beyond the precise, neat lawn and over the top of an enormous glittering concrete wall, the roofs of the rest of the Science District were just distinguishable. It was such a shame it was pouring, as it was difficult to see the garden through cascades of water drenching the glass facades. Below her was a step down to the main seating area. Here three low-slung charcoal-grey settees arranged at right-angles to each other were the perfect backdrop to a fire-pit with no obvious chimney; it was bigger than her bed. Huge black and sand cobbles glowed a rich magenta and orange hue, though there did not seem to be any warmth radiating from them into the grand, airy space.

Quill savoured the immaculate simplicity and sheer elegance of the place. An image of the Master's chaotic study came to mind, and she brushed a palm across her features, washing it aside. Quite why the Master saw the apartment as a glass monstrosity wasn't clear in the slightest. She could look at it all day.

"Right girl, where did you say Wit had left his diary?"

Quill jumped at the sound of the woman's voice. So engrossed in opinions about the accommodation, it took her a while to register the particular nature of what Mrs Hawkin had asked. Nobody usually referred to the Master as Wit, which only added to the confusion. At last able to gather herself, she realised she had no idea where the appointment book might be, having not waited long enough to ask.

"Goodness me, another idiot," declared the woman in response to the silence. Feeling the glow of flushed cheeks once more, Quill had to admit her ignorance.

Eyes rolling and tutting loudly, Mrs Hawkin continued, "Well, I haven't seen him for at least a week, so I assume he met the Professor when I wasn't here. To be honest, I haven't seen my husband yet this morning as I felt dreadful yesterday evening and was still sleeping when you saw fit to disturb me. Follow me, I expect he is having his customary double espresso."

Mrs Hawkin led the way, and Quill followed at a respectful distance. The woman luxuriated in damson linen, a tailored two-piece suit worn like a bespoke second skin. Hair now flattened and twisted into an elegant chignon, the smooth sashay toward the kitchen interrupted at intervals by stumbling as Mrs. Hawkin tripped over her feet and had to steady herself before continuing. A sickly, sweet aroma, like fruity vomit, permeated the air. Perhaps it was expensive perfume? Though that seemed unlikely. Quill banished thoughts that the lady of the house must have been handsome as a young woman, as she remembered that focusing on a persons' appearance was shallow and vulgar. Why was she such a terrible person? Reaching for the raised brown stain on her face, she rubbed and pinched it, cursing herself. It was a punishment, ugliness on the surface showed what lurked inside. No wonder her father had taken off.

Arriving at the far end of the apartment, Quill experienced that unnerving sensation of having no clue about the details of the journey. Despite expecting an earthy waft of coffee beans, the replacement chemical taint of bleach disappointed. Surrounded by high polished stainless steel cabinets and every kitchen-gadget you could imagine, Mrs Hawkin checked and re-checked her watch, as if it might at any moment display a long held secret. "That's odd," she said. "He never misses his morning shot of caffeine, no matter how busy he is. Where has he got to? And where is that damned servant?"

Quill ran a hand through the short, cinnamon brown hair, perceiving a tightness in her chest and the beginnings of a bead of perspiration on the left-hand temple. What was happening today? People and their belongings were not where they should be. It didn't help that Mrs Hawkin clearly did not know where her husband was, nor the sense to come up with an educated guess.

"Is there anywhere else he could be? Maybe he already started work?" Quill asked, stood rigid, fidgeting with her fingers. Reminding the woman that every other person in the city had begun working hours ago might have been a mistake.

"Of course, how remiss of me. No doubt he's busy in the lab. Follow me." The woman turned ninety degrees and headed along another glass passage. From here, Quill could see more of the garden. After taking a sidelong peek at the green open space, she longed to step outside to explore the sights and sounds more closely. The Master forbade plants and all forms of living material in the library for fear that their moisture might lead to the oldest, most fragile manuscripts deteriorating. Quill knew little of the different species of trees and shrubs and made a mental note to add it to the long list of research topics. She basked in the joy of knowing that, with her father's guidance, she'd bucked the usual Defecto trend and learned to read, continuing to study on the sly, even after he had left. Nothing could match the feeling. At the end of each day, chores complete, she resumed studying the latest pile of books stashed under the bed. One day she might find the courage to tell the Master the secret and persuade him to teach her everything at his disposal.

Finally, they reached a solid metal door at the far end of the L-shaped apartment. It blocked their path, jealously guarding the secrets of what lay on the opposite side. "This is the laboratory," Mrs Hawkin announced, as if giving a guided tour. "We'll have to knock and wait. The Professor is ultra security conscious about his work so always locks this door."

The upper-crust woman knocked with firm strokes, a perfect rhythm, and the loud sound ricocheted around the corridor. But, not for the first time that day, no-one replied. Quill grinned, downcast eyes bashful, and tried to stay level-headed. Somewhere close a clock ticked—tick, click, tick, click and her toes followed the rhythm. A crowd of irate scholars shaking their fists jumped into view, and she clamped her eyelids shut to banish them.

For a few moments Mrs Hawkin appeared paralysed, frozen by indecision. Then without warning she emerged from the dithering, growing a few inches taller, straightening some extra vertebrae in her spine and with a look of determination she grasped the door-handle and pushed it downward. A rush of air escaped her with a whoosh as the heavy door swung free on its hinges and she launched forward at speed into the lab.

With lightning reflexes Quill grabbed a handful of Mrs. Hawkin's jacket, together unfortunately, with a handful of back fat, saving the woman from the ignominy of falling flat on her face. Mrs. Hawkin adjusted the garment, brushed it smooth and adopted a mask of calm, pretending that everything was as it should be. Unfortunately, it was impossible to hide slack-mouthed disbelief as she rubbed her temples, unable to grasp the scene in front of them. Before the woman had the presence of mind to censor any thoughts, she warbled an important question, "What—happened—here?"

Chapter Four

Deputy Red savoured the tingling sensation of weightlessness in his thick limbs as he ventured into the familiar Law and Order District. It was as recognisable as the features of his own face in a mirror. Law was in the blood, his father and grandfather were both lawyers and their fathers before them. It had been a calculated risk, becoming a guard and he still believed father did not approve.

The early morning sunshine had disappeared, and rain pelted every surface. A skyward glance showed thick grey clouds crowding in from the north. It appeared unlikely that the torrent could end anytime soon.

To begin enquiries in the Science District made sense for two key reasons. First, if the reports were to be believed, that was where the first two missing servants lived and worked. And second, and most important, by staying away from Law and Order he was less likely to get caught meddling by the Chief. It was fortunate that Science was just north of the legal district, and as the

Guard HQ building was roughly central, he reckoned it might only take thirty minutes on foot to reach it. Were cars allowed, the journey would have been quicker, but banning them on the grounds of public safety was already a distant memory. To keep the moisture at bay, he pulled his navy blue uniform jacket tighter around his broad torso and fastened the gold buttons. Across the tarmac street, Red caught sight of himself in the mirrored glass of an office tower. With a wide, tombstone filled grin, he thrust out his powerful chest and drank up the view. He looked good. Young and athletic, he ran to stay fit, and it showed in the muscular build of his legs in the tight fitting garb. At five foot six in his boots, he'd long ago accepted it was never his destiny to be a tall man. But it didn't bother him, and what he lacked in height he compensated for with breadth. Red knew Scolarians frowned upon the appreciation of physical attractiveness, but had never understood that rule. It was stupid. Life was meaningless without having a fondness for fine things, though he could never admit to these thoughts. The prospect of his mother's reaction if she could read his mind made the hairs on the back of his neck stand proud.

As Red marched, purposeful through the rain-washed streets, it occurred to him he did not know where to start. If there had been reports of missing Science personnel, then that should have been easy. To start with, there ought to be full names and addresses. But these were servants—Defectos, and there were no central records of either. Unless you were lucky enough to serve a Protector, you settled in the Defecto quarters connected to the district you served. Dry mouthed, heart pulsating, he stopped to wipe away sweat and raindrops, contemplating the fact that he had yet to set foot in a Defecto region.

Defectos in Law and Order lived on the far eastern side and it was a reasonable assumption that the same should be true here, in Science. Out of sight, out of mind, was the thought that first appeared. What if he lost his way, or worse?

The pavements of the Science District were empty. Everyone hard at work in the myriad of laboratories and chemical plants that lined the way. Acrid, astringent fumes assaulted Red's nose from every angle. Coughing and spluttering, water streaming from his eyes, he fought through plumes of charcoal vapour, counting himself lucky that he did not have to live and serve there. Hunkered low against the atmosphere, he continued eastwards through the cobbled highways, hoping to find the Defecto quarters based on nothing more than a hunch. He still didn't know what to do when he arrived.

As the precise utilitarian buildings of the hub of the district turned to ramshackle makeshift units, he was at first relieved. The inkling was correct. Relief didn't last long. Precarious looking, the homes were constructed with an endless variety of materials, none of which were necessarily meant for that purpose. Bits of old wood, concrete blocks and sheets of tin clung together like terrified children, and the clean cobbled streets gave way to dirt tracks. The startling contrast forced a study of the shine of his black boots. That view preferable to facing what was in front of his eyes. Red had not noticed the conditions in the servant's quarters attached to his district, but assumed they were similar. How did people live like this?

Focused on the notes scribbled earlier in the notebook pulled from a pocket, Red blew out every molecule of breath held in his lungs. But, in all honesty, the scant details weren't much to go on. There were two names. Bill had been the first Defecto reported missing, roughly six weeks ago. And Finn, about a week later. That was the extent of the intelligence. He bit the inside of his cheek, huffing and grumbling through gritted teeth. Despite the hundreds of hours spent studying books on investigation techniques, whoever had taken these reports was a total incompetent. Though on reflection, the Chief's approach to the whole situation suggested it was less about competence and more about total indifference. Doubtless this was going to be an almost impossible exercise, and he suspected that no-one, including Chief Ross, would thank him for it.

Whilst wondering whether continuing served any meaningful purpose, Red saw a woman doddering along the dirt track towards him. Her customary brown tunic soaked up the deluge like a blood-sucking leech, hugging a brittle body. "Excuse me madam," he called, "may I ask you a few questions?"

The elderly lady flinched at the sound, refusing to look up from the ground, scurrying past like her life depended on escape. "Madam, ma'am. I need to speak to you." Red shouted, voice competing with the rainfall.

Ignoring him, the woman shot into a shack he had passed moments before. Determined not to give up at the first obstacle, Red followed.

Logs tethered with an orange plastic rope formed a makeshift front door. Painted on it, in lime green paint, the number 43 and the initials DSQ. 43 Defecto Science Quarters. As Red inspected the closest units, he recognised similar markings, though no two in the same colour. An address system existed, after all. Red banged on the log entrance and flinched, shaking the hand as he peered at a needle-sharp splinter embedded into the knuckle of the middle finger. As he sucked the wound, the door opened, revealing the top half of the woman he was expecting. Her slumped shoulders and voluminous eye-bags were tough to miss. Anaemic-looking, she surprised him with the force of her rough greeting. "What d'ya want? You don't live 'ere!"

"Sorry to bother you, ma'am," he said, causing the sickly lady to search around and behind, as if he was speaking to somebody else. "I'm Deputy Red with the City Guard. We're investigating details of missing men from this district and need you to answer some questions if you have a minute?"

She snorted, "Don't ask me. I don't know nothing about no men gone missing. Like I say, you don't belong, you ought to leave."

The makeshift door began closing, but Red's reactions were too fast for the worn out woman, and he just squeezed the toe end of his left boot in the gap.

"Jus' go away and quit bugging me," she insisted.

"Please, I need your help. The two men are Bill and Finn, but that's the only information I have. I must make sure that they are okay."

"Why d'ya care for a couple of missing Defectos? Nobody else does."

"I'm just doing my job," he replied. But then, seeing her pained expression, added, "And, more importantly, they are people just like you and me and if they call for aid, then they should get it."

The grim set outline of her jaw softened, and after a few seconds she relaxed the firm grip on the door. "I'd invite you in for a tour of the Palace," she smirked, "but if anyone sees you coming in, the neighbourhood tongues might wag. That could cost me my place." She directed him, with rapid eye movements, to the other units nearby, and Red noticed they were being watched.

"Look, that's the last thing I want to happen. But, is there anything you can tell me?"

The moment of silence felt as if it lasted for hours as the old woman chewed her bottom lip. And then she sighed and said, "There's not much to tell. All I heard is about six weeks ago Bill didn't turn up for work. He works at the same lab as me on High Grove Square. As for Finn, I haven't got a clue. And that's all I got, now mister, please remove your shiny boot from my doorway."

"You've been truly helpful, thank you. Just one last quick question. What's the name of the laboratory?"

She glanced around, fierce eyes darting in all directions, thin lips rigid and whispered, "AccuDiagnostics," and then the door shut firm in Red's face.

Red grinned, punched the air, replaying the conversation with the old woman. Despite her obvious mistrust, he'd extracted some useful information. Maybe studying all those books had not been such a waste of energy. It was regrettable that the thrill of the moment was fleeting. He chewed his fingernails, realising that he had neglected to ask for the most basic of details: How old was Bill? A description and his home address. To make matters worse, he'd not even taken the woman's name. What an idiot!

Red raised an oversized fist, planning to knock again, but soon decided against the idea, afraid to push his luck any further. If necessary, he might return after dark when the twitchy neighbours were in bed.

In the significant excitement he'd almost forgotten about the rain, but now his body trembled, shivering as the damp and chill penetrated through to the skin. The saturated blue uniform no longer keeping him warm and dry. No doubt the Chief would expect the imminent arrival of his favourite triple-layered meat sandwich. Topped off with a solitary lettuce leaf, all in the interests of good nutrition. And, not forgetting the perfect accompaniment, a litre of thick, caramel-infused, gut-buster hot chocolate. To disappoint the man was risking a verbal onslaught. The sensible course of action was to head back to HQ. Leave things alone. He had tried to investigate, and that was more than anyone else could claim.

But his conscience drove him forward. Red couldn't help thinking of the elderly woman's dreadful living conditions and her conviction that nobody cared for Defectos. She'd entrusted him with the identity of the laboratory, despite the personal risk. He had to prove to her, and more importantly to himself, that he was trustworthy. If he hurried, there should just be time to check out AccuDiagnostics and still find the Chief's lunch.

Chapter Five

Quill adopted an exact impression of Mrs Hawkin's frozen, bug-eyed expression as, exchanging glances, they shared a moment's solidarity.

The laboratory wasn't just a wreck; it resembled the scene of an industrial accident. "Alexander, Alexander, are you here? Are you hurt?" Mrs Hawkin cried, hurrying into the devastation. With the unmistakable sound of crunching under the woman's low-heeled shoes, Quill observed hundreds of glass vials scattered and smashed across the floor. The majority leaked their unidentified contents onto the polished white tiles. As she ventured further into the room, tiptoeing to avoid the broken shards, an immediate, thick, cloying aroma disabled her. With her head spinning, bile rose in her throat as she prepared to faint. Cupping palm over nose and mouth, she stumbled towards the far side of the lab, thinking to open a window. But to Quill's surprise, the sliding doors there were wide open, and she felt the draught of air coming through them. Unable to fathom how such a revolting smell could linger, she choked, saying "What is that awful stink?" somewhat louder than intended.

"What smell? What are you wittering on about, girl? Where is Alexander, that's the question that needs answering? And what or who caused this terrible mess?"

The workspace was a perfect rectangle in which there were few places to hide. Irrespective, they continued a fruitless search for Alexander Hawkin amongst the neat rows of conical flasks, measuring cylinders, funnels, and test tubes. But, it was clear; the Professor was not in there. As Quill tightened a dripping tap, she noted a trail of mud between the wide-open exit and the central workstation. Were there footprints? Maybe, but the wet ground made it impossible to be sure.

Quill's attention turned to the disarray on the central countertop. Scattered over it were scribbles, notes, graphs, plans, and diagrams in various stages of completion. They were intriguing, but deciphering their meaning proved futile. Perched on the right-hand corner, at the front, a half-eaten plate of roasted vegetables and rice congealed into an inedible palate of colour. Likewise, three wine glasses, stained by deep crimson dregs which clung to the sides, framed the crusted remnants. Amid the chaos, the bottoms of her feet registered an icy chill and, lifting a shoe, the dark shadow of a damp patch spread along the sole. Whatever had been in those bottles was now seeping through the moccasins. Quill wrinkled her nose and hopped in a circle, searching for the nearest dry spot.

Without warning, the hairs on the back of her neck rippled and the pulsating throb of blood rushed through veins. Struck by the sudden sensation of reality freezing in her small barren square of laboratory, the rest of the world sped up around her. Quick to catch up, Quill's brain processed what her eyes had perceived seconds earlier. At the centre of the heap of papers, resting proudly on top for everyone to see, a green leather-backed book, embossed in gold with the initials 'M.W.'.

The relief and elation at finally finding the diary evaporated in an instant. Alongside the moment, Quill registered Mrs Hawkin's hard eyes, drilling into her. Was it too much to hope she hadn't noticed the book in the chaos?

"Well, well. I appear to have lost the Professor, but you found the elusive diary." The woman's pointed remark was a hammer blow to those hopes, crumpling Quill like a useless scrap of paper. Something untoward had happened in that room. But what? A long list of questions formed: Where could the scientist be? And why did the Master's diary have to be right at the centre of this turmoil? Quill's head swam again, battling with the mysterious smell, trying to keep a hold on reality. But the whole situation proved impossible to fathom. She kneaded her temples, the beginnings of a headache tightening like elastic above her eyebrows.

What Quill required was a second to think, to regroup. But the minutes marched onward, and the situation called for decisive action, and fast. Then it came to her. As a servant she needed to play to the stereotype, summed up in one word—clueless.

Without hesitation, she grabbed the appointment book with both hands. "Thanks for your help, Mrs Hawkin. I must return to the Master," she chirped in the most innocent sounding tone she could muster. And then she ran. Pumping her slim legs and pounding the floor, racing out of the lab, through the sleek apartment, along the passageway, across the cobbles and back to the safety of the library.

Leaned back, chest heaving, Quill panted, resting against the interior of the thick oak door. With the green diary clutched to her chest, she tipped her eyes skyward, willing the tension to subside, revelling in the solidity and security of the surroundings. Gulping a huge lungful of air, for a moment she thought she might be sick. All this physical exertion was taking its toll. If she could just catch her breath, everything would feel better. Quill whispered, "Thank you," to no-one in particular and tried to ignore the nagging negative voice asking how best to break the news that the Professor was missing.

The Professor was missing. She let that thought percolate for a few moments as her breathing continued to lengthen. Nobody went missing in Scolaris, unless you counted her father. No, that was different. He left. Everybody had a place, a role and purpose, and nothing ever changed. Life was fulfilling, happy, and safe. There had to be a reasonable explanation for the man's absence. Buoyed by that logic, she headed back to the Master's rooms.

Hard at work, his head in a book as usual. Not even the sound of her return caused him to look away. "Did you bring the diary, child? Pass it here will you, I need to check today's appointments."

Quill wondered if he even realised the length of time it had taken to complete the errand as she passed him the troublesome book. He leafed through the pages until he found the right one. "Huh," he grumbled, "after all that I don't have any dratted appointments."

Quill forced a smile despite the clenched jaw muscles, holding her tongue to avoid uttering the complaints that formed behind upturned lips. Knowing she had no choice other than to explain the details of the visit to the Hawkin's apartment, she still could not decide how to broach the topic. As she stood, curling hair around fingers, contemplating what to say, she winced, the study reminding her of the devastation left at the apartment. Bowls of unidentifiable globules protruded from under stacks of pamphlets. And piles of threadbare robes dangled limp over the slick sheen of bedstead, despairing of ever being repaired. Hung on the coat hook at the right-hand edge of the room, his olive green oilcloth coat and peeping out from under it the muddy tips of a pair of black boots.

"Good grief, look at the time," exclaimed the Master, peering up at the clock on the wall. Made from burnished metal, strange indentations marked its surface, resembling the dimpled peel of an orange. Not only did it signal the hour and minutes, but, in the centre, ornate bone tiles displayed the expected arrival and departure of the tide in red. Quite why he needed to know when the tides were high or low, when no tidal water existed for hundreds of miles, was an enigma.

"For goodness' sake, child, will you ever stop daydreaming? Where have you been all this while?"

Quill took a sharp breath, preparing to tell him every detail of the extraordinary morning, but before she could begin, he shouted, "Don't tell me now. We don't have a minute to lose. Hurry, follow me, we must get the reading room open now the spring clean is complete."

With a curt nod, the locked room made sense all of a sudden. Quill avoided making eye contact, hoping that he might not realise that she had forgotten this job in the confusion. Like a pet, she followed the hunched, bony frame of the scholar as he loped ahead.

As they arrived at the locked door, he fumbled inside the deep pockets of his robe. Quill decided that now might be the best moment to announce news of the absent man. She hoped that his attention being elsewhere might lessen the blow. "I'm sorry I was so slow getting the appointment book, but I wasn't certain where to search. It didn't help that the Hawkin's servant, Ezra, wasn't around to track it down. It was ever so weird because Mrs Hawkin couldn't locate her husband, either. We checked in his lab, but he wasn't there. Also, it was a real mess as if there'd been an accident."

"Oh, I'm sure it's nothing to worry about," he blurted, waving his fingers in front of his face, as if swatting a fly. "I expect Alexander and Ezra are together, doubtless stargazing. And in any case my study is a mess."

The old man sounded nonplussed, unmoved by the story, and she feared she had misread the scene. The suggested explanation was straightforward and made sense. And Mrs Hawkin had been acting strange, so maybe the woman overreacted.

At last, from an inside pocket, The Master produced a set of keys. To identify the correct one, he held them up to the light, examining the shapes of the small brass keys in more detail. Muttering to himself, he inserted it into the lock and opened the door. More book shelves supporting yet more study material cocooned the reading area on every side. At the far end, windows stretched from one side to the other, welcoming in all the natural light necessary for research. A comforting smell of beeswax filled the air—spring-cleaning completed. All that remained were thick white dust sheets thrown over the furniture that occupied the room.

"Here," Quill said, removing the drop cloths, "let me." As she stepped forward to remove the final cover from the mahogany table in the middle of the space, her right big toe collided with a solid object on the ground. Perturbed, she stared downward and there, sticking out from underneath the table, hidden by the dust sheet, was a shoe-less foot. Eyes wide, mouth slack and dry, a piercing scream shattered the peace and tranquillity. Confused, looking for the source of the dreadful sound, it shocked her to discover that it came from her. Unable to stop, the deafening sound continued until, at long last, regaining control, she clamped a hand across her mouth.

Face down on the carpet in front of them was a naked body.

Chapter Six

The Chief of the City Guard examined the corpse. The Master had called the Guard at once, following their disturbing discovery. His instinctive ability to do what was necessary in such unchartered circumstances had surprised Quill. Since then they both sat, numb and speechless, at the far end of the table under which the body lay.

"Master, can I please ask you to take a closer look at the deceased?" The Chief's gruff, gravelly tone broke the eerie silence. The scholar bowed, shoulders slumped in silent resignation as the guard added, "I need you to tell me if you recognise him."

As the head guard pulled back the dust sheet, the Master stole a glance at the inanimate, sleeping figure. His mouth twitched, the blood draining from his papery complexion as he croaked, "It's the Professor, Professor Hawkin."

Quill turned away, eyes clenched tight, hoping it was a dreadful nightmare. A tremor seized her entire frame as she searched the options for an escape. Life looked so bright and positive that morning. When did it all go wrong?

"What—? He—How did he die?" Quill stammered. The middle-aged guard peered along his stumpy nose at her and, shaking his head, shifted his attention back to the Master, who remained rooted to the spot.

"We'll need to examine this area with exceptional care. But it looks to me as if someone hit him on the back of the head with this." And he grunted, struggling to lift a solid brass bookend. Butterfly-shaped, its outstretched wings ended at four pointed corners, all of which looked deadly. The irony of the spectacle struck her. Two butterflies and two dead bodies presenting themselves in the same morning? She should have expected that something awful was coming. Curiosity overcame the initial shock, and she edged closer to the business end of the study table. Intrigued, Quill noticed a dark patch on the deep-burgundy carpet, next to the lifeless bald head. Why hadn't she spotted it a moment ago?

"Hawkin is a Protector, correct?" the Chief asked the Master, ignoring Quill as if she were invisible. The scholar nodded, and the guard guided him back to a chair, asking, "When did you last see him?"

"Oh, I don't know, a good few days ago," the ancient man mumbled.

Quill was about to correct him, but straightaway experienced second thoughts. The Master was in shock, no doubt confused. Yet a familiar voice in her head kept chirping that he was far too smart to get something that straightforward wrong. She didn't want to interrogate him, though, in front of the lawman, especially as there seemed little doubt that the guard held an extremely dim view of servants. More worrying were mounting suspicions that investigating a crime was a first for him, not least because he'd picked up the bookend with bare hands. The assumption that he was qualified to solve the mystery of the Professor's death was vanishing. And the last thing she wanted to do was make a rotten situation worse. In the end, there seemed no sensible option other than to keep quiet and find out more in private.

The investigator paced around the table, fingertips tapping lips, his regulation boots creaking and squeaking with every step. "Sorry to ask so many questions, but you said that this room was locked. May I ask, who has keys?"

Quill was reasonably sure that only the Custodian possessed keys to each room in the library. So it surprised her when the Master replied with the revelation that the scientist owned his own key.

"Hmm, so he could have let himself in then?" the Chief mused to no-one in particular. "The key question then is, when?"

"They cleaned the reading area yesterday afternoon, and I locked the doors just before supper, as usual. I can't imagine he was here, like this, when they cleared the room or the cleaners would have discovered him," responded the elderly scholar, trying his utmost to avoid looking at the prone corpse.

Quill concurred. The facts pointed to the unfortunate man letting himself in sometime yesterday, after dinner. But it did not answer any of the other pressing issues.

What was he doing here at that hour of the day? How had he suffered a blow to the head? And where were his clothes and the collection of keys, assuming that he owned a set? At once, she remembered the scene at the Hawkin's lab. Stupid idiot, how could anyone forget? It must be the effects of such an unusual morning. If the Professor died here, on the reading room carpet, what had happened in the laboratory and how was it connected?

Quill's stomach felt as if she had swallowed a rock as she fought back the sobs that threatened to overflow. The growing realisation that nothing added up proved difficult to bear. Could life ever be the same again?

"You'll have to excuse me Master, I've received a radio call from HQ and need to be somewhere else right now." The Chief's statement penetrated Quill's thoughts and brought them at once back into the room.

Suspecting that recent developments now called the guard to 1 Courtyard Place, she debated again whether to recount the facts of that morning. To be frank, weighing the pros and cons, she was still against the idea. Quill needed a moment to speak to the Master, figure out why the elderly man failed to mention visiting the Professor yesterday.

The Chief left, replaced by a swarm of guards, every man in the regulation blue uniform, red stripes across the shoulders and along the arms like scratches. In silence, they worked as one. Doubtless, this was also a first for their ranks.

"Quill, let's leave them to their duties," whispered the academic, ushering her away from the upsetting scene to return to the warmth and comfort of the study.

As he lowered himself inch by inch into the embrace of his favourite armchair, it reminded her of his advancing years. The morning's events had aged them both, and he propped his head upright as if possessing no more strength to hold it unsupported.

"Do you feel unwell?" Quill asked.

"No, child, but I am a little weary. We have both suffered a horrible shock."

It comforted that he recognised the terrible effect of the morning on them both. But this soon morphed into concern. Despite his age, the old fellow never once admitted to being tired.

"I think you should lie on the bed. Rest," she suggested.

"There's no time to doze. You know I have work to do," he sighed with weary resignation.

"You work too hard. A few hours' sleep should help."

The old man nodded, and she eased him from the chair and onto the bed. "Why did you say you hadn't seen the Professor for a few days? You were there yesterday with the diary," Quill said, trying to keep a calm and even voice, despite the rocks in her stomach.

The fatigued scholar twisted away, face shielded from view, fidgeting around, incapable of getting comfortable.

"Do you know what happened in the Professor's lab? Only—your diary was in the lab on top of the mess. It looked—well—suspicious." Without thinking, Quill had said more than intended.

"I don't know what you're talking about. Stop asking me all of these foolish questions. Who are you to question me? I am the Master and you are just the servant. Now leave me in peace."

Quill stiffened, gripping the bedcovers to her chest. Those words stung, aggravating the childhood wounds that already festered within her. Perhaps it was naïve to imagine that he genuinely cared for her. She longed to quiz him further, to understand. Whilst unable to accept that he had anything to do with the Professor's death, he was clearly hiding something.

Left to her own company, Quill reverted to catastrophising. If they caught him in a lie linked to the scientist's demise, it might not only affect him. She depended upon him for everything. The job, home, her life. Everybody sounded determined to remind her she was just a servant, but deep down there was more to her than that. She was not stupid, she'd proved that by continuing to study, even without her father's support.

What if it turned out that the Master caused this nightmare? Could it implicate her? Quill shuddered, sweating, nausea building, the rushing of blood whispering of impending doom. She could not figure out what to do. Maybe she was crazy? With closed eyes, taking full, controlled breaths, she fought the panic. The prospect of doing nothing was just as maddening. Who was she kidding? She had to find out what he'd got himself into, and there seemed only one logical place to start.

Chapter Seven

The AccuDiagnostics laboratory resembled a white concrete box, a single storey rectangular building with a flat roof. The owners seemed to value their privacy, as there were no windows at the front. A dark grey band running along the centre of the length of the cement walls contained the initials AD in neon green, the building's only distinguishing feature. The only sign that something or someone was inside was a continuous plume of white smoke pumping from a solitary steel chimney at the far end.

"May I help you, sir?" asked the middle-aged man protected from head to toe in green overalls, greeting Deputy Red on entry to a tiny reception.

"I hope so, Mr?"

"Mr Hamata, I am the lead technician at AccuDiagnostics, and who might you be, sir?"

Mr Hamata was a wiry, intense looking man. Balding on top, he had a strip of coarse silver-grey hair stretching from one ear to the other. A bizarre echo of the exterior of the building. He spoke meticulously, every word enunciated with precision, but so quietly that in order to hear him, Red had to study the motion of the man's purple lips.

"I'm Deputy Red of the City Guard. I should like to ask you a few questions about one of your employees."

Mr Hamata's chestnut eyes widened for a second but then he raised his shoulders and palms and said, "I can't think who you might mean or how I could assist but ask away."

"The City Guard has received a report that a man named Bill, a staff member here, didn't show up for work approximately six weeks ago. Furthermore, no-one has seen him since then. What can you tell me about this?"

Hamata's gaze dropped to the reception desk as he hyper-focused on the re-arrangement of multi-coloured paperclips collected in a heap. "I don't believe that I can tell you a thing, unfortunately. I think I ought to have remembered an employee not showing up for duty. Are you sure you have the right lab? May I ask where this information came from?"

Red shook his head. It was possible the old woman had lied just to get rid of him. Thinking of the elderly lady, though, had given him an idea. I wonder, he thought, "Afraid I can't answer that, Mr Hamata. Perhaps I should've mentioned that Bill is a Defecto."

A slow smile spread over the man's features, and his hunched shoulders relaxed. "Ah, well, yes, that certainly makes a difference. Defectos serve so a strict interpretation of the law is that they're not employed. For that reason I don't pay them much consideration."

"Does that mean Bill could have worked here?"

Mr. Hamata paused, shifted the weight from one leg to the other, as if standing on molten metal, before answering, "I suppose it's possible."

Red pressed on, "I need to see your personnel records please."

"You are welcome to look at them, sir, but as I'm certain you know, regulations do not specify the keeping of lists of Defectos."

Red cursed, the heat rising in his cheeks. He should have known this and, not for the first time that day, felt more than a tad stupid. It crossed his mind that he couldn't ignore the possibility the scientist was lying, but didn't want to humiliate himself any further, so chose to accept his word for now.

It was becoming more and more plain that the city's approach to Defectos was an impediment to investigating. He ought to check the regulations back at HQ. Not having to keep documents on which Defectos served where was inconvenient, to say the least. And he got that same feeling of deep unease about their treatment. In a society where knowledge was so highly prized, how did no-one appear to know any details about one particular group of people and how they lived? It really didn't seem right.

"Is there anything else I can help you with, sir?" said the technician, interrupting his thoughts.

"Err, no, I don't think so. Thank you, Mr Hamata, you've been so helpful." Red replied with more than a hint of sarcasm and left, burrowing into the blue jacket, submitting to the taunts of the driving rain.

As soon as Red stomped out of High Grove Square and out of view, he halted, replaying over and over the fruitless conversation. Perhaps he should have followed in his father's footsteps. Red dreamed of being a guard ever since seeing them parading the streets of Law and Order. Imagined marching in the smart blue uniform. Guards took action, they weren't just stuck behind a desk the entire day poring over wordy documents. Or that is what he expected before becoming one. The belt of fat around the Chief's waistline suggested he had seen no action in many years.

Despite a reluctance to do so, Red saw that the morning's work had got him precisely nowhere. The decision to investigate a person's disappearance, someone who might not even exist, was a thankless enterprise.

The sudden arrival of hundreds of workers interrupted the flash of self pity. It was as if an unknown power had wound up the keys on a set of mechanical toys and set them off as one. The silent streets filled in an instant with the hustle and bustle of crowds searching for lunch. There were two distinct groups, those in lab coats and overalls and the rest, the Defectos in the regulation brown. Not only their clothing set them apart, something in their demeanour added to the picture, and not in a good way. Only a quiet observer might detect the subtle nature of the down-turned eyes and trudging gait of the servants. It looked as if they were trying to disappear into the pavement, making themselves smaller and less conspicuous. Guilt germinated out of sadness. Why had he never recognised these problems?

"Hey, Mister."

Red whipped around, surprised by a childlike voice at the rear, expecting to discover the face of a small boy. Instead, the physique of a young woman greeted him. Slim and willowy, like a sapling bowing in the wind, her wide amber eyes implored him to pay close attention.

"Don't speak," she urged, "just listen to what I have to say and then leave."

Red nodded, waiting, struggling to stay patient as the young woman jerked her head from side to side before adding, "I worked with Bill. I heard you, with Mr Hamata. I don't know why he lied to you, saying he didn't remember Bill. He was cross enough when he didn't turn up for his shift. There was another one too, his name was Finn."

Red tensed, drawing his arms in tight, shrinking so as not to draw attention to them. Then he nodded for her to continue.

"They vanished, roughly within a week of each other. Something must've happened to them. It's a good job at the lab even if we have to handle pretty toxic stuff. No Defecto could afford to just give up a job like that, not unless they were really stupid. And they weren't, you know, dumb."

Red nodded and replied in a whisper, "Thanks for trusting me with these details, Miss?" he asked, followed by a pause in which he hoped she'd fill in the blanks. But the girl ignored her cue, and impatient for answers, he continued, "Can you tell me anymore? Could you describe the two men? Do you know where they live?"

Suddenly Red realised that her body shook, hands jammed into armpits. But the brave girl continued, quieter than before, "You have to promise you won't tell Mr Hamata that I spoke out. Those men looked out for me, so I feel I owe it to them to help you find them."

"You have my word."

"Bill was the oldest, I reckon late fifties, sturdy, roughly my height." She showed with a hand gesture and Red estimated that to be a little shy of five foot eight. "And he had a thick grey beard. Bill always looked quite pale, with bright red cheeks. Hair short on the sides, dark brown with patches of white, curly on top. Oh and glasses, and he had a raised black mole on the right cheek. He was always cheerful, liked to tell a joke." Her voice faltered.

Red reached out his hand, offering support, but she recoiled, taking a step backward. The young woman took a deep breath and continued. "Finn was younger, say late twenties, early thirties, golden-brown skin, much like yours. Short hair on top and clean-shaved on each side. It was jet black. He was taller than Bill and lean. But his eyes were wide on his face, hazel eyes. A ragged scar on the left side of his neck bothered him, from a chemical burn that happened in the lab a few years ago." Her expression sparkled as she spoke of Finn, and a pink flush burned on her neck.

Red wished he could reassure her that everything would be alright, that they would locate him, but that would be unprofessional. And so he held back.

"Bill lived at 72 DSQ, but I have no clue about Finn. I never plucked up the courage to ask him. Please, find them," she begged.

"I'll do my absolute best, Miss?" Red asked, not wanting to make the same mistake twice and leave without getting a name.

But the youthful woman didn't answer. Instead, she grasped his forearm, squeezing it tight, and held his gaze. A moment of understanding passed between them, and then she turned and hurried away.

Finally, Red had a lead.

Red's elation broadened his smile and, to improve the mood further, the relentless morning rainfall subsided. Now, no doubts remained in his mind that Bill and Finn existed. They were living, breathing people, and something might have happened to them. For that reason he needed to press on, investigate the cause of the disappearances. The thought of searching Bill's unit gave him goose bumps.

As the crowds dispersed, the realisation struck Red that the residents of the Science District had finished lunch. Thoughts of a brooding Chief followed close behind, impatient, shaking his head and awaiting a sandwich. In all the excitement, he had completely forgotten. It was time to get back to the office and, while there, he should check on those regulations and Mr. Hamata. The interruption needled, but there appeared to be no choice. Bill's place would have to wait.

Chapter Eight

The penetrating sound of raised voices came from inside the apartment. The front door was wide open, giving Quill the ideal opportunity to sneak herself in, unannounced. As she slipped into the building, the voice crescendoed. The guttural cries were chilling in their intensity and Quill lingered, head cocked to one side, listening, preparing to step out into the open.

"No, no, it can't be true," sobbed Mrs Hawkin. "Ezra, ask Ezra! Ask him where he's been. He did it, it's him—filthy Defecto." Spittle flew from her lips as she spat out her last words of hatred. An instant transformation from grieving widow to vengeful wife, Quill glimpsed the real woman underneath the polished facade. It wasn't pleasant.

"Mrs Hawkin, I've brought you this strong, sweet drink. It's the Master's favourite blend," Quill announced, striding into the room as if she had never left. Before leaving, she had filled a tin flask with the steaming hot brew that simmered day and night in a copper vat. To be frank, Quill could not stand the stuff. The stink of the blend reminded her of old grass cuttings and wet leaves. But, the Master drank it by the gallon and, for an octogenarian, he was looking healthy on it.

Quill's plan was to ingratiate her way into Mrs Hawkin's confidence. The woman's curling lipped response to her arrival suggested that might be difficult to accomplish. However, at the mention of refreshments the widow soon swapped the sneer for radiant superiority. The prospect of being waited on in her darkest hour was too tempting an offer to ignore.

"Perfect timing, girl," she replied. The sobbing and wailing had vanished, and she was reborn, refreshed and composed. The sudden change was unnerving.

As Quill stepped below into the main seating area, she noticed the Chief, sat with his back facing her, on one of the sleek grey sofas. They were so low to the ground that the man had folded himself virtually in half at the waist to sit and his kneecaps were rubbing his ear lobes. The middle-aged guard glared as Quill stifled a snort. It suggested the sofas were for show, not designed for sitting. Confirmed by the fact Mrs Hawkin, even in a state of clear distress, had remained standing.

Quill took ample time pouring the tea, a desperate measure to disguise the effort to settle her nerves. Mrs Hawkin had opted for something stronger which, at that hour of the day, was alarming, until she reminded herself that the poor woman had just lost a husband. The widow had by now knocked back two pomegranate martinis and, guzzling the syrupy fizz through a crusty sugar-rim, was sporting a distinctive pink moustache as proof.

As the Chief slurped a first sip of tea, Mrs Hawkin began waving her glass around, pointing toward the kitchen. The widow's mouth opened and closed in quick succession, but nothing came out of it. Quill could just make out a disembodied pair of brown trouser legs heading towards them through the glare of the cobblestone fireplace.

"Ezra, Ezra. It's him, he's returned to the scene of his crime. Don't just sit there Chief, do something will you man." Mrs Hawkin ordered.

It took the guard a considerable amount of time and effort to unfold his body and lever it out of the chair. Though he didn't resemble someone who favoured hurrying to accomplish any endeavour. "Try to remain calm, Madam. I don't think he's going anywhere, for a start he's headed toward us."

Ezra's skin was haggard and gnarled like tree bark. Deep channels formed around a hooked nose and extended from his chin to the base of his neck. A sour scowl suggested a bitter lime lodged permanently in his mouth. It was remarkable how old his features looked compared to the youthful way in which he moved. His hooded eyes were impenetrable from a distance, but as he drew nearer, she saw they were a striking frost-blue. "What's happened in the lab, madam? Where is the Professor?" he asked.

"Don't play the innocent," shrieked Mrs Hawkin, returning to her earlier hysteria. "How could you, after all we've given you, you miserable excuse for a servant? And where have you been? I had to answer my own front door this morning. The humiliation—" Wracked by sobs at last she ceased the ranting.

Ezra's thin lips spread wide, but it was his turn to lose the power of speech. The Chief gave the widow a stern look and shoved her onto a sofa, as if manhandling a disobedient child. "Please madam, leave the questioning to me." he ordered.

Mrs Hawkin's cerulean eyes pinched and Quill admired the man in secret, doubting that anyone had ever told the posh woman what to do. The look of surprise and indignation on her face was priceless.

"Right, everyone needs to stay calm. Ezra, you need to give me a satisfactory answer to my questions."

Ezra nodded, but the scowl remained.

The Chief went on, "First, I need to hear where you have been in the last twenty-four hours?"

"Yesterday morning, the Professor asked me to contact a Mr Dodds from the Engineering District. He wanted me to quiz the engineer about a new project. I went just after serving lunch and was due to meet Mr Dodds in Central Square at 2:30 pm, but he didn't show. It was really important to the Professor, so I waited the entire afternoon in case there'd been a mix-up about when the meeting was due to take place. By the time I decided that he definitely wasn't coming, it was getting late. My younger sister, Val, lives in Engineering, so I figured I'd pay her a visit. But, when I turned up at her place, there was no answer. I have a set of keys, so I let myself in. Must have fallen asleep on the sofa because the next thing I realised, it was morning. I assumed she must've left me to sleep and gone to bed but, when I checked in her room, she wasn't there. She couldn't have slept in the bed. Nothing looked out of place. I've spent most of the morning knocking on the doors of her neighbours, but no-one has seen her. It's such a worry. She's much too young to be by herself. Can't figure out where she is and then I lost track of time, that's why I'm so late back."

The Chief cupped his chin and paced around in a circle, taking in everything that Ezra had said. "This Mr Dodds, why didn't the Professor just call him?"

"You'd have to ask him that. I'm not paid to ask questions, I just follow orders." he said, a small tight smile forced to the surface.

It was too much for Mrs Hawkin to take, and she launched herself towards him. "You know full well we can't ask him, you thieving wretch. He's dead, and you killed him."

The colour drained from the Defecto's cheeks and he had to steady himself against the back of the settee. "What? Where? Is that why the lab is such a mess?" Ezra vomited a jumble of thoughts, mouth struggling to keep pace with the brain.

In contrast, the Chief was florid, nostrils flaring, cracking his knuckles. Quill held her breath, waiting for an explosion as he shouted at Mrs Hawkin. "Madam, I must ask you to restrain yourself. If you cannot keep quiet, I'll have to order you to leave the room."

The widow lifted her chin and gazed at him in an act of quiet defiance. But the rebuke had worked and, shrinking back into the chair, functioning on automatic, she reached for the pink pitcher.

By this time, Ezra appeared to have composed himself, and the Chief proceeded with the interrogation. "Can anyone confirm your story?"

"Well, I suppose you could speak to Val's neighbours. They spoke to me this morning. And here, these are Val's keys." He thrust a series of silver keys hanging from a rusty twist of wire into the man's hands.

"So, let me get this straight. Yesterday you travelled to visit a man you've never met." He paused for effect and scratching his stubble continued, "He didn't show up, so then you left for your sister's, and she wasn't around. Then, you conveniently fell asleep and didn't wake until morning. So, no-one can account for your movements from yesterday's lunch until you arrived back here moments ago? And yes, I can check out these keys," he said, squinting and holding them up to the light, "but they don't actually prove a single thing, do they?"

Ezra slumped further against the seat, a vacant look in his downcast eyes, and Quill pitied him.

"And then, there's the question of these," the Chief announced, pulling out a wad of papers from the interior of his tan coat and thrusting them aloft like a trophy. "I took the liberty of searching your room as no-one knew where you were and I found these letters from your sister. This one's particularly touching." He cleared his throat and proceeded in a parody of a woman's voice. "'Please be careful Ezra, I understand that you're unhappy and that you hate your job, but don't do anything you might regret..' What did she mean, I wonder?"

The room fell silent as three pairs of ears listened, intent on sticking around for an answer.

"Why were you in my room, going through my personal things?" Ezra growled, raising himself to his full height. Quill reflected he wasn't helping himself.

"You are a Defecto. You don't have any rights and you know it. Stop avoiding the question." The Chief's reply was frank, and Quill backed away, horrified. Was that true? Defectos didn't have the same rights as everyone else?

Mrs. Hawkin, unable to contain herself any further, blurted out in her harsh tone, "I know why he hates me. He's been stealing food, and I reported him to the Professor. After everything we've done for him. Giving him a room in our home. I tell you he's responsible and I want him to pay for what he's done."

On this occasion, the Chief received Mrs. Hawkin's outburst with a knowing smile. "I think it best if you come with me to HQ. We'll need you to give us some further information." And with that, he grabbed Ezra's arm and dragged him away from the living room.

The Defecto struggled against the man's grasp and, turning his head in their direction, shouted, "I stole nothing, you stupid old bat, admit it, you ate it while you were drunk. Let's face facts, half the time you don't recognise what day it is. No wonder the Professor couldn't bear the sight or the smell of you!"

Quill did not believe what she was hearing and turned to Mrs. Hawkin, expecting her to retaliate with the immense force of a woman holding every ounce of power in the room. In contrast, she just shrank, looking old and defeated and, through a pink 'tache, just forced out a whisper, "Get him out of my house," as the Chief yanked him away.

For the second time that day, Quill found herself putting someone to bed. Mrs Hawkin was ashen and a tinge of green kissed her complexion. A thin sheen of sweat formed on the woman's creased forehead, and Quill wondered if she was going to be sick. The widow acquiesced with no argument, and Quill left her curled into the fetal position.

The apartment seemed clinical and soulless, with no inhabitants, but Quill embraced the solitude. A moment to herself to mull over everything she had seen and heard lightened the mood. Her head was spinning with possibilities. Had Ezra killed the Professor? His sister Val's letter certainly suggested that he might have a reason. On the other hand, something he said about the widow drinking too much struck a chord. The faintest hint of pink in an otherwise empty pitcher tallied with the accusation. But she couldn't be sure, especially having no first hand experience of alcohol.

Doubtless it might be best for her and the Master if Ezra turned out to be the culprit. But nothing so far explained the mess in the Professor's lab, or the fact that the diary had been on top like a red flag. If Ezra was a killer, why did he come back to the apartment? The puzzle grew more and more complicated with each passing moment.

Quill ached, a heavy-limbed longing to return home, and hoped that the Master was still sleeping. Even though the widow treated her with disdain, she couldn't help pitying her. After all, she had just lost a husband and suffered insults in public from her own servant all in the same morning.

Quill gathered up the pitcher, a half-drunk cocktail glass and the teacup and saucer and carried them through to the kitchen. Sniffing the remnants of the pink martini on route, she immediately wished she had not. Bile rose in her throat, stomach lurching at the cloying, bitter sweetness.

Perturbed to see that the herbal brew left behind a dirty green stain in the bottom of the otherwise pristine cup, she obsessed over the menial chore of cleaning. Scrubbed and scrubbed, trying to erase it and all her troubles and failing miserably.

Out of nowhere, a thought floated upward with the soapsuds. Ezra came this way. Did that mean the laboratory door still stood open? The Chief must have known about the wreckage in that room. So why had he left without collecting evidence? Perhaps she had over-estimated his ability to get to the truth.

A quick glance around to check she was still alone confirmed that she was, and then Quill reached a decision. This was a perfect opportunity to take a closer look. If she hurried, no-one would ever know. With her mind made up, she discarded the stained teacup on the drainer and rushed towards the lab.

Chapter Nine

Red climbed the twenty-three steps, bounding along like a mountain goat clutching the Chief's sandwich. Half-way up, he wondered at the commotion. A rumble of voices signalled that something other than approved reading was going on inside the office.

"I wouldn't want to be in your shoes when the Chief gets back. Where have you been?" Guard Jackson's droning voice vibrated through him the instant he stepped through the door. Of all the men under their command, he was the only one who succeeded in getting under Red's skin on a daily basis. At six foot seven, the stick thin guard towered over everybody and seemed to think that gave him a license for just about anything.

"I've been getting this sandwich." Red held the brown paper bag aloft, visible proof of the success of his errand. "What's up?" he asked, changing the topic of conversation.

Red's tactic appeared to work, and Jackson became animated, jerking like a stick insect in a noose. "You're not going to believe it. We've got a case. The Protector for the

Science District, Professor Hawkin, was found dead this morning, at the library. We're waiting for confirmation but it looks like foul play."

Red was dumbstruck. Murder? In Scolaris? He wondered if he was dreaming, expecting to wake up at any moment and find that none of it was true. He chewed his bottom lip. Had he made such a terrible thing happen? He had longed for this mundane existence to change. Don't be ridiculous, it's nothing to do with me, he told himself, smoothing his uniform with sweaty palms. Deep down an inner critic insisted otherwise. But this was the opportunity to prove that this job was worthwhile and maybe even persuade his parents to forgive him for not following in his father's footsteps.

"Do we know what killed him?" Red asked.

"Like I said, we are standing by for verification, but so far a hefty bookend found at the scene is looking the most likely culprit," the irritating man replied, a huge smirk on his pockmarked face.

"Enough of the jokes Jackson, if this death is a murder case it's no laughing matter." Suitably admonished, the lanky guard turned his attention back to his desk, and the buzz of chatter silenced.

There didn't appear to be much doubt that Professor Hawkin had been murdered. That was incredible and the fact that the murdered man was a Protector struck right at the core of everything. The entire city would be reeling, so they needed to find whoever was responsible, and fast.

The office door whined on its hinges and Red observed the shiny, dripping form of Jim Ross, dragging behind him an unfamiliar male.

"Where—have—you—been?" the Chief demanded, wheezing between each word. The boss looked dreadful, a usually pristine set of uniform crumpled and twisted under his old tan overcoat. A sweat patch began rising from the midriff, staining the blue jacket and proving hard to ignore. The fellow was a walking heart attack.

"Sorry, Chief, the usual place didn't have your favourite, so I ended up in the Science District. I managed to get it though." Red held up the sandwich bag again, forcing a smile and holding his breath. It wasn't exactly a lie, just not the complete story.

Fortunately, the Chief's hands were full with the unknown man and he looked eager to move on from the details of Red's whereabouts.

"Jackson filled me in on this morning's developments. I assume this man is a suspect? What do you need me to do?"

"This is Ezra," the Chief panted, shoving the man into the nearest wooden chair. "He works for the Hawkins and is going to be assisting us with our enquiries."

A hard-nosed scowl suggested Ezra had not willingly volunteered any help. The suspect fumed and pouted, guarding his chest with crossed arms. He wore the familiar brown Defecto uniform, which sparked a connection in Red's mind. A murder and two Defectos disappearing linked to the same district. Surely that was too much of a coincidence? He could not mention it without risking revealing where he had really been all morning. The Chief could work the facts out for himself, and what was there in truth to tell? It wasn't the right moment; he needed something more concrete, otherwise, he might just look like an amateur.

"Hey, sunshine, back in the room," the Chief snapped his fingers. "Go over to the Hawkin's apartment. I didn't have time to question Mrs Hawkin about her movements yesterday. And while you're there, be sure to get more information about what went on with this one," he nodded towards Ezra and then continued, "She mentioned he was stealing from them. I haven't got time to get into it with you, just head over there, and no more vanishing acts. Are we clear?"

"Yes Chief, you can count on me." Red responded, clicking boot heels together as he saluted. Adrenaline pumped around his veins, propelling him at speed towards the Hawkin's residence. It was not a dream. This was it. What he'd been waiting to happen. A real live case.

Chapter Ten

Professor Hawkin's laboratory remained a scene of utter devastation. So far as Quill could tell, no-one had moved anything other than the diary. Time was of the essence. She needed to hurry, to examine every detail. If they caught her snooping around, it would be almost impossible to explain. She started with the sea of papers on the central workstation. Nothing about them made any sense earlier, and looking close up did nothing to improve the situation. Numerous charts and graphs of data written in meticulous handwriting dominated the piles. She assumed they were the Professor's work, but she did not know where to start to make head nor tail of them. What was he working on? Tucked underneath all the data sat a much larger sheet, and on it a detailed line drawing of a domed building. The item looked like a blueprint for something. But again, she had no clue what that might be. Someone had recorded in the top right corner, in a different hand from the rest, a fuller cursive script, "Proprietorial rights to Professor A Hawkin. Authorisation pending. Certified by K. Ginsburg."

Whatever this was, clearly represented an important project that required a permit. Authorisation from who? And who was K. Ginsburg?

Quill rubbed her eyebrows, perplexed, mind churning. It was no good. Nothing on the sheets got her anywhere. Her attention turned to the rest of the room, and she noticed that the nauseating odour had disappeared, which was not particularly surprising as the sliding doors remained wide open. Perhaps she imagined the smell earlier? The soles of her feet registered a creeping cold and damp sensation once more, a reminder of the smashed vials. Quill squatted, inspecting the floor. A thin layer of translucent liquid extended across the surface like a miniature lake. With delicate finger tipped strokes, she rippled its surface. The unknown viscous, syrupy substance shimmered close up, flecks of phosphorescent colour running through it. Lifted towards her nostrils, they crinkled, detecting the same sickly odour that threatened to overwhelm her earlier. So it was real. She had not imagined it and strangely, exposed now to a considerably smaller quantity, the effect drew her in. Intoxicated and seduced, she inhaled again, deeper. Nonetheless, an undercurrent remained, a hint of corruption under the surface, but intense sweetness heavily outweighed that. What was it? She contemplated collecting a sample, taking a tiny amount away with her, but, searching around, could turn up nothing to use for the job. And, in any case, having no experience with chemicals, how would she possibly work out what it might be? With nerves still jangling, confused by the magnetic pull of a substance that made her feel so unwell before, she made a conscious effort to move elsewhere and continue the search.

To get a closer look at the trail of mud, Quill stepped towards the open doors, wiping the residual stickiness on the front of her tunic as she moved. Now stood closer, able to see more clearly, convinced her it was a set of muddy footprints, though whether they headed into or away from the mess was not so obvious. Tight-chested, pulling at small clumps of her brown hair, Quill paced. She was no expert, but it didn't take a genius to realise that physical clues deteriorated as each second passed. Where was the Chief? Shouldn't he be here gathering evidence?

Taking a deep breath, Quill rolled away the tension, burying her irritation, thinking that way did not change the current situation. She could only control what she did. As she surveyed the scene once more, an impressively proportioned glass aquarium in the far corner grabbed her attention. Perched on top of the waist-high storage cupboards which ran around three sides of the space, the object had blacked out sides and, looking down through its glass lid, she expected to encounter a whole shoal of brightly coloured fish. No such luck. Her spirits dropped, along with her expression. The tank provided a home to a pile of dried black husks and dusty old twigs.

Quill ambled back to the expanse of notes, squashing the disappointment. Thrown forward without warning, she grabbed for the edge of the work-table, narrowly saving her face from injury. Whatever had caught her foot hid from view in the shadows cast by the countertop's overhang. She squirmed, back arched, lips clenched, stifling the hiss threatening to escape her lips as her left big toe throbbed from the impact with an unseen object.

Suddenly confronted with the fear of turning up another body, she froze, fighting the paralysis with logic. Two deaths in one day were hard to contemplate, but the probability of a third was surely mathematically impossible. Persuaded to investigate, she crouched, bringing her face to face with a metre long brass tube, roughly twenty centimetres in diameter at one end, narrowing to a five centimetre eyepiece at the other. Somebody had decorated this glorious example with ornate spirals which punctuated the otherwise smooth surface. Quill marvelled at its construction, having only ever seen telescopes in a book. Every inch of her body tingled as she peered through the transparent ends, trying to make out the combination of refracting mirrors which hid inside somewhere. But they were not visible. Even the tripod which lay behind looked astonishing. Its owner left free to adjust its combination of metal and wood reticulated legs up and down with securing bolts which slotted into hand-carved holes. This example resembled a fantastical, mechanical spider. She pictured setting them up, gazing into the night sky above the City, studying the array of stars in more detail than anyone should ever hope to see with the naked eye. Pulse-racing moments like this reminded her exactly why she wanted to become a scholar. This, a dream that would probably never come true. But her spirits soared with each new piece of knowledge or experience, and nothing else even came close to matching the feeling. She would go on dreaming.

The thrill of the discovery evaporated as she noticed a scant smear of a dark brown material around one half of the widest end of the telescope. The unidentifiable smudge had dried on and didn't transfer to her fingertips. Over and over she swallowed, her mouth dry and devoid of saliva. Could it be blood? If so, how did blood end up on the telescope? And, assuming all this was true, and the Professor sustained an injury with the telescope here, where was the rest of the blood and how did he end up in the reading room? That seemed an unlikely sequence of events. Perhaps she was letting her imagination run away with her. So far, she generated more uncertainty and peace of mind fast became a distant memory. Quill scratched her cheeks, bewildered. Maybe this was a job best left to the professionals. Or it should be, but where were they? And to make matters worse, it was difficult to forgive the Chief's repugnant attitude towards her.

Lost in growing scepticism at the man's detecting abilities, she froze at the unexpected sound of muffled voices and shuffling footsteps coming from inside the residence, beyond the open lab door. A glance to the outside world affirmed that the morning's rain had given way to a blanket of pale white cloud. She wondered how long she had been in the lab and cursed herself for losing track of time. What was she going to do? Without question, the sounds grew louder and more distinct with each passing second, which only meant one thing. Whoever was in the apartment headed in her direction. How would she explain her presence? Quill struggled, unable to think straight, no-one could find her here.

The voices were now so loud that it was possible to identify Mrs Hawkin's high-pitched, upper-crust diction. She isolated another voice too, deeper, velvety smooth, but it wasn't recognisable. Whoever it was, they would discover her in a matter of seconds, and she had not the faintest clue what to do. Quill was in deep trouble.

Chapter Eleven

In a moment of clarity, Quill darted across the lab and, throwing open one of the cupboard doors, was lucky enough to find the space inside almost empty, save for a solitary bright yellow high-heeled shoe. She threw her body inside as if tossing away dirty dishwater. Just in time to pull the door to with outstretched fingers as Mrs. Hawkin and the unknown man stepped into the carnage.

As they passed in front of the impromptu hiding place, Quill pushed the cupboard door open a fraction, planning to eavesdrop on their conversation. With a slice of luck, she might gather useful additional material to help untangle the situation.

"This must've been a terrible shock for you, Mrs Hawkin. We are all truly sorry for your loss and we'll do whatever we can to get to the truth. Does the Chief know about the mess in here?"

So, she pondered, the unidentified man must be a member of the City Guard, but clearly not the Chief. From her vantage point, she just glimpsed the lower half of a pair of legs in a blue uniform and polished black boots. The bulge of muscular calves was unmistakable and to be truthful, it was inconceivable that those limbs belonged to the Chief. Unable to see any more of the man, nevertheless from the vantage point cowering in the cupboard she enjoyed listening to the smooth melodic tone of his speech. And the sympathetic quality of his questioning made a refreshing change.

"To be perfectly honest, young man, I'm sorry I don't recall your name," replied the widow, her voice thick as if her tongue filled her mouth.

"Please don't worry, you've had an appalling shock, and it's a lot to take on board. It's Deputy, madam, Deputy Red."

"Thank you, Deputy, you're very thoughtful. As I was about to say, to be honest I really don't remember whether the state of the lab came up. I was so shocked when the Chief told me the Professor was dead. The rest of our conversation is all a bit of a blur. And then, of course, that filthy Defecto Ezra turned up. I still can't believe the nerve of the man."

"Let's start afresh. You can tell me all about it and I will report back to the Chief. Perhaps you can start by telling me who has access to the lab?"

"The Professor is—err—was—very particular about security, particularly regarding his work. That's why it was so odd this morning,"

"Odd how?" the Deputy interrupted. Quill sensed an excitement and enthusiasm for his work. In short, a stark contrast to the Chief's style. "Sorry for interrupting madam, please continue."

"Please, call me Lucinda," the widow replied in a girlish, giddy tone, which sounded truly revolting for a grown woman, let alone one whose husband had just been found murdered.

"As I was saying, it was odd that the entrance to the laboratory was unlocked. The Professor was nowhere to be seen, and the lab was in this mess. Only Alexander and his assistant, Mr. Penrose, have a key." Mrs Hawkin interrupted the pause that followed her revelation, adding breathlessly, "It's only just occurred to me that Theo owns a key. I'd completely forgotten. Perhaps you should talk to him."

"Rest assured, madam, we will talk to anyone who might have pertinent information. Moving on, where were you from yesterday lunchtime onwards?"

"Why do you need to know? You're frightening me. Surely you don't think I had something to do with the Professor's death?"

"These are routine questions. We always ask them in such cases. Please try not to worry."

Quill found it difficult to put her finger on it, but something about Mrs Hawkin's response to being interviewed did not ring true. Here was a woman of intelligence and discernment, holding a position of power, acting like a scared child. And, from what she had witnessed of the woman so far, it seemed almost absurd to believe anything would frighten her. But the widow projected a different persona, a pretence at being someone who didn't understand what was happening and why they were being questioned. More importantly, either the Deputy was a talented actor, or the charade had him fooled.

"Thank you so much. You are so very kind. Now let me think, yesterday, hmm, yes, I pottered about here in the morning and after a spot of lunch I visited a friend. We had dinner together and then I returned home. I don't think I returned much later than about eight but I felt tired so I went straight to bed."

"And where was the Professor?" the Deputy asked.

"I don't know. I assume either in the lab working or out somewhere with Ezra. They often travelled together looking for suitable sites for stargazing. I'm certain he wasn't in bed when I turned in for the night." Mrs Hawkin paused and Quill had to strain to hear what followed as the woman whispered, "Between you and me he rarely came to bed at all. He never stopped telling me how his work was too important to waste precious minutes, you know—resting."

Quill squirmed, cringing at this tidbit of marital information. The story being told to the Deputy sounding not quite the same as Mrs Hawkin had re-counted to her. It wasn't as if she withheld details about personal matters. So what was she hiding?

"You've been very candid, madam. In a minute, I will need to take a thorough look through the lab and catalogue everything here for evidential purposes. Before I start, I will need the name of your friend so I can contact them to confirm your whereabouts."

The silence that followed was long and painful. Quill could only imagine the scene playing out beyond the cupboard door.

"I'm afraid I must decline to answer your question, young man." Her tone remained polite but superficial. But something about the way she emphasised the rejection signalled she had no intention of answering the question. "Need I remind you to whom you speak?" the widow added, her voice flat and devoid of emotion.

"I am aware, madam, of your position, but we must not forget your husband is dead, and the job of the City Guard is to find out why. I will do whatever it takes to fulfill my duties."

Quill admired the response. The Deputy appeared to be a guardsman worthy of respect.

"I'm not likely to forget that he is dead, Deputy. Just don't you forget the City Guard is directly responsible to the Protectorate. My husband was a key member of the council and as his wife I have considerable sway with its members. I do not propose to discuss this any further. I suggest you turn your attention to this mess. The Chief already has the culprit and what you need to do is to uncover the evidence to support what I already know; Ezra, a common thief, a Defecto killed the Professor," she said, spitting the words out as if removing a swallowed insect. And Quill was just able to make out Mrs Hawkin's black court shoes as they flounced out of the lab.

Quill still saw the outline of the Deputy's neat calves and thought she could hear the faint murmur of his voice. It sounded as if he was talking to himself, though it was impossible to catch any exact words. At least that was the case before he announced to the empty room, "Hideous woman."

Quill grinned, pressing a fist against her lips, blocking the escape route of an unruly chuckle.

The flash of pleasure soon passed and in its place the nagging throb of doubt curled Quill's slim body into a defensive ball, knees hugged in tight to chest. Threatened by the intense hatred aimed toward her social class, she was totally ignorant of the fact that people felt this way about Defectos or why. It was possible their views were justifiable. After all, Ezra might have been stealing food. And then there were those letters. Maybe she was different to other Defectos, and they all caused trouble? Confused and conflicted, why was she so downhearted? If it transpired Ezra was the killer, then the Master was innocent, and that could only be positive. Faced with the reality that she had been living a sheltered life, ignorant about the world outside the library doors, she wished she could turn back the clock, go back to yesterday, before everything irrevocably changed.

Quiet and deliberate, Quill exhaled deeply as the Deputy's well built legs left the lab, heading back into the apartment. Without a moment to waste, she nudged the cupboard door and edged out. The coast was clear. Knowing that there might not be another chance, she scanned the scene, stamping it forever on her memory.

Quill drew an imaginary map of everything: notes, data, graphs, the building plans, broken vials and slick of shimmering liquid, the telescope and tripod and a trail of muddy prints. She needed to remember every detail, because it was entirely possible that one or more of these items might hold the key to the mystery.

Chapter Twelve

"And what do you think you are doing in here, girl?" came a piercing voice from behind her.

Quill twitched. Black spots darted across her vision as Mrs Hawkin's indignant shriek echoed inside her skull. How had she ended up in this predicament?

Turning on the spot, it surprised Quill to see that Mrs Hawkin was not alone. A man in a blue uniform who she assumed was the Deputy accompanied the widow, together with another gentleman who she had never seen until that moment. Focused on keeping her features devoid of any expression, she wished she could tell whether it was working. "I thought I could clean up the mess for you. It must be so difficult for you, what with the terrible shock of losing the Professor and of course not having Ezra to manage the house for you. I wished to serve." With fingers crossed in secret, she hoped that her dutiful little speech might appeal to Mrs Hawkin's sense of superiority, despite recognising that the ploy only went so far. Her tale didn't explain how she had wound up in the lab and where she had been in the interim.

"How refreshing, a Defecto with a conscience. Unfortunate timing though, so maybe not such a good idea. The Deputy here needs to examine the chaos in more detail and take away any evidence."

Quill realised she had been holding her breath, anticipating being caught lying. It seemed, however, that she had at least fooled the widow. Sadly, the same could not be said for the Deputy, whose intense gaze suggested a suspicious nature. He appeared to be sizing her up, debating the veracity of the story.

This presented the first opportunity to put a face to the shapely calves visible from her hiding place in the cupboard. He was a few years older, perhaps in his late twenties, but only a few inches taller than her petite stature. Broad shouldered and sculpted all over, his brown skin highlighted by a copper undertone, contrasted with clipped jet black hair framing a forehead free of lines. And dark, almost black, inquisitive eyes reminded her of the black holes that were so captivating, sucking her willingly into the pages of her favourite cosmology books, never to return. Lightheaded, the hairs on the back of her neck rose, and she struggled to drown out the pounding of her own heartbeat.

Quill forced her gaze to the other individual. The contrast was startling. He looked older than the Deputy, possibly mid thirties. Diminutive and obese from the collar down, he resembled the shape of a pump action spinning top. A long brown rat tail of hair tied in a ponytail was so wispy that she imagined it falling off if anyone blew on it. His eyes were pinpricks, despite them being magnified by the biggest, roundest pair of wire-rimmed spectacles. This fellow was wringing his hands, hopping from one foot to the other as if his shoes were on fire.

"What has happened to my lab?" the little man squeaked. Stunned by the high-pitched cry, it didn't fit well with his rotund body.

"May I remind you, Mr Penrose, that this is not your lab. My husband may be dead but everything here is still his property and now is not the time to be carving up his possessions."

So, thought Quill, this was Theo Penrose, Professor Hawkin's assistant and supposedly the only other person, apart from the dead man, who had a key to the laboratory. She needed to concentrate. If she merged into the background again, she might overhear key details. Edging over to the side of the room, she hoped she was out of their line of sight.

"Of course, forgive me, I am sorry that the Professor is dead but I can't help thinking of this lab as mine, having been here for over ten years and instigated many of the projects we worked on together. I must have my work and expect to be appointed to take over from the Professor by The Protectorate in due course." Theo Penrose's squeaking pitch combined with Mrs Hawkin's sharp retorts was unbearable, and Quill had to resist the urge to cover her ears with her hands. Penrose's face was getting redder and more screwed up by the second, and his eyes disappeared into their minute sockets.

"Mr Penrose," the Deputy interjected, "You cannot take a thing. Everything in this room is evidence. I'm about to catalogue it all and take it away. If you want to tell me what you claim is yours, then I will make a note of it. Once the case is over, the guard will surrender it to you if you offer proof of ownership."

"This is outrageous," the little fellow screamed, veins threatening to escape from the mottled skin on his neck. "I need my work. What am I going to do in the meantime? At the very least, I must take the building plans for the new observatory. They represent the culmination of five years of planning on my part. The Professor promised to support me but this was my project. I must insist that you find them and hand them over," he added, jabbing a finger toward the Deputy's face.

The Deputy brushed a hand across his face, sweeping aside the attack with ease, and shifted to the confusion of scattered papers. Quill recognised the baffled expression as the guard puffed his cheeks and then released them, expelling a hiss of air. And then a flicker of recognition. He must have spotted the detailed drawings. The plans now made more sense. It was going to be an observatory, a place to venture out into the cosmos and discover more knowledge than anyone could ever imagine. "Do you mean those?" the Deputy asked, pointing towards the mass of papers.

Theo Penrose darted forwards, his hand outstretched like a greedy child.

"Mr. Penrose, do not touch anything," the Deputy barked, stepping into his path, blocking the way. With a withering look, the lab assistant deflated, visibly shrinking under the ferocious stare. "Please Theo, may I call you Theo?" asked the Deputy, now that the situation was back under control. Penrose nodded his agreement, and the guard continued. "You can look at these papers for the purposes of identification, but we cannot touch. Do you understand?"

Theo nodded again, resigned to the fact that the Deputy was in charge. All three of them, perched on their tiptoes, peered over the workbench, studying the papers more closely. "What the?" Theo Penrose's fat lips fell open in disbelief, rendered speechless.

"These plans say that they're the property of Professor Hawkin. I'm afraid I can't release them to you even if I wanted to."

It was too much for the spectacled man to take. "The lying, thieving. How could he? How dare he!"

And then it was Mrs. Hawkin's turn to lose her self-restraint. "Mr. Penrose, how dare you," and she thrust a perfectly manicured lilac fingernail hard into the centre of his chest. "You odious little man. I never did like you. Fancy, trying to steal the work of a dead man. Mark my words, I will be speaking to the Protectorate about the appointment of the Professor's successor and rest assured I won't be recommending you!"

Well, this was all very interesting. Just when Ezra appeared to be the most obvious answer to the mysterious death, a new suspect had emerged. Penrose clearly had his sights set on the Professor's job and then the question over whose work those plans really represented couldn't be ignored either.

"I think it might be best if you left now, Mr Penrose, you're upsetting Mrs. Hawkin. Let me show you out. I'll need your personal details and your lab keys please." the Deputy said, holding out his hands in a businesslike manner and Theo duly obliged, dropping a set of keys into his palm. So, it was true, Mr. Penrose had access to the lab too, and with that discovery he had climbed to the top of Quill's list of suspects.

Lucinda Hawkin stared into space. At first, Quill thought she was still pondering the mess, but soon realised that the widow gazed instead out at the garden. Trance-like, Quill wondered what she was thinking. She could not imagine what torment the woman must be suffering, and on top of that she was impossible to read. Perhaps maintaining appearances and managing power and position was not without its downsides. Maybe she had been too hard on the woman. After all, she had no experience of what it felt like to lose a husband. The only bereavement she had suffered was that of her mother. Even so, was it really possible to understand the loss of someone that you never knew in the first place? It was arguable that not seeing her father for the last fifteen years might count but she refused to acknowledge even the minutest possibility that he was dead. Swallowing the lump in her throat, she repeated a whispered mantra, 'He will return, one day, he will.'

"Madam, madam," it was the Deputy, returning from escorting the lab assistant from the premises. "Truly sorry to intrude on your grief, and about the scene with Mr Penrose. I should've handled that better. I've instructed him to come to HQ later, to answer further questions but, in the meantime, I need to get on with the close examination of this lab." Just as he was finishing the sentence, the Deputy looked in Quill's direction, his probing, analytical expression revealing that he noticed her loitering in the shadows. Quill averted her gaze, shrinking in an act of submission, and hoped that he would not speak to her.

As if reading her mind, he turned back to Mrs Hawkin and continued, "Before I begin, I need to ask you if anyone has moved anything since you first found it like this?"

The passage of time stuttered, and Quill fought the urge to flee. It was as if the widow had finally deciphered the Deputy's face, reminded that someone else loitered in the room besides the two of them. Mrs Hawkin swung on her heels and Quill found herself face-to-face with disaster. Paralysed, dangling off the edge of a precipice by the fingernails, Lucinda Hawkin was preparing to stamp on her knuckles. Delighted to let her fall, there wasn't a single thing she could do to stop it.

"Quill, I'd almost forgotten you. Standing there, hiding in the background," the predatory woman said, drawing out each syllable, enjoying every second. "But that's not the only thing I'd overlooked, is it, girl?" she suggested, hands rubbing together, wet lips parted as if she were ready to devour her.

Quill held her breath. Why had she run away with that stupid diary? To be honest, she had a horrible feeling her face had guilt written all over it. She had hoped against hope that nothing would bring the Master's name into the investigation, but what came next was inevitable.

Lucinda Hawkin turned to the Deputy, a wild-eyed, triumphant expression across her features, and announced, "I must thank you for reminding me. This Defecto girl, who's been loitering in my home, getting up to goodness knows what, arrived in a panic first thing this morning looking for a diary that belonged to her Master. Master Wittgenstein no less. And where do you think we found it?" she inquired, a rhetorical question for effect, "right there, resting proudly on top of all of this chaos." She answered, throwing her arms wide open. "And do you want to know the strangest thing? She didn't even stay to help me look for the Professor, she just grabbed the book and ran."

The gloating chuckle that followed made Quill sick to her stomach. But nothing she could do or say would change the situation. The secret was out.

Chapter Thirteen

Red knew that time was against him. He needed to get back, report everything that he'd discovered at the apartment. On edge, he should still be there, cataloguing the evidence, but the entire afternoon something whispered to him. Struggling to hear its message, it eventually made sense when showing Penrose the door. The enjoyable view across the garden had granted a glimpse of the roofs of the Science District, a reminder of just how close they were to the AccuDiagnostics lab. The only murder that had ever taken place in Scolaris and Bill and Finn's disappearance, three unusual events connected to the Science District.

Jackson could collate the evidence. That should give the joker something meaningful to do and, in the interim, it made sense to examine Bill's unit whilst he was still here. Afterwards he should brief the Chief on everything. Red felt positive that the man ought to listen this time, but the more information gathered, the better.

Even on foot, the journey to cross the district did not take long and, arriving back in the Defecto quarters, he located 72 DSQ with ease. It helped enormously that Red knew to look for the painted on arrangement of numbers and letters. And much to his relief, on this occasion, his arrival coincided with late afternoon melting into dusk. This allowed him to keep to the shadows cast by the hodgepodge of units, as he preferred not to alert anyone to his presence.

He skirted the perimeter of Bill's unit, trying to find a means to get inside unseen. Only one narrow window pierced the back wall, though calling it a window somewhat stretched the truth. Someone had created it by recycling a sheet of thick plastic, which was not altogether translucent. Red pressed his refined nose against the hard surface, straining to see inside, but the darkness within remained impenetrable. There was nothing for it. He would have to break in to the place.

The bottom left-hand corner of the piece of plastic obligingly stood proud of the sheets of tin that made up the walls. Red worked his fingers under and around the corner and next, moving along the left-hand edge, created enough of a gap to take his entire hand inside the hole. Then, grasping the dense plastic with both hands, he pulled towards him and the whole window slid out with relative ease. Bill's unit's security left a great deal to be desired. Though he was beginning to understand that being born a second-class citizen did not lend itself to notions of wealth, health, happiness and security.

If Red thought that the Defecto units looked poor from the outside, the inside was much worse. Climbing headfirst through the gap, it was obvious at once that he was looking at one solitary room. Stood on bare earth, the lack of a proper floor no doubt an unwanted feature. A tatty mustard armchair, the only visible item of furniture, decayed in the half-light. Its arms were threadbare and a rusty spring protruded out of a large hole at the back of the seat like a crusty tongue. No doubt this was where Bill relaxed, ate his meals, and slept. How was this allowed to happen?

Red found a sink with running water, much to his surprise, though the precarious pile of dirty plates and chipped cups suggested either Bill hated washing up or he'd not been home for several days. In the corner, next to the front door, stood a modest, single gas stove, which he suspected also doubled up as a heater.

Red wondered if this was another dead-end. What did he expect or hope to find? And then, just as he thought of giving up, something caught his eye. A crude wooden shelf behind the battered armchair displayed a photograph. A beaming middle-aged man, his arm tight around a much older fellow. On closer inspection, the two men looked alike, despite the age disparity. The younger of the two showed off dark, curly hair, pale with pink cheeks and a playful grin. Almost certainly Bill. He fitted the description given by the young Defecto woman and, whilst Red could not be sure, a similar look about the older man suggested he was most likely Bill's father. The shot made Red smile, imagining what it should feel like to have that bond. The two men epitomised the happiness and contentment to be found from a strong family connection. Whilst it was plain that Bill had little in the sense of material wealth, the man possessed something that Red could only dream of, a loving father.

As he picked up the photograph, planning to take it to show the Chief, Red spotted a small glass container that had been hiding behind it. With a thumping heart, he forgot his envy, suppressing the urge to leap around the room. Red could not be confident, but it looked very similar to the glass vials that were smashed all over the floor of Hawkin's lab. As he held it up to the hole where the window had been, searching to find sufficient light, it was disappointing to discover that it looked empty. Its glass stopper offered no resistance, and a tentative sniff suggested a hint of something, but maddeningly it was too faint to identify. Never mind, it was coming back to HQ for analysis. If Red could prove a link to the Professor's lab, the Chief would finally have to listen to him.

Chapter Fourteen

Trouble headed toward Quill at a canter. Its eventual arrival was inevitable, and it was all her fault. The bounce in the Deputy's step as the widow delighted in placing the diary bang smack in the middle of a crime scene had left Quill in no doubt. It was impossible to erase the way he looked at her out of the corner of those liquid black eyes as he scribbled the details in a notebook. If she had just stayed with the woman, not gone running back to the Master, she might not have drawn so much attention to the appointment book's position. A hideous black beast lurked in the pit of her stomach, threatening to climb up and out and devour her.

Quill fought against it, punching it with clubbed fists. But the challenge was exhausting. It felt like a lifetime ago that she sat in her cozy little room poring over her latest favourite books. The shadows created by the variegated border shrubs were lengthening with every passing minute. Late afternoon ebbed and evening was fast approaching. The day had passed in a blur and she longed to curl up under the star covered blankets, which lay waiting on the bed. Quill knew, though, that she had more to do before that was going to happen. She needed to head back to the Master, to warn the old man and ask for forgiveness for making a dangerous situation a hundred times worse.

"Is there anything more I can do for you, madam? Really, I should be getting back. The Master will be waiting for his supper," Quill said, surprised to see the woman slumped onto one sofa, shoes discarded, resembling a broken and worn rag-doll.

"As a matter of fact, yes, there is an errand I need you to run for me, girl. I'm tired but very much suspect that I won't be able to sleep. I hate to admit it, but this whole thing is rather frightening. What if Ezra comes back?" she stuttered, shaking uncontrollably. "Listen carefully, I want you to fetch Doctor Cooper, insist that he comes at once. Tell him that I'm in dire need of something to help me relax. Now don't just stand there gawping, get going!"

Mrs Hawkin truly was an insufferable woman. But as much as Quill wanted to get home, the lady had already proved how capable she was of causing trouble. For that reason alone, it was imperative to keep on the widow's good side. Added to that, Quill reminded herself once more that the woman had just lost a husband.

With numb, heavy-limbed resignation, Quill capitulated and replied through a fake smile, "Of course, madam, it would be a pleasure."

Chapter Fifteen

"What time do you call this, sunshine? And who gave you the authority to order Jackson over to the Prof's place to catalogue the lab? I sent you to do that job." The Chief's sweat inducing outburst left Red in no doubt he had some explaining to do. His earlier self-satisfaction and confidence evaporated in the onslaught of the inimitable Jim Ross. The boss's temper was legendary, but fortunately, until that moment, he had never been on the wrong end of it. Red had always believed that the rumours were exaggerated. Yes, he was a grumpy old man, but nothing more. This view changed in an instant, he'd been very wrong and, if anything, the gossip had been too kind.

Red faded into the door-frame of the Chief's office as the boss berated him for a full fifteen minutes without pausing to take a breath. After the first five minutes or so, he switched off his ears. There were only so many personal insults anyone could take. Aware of the odd word, 'stupid, incompetent, arrogant, lazy,' what he chose not to hear were the actions that linked this list of delights. At last, the

Chief had to draw breath and, in doing so, fell backwards into his swivel chair. Propelled by his ample bulk, the seat immediately spun an entire three hundred and sixty degrees. When the chair finally came to a stop and the Chief recovered from the disorientation, eyes rolling like marbles, he said more calmly, "We've had confirmation. The Prof didn't die of natural causes. We are still waiting for the exact cause and time of death but we are looking at roughly somewhere after 11 pm yesterday and before 6 am this morning. And then, assuming we believe their story, Master Wittgenstein and his Defecto discovered the body at approximately 9. We're still holding the Hawkin's Defecto, Ezra. He has no alibi for that window of time and Mrs H says that she caught him stealing food. I can't help agreeing with her. It would make sense for this to be the work of a Defecto. After all, we all know what they're like."

Red knew that it might be best to keep quiet but couldn't stop himself. "What do you mean, what they're like?"

"Lay-abouts, jealous, dirty thieves."

Red couldn't altogether believe what he was hearing. The first rule of investigation was to keep an open mind. They had all read the same manuals about a million times. It sounded, though, as if the knowledge recorded in all those books had not wielded enough power to smash through the prejudice that ran through the core of the boss like a black canker.

"If that's true, why aren't we kept busy dealing with Defecto crime?" Red asked.

The Chief sniggered, shaking his balding head. "What do they teach recruits these days? The Protectorate ensures nothing can interfere with the gathering of knowledge, nothing. All civilians know that and when Defectos step out of line it's dealt with in the correct manner."

"Dealt with, how?" asked Red, uncomfortable at the direction the conversation was taking.

"With impartiality, by the families or businesses they serve, in private. That's why we never need to be involved."

"Then what's the point of the Guard? What use are we?" asked Red, mouth dry, swallowing hard, childhood dreams disappearing in the face of reality.

"Good question. Until today I might have said we're the ultimate deterrent. One hundred per cent successful at persuading the good citizens of Scolaris to behave. And, once they see what happens to the Defecto that murdered the Prof, it will remind everyone why they follow the rules."

"Even more reason to suspect that there's more going on here than petty theft," Red suggested, knowing it was a gamble, but still determined to change the Chief's mind.

"I'm not sure I understand what you mean?" said the boss.

"If justice behind closed doors or the thought of being taken by the City Guard is such a deterrent, why should a Defecto commit murder for the sake of a few food scraps? And that's not all, the manservant isn't the only person who might have had a reason to hate the Professor."

"Okay, sunshine, best you tell me everything you've got and then I'll decide what we're going to do with it."

Chapter Sixteen

Quill soon replaced the frustration at being sent on yet another errand, when all she wanted was to get home, with enjoying a moment to herself in the fresh air. Darkness descended like a thick, woolly blanket, and although the day's rain had ended some hours earlier, large pools of rainwater remained standing on the cobbled streets. A freshness to the air wafted like clean linen hanging on a line, and whilst an icy chill penetrated her tunic, she didn't mind. The brisk breeze enlivened her.

Quill had visited Doctor Cooper's for the Master on regular occasions to collect medicinal herbs to add to his favourite brew, so knew the way. To the north-west of Science lay the Physician's District, and she walked briskly, hoping to deliver the message and return to the Master in time for supper. The streets were empty, an entirely normal state of affairs at any hour of the day. Whilst the City was a hive of enterprise, most of it took place behind the closed doors of the labs, workshops and offices of each district. The pursuit of knowledge never slept and residents worked in shifts round-the-clock.

After walking for about twenty minutes, the cobbled roads and low rise labs of the Science District made way for an entirely different scene. The Physician's District was homely, doctors practised from private clinics within their own grounds and they designed the outside environment to encourage relaxation and healing. Green spaces proliferated here, unlike anywhere else in Scolaris, and if she could choose where to live, this district is where she belonged.

The solitude of the walk filled Quill with joy. For a moment, it cleared the mind of everything that troubled her. Almost disappointed to arrive at the destination, Quill stood at the waist-high wrought-iron gate to number 15 Serenity Gardens, Doctor Cooper's home and clinic. The gate nestled between two red brick pillars which formed part of the low brick wall surrounding the grounds. Through the gate sat a front courtyard, tastefully lined with small white stones and interspersed with perfectly manicured circular flowerbeds. The whitewashed face of the house complimented a pastel-blue front door framed by a marble pillared porch. The whole of the front elevation lit up from the ground to the roof. A gentle splash splosh of water bubbled up from the stone fountain in the centre of the courtyard as she stepped through the gate. She'd always wondered which had come first, whether the serenity of the house and its grounds had inspired the name of the street or vice versa.

Lights shone through all four of the downstairs casement windows. But Doctor Cooper's clinic sat at the back of the property, so it was impossible to tell whether he was in the clinic or at home.

The brass door-knocker had always fascinated her, and that evening was no exception. Moulded into the shape of a large fish, which of itself wasn't particularly intriguing, the aquatic creature had bulbous eyes protruding from the top of its head. Eyes that might have looked more at home on an insect. Added to that, the animal had protuberant lips, through which it spat a jet of water. It was comical, to say the least, to find such an odd creature amid such perfection.

Quill snickered, grasping the cool metal, and knocked rhythmically on the front door. The sound vibrated through her fingertips, followed by a sonorous echo reverberating deep into the home beyond the closed front door. It was solid and comforting, an echo of the dwelling itself.

The young man who opened the door was a stranger. She had been expecting old Jed, Doctor Cooper's Defecto, so it was a surprise to observe a new face. This individual still had the plumpness of youth, but subtle hints of emerging adulthood existed in the beginnings of defined cheekbones. His ochre skin looked smooth in the lamplight and his motionless eyes were the colour of liquid gold. "Can you identify yourself, please? How can I help you?" he said, gazing past her towards the horizon.

What an odd thing to ask. Why didn't he look at her? Quill's ears burned. The mark on her face was unusual and often led to curious stares. But this was a novel experience. Was he so repulsed that he couldn't bear to glance at her?

"Hello, hello, is anybody there?"

How rude, he mocked her as if she were a child. Stupid boy, she didn't have the time, inclination or energy for games. Quill glared, rising to meet his gaze, ready to launch a verbal attack. And then all of a sudden everything made sense.

He was blind.

"Sorry, sorry, I've never met anyone who was, um."

"Blind? It's okay, you can say it."

"Yes, sorry, blind."

"Well now you have, you can cross it off your to do list."

Unable to work out whether he was making a joke at her expense, Quill fidgeted, arms crossed tight over her chest.

The boy paused and then asked, "Please, tell me who you are and what you want?"

"I'm Quill, I work for Master Wittgenstein. Are you new here? Where's Jed?"

"Great to meet you." He answered, offering his hand to her to shake. "I'm Kai. I started working here a few weeks ago. Jed's been struggling to keep up with her duties, so Doctor Cooper decided he needed an extra pair of hands. And here I am."

"Right, err,"

"I know what you're thinking, you're wondering what use I could be when these don't work," he said, touching the corners of his eyelids, "but you'd be surprised what I can do. There's much more to seeing than having functioning eyes."

Quill did not entirely understand his last remark, but it embarrassed her that he sounded as if he had read her mind and decided not to ask any more questions. She needed to focus on the job at hand, deliver Mrs Hawkin's message, and get home.

"Sorry—I just need to talk to Doctor Cooper."

"I'm afraid the Doctor is still seeing patients. Can I give him a message?"

"Could you tell him I'm here? Tell him that Mrs Hawkin sent me. It's urgent that I speak to him. Please, it really is incredibly important," she begged, worried that Kai might not register her desperate tone.

"Look, I don't normally dare interrupt the doctor during clinic hours, but as the Hawkins are very important patients, I will try to catch him. Wait here."

Kai closed the door behind him, and the shuffle of footsteps faded into the house. Faced toward the gate, Quill admired the natural feature of Serenity Gardens. The road itself formed two adjacent sides of a rectangle enclosing a green. On the remaining sides, well-established lines of oak trees formed a natural barrier from the elements. They stood, lofty and imposing, silent watchers in the dark.

Without warning, something or someone blocked the light coming through the downstairs window, the first to the right. It was rude to pry, but as Quill had nothing better to do, she decided a closer look through the window might prove interesting. She sidled up to the edge of the window and peered in, hoping not to be seen. The main house was a mystery. Jed always took her around the back, through the garden and into the clinic to collect the herbs. This room reminded her of the Master's taste in décor and furnishings. There were a multitude of chairs, each one different shapes and sizes. Armchairs in rich red velvet with high winged-backs and low seats, finer dining style chairs with elegantly turned legs and oat-coloured damask upholstery. She loved the assortment of odd little stools. They were oval shaped and covered in a quirky olive-green and cream check. All things considered, having studied the room in more detail, it did not fit with the pristine, elegant façade of the residence. It was much more individual and more than a tad muddled in personality. Perhaps it was Doctor Cooper's private living room? And then, as if to confirm that thought, there he was.

Even though only his back was visible, crossing diagonally from the front of the house to the far corner of the room, the pale blue scrubs were a give-away. As he scurried back and forth, Doctor Cooper reminded her of a squirrel hiding its food store for winter. It always struck her how bony he looked, sallow skin and a gaunt face in stark contrast to a thick slick of jet black hair swept back from the forehead. To be blunt, he looked as if he needed to consult a doctor. What was he doing?

To get caught snooping would prove disastrous, but she couldn't tear herself away. And then the skinny man suddenly stopped, fixated on a grand terracotta pot tucked inside the hearth of the brick fireplace. He produced something out of his top pocket. It was small and almost impossible to detect. What was it?

As Quill pressed against the glass, he whipped around, forcing her to duck out of sight, but not before glimpsing a metallic glint in the firelight. Crouched beneath the sill, panting, she waited a few seconds, gathering the courage to resume spying. As her eyes edged into position, she was just in time to witness him throwing the shiny object in the pot and dash off. No-one must find her staring into the window, so she took his lead and darted back to the front door, expecting him to appear at any moment.

When the door finally opened, it wasn't Doctor Cooper; it was Kai.

"Um, mm, err," he said, fiddling with the hem of his tunic. "The Doctor's busy with patients. He's asked me to inform you he will call Mrs. Hawkin at the end of his clinic." Kai grinned, looking sheepish, and the hunch of his shoulders relaxed a little.

None of that could possibly be true. The Doctor was not assisting patients unless he had developed an ability to be in two places at once. What was going on in there? Unfortunately, the prospect of explaining what she had been doing staring through the windowpane made her cringe. And having only just met the boy, she wasn't about to confide in him.

"Oh, err, really? Okay, are you sure?" she asked. "Did you actually talk to him? Did you explain the urgency? Mrs Hawkin needs to see him this evening." Quill didn't know what to say.

"Of course, I'm blind, not deaf," the boy fired back, hands on hips, "I told him it's urgent. He works very hard, he's totally dedicated to his patients so I'm positive he'll ring her."

"Of course, sorry I wasn't suggesting you were, you know." She was tongue-tied, getting more and more muddled about what she should or shouldn't say with each passing moment.

Kai leaned back, laughing out loud, a deep manly laugh, providing a snapshot of the man that should emerge from the shell of the boy. The joyful sound took Quill by surprise and it thankfully broke the tension. "Don't stress over it. It's fine, I get a bit uptight about it. It's bad enough being a Defecto without having an obvious defect to add to the pile!"

The truth of this observation struck home with a clenched fist. Quill's first opportunity to consider the possibility that the term Defecto and the notion of being defective were connected. Was it intentional? Is that how people thought of them? In response she retreated inside, mentally crumpling under the weight of self-realisation, turning aside, grateful that the boy could not see her.

"I'm sorry he didn't come to the door, but it was good to meet you. I don't get to meet many young Defectos. It would be good to make a friend and you could be it."

Quill recognised the loneliness in his straightforward declaration, but wasn't sure how best to respond. "I'm sure I'll be back soon for Master Wit's herbs. Perhaps we can talk more then?" she said, with little conviction. She didn't need a friend. Working for the Master gave her everything, the two of them against the World.

"Great, see you soon," Kai replied, and the tooth-filled grin spread across boyish cheeks was the last thing she saw as the door closed behind him.

Chapter Seventeen

Red had to hand it to the boss. He was a very attentive listener when the mood was right. Red detailed each discovery. Two trips to the Defecto Science Quarters, disappearances of Bill and Finn tentatively confirmed and their connection to the AccuDiagnostics lab. And, not forgetting the revelations on Theo Penrose's ambitions to take over from the Professor and the lab assistant's assertion that the dead man had stolen his work. All of this he concluded with the suspicious removal of Master Wittgenstein's personal diary from the crime scene at the laboratory by the old man's Defecto.

The pair sat in silence; the Chief kneading his temples with fingertips. No doubt force-feeding every single scrap of information to starving brain cells. Red's confidence grew. The evidence was coherent and compelling. Chief Ross ought to take the disappearances seriously.

The Chief's gravelly growl attacked the hush. "I don't know who you think you are, sunshine, or what you think you've been up to, but I've a good mind to have you on toilet cleaning duty!" And with that, he battered Red's hope into submission. "How many times do I need to tell you? There are no missing Defectos. What we must do is concentrate our attention on Hawkin's death. Have you any idea how much pressure I'm under from The Protectorate to get this unsavoury business resolved as quickly as possible? The last thing I need is you adding unnecessary complications. This is your last chance, sunshine. Follow orders, nothing more. Do I make myself clear?"

"Yes, Chief." What was the old dinosaur's problem? This blatant prejudice against Defectos was so deeply ingrained that his mind was closed off to any notion of them as victims. The only choice left available was to go along with everything the boss asked. But Red wasn't about to give up. A hand instinctively reached for his left trouser pocket, tracing the outline of the glass vial taken from Bill's unit. Concealed dread tingled in his chest. Getting caught was not an option as the prospect of a future slopping out the gents filled him with horror.

"First things first," said the Chief, rising from the chair, "In the morning we'll speak to the Hawkin's Defecto. With any luck, he'll tell us what we want to hear. In the meantime a night in the lock-up should refresh his memory." And with that, the Chief gathered his overcoat and, leaving Red in no doubt who was in charge, the working day over, he left the building.

Chapter Eighteen

By the time Quill had walked back from Doctor Cooper's, the clock read after 11 pm. Her feet chafed, damp with sweat, and both calf muscles twinged and complained of fatigue. She expected the Master to be up and working, which would give the perfect opportunity to warn him that the guard knew he had been in the Professor's lab yesterday. But the bulge in the bed covers signalled it was too late. The old man was already asleep. Unsure whether to feel frustrated or relieved, she decided it would be wise to wait until the morning, anyhow.

Disturbed and restless, the Master shifted from one side to the other. Maybe he was dreaming?

"Don't get caught, no... Mustn't... Not now," he muttered, eyes closed, sleeping.

Quill froze, tuning in to every utterance. Could this day get any worse? It meant nothing, don't get carried away. This had to be a dream. Who did he expect to catch him, and for what?

Stifling a yawn, Quill stretched aching limbs as sleep beckoned. The situation might look clearer in the morning. As she trudged towards the study door, the Master's boots peeped out from under his coat in the exact spot where they sat that morning. But it was like seeing them for the first time. They were still dirty, but on this occasion, all she could think of was the muddy trail of footprints in the laboratory.

Quill could not ignore the signs. It looked more and more likely that the Professor's death involved the Master somehow, and that meant nothing but trouble for them both. She struggled, not knowing what to do for the best, but reluctantly decided that doing nothing might prove to be a horrendous mistake. Tiptoeing over to the boots, she gently eased them from under the coat, hoping that he wouldn't wake.

Just as she thought it was safe, the scholar sat bolt upright like a jack-in-the-box, staring straight at her, glassy-eyed. With lips clamped tight, she stifled an escaping gasp and froze. Seconds felt like hours, and then, just as she felt her lungs might explode, the old man lay back on the pillows as if nothing had happened. The crisis passed.

On the far side of the study, another door led to the kitchen, if they could call it that. To be truthful, it was more of a large cupboard, but it sufficed for their culinary needs. The Master lived frugally on a diet of bread and cheese, mainly because it was the quickest and easiest thing to eat whilst working. A plate of crumbs lay in the sink, a sign that he had, at least, eaten supper. Quill substituted the dish for the wellingtons and set about getting rid of the mud. They were large boots for large feet, sturdy with thick rubberised soles. The muck ensconced in the deep grooves which crisscrossed the rubber was stuck tight. It proved difficult to dislodge, and she was weary. Even bashing them together had no effect, and she had to resort to levering out solid clumps with a bone-handled butter knife.

When they were as clean as she could hope, she shook them, eager to remove as much of the water as possible, and then left them to dry on the kitchen floor, in front of the blue and green tapestry hanging on the back wall.

Quill wandered back through the library, stumbling a little with exhaustion, desperate for the comfort and oblivion that sleep should bring. She had always loved the library at night. To explore all its avenues in solitude was exhilarating. But that evening, the shadows were ghosts brought to life by a vivid imagination, and the tapping and scratching of murderous branches on the stained-glass windows set her nerves on edge. Alone in the building with the Master, was she in danger? What if he was a murderer?

Black thoughts sent Quill hurtling into the bedroom. She slammed the door, leaning against it, waiting for the rapid breathing to slow. This was ridiculous. The Master had been nothing other than kind. It reminded her of Kai. He acted mature for his age, like he had life worked out.

Collapsed onto the bed, throwing off damp shoes, Quill sought to clear her mind and sleep. But the harder she tried, the more frustration grew. A blurred and faded image of her father crept painfully into her consciousness. The details of his face withered as each day passed. With eyelids squeezed together, she pushed beyond the distant recollection of his physical form and conjured instead the lilting sound of his voice. A core memory of being soothed to sleep, the perfect remedy for a restless child with an overactive spirit. He had harnessed an obsession for cosmology, taking them both on a magical flight. A journey in words which took them orbiting around stars and soaring through galaxies, into the depth of black holes and to sleep. Quill followed the warm, rich tone, floating into space, drawn willingly into the infinite darkness.

Chapter Nineteen

The distinctive song of the Lilith birds perched on the ledge outside the window woke Quill early, as they always did in spring. The noise was a bitter-sweet sound, a reminder of a mother who died in childbirth uttering the name 'Lilith' with every urgent ragged breath. Her father had recounted the story only once, and she understood from what he could not say that the pain remained raw and visceral. Yet it was useless to think of herself as Lilith. The name Quill had belonged to her forever, her father's 'little bird'.

To watch their body bobbing, tail-wagging courtship through her window remained an endless source of pleasure. Roughly fifteen centimetres long, their tails were comparatively short. The male of the species looked distinguished with black cheeks and a matching eye-stripe on a grey crown whilst the females dazzled with orange cheeks and a chestnut eye-band. Besides their pied plumage, both sexes had a striking white rump with a blackened 'T' shape on their tail. And then nothing could beat their song—a distinct mix of full-bodied notes interwoven with a series of ascending, plaintive trills. It was mesmerising to hear them calling and singing to each other, trying to attract the amorous attention of a potential mate. She revelled in the sound. The only music that The Protectorate couldn't outlaw. Though it pained her that there were periodic culls of the poor creatures, usually done under the guise of reducing the spread of disease. The brutal slaying didn't seem fair, especially as nothing she read about the birds suggested they were disease carriers.

Quill's usual excitement at the prospect of each new day deserted her. She had slept soundly, but every bone from the waist down rubbed painfully against its neighbour, and the muscles attached to them throbbed and shivered in the fresh morning air. Teeth chattering despite the layers of bed-covers, the repeated soaking in yesterday's rain appeared to have brought on a chill. Chores couldn't wait for her to be ill, she told herself. Short of breath, chest feeling heavy and uncomfortable, she wracked her brain for a solution. The Master would say fast today and replace all meals with gallons of his foul tasting brew. Just this once, she might have to take the advice.

Quill's favourite way to start each day involved indulging in the delights of the secret stash of books. But as thoughts of the previous day's events swirled around, Quill knew the texts would have to wait. The priority was to get the facts down on paper. Anything to comprehend the full extent of the trouble she faced. With outstretched fingers reaching under the bedstead, she shoved aside the pile of publications and felt for the corners of her prized possession, her only possession. She had no idea where the box came from, only that she didn't remember ever being without it. And despite trawling her memory, struggling to find an occasion when her father discussed it, found nothing. She had asked the Master a few months after her father's disappearance, but it was another one of those topics that the scholar skirted around. Now she appreciated how secretive he was about a lot of things, and maybe she didn't know him quite as well as she thought.

With the casket on top of the bed, she traced the outline of the carving on the lid. A simple thing, but that was part of its charm. Over the years she tried to identify the tree from which it originated, but could never quite match it to anything in the texts on plant species. The warm, honey-brown wood shone, and each surface was perfectly smooth. The only aspect she had identified were the small jet-black pieces set into the etching on the cover. In the upper right-hand corner perched an exquisite Lilith-bird. It's black eye markings and tail picked out in ebony. But this was no ordinary Lilith. A swirling symbol filled the fledgling's body, reminding her of a letter G, and from the creature's beak, a spray of ebony dots fanned out across the top. It made sense that the symbols somehow related to the birdsong. But she had never been able to prove her theory. She knew that there were texts about music and verse, but they were off limits, locked away by a ruling of The Protectorate.

Quill lifted the lid and admired the interior. The wood grain resembled the ripple effect caused by dropping a pebble into water. Concentric circles flowed outwards from the centre. Whoever crafted the case had been exacting when choosing the materials. It always pleased her that no one had chosen to refine its appearance by adding a lining. The case was absolutely perfect, just as it was.

The contents, in comparison, were eclectic. In homage to the fowl on the cover, she collected feathers from the live variety that sang on her windowsill. There were various colours, grey and brown and orange, but her favourite was an exceptionally splendid inky tail-feather. Held against her face, running it down her cheekbones, it felt soft. And yet the plume possessed a solidity, a strength which she found compelling. She couldn't help looking at herself in the narrow piece of mirrored glass hanging from the wall. And, at the same time, resting the feather firmly against her cheek, the one that bore the mark. The raised brown stain she struggled to pretend wasn't there bore a remarkable resemblance to a Lilith tail-plume. This was the only story that the Master had ever told her about herself. A motherless child with a feather-like blemish on her face, and a father who, unable to speak her birth name, chose instead to call her Quill. That was all she owned, her name and this box.

Apart from the collection of plumage, only one other item nestled inside, an old leaflet, dog-eared and wrinkled. The paper faded, and Quill tried not to look anymore, afraid that exposing it to the light might render the image invisible forever. And on the page, a picture of a building, though very little appeared in the background or foreground to suggest where the place might be. Over the weeks and months she visited most of the districts of the city, and saw nothing like it. Had even recovered an original map of Scolaris, which predated the place as it was now, tucked inside an ancient scroll in the architecture section of the library. The Scolaris that she knew lay over the top of the older city set out on the map. Like a fine veil, the new city added decoration, but could never completely hide what lay underneath the foundations. Whenever Quill returned from running errands for the Master, she would cross off the areas visited, hoping that one day she would find evidence of the building in the picture.

To the left, the construction appeared circular. And to the right of the round end was a wide rectangular section, reminiscent of the central corridor of the library, as if giant hands welded together those two anomalous pieces. The tips of leaves and branches overhung the circular end, but it was impossible to see the trees they sprouted from. The image didn't capture the inside, but full height windows dotted the outside at frequent intervals. Quill spent hours imagining how light and inviting the internal space would be, particularly on a bright spring day with the sun streaming in from all angles. She still hoped that in the future she would discover the place and experience it for real.

The mechanical voice of the six am alarm call broke the silence and jolted Quill into action. How many hours had she wasted? The thought of arriving late again touched a nerve. Grabbing a thick sheaf of plain paper, ordinarily used as camouflage for the prized box, protection from an undefined threat, she scrawled. The list in fine slate-grey pencil borrowed for secret studies, represented a regurgitation of everything discovered that might be relevant to the Professor's death. When finished, they resembled the ravings of a madman. Worse still, it was essentially a tally of everybody she had come into contact with the day before, except for the guards and Kai. Quill meant the exercise to narrow the field, but it obviously wasn't going to be that simple. More worryingly still, nothing so far suggested that the Master shouldn't be recorded there too.

Dejected and confused, even a half decent night's sleep had not allowed her brain to deal with the conflicting information. The fact Quill knew how to read and write didn't make her a genius. Nothing about this situation was easy, and fear screamed at her to give up. It was for the best. Leave it to the experts.

Her mind made up, Quill dawdled, tucking the notes one by one into the box and hiding it back under the bed, behind the stack of reference books. What was the point of keeping them? It wasn't important, she should dispose of them when this was all over. With one last look in the mirrored tile, Quill told the green-eyed reflection with as much conviction as she could muster that today would be that day. The City Guard would identify the killer, exonerate the Master, and everything would go back to normal.

Chapter Twenty

"Mother," Red said, nodding politely as he passed her on his way to the far end of the seemingly endless dining table. Every week he wondered why he continued to show up to this farcical meeting over breakfast. To be clear, he needed to get out of that house. But since finishing guard training and taking on the privileged position of second in command, he just hadn't found the right moment to search for something suitable. At least that was the unconvincing story he told himself.

Red had worked since the early hours, interrupting a fruitless hunt for leads to stay in his mother's good books. She was not a woman who took kindly to playing second best at anything.

"Red, Where have you been? I never see you."

As Red stood at the whitewashed sideboard, spooning pink grapefruit and yoghurt into a bowl, he was glad she could not look at his expression. The stentorian tone left no doubt that she disapproved of his career choice. Thank goodness she was oblivious to his gritted teeth and rolling eyes. "I'm fine. Honestly, you don't need to worry. I was at the office. There's a serious investigation so I'm going to be busy for a while, in case you're wondering where I am."

The silence that descended squirmed as they sat on opposing sides, cradling the breakfast. Red sensed her judgmental eyes boring into him but blocked the discomfort, hyper-focused on the bitter pink flesh, a welcome flash of colour against the white of the room. The focus of the early morning sojourn to HQ had been a simple one. To confirm Mr Hamata was wrong, that employers were required to keep records of Defecto employees. Much to his chagrin, he had only managed to discover that the opposite was true. To make matters worse, a double check of the incoming call logs disclosed nothing new. There were no names for those missing Defectos from the other districts. Red found himself in the unenviable position of investigating thin air.

"What is it? What's troubling you?" His mother's stern voice nudged his attention back to the present. It was unusual for her to be so intuitive, or at least to ask after his welfare. Superficial conversations were more the norm in their household.

Finishing a mouthful gave him space to contemplate whether it was wise to try a new style of conversation. And having reached a decision, he said, "It's difficult to talk about, because it's related to the case. But, why do we treat Defectos so–-differently?" Red had wanted to say 'treat them so badly', but checked himself, sanitising the question.

A raised left eyebrow was the only sign that the query troubled her. The matriarch pushed aside remnants of avocado on toast, wiping both corners of her mouth with an embroidered lace napkin, and laid it on the table. Her mouth opened twice as if to speak, each time stopping before she had started. Finally, she said, "I'm not sure I agree with you. This family has always treated its Defectos with consideration and kindness. They have shared our home and our lives."

"You make it sound like they should be grateful. As if there's a reason they don't deserve respect and decency. Have you seen their quarters? The way they have to live. It's inhuman. Scolaris is supposedly an enlightened society, working towards a common goal. We've amassed all this knowledge but we can't even take care of every person who lives here." Breathless and perspiring, he had surprised himself with his strength of feeling about the plight of the Defectos. Furthermore, acknowledging his mother's wide-eyed gape, he could see that he wasn't the only one.

The proud woman stood in one graceful motion, the palms of her hands forced flat onto the tabletop, knuckles white from the pressure. "I don't know what guards chat about—-at work." She added, stumbling over the last word as if it was poisonous, "but I will not have such a conversation in my home."

In an instant Red was a small boy, head hung low, chastened. She didn't wait for an apology or indeed for any response. The frigid woman dismissed him in the usual manner, silently turning away and leaving him alone.

"Who has my pen?" Red growled at the room of idle guards who, as usual, had nothing else to do but read another book. The breakfast with mother soured his mood, again. Why did she have that effect on him? He was a grown-up and could never understand why she reduced him to a gibbering wreck with a single look. It made him furious. And not just with her.

"Someone got out of bed the wrong side," sneered Jackson in a caustic manner as he threw a pen across the office, landing it with a strategic plop, straight into Red's coffee. The rest of the men erupted into laughter and took it in turns to congratulate the prankster with an array of back slapping and fist bumps.

"Hasn't anyone got work to do?" he scolded, reducing the men to childish tittering and muttering behind their palms. As peace descended upon the place once more, he returned to the call logs, which he had been scrutinising since arriving first thing that morning. He wasn't sure what he thought he was going to see. It didn't matter which way he looked at them. They were useless. On each occasion that someone had reported a Defecto missing, the log only showed the date and time of the report and which district the absent Defecto served. No-one making a report had been willing to leave their details and so the guardsmen logged them as a 'Call 0', in layperson's terms, a bogus call. As a result, the records revealed nothing else of any note.

Frowning and holding his head in his hands, the sudden ringing of the telephone startled him. An orange light flashed on the unit, signifying an internal caller, and he snatched up the receiver in anticipation. "This is Red. What have you got?" he said, fingers drumming at his side.

"Morning, Red. How's your mother?" The clipped, nasal speech of the man on the line was instantly recognisable. Dr. Virgil Fox, the forensic pathologist, one of his father's oldest friends. The two men had been at school together, yet Fox had also broken with family tradition, choosing science over law. The scientist always asked after his mother rather than his old friend, which raised too many issues that Red did not want to contemplate.

"She never changes," he replied, trying to sound upbeat. "Are there any test results yet?"

"Nothing that's going to prove much use, I'm afraid. That vial that you submitted; unfortunately, the analysed sample revealed no significant information. To be honest, if there was anything inside the bottle, it had evaporated away to nothing."

"What about the container itself? Can we link it to Hawkin's lab?"

"Afraid not, sorry. It's a standard glass vial, not in any way out of the ordinary. I've got hundreds of them in my stock cupboard."

Red grumbled, finger-tapping the desktop. "How are you doing on the body?"

The opportunity to get some practical pathology experience thrilled the doctor, who usually had no choice but to concentrate on private practice.

"Nothing conclusive, though he does have a very distinctive tattoo behind his right ear. It's hidden beneath his hairline. Unusual to have one there, not certain what it is though, like a black swirl. Probably best if you check it out for yourself. In the meantime, we're still waiting on the comprehensive chemical screening. There's something in his bloodstream that we can't identify. And it's odd, but the corpse isn't decomposing in the manner I'd expect. It may be nothing but we have to be certain."

"Of course. Keep me posted and I'll update the Chief."

"Will do. Oh, and don't forget to give my regards to your mother."

"Who was that, sunshine?" barked the Chief, sauntering into the office.

Red rose and followed him into his room. "That was the forensics lab. They're waiting on further chemical tests on a substance they found in Hawkin's blood and they need us to take a look at an unusual tattoo. Nothing concrete at this point."

"Huh," he grunted as he threw off his well-worn overcoat. "Really don't know why they're bothering. Couldn't be more straightforward if you ask me. We have a dead man with a bookend shaped wound in the back of his skull and the culprit in custody. Job done!"

"I don't believe we should make any assumptions just yet. We need to wait for the completed report at least, don't you agree?"

A vein on the Chief's forehead pulsed and twitched a warning signal as he placed his hands flat on the desktop, leaning toward Red. Looking down his nose, seething through bared teeth, the boss asked, "Are you questioning my decisions, again, sunshine?"

The threat level in the place shot up and a vein in Red's head synchronised with the throb of the old man's. As if reading the discomfort, the older man's mouth broke into a huge grin, and thumping the desk with a clenched fist he added, "Yeah, I didn't think so. Anyway, we haven't got all day, let's go and net ourselves a Defecto killer. By now he should just about be ready to tell us anything."

Chapter Twenty-One

The lockup lurked underground beneath headquarters. Accessed by an elevator which could only just accommodate two occupants, it was a vertical coffin standing on its end. The Chief stepped in first and Red jammed into the minute spot that was left over. The journey through three floors and then into the basement felt like a million miles wedged up against the Chief's girth. As his body registered the recognisable shudder of the enclosed box grinding to a halt, Red breathed a sigh of relief and relaxed. That was a big mistake. The door flew open, and all at once he found himself grasping for purchase on the inner walls, the force of gravity propelling him backwards towards the cellar floor.

"Stop messing around, will you, sunshine? There's work to do." said the Chief, pushing past him.

Red longed to complain about the callous response to this near miss, but thought better of it. Stood at the entrance to the cells, it was impossible to forget the mind numbing hours of boredom sat in front of that same metal gate. The recruit on duty lay slumped on the small, round wooden stool that was the only item of furniture available. Pushed against the wall to create the next best thing to a backrest, the young man's head draped over his right shoulder. His mouth, wide open, tongue hanging and drool dripping from its tip, created a dark patch on his blue trousers.

The Chief bent at the hips until his lips were millimetres from the inexperienced man's ear and screamed, "You're finished!"

The comatose recruit launched into the air, as if fired from a catapult, dislodging the seat, clattering on to the hard concrete floor. "Chief, Sir, Chief," he bellowed, head jerking left and right. At the same time he tried to salute, but it looked more like face scratching, and Red had to turn aside, stifling laughter.

"Get out of my sight you useless piece of—" the boss said, mumbling the rest of the diatribe into his chest.

The unfortunate young man just nodded, crestfallen, handing the keys to Red and sped up into a sprint over to the lift and escaped.

There were only four cells organised into rows of two which faced each other, separated by a narrow passageway. As far as Red knew, this was the only occasion in history that a suspect had occupied any of them. Thick stone walls divided the chambers, and a solid steel door accessed each one. A musty aroma reminiscent of wet socks hung in the atmosphere, stubborn and unrelenting. They placed the pens in the basement for one reason—grinding down the resolve of prisoners with the reality of eternal night. A memory of childhood punishments, hours spent shut away in the cupboard under the stairs, invaded Red's consciousness like a contagion. He shuddered, thinking about spending a few minutes in solitary darkness, let alone many hours. If any single thing could be considered the ultimate deterrent against crime, this was it.

The deep groan of iron hinges followed the hollow clunk of the key, unlocking the first cell on the left-hand side. The compact area beyond the cell door welcomed the little light that seeped in, like blood congealing over a wound. On the far side of the box, buried into the rock, was a wooden bench upon which lay a brown bundle. And from the heap of beige came the soft purr of snoring.

"What the—?" inquired the Chief. Even in the basement's gloom, Red couldn't miss the deep scarlet rising from the irascible guard's collar along a saggy neck and clenched fists beating an urgent rhythm on his thighs. "Get up you filthy—"

Red was certain that the sentence ended with the word Defecto and that he had somehow stopped himself. As if to aggravate the boss further, Ezra stretched to full height, horizontal on the board, and yawned, the sound loud in the confined space. Then the manservant made a great show of rubbing his face and arranging his clothes before swinging both spindly legs around to face them.

"I could get used to having a lie in," Ezra said with a glint in his striking eyes.

By this point the irascible head of the guard was attacking his own lip with his teeth, face crimson from forehead to chin. "That can soon be arranged, sunshine. Get moving, it's time to answer our questions."

"Ask away. I've got nothing to hide. There's nothing more to tell you than I've already said."

"I'll be the judge of that," replied the Chief, grabbing Ezra by the sleeve and dragging him into the half-light of the cellar corridor.

"I don't think the night spent in the lock-up had the desired effect, Chief," Red said as the two men sat facing each other in the boss's room.

"If you're trying to irritate me, you're doing a superb job," the older man grumbled.

Ezra's interview had uncovered precisely nothing new. The Defecto denied stealing from his employers and repeated the lurid account of Mrs Hawkin's drinking habits. Seemingly, here was a fellow with few regrets who was not ashamed of the letters written about the Hawkin family. The one crack in the armour was an abundance of fraternal love and affection for his younger sister, and Ezra had devoted a disproportionate amount of the interview begging the Chief to search for the girl. The memory of the Defecto prostrate on the basement floor, clinging to the hem of the Chief's trousers, would haunt Red for years to come.

"Look, I realise you weren't keen before, but we can't afford to ignore what he's telling us about the sister, Val. We've never had a major crime, any crime, and now there's a murder and missing people. I'm sure they're connected, we just need to consider the facts more closely," Red ventured.

The boss studied his fingernails as if the answer might be recorded there in miniscule lettering. After a protracted awkward silence, he began tapping out a disjointed rhythm with the index fingers of each hand. Unusually, his face was a sea of calm, and Red brooded, smoothing his hair, waiting for a response.

"I thought we had an understanding," the older guard replied, emotionless. "But here I am repeating myself. I'm the Chief so I make the decisions," he added, voice rising in an alarming crescendo. "I give the orders and you follow them. This is your last and final warning. If we speak about this again, there will be serious consequences. Now get out of my office."

Red just about mustered a nod in agreement, followed by a slow retreat. Just as he was heading through the doorway, relieved that the conversation was over, the boss added for good measure, "And Red—so you know, I'll be speaking to your father."

Chapter Twenty-Two

"Ah, Quill, child, there you are. I've been waiting for you —again. I've been up for hours, trying to finish this new text charting the history of our wonderful city."

The Master sat in the usual place, hair tamed and smooth for once. Nothing about this demeanour hinted that, yesterday, they had found a dead body literally yards from his rooms. It was astonishing and infuriating. Whilst she'd decided to leave well alone, pretending it had never happened wasn't quite how she envisaged their lives moving forward.

"The City Guard have completed their work in the reading room and gave permission for it to be reopened along with the rest of the library," the elderly scholar declared, beaming a contented smile.

Quill couldn't altogether believe what she was hearing. He made it sound as if they'd been doing some private research. As opposed to the truth that a man's lifeless body had been laying on the carpet waiting to be discovered.

"We will return to business as usual. First, check the reading area and make sure everything is in order in there, and next, open the central library doors."

Unbelievable, he wasn't even going to ask about yesterday. If he wouldn't discuss it, she would have to broach the subject. "Master?"

"Yes?" he mumbled without looking up from the desk. "This isn't going to take all day, is it? You've got work to do and so have I."

"You do remember what took place yesterday?" Quill asked, shivering, still feverish.

"I may be old, but I'm not an absolute idiot. Of course I remember. But what's the point of dwelling on such matters? Each of us has a job to do and that must continue. The Guard will do their duty and we must do ours."

"But, your diary—"

"Yes, child, it's a green book. What about it?"

"I tried to tell you yesterday. Professor Hawkin's lab was a total mess. Glass chemical containers smashed all over the floor, his scientific papers scattered everywhere. It looked like someone had broken in and wrecked the place. Only, the doors were all unlocked, wide-open. It was difficult to figure out how to deal with the situation."

"Well, like I said, we don't have to piece it together. You need to stop filling your head with affairs that are none of your business," he replied abruptly.

Exasperated, Quill crouched down in front of him, staring straight up at his face, desperate for him to pay attention. "You don't get it. We didn't find your appointment book in the apartment, and that's what led us to search in the lab. That's how we discovered the mess. But that wasn't the worst of it. When we found the diary, it was right in the centre of the shambles, on top of the Professor's papers. The truth is, it looked strange, so I panicked, grabbed it and ran out of there as fast as possible. I'd hoped that the widow didn't notice, but I'm afraid running away made the appointment book being there look even more suspicious. And then circumstances went from bad to worse. Mrs Hawkin made a point of informing the Deputy all about the discovery and no doubt he's told the Chief. So cutting a long story short, they'll know you lied about the last meeting you had with the Professor. Why did you say you hadn't seen him for a few days? Why did you lie?" And finally Quill stopped. Every anxious thought that had been fermenting blurted out all at once. Breathless and panting hard, she had used up every ounce of energy, verbalising this tangle of thoughts.

The Master didn't respond immediately, didn't even glance up from his studies. And then, leaving her with no ambiguity as to his mood, responded in a low threatening tone, "Are you quite finished? I thought I had made myself very clear yesterday. Mark my words, I have no intention of answering such ridiculous questions."

"But, you need to understand that you're in danger. Even if you can't give me an answer, you should prepare one. The Chief is going to want an explanation. It looks suspect, as if you have something to hide. And I nearly forgot your boots. There were muddy prints on the laboratory floor and I,"

"You made a massive assumption," he cut-in, voice raised, emerald eyes blazing, "How dare you! Who do you think you are? I'm starting to think that I've been too lenient. We will not be discussing this any further. This conversation is over. You will prepare and open the reading room, followed by the main library. Once you've done, return at once to the Hawkin's residence. Lucinda needs help and support. She has lost both a husband and a servant. You are to replace Ezra for as long as the widow needs you. Do I make myself clear?"

And that was that. The firm set jaw and the inscrutable look around the corners of his eyelids confirmed his words. The topic was closed, and personal experience told her that continuing to press would risk alienating him further. As he was all she had, that risk was not worth taking. An image of being offered to the bereaved woman as a permanent fixture refused to budge. If that happened, there would be absolutely nothing she could do about it.

Nevertheless, staying put wasn't going to achieve anything useful either. A warning that the guard would be looking for answers was the best she could manage, and that had to count for something. During the heated exchange, a new plan emerged. The task would not be easy, but she wouldn't let fear stand in the way. If she had to serve the widow, then she would just have to make the best of a bad job. It might not be so terrible. After all, spending a few more days in that apartment sounded like a dream come true. And if she happened to work out what the Master was hiding in the process, that would be even better.

The overwhelming sense of déjà vu was difficult to ignore as Quill came to the outer courtyard on the north-eastern corner of the library, just as she had a day earlier. Relieved that yesterday's heavy rain had passed, the mid-morning sky filled with clouds, but they were the non-threatening, voluminous white variety. A strong breeze hugged the pentagonal perimeter. Bold and invigorating, she stood in its path for a few moments, grinning as it threatened to push her over. The feverishness seemed to evaporate with it, but remembering the poor dead butterfly darkened the mood once more. An internal magnetic force compelled her to look for it, even though she had no desire to see its broken body again. But it was nowhere to be seen, and she wondered if the current had carried it off, no trace left behind of it other than specs of multicoloured dust.

A repeated tapping vibrated through the passage. Confused, Quill searched all around for the source, but was entirely alone. The sound was rhythmical, beating louder, synchronised with her heartbeat. As she entered the shelter of the glass passageway, leaving the brisk squall behind her, the cause of the noise became clear. A woman in vertiginous heels headed away from the apartment and in her direction. The click, clack, tap of stiletto on polished concrete echoed through the glazed tunnel as if an army of women tottered towards her.

The female stared at the floor ahead, tracking every foot placement, an abundance of perfectly formed ash blonde shoulder-length curls hiding her face. Cuffs from a cream blouse poked out at the wrists of a navy blue tailored suit which hugged a voluptuous frame. The skirt was so narrow that it forced the unknown woman to take bird-sized steps, more than doubling the number of heel clicks and taps. The singular detail that distinguished her from the usual crowd of blue suits was those shoes. Not only did they add about five inches to her height and accentuate already shapely legs, but they were bright crimson with a silver heel. They were definitely a statement, although of what it was impossible to tell.

As they crossed on opposite sides of the walkway, the lady stole a glance across. The peek revealed a glimpse of flawless ivory skin beneath the golden ringlets. Quill covered her cheek, the shame of her own marked complexion rising in response. She couldn't help it. Whoever this person was, she was beautiful. The suited woman's shoulders rose and fell with each tiny step as she brushed something from her eye. Perhaps that was the reason for the hidden face. Maybe she was a grieving relative.

To prepare for what lay ahead, Quill took a deep breath. Arriving back at the front door of 1 Courtyard Place, she knocked and waited for an answer. As Quill lingered, she could still detect the blonde hair of the unidentified female, stopped in the exterior yard. It was fortunate that the glass walls of the passage afforded her an uninterrupted view. What was she doing? Quill teetered on tiptoe, craning her neck, trying to discover what the businesswoman was up to. After thirty seconds of inaction, the blonde's head turned in all directions and then she took an object out of a large leather briefcase. Strangely, it looked like another bag, though it was a distinctive orange colour. And then the object disappeared, and the woman hurried away.

"I was wondering when you'd get here, girl. Wit said he would send you over, and here you are. Don't just stand there, there's lots to do. I need you to help me clear out the Professor's things. The refuse collection is tomorrow and so it's sensible to get everything sorted today." Before she had even had a chance to draw breath, Mrs Hawkin shooed her, like a stray animal, into the room to the left of the entrance hall.

Ignoring the array of personal papers and effects piled high in a heap in the corner of the bedroom, it was a room of two halves. An imaginary line bisected the space along the centre of a queen sized bed as if two warring countries had built an invisible wall between them. Festooned on one side with a huge number of silk-covered turquoise cushions, while on the other sat a single crisp, cream pillow. The cushioned half complimented a mirrored bedside table covered in crystal bottles of scent and brightly coloured pots and tubes of face creams and anti-aging serums. It surprised Quill enormously to see these items, and she had no idea where the widow could have got hold of cosmetic products. Not legally, anyway. In contrast, the black table on the other side lay bare, all except one item, an inconspicuous brown leather-strapped wristwatch. Laid out over every single inch of the vast bed were the Professor's clothes. A lifetime's selection of suits, starched shirts and lab overalls. "We'll start by separating them into good quality recyclable items on the left and the older pieces for disposal on the right." And the widow pointed to either side of the bed.

Operating on auto-pilot, Quill began dividing the array of clothing as instructed. Was this actually happening? Mrs Hawkin was already removing all traces of her husband from their home. She knew that grief affected people in different ways, but this sounded highly unusual. "Oh, madam, I passed a young woman just now in the passage. Is she a relative? Only, she looked upset and so I assumed, you know, that it was about the Professor." Quill tried to inquire as nonchalantly as possible.

"You do have a habit of asking a lot of impertinent questions. The Master warned me."

Quill's toes curled, a lump in her throat which refused to budge.

"Not that it's any of your business. I assume you are referring to Ms Ginsburg. She's the family lawyer and visited to discuss the Professor's estate. I can't imagine what could have troubled the woman. The only relationship she has with our household is a professional one. Wit told me you have an active imagination so I suspect you were mistaken. Now, if you're finished with the interrogation, put the old items into this sack." And with that instruction, Mrs Hawkin handed over a bright orange pouch.

Instantly, the eye-catching citrus bag transported Quill backward an hour or two to the strange scene in the courtyard. A city rubbish sack. The lawyer must have been putting something into one of the many refuse silos that were dotted throughout the city. What seemed altogether illogical was bringing a bag of rubbish along to an important business meeting, and why dispose of it there? It was all very odd, but Quill was certain about what she had witnessed. Irrespective of Mrs Hawkin's opinion on the subject, the fascinating young lady had been crying. Quill just needed to work out why.

Chapter Twenty-Three

"I'll get that, madam," said Quill, heading toward the front door.

The loud knocking had made both of them jump, mainly because they were so engrossed in sorting the dead man's wardrobe. Stood on the threshold, the Chief of the Guard picked at his fingernails. The man's top lip curled into a sneer as he pushed past, not sticking around for an invitation. "Erm, Chief, excuse me, please wait while I check if Mrs Hawkin is available," Quill pleaded, trying to edge in front to force him to stop and wait. It was as if he couldn't hear her, or, more likely, chose to ignore her. The rude man strode into the living room and stood staring into the garden through the expanse of glass. He glared, sweating profusely, "I haven't got all day, just tell her I'm here."

"Chief, to what do I owe this pleasure? I really am rather busy, so would be grateful if you could tell me what you came to say and then be on your way." Mrs Hawkin appeared behind them in the hallway, causing them both to turn in the voice's direction in surprise.

"Good morning, madam, it's a pleasure to see you too. I thought you would want to be the first to know that we have had the preliminary findings from an examination of your husband's body. But, if you're too busy, then I will, of course, come back later."

Quill fiddled with a shirt collar, desperate to avoid this overly polite exchange. If it wasn't for the fact that something useful might crop up in conversation, she would have happily gone back to sorting clothes. Mrs Hawkin smiled a deprecating smile, and the guardsman took that as his cue to continue.

"I'm afraid it's my sad duty to inform you your husband did not die of natural causes. This is now a murder investigation!"

He's milking this, thought Quill, working ever so hard not to roll her eyes at the absurd announcement. Surely he didn't think finding a naked gentleman with an enormous dent in the back of his head usually suggested death by natural causes? Mrs Hawkin's face was stone-like, unreadable. To be honest though, that wasn't surprising as, apart from the odd moment, Quill saw first-hand how adept she was at maintaining an illusion of perfect grace and poise.

"Early indications are that the cause of death was a blow to the back of the skull, most likely inflicted with a bookend. And time of death, sometime between 11 pm and 6 am. These findings are all subject to change and, in particular, we are still waiting for various chemical tests."

"The only question that you haven't answered is whether you've charged Ezra with the crime, and if not why not?" Mrs Hawkin asked, fixing him with her sternest glare.

"Rest assured, my deputy is continuing to question the Defecto and I'm confident we'll soon charge him. But while that's going on, there remain a few loose ends that I need to tie up. First, it's vital to understand the Professor's movements and work commitments in the days leading up to his murder and wonder if you can point me in the right direction with this?"

Mrs Hawkin rubbed her hands down the front face of a black silk dress and, after a few moments of thinking, said, "I don't know what to tell you. He didn't involve me in his work and I didn't ask. I cannot understand why you think any of these details are important. You're holding the guilty man, just hurry up and prosecute him so we can all return to normal."

"It's just procedure, madam. Perhaps the Professor kept a diary?"

Quill gulped hard at the mention of a 'diary', goose bumps erupting on her arms and legs. The sound was so deafening in her head she was positive the others had heard it, too. A quick glance around confirmed they were not even aware of her existence anymore. She was a Defecto and thus irrelevant.

"Yes, now you come to mention it. He kept a log of appointments. I'll fetch it for you." Mrs Hawkin glided back into the bedroom and returned a few minutes later with a palm-sized brown hardback book, with the word 'appointments' etched onto the cover. The Chief took it from the widow and flicked through the pages, stopping every so often to study an entry. "Who is DC and who is MW?" he inquired.

A blood vessel in Quill's right temple pulsated, and she rubbed sweaty palms on her tunic, seeking to dry them.

"Mm, I can't be sure but would assume that DC stands for Doctor Cooper and the other entry is Master Wit." As Mrs Hawkin translated the initials, her gaze locked onto Quills, but it was over in a second.

"There are several entries for DC in the weeks in the run up to the murder. Any idea what they were meeting about?" he asked.

Mrs Hawkin tapped her right foot and sighed, "I've told you, I do not know," she said and stalked back toward the bedroom. The bereaved woman signified the end of their conversation.

Unwilling to accept the snub, the Chief followed, questions addressed to the woman's back. "And MW is in the diary for the day before yesterday?" he asked, throwing a knowing glance in Quill's direction as she brought up the rear. "I learned from Deputy Red that the Master's diary was in the lab, on top of the papers, and that this Defecto," he said, features distorted, a choking sound in the back of his throat, "removed it from a crime scene."

"Yes, that is correct. I can't state for definite that Wit was here, but it seems a reasonable assumption to make. Anything else and you'll have to ask him. Now, if that is all, I must go back to spring cleaning," Mrs Hawkin trilled, opening her front door and ushering the Chief through it.

"Oh, I almost forgot," the head of the guard added before the door had closed. "Forensics found an unusual mark under your husband's hair, behind the right ear. It's difficult to describe, like a swirl perhaps, in black. Any clue what it could be?"

"Absolutely none. Now good day." And Mrs Hawkin slammed the door shut.

Placing the last of the old clothes into the orange pouch, Quill mulled over the new snippets of information. There was no getting away from the facts. The Master faced a lot of tough questions. She remained hopeful that he would be more forthcoming with the Chief than he had been with her.

The fact the Professor had met with Doctor Cooper on several separate occasions didn't seem that unusual. People consulted their doctor for any number of reasons, none of which would be considered suspicious. On the other hand, she'd witnessed the physician's exceptionally strange behaviour with her own eyes and so made a mental note to find out more.

With the sack's handles tied into a tight, perfectly formed knot, it struck Quill suddenly that she was being presented with a perfect opportunity. "I'm taking the rubbish out now. While I'm there, I'll check on the Master and then I'll be back," she shouted to the widow and let herself out of the front door.

The sack was misshapen and cumbersome. It banged against Quill's shins as she held it out in front of her in both hands. Not wanting to draw attention to herself, she tried to walk slowly and steadily, but couldn't help breaking into a trot, eager to discover what the lawyer had thrown away. With any luck, the silo would be relatively empty, as she wasn't keen on the idea of rummaging through bags and bags of rubbish.

A heady floral scent saturated the air as Quill rounded the corner of the passageway and entered the courtyard. Occupied with thoughts of suspects and balancing the heavy orange bag, she barged straight into someone. Pitched off balance, she stumbled sideways. And, despite assuming she'd done an exceptional job with the knot, the contents of the sack spilled out all over the pavement. By the time she gathered herself and the unwanted clothes, whoever she bumped into had vanished.

The silo was a rectangular box with a semi-circular lid which lifted away from anyone disposing of their trash. It was wide enough to take the body of a grown adult, though where that thought came from she didn't know, and she struggled to push it aside. As she swung the cover wide open, Quill heaved a sigh of relief, greeted by the sight of only three orange sacks. A sickly, rotting smell of days' old food remnants soon clogged her nostrils, threatening to make her gag, but she pressed on regardless. As she grappled with the tie in the first sack, she questioned what she thought she was going to achieve. In all honesty, throwing rubbish out wasn't particularly revealing. After all, she was about to do just that. The disintegrated potato peelings and mouldy cabbage leaves told a story, but not one anyone was interested in hearing.

Quill was about to give up when she noticed that the last pouch looked quite different from the other two. Plumper and curved, more like the bag she was about to throw away. Content she'd nothing to lose, she swapped her sack for the one she had yet to explore.

The knot slipped open almost at once. She was right. This bag also contained clothing. Pulling out the uppermost garment, it had a stiff collar and cuffs, much like the Professor's shirts. And yes, there sat his monogram, 'A.H.', embroidered in red on the top of the pocket. Perhaps Mrs Hawkin had already flung out a few items before she'd arrived.

Quill teased the shirt out, stepping backward, holding it at arms-length, creating as much distance from it as possible. Her mouth dropped open, and she felt as if somebody had deflated her with a single blow. A reddish-brown stain covered the rear of the garment from collar to hem, thicker at its outer edges than in the centre. With a racing pulse, she screwed the item into a tight ball, shoved it straight into the refuse sack and, ignoring the rest, sprinted back to the library.

Chapter Twenty-Four

A numb, icy chill expanded from Quill's core, seeping into every living cell as, collapsing onto the bed, she realised that her hands still clutched the orange bag. White-knuckled fingers gripped the garish plastic, as if survival depended on its preservation. In the overwhelming panic and fear, she had unintentionally brought the incriminating evidence with her. What was she going to do now? The right thing to do was to turn the sack over to the guard but, how would she explain herself? The Chief's low opinion of Defectos would be an obstacle. She pictured the scenario; explaining that a well-respected lawyer throwing out the rubbish had looked odd and as a result she'd rummaged through a silo and by complete coincidence found the Professor's bloodstained shirt. Even knowing that it represented the truth, the story sounded utterly ridiculous.

Quill thought about putting the sack back, but couldn't ignore the worrying thoughts about being seen. As her breathing slowed, she saw things more clearly. Faced with no other choice. She would have to hide the bag in her room and wait for a better opportunity to get rid of it. The idea troubled her conscience. She knew the plan was wrong. If anyone had asked her a couple of days ago if she'd suppress key evidence relating to someone's murder, she would have had no problem answering with a definite 'no'. How quickly everything changed. It seemed that life wasn't as black-and-white as she'd always assumed. People weren't as straightforward as they appeared, and the city in which she lived had problems. All of which came as a total surprise.

Quill couldn't just hand the sack over. That option was too dangerous, both for her and the Master. Resigned to the impossible choice she faced, Quill lay face down on the floor and pushed the pouch under the bedstead as far as it would go. The plump shape nestled snugly against the Lilith-bird box, behind the pile of library books which still needed to be returned. No one ever showed up here, so discovery was improbable, and there seemed no reason that should change.

Chapter Twenty-Five

The indistinct murmur of voices inside the study was enough to stop Quill in her tracks. Tuned into the unfamiliar sounds, she strained to make out who the voices belonged to, but it was impossible to tell. The Master receiving visitors wasn't an unusual occurrence, so why was she getting that sweaty palmed feeling?

She knocked and let herself in, keeping her gaze at her feet. The Master had taught her well. He only invited the most important members of Scolaris society into his private rooms and they all demanded the utmost respect.

The Chief's physique was recognisable at once, draped in that dreary tan overcoat. Quill swallowed hard, hands clasped together, taut like a compressed spring. No one noticed her arrival, as usual, and she concealed herself in the best spot, watching the action from the shadows.

"Professor Hawkin's log suggests you met at some stage on the day of the murder. You didn't mention that. I need you to explain why," the Chief asked.

"I've told you everything I can remember. What else do you want me to say? I may have seen him, and maybe I didn't. Sorry, I just can't be certain. Every detail I've given you is the truth to the best of my recollection."

Quill clamped her lips together to prevent herself from interrupting. Why was he pretending that he was a forgetful old man? He was as sharp as a shard of glass and knew full well that he'd seen the Professor on that day. He'd said as much to her when he sent her to collect his diary. What was he up to?

"So here's the problem. We have the Prof's appointment book which tells us that the two of you were due to meet. And then, Mrs Hawkin informs us that your diary was in the lab on top of all the Professor's papers. Now, the physical state of that room suggests that some criminal activity took place there. And for the time being, we're assuming whatever happened is related to the crime. So, I'm asking you again, think carefully, don't rush, what were you doing with the Professor in his lab on the day of the crime?"

"How can I make myself any clearer? I cannot recall meeting Alexander on the day in question. No idea why my diary was there. What I can say, however, is that any discussions between myself and the Professor are protected. The long established rule of privilege extends to all dealings between representatives of The Protectorate. I am surprised, Chief, that a man in your position is ignorant of the law."

The Chief's raised eyebrows echoed Quill's surprise. Everybody knew about these rules, but did they still apply for a murder case?

The middle-aged guard stepped towards the Master's desk, closing the physical distance between the two of them. "Thank you most kindly for reminding me about the rules," he teased, "though correct me if I'm wrong, while you don't have to disclose what you discussed, I don't think you can avoid confirming one way or another whether you met."

The Master paused, fingertips pressed to his lips, and added "You are quite correct but I believe I have answered those queries to the best of my ability."

Nobody spoke or made eye contact for a few awkward moments of total silence. A tiny speck of hope germinated. The Chief seemed to have run out of questions, and the Master's superior grasp of the legislation had thrown everyone off balance. The two men arrived at an impasse and the minutes paused as, muttering in whispers under her breath, she willed him to leave.

But then, a young man in blue dashed all those hopes in an instant as he rushed in from the kitchen, sporting a knowing grin and holding aloft a large pair of soggy black boots.

A gasp rushed from Quill's mouth at such speed that nothing she could do could prevent it. All three gentlemen turned, alerted to her presence. It didn't last, and their attention quickly returned to the matter at hand. "Chief, I found these back there. They look like a match for the footprints on the floor of the laboratory. Someone's tried to clean them, there's a muddy mess in the sink and if you look closely, they didn't do a great job. See, there's still bits of mud stuck in the tread."

Quill couldn't believe it. How had she been so brainless? What fool tries to remove evidence, fails in spectacular fashion and leaves more clues in the process? She had to say something, "Please, it was—"

"Quill, be quiet. No-one asked for your opinion." The Master interrupted before she confessed her clumsy part in the clean-up operation. And the glare told her that this was deliberate. Why didn't he want her to own up?

Before she had any chance to ponder further, the Chief reached over the desktop and, grasping the old man's left arm, smiled and said, "You'll be coming with me now."

If the change of circumstances alarmed the Master, it didn't show, and another withering scowl let the guard see he didn't appreciate being manhandled. The scholar rose slowly, straightening out the desktop, ensuring all was in order, something he rarely bothered with under normal circumstances. Preparing to go with the escort, he turned to Quill and added, "You're in charge until I get back. Everything must continue just as it always has. Understood?"

Quill nodded and whispered, "Yes, Master. You can count on me."

The elderly man forced a thin-lipped smile and just as they headed out of the door he called out, "And don't forget to wind the clock. You remember how it loses time otherwise." And then they left, leaving Quill all alone.

A perfectly formed teardrop fell onto Quill's right cheek. The sudden dampness startled as she slumped in a melancholy stupor on the faded study carpet. The water droplet trickled along the length of her face and pooled in the crevice at the corner of her mouth. A salty tang invaded her taste buds, and repulsed, she swiped the tear away. Every so often, the thought of her father was sad, but she had learnt not to dwell on it. To be honest, often she blamed herself for him leaving, but this was different. There could be no doubting that this disaster was all her fault. Fear threatened to breach her defences. Those she'd erected over the years since his disappearance. With knees clamped to her chest, retreating from the pain, she crawled into the forest of carpet fibres, willing the moment to pass.

The sound of rain battering the window behind the desk woke her and stiff limbs and a glance toward the soft tick, ticking tidal timepiece confirmed Quill had slept through lunch. What did the Master mean about winding that clock? He'd expounded on countless occasions what a feat of engineering it was, run on the expansion and contraction of nothing more than a volume of air. The strain had surely gone to his brain. Struck by a sudden pang of guilt thinking of him, she wondered if they fed prisoners. He ate little, but she wished she'd the sense to feed him lunch before the Chief so unceremoniously took him away.

The emotional crisis ebbed, watered down by sleep. But fear remained, nibbling at Quill's edges with razor-sharp teeth. What would become of her? If they found the Master guilty, they would strip him of his place on The

Protectorate and remove him as Custodian of the Library. And where would that leave her? Perhaps they would allow her to stay? She shook her head. The chances were that she would end up being dragged into this mess. Not least having made things worse by running off with the diary and the half-hearted attempt at cleaning. Why hadn't she listened to the old scholar, not interfered? Panic drove her to acts of total stupidity. As Quill searched her conscience, the realisation that fear might not be entirely to blame rose to the surface. She had honestly believed that she was clever enough to solve the murder, and that arrogance might haunt her forever. Knowledge was King and seeking it was one thing, but what you did with it, another.

The pounding of the rainfall lessened, and with it descended a sense of quiet determination. Quill had a list of plausible suspects: Mrs Hawkin, Ezra, Theo Penrose, Ms Ginsburg, The Master and Doctor Cooper. All she needed to do now was decide what to do with it.

Picturing the stoic look on the venerable man's face as they'd carted him off, reminded Quill that the Chief mentioned recent appointments between the Professor and the Doctor. She kept coming back to the memory of the sickly man acting suspiciously in the living room. And that reminded her of Kai and an offer of friendship, something she'd readily dismissed. But perhaps that had been the wrong decision. A friend might be very useful right now. Quill made a vow to be much more careful, to plan her actions and consider their consequences. If she worked methodically, it was just possible that the situation was salvageable.

Chapter Twenty-Six

Quill trudged to Serenity Gardens, the distance seeming to have doubled in less than twenty-four hours. Arriving at Doctor Cooper's, she fought the urge to turn and run. "Hi," she said to Kai, voice cracking as he appeared at the front door.

"You're back," he replied, a relaxed look spreading down from his lips through his shoulders.

"How could you tell it was me? Wait, don't say anything, I know, there's more to seeing than using the eyes."

Kai beamed. "Glad to find out I've taught you something. So, is it medicinal herbs or my charming company you're after?"

Quill laughed, and it felt good. The sensation was unfortunately fleeting, as the seriousness of the situation brought her crashing back to reality. Somehow, and she really had no idea how, the boy did the mind reading trick again as stepping outside he asked, "Are you okay? What's happened?" Pulling the door to, he stood so close that the warmth of his breath tickled her face. So with closed eyelids, Quill tried to experience the moment as he did.

Quill shook her head, eyes open once more, freeing herself from the unknown sensations. She liked him, but could he be trusted? Recent experience suggested it was unwise to trust her own instincts, let alone someone else's. Now it was important to tread carefully. "I suppose you've heard about the murder?" she inquired in an even voice, the tone conversational.

"I can't imagine there's anyone who hasn't. People assume this district is all peace and relaxation, but I don't think that covers a murder. And, I had to deliver Mrs Hawkin's sleeping remedy. She insisted I come in and told me all about it. At first I assumed she was just like all the rest, treating me like a pity case, but then, I don't know. I got the impression she was genuinely lonely, and that's how life had been for a long while."

And there it was again, this innate ability to see through to the heart of people. How did somebody so young get to be so perceptive? The talent was admirable, but also on the wrong side of terrifying. It had been shallow before, to be glad that he was blind so he couldn't see her marked cheek. But worse still was the growing realisation he might already have seen that she was as ugly on the inside as outside.

"Whatever's gone on, it can't be that bad. Come on, you can tell me. Like I said the other day, it would be great to have a friend and you can count on me. I'd be a great friend to have."

Perhaps he hadn't worked out her flaws quite as well as she'd thought. He seemed to be genuine and at that precise moment, there weren't many other options. So, sitting side by side on the doorstep, looking out onto the green, Quill explained the whole sorry story.

"What are you going to do?" Kai's voice broke the silence that clung to the air between the pair like dense smog. The tale of woe took surprisingly little time to tell, but by the end it had sapped her of energy. With nothing left to give, the question hung in the ether. But he didn't seem to mind the quiet, and Quill sensed the faint touch of his arm against hers. Eyes closed, she imagined absorbing energy through the minute point of contact and with relief, that soothed and she grew lighter, re-energised.

"Who knows?" said Quill, shoulders shrugging. "Can't just sit around watching my entire life disintegrate. If the Master is guilty, it'll mean losing everything. This might sound stupid, but I need to find any information that could prove his innocence. I don't want to put you in an awkward position but wonder if you know anything about the Doctor and the Professor meeting up over the last few weeks?"

"Hey, I want to lend a hand, but I need this job. You can't imagine how tough it's been trying to find someone to give me a chance. If I help out, you need to promise to keep my name out of it."

Kai was a contradiction, a boy hidden under an independent outer skin, worn as a coat of armour.

Embarrassed, she hadn't even stopped to consider the consequences of involving him. So much for being more careful, "I'm so sorry, forget that I asked,." Quill said and rose from the doorstep, preparing to leave.

Kai grasped her hand, pulling her backward. "Stop, why are you running away? I didn't say I wouldn't help."

"I'm not running away. But I shouldn't have expected you to get involved. That was selfish. You're still a boy and a blind one at that. Honestly, I don't know what I was thinking," Quill said, words tumbling out, unfiltered. To her dismay, she felt his grip loosen, the realisation of what she'd said hit home. But it was too late. The words couldn't be unsaid.

The gap between the two widened into a yawning chasm and she wished, at that moment, to throw herself off the edge and free fall into space.

"If you've quite finished, I said I'd back you up and I will. I might be blind but I'm not useless." Kai's defiant statement cut through like a jagged blade and then plunged in deeper. "Why are you so angry? You do know that mark on your cheek isn't a big deal? And, to be honest, it's sort of well," and then he added in a whisper, "beautiful."

"What?" Quill asked, hand darting to cover cheek. "How? I assumed you couldn't see me. I don't understand," she added, a hot flush creeping upward from the base of her neck.

"You're right, mostly I can't. But when we're close, like this, in the daylight, I can make out contrasting colours and sometimes even shapes."

"Why didn't you say so before? You said you were blind," she said, fighting back bitter tears.

"I am blind. You just chose your version of what that means. I bet you do that a lot. Make assumptions."

"Thanks for the character assassination," she replied, like a petulant child. "And as for the offer of friendship, you've got a funny way of going about it."

"Perhaps it's your idea of friendship that's wrong. Friends tell each other the truth, no matter how difficult that might be. Don't you agree?"

Quill sat, contemplating, "Maybe. I'm not sure I've ever considered the details because, well, I've never had one."

"Me either, but I've spent a long while imagining what it would be like. I really do want to be friends and look, I'm sorry for offending you. Maybe we should just get back to the murder?"

The irony! It was less complicated to talk about a murder than about becoming friends. Quill nodded, and the young man continued. "The Professor and the Doctor have been meeting during the last few weeks. I let him in at least half a dozen times and, to be honest, should've realised that it was odd then."

Interrupting, she asked, "What do you mean odd?"

"Well, he smelt weird, the Professor, like he was wearing ladies' perfume weird. And, most of the meetings took place in the doc's private living room. In fact, come to think of it, I never took Hawkin through to the clinic where patients are usually examined. And that's not all. They always shut the door, but for the last couple of weeks I'm fairly sure they were arguing. At least, I heard raised voices. Just wish I could explain what they were shouting about but I don't know."

"When you say his private living room, do you mean this one?" Quill asked, realising at once that pointing was useless and improving the description might yield better results. "The room to the left of the front door, at the front of the house, looking out onto the courtyard?"

"Yeah, how could you tell? No one's allowed in there."

"I have a confession to make. That last evening I was here, while you passed on the widow's message, I might have been nosing through the front window." She shifted weight from one foot to another and, focusing on her feet, dug down into the white courtyard stones with alternate big toes. "What I saw was strange. Supposedly the Doctor was too busy with patients to come to the door but I watched him, in that room, hiding something. Your boss put whatever it was in the big terracotta pot on the right-hand side of the fireplace."

Kai looked up towards the sky and she assumed he was examining the information, but what came next was not at all expected. "Is that why you're annoyed?"

Quill frowned. "What? Why would anyone be cross about the doc hiding something?"

"That's not what I meant. You assume I lied to you, that I knew the clinic wasn't busy."

The revelation was startling. Yet again, he knew her thoughts even before she did. Kai was correct, she'd jumped to the conclusion that he was a liar. "I'm not one hundred per cent sure what I believed. It wouldn't be the first time that a servant received instructions to stretch the truth in the name of duty. And anyway, why are you being so defensive? Everything I learned about the crime, I've told you. So I can't have decided you're that bad, can I?"

"Mm, I suppose not. Anyway, no doubt that was a fair conclusion to reach. But I swear it wasn't a lie. The doctor told me he was busy in the clinic and couldn't speak to you. Come to think of it, there are two separate doors into that room. One from the main hallway which leads here, to the front door, and another one on the far side of the room. So, he must've used the other entrance or I would've heard him following behind in the corridor."

Quill realised at once that he was telling the truth. It explained how the doctor had turned up in a corner of the room furthest away from the hallway.

"Wait there!" Kai dashed back inside the house, navigating like an expert, with outstretched fingertips.

"Kai, Kai, wait. What?" she called after him through gritted teeth, but it was a waste of breath as he'd already vanished. Quill paced, chomping at already ragged cuticles. What was the boy going to do? And then Kai reappeared, brandishing a small object.

"This, this was in that pot. It's a key, but a key to what?" Kai asked.

"Are you mad? What were you thinking? You'll get caught," Quill said, peering around the side of him, expecting the doctor to appear at any second and catch them.

"You wanted to see what he was hiding? Well, here you are," he said, handing over the key. It was small and brass and definitely looked like a key to the reading room, but unless she tried it in the lock, there was no way to be sure. She shouldn't take it though, should she? Reminded of her recent solemn vow to stop making hasty decisions, the answer was obvious. No, taking the key was far too dangerous. If Doctor Cooper discovered it had gone, the consequences for Kai would be too catastrophic to contemplate. Another opportunity might arise, but not today. So, seizing his left hand, she pressed the key into palm, closing four fingers gently around it. "Thanks, now go. Put this back in the pot."

He smiled, nodded, and turned away, heading toward the door. "And Kai," Quill said.

"Yes?"

"Be careful."

"Careful's my middle name," he said, winking as he served up a fresh serving of boyish grin.

Quill chuckled. Kai was annoying and rude and ridiculous, but she couldn't help herself.

Chapter Twenty-Seven

Ever since the Chief's return from 1 Courtyard Place, home of the Hawkins, the entire contingent of guards had been subdued. Heads turned down, studying the array of paperwork generated by the murder investigation. The fact the boss hadn't spoken to anyone since returning, remaining holed up inside his office, banging and slamming filing cabinet drawers, suggested there might be a problem. Red decided to leave the man alone, allow him a moment to calm down, even though a curious nature urged the opposite course of action.

In the meantime, several house calls to residents of the Engineering District confirmed their prime suspect had talked to Val's neighbours that morning, trying to track the young girl's whereabouts. That part of Ezra's account was true. As Red finished writing up detailed records of those conversations, the boss emerged, a brown hardback pressed to his chest, looking grim and heading his way. "What's up Chief?" said Red.

"This," the old fellow replied, throwing the book down onto Red's notes, sending them flying, "it's the Prof's appointment log. On the day of the murder a couple of interesting entries appear, one is a meeting with Master Wittgenstein and the other is for a Mr. Dodds, 2.30 pm, Central Square. Next to that entry it says, 'Ezra?'. I hate to admit it but maybe a meet-up took place after all."

Red nodded and added, "I agree. And I've been able to confirm that Ezra spoke to Val's close neighbours first thing yesterday morning. Which means, so far, the whole statement checks out."

The Chief huffed, blowing air into his cheeks and forcing it out again, hissing through clenched teeth, "The Defecto must be guilty of something. Keep searching. If we can't find holes in the story soon, we'll have to release him."

"Yes, sir," said Red, acknowledging that this was the first sensible contribution the Chief had made since the start of the case. Perhaps he wasn't as stubborn and stuck in old-fashioned ways as he appeared.

Chapter Twenty-Eight

The curved wooden slats of the bench caressed Quill's lean legs, spine pressed hard against the backrest. With an upturned gaze, a gentle breeze kissed her cheeks. The seat reclined, tucked away under the tallest of the immense trees that lined the green in front of Doctor Cooper's home. Stumped where to go or what to do next, the spot looked so inviting. White pillow clouds scudded across the stratosphere at speed, but the tree line offered protection, shielding much of the force of the wind. The sky wept spring blossom. It filled the air and coated the ground with white ashes. She glanced toward the house and couldn't help wondering where Kai was, hoping everything was okay. The youthful man had struck more than one raw nerve, and she still felt the effects of their exchange. According to him, the mark looked beautiful, and she hadn't questioned it, not even cautioned him that the law forbade such talk. Through her subconscious she probed, trying to learn why, but struggled to turn up an answer. In any case, Kai talked nonsense. To be blunt, the blemish was a stain, something she dreamed of wiping away. The expression on strangers' faces was always the same, a mix of horror and morbid fascination. Deformed, she challenged the fabric of society. People who accepted that celebrating beauty was crass, unsure how to react to the complete opposite—ugliness in its crudest form. Was it even allowed? To be disgusted by disfigurement and say so? Especially when the rules demanded all Scolarians to abandon the pleasures of pretty things in favour of intellectual progress. This summed up the paradox that her existence posed.

Kai had been correct. It wasn't fair, and she did get angry. Nobody chose to look this way, but then neither had he asked to be blind. They had more in common than she wanted to admit. What had he suggested? Something about the peril of being defective and a Defecto. Now she understood that applied to them both.

Memories of Kai brought back thoughts of the hidden key. Quill was about as sure as anyone could be that it would unlock the reading room. A few days ago she'd assumed the Master alone possessed one, but now here she was contemplating not only the Professor having a key but also Doctor Cooper. Hawkin owning one made sense. After all, a Protector should enjoy certain privileges, but why the Doctor? Despite wracking her brain, no obvious explanation emerged. The list of unanswered questions grew longer and longer, with no end in sight.

The rare sound of whistling crescendoed through the open air, an open statement of defiance. Vision strained, scanning the grass and across to the road. The tune came from a lone figure in the trademark brown uniform, striding along, leaning into the draught. It must be Old Jed, she decided. But as the individual drew closer and Quill's eyesight adjusted, it became abundantly visible that she was mistaken. To her dismay, astonished, she saw the last person she expected.

Ezra? It was Ezra; the guard had released him!

"Wait, wait, Ezra, stop," Quill shouted, running after him until her eyes watered and lungs burned with the exhaustion and she could run no more. Hands on knees, bent double, gasping for every breath, she rubbed away the effects of the lactic acid build-up in her muscles. "Please, I need to talk to you," she gasped, one final desperate attempt to get the man's attention.

Finally, Ezra stopped and turned, a frown creeping down to his chin. "Oh, it's you. What do you want? I'm in a hurry."

Then Quill remembered the grimace was more like a permanent scowl and wasn't truly an indicator of anything other than a sour disposition.

"I thought you were at Guard HQ, answering questions?" she said.

"I was. And now I'm not. What's it matter to you?"

What an unpleasant individual, she reflected. "I just wondered if you saw Master Wittgenstein while you were there? Have they freed him too?"

Ezra scoffed. "Why would they release a murderer? I didn't see him, but from what I overheard they're pretty confident they've got the right man, which means I'm off the hook. And here I am!" He threw his arms open and angled his face skyward, as if announcing his freedom to the entire universe. "To be honest, I can't say I blame him. I wish I had killed him. I wouldn't mind putting an end to that stuck up wife of his either."

Light-headed, Quill questioned if she was hearing things. Had he honestly just admitted to wanting to wipe out the Professor and his wife? Released? How? Why? The whole situation was unbelievable. Never mind, the details were irrelevant at that point. Ezra was free, and that was that. Concentrate, she told herself, glean whatever information might be relevant. "Right, I see," she responded, remaining calm and appearing non-judgmental. "Why do you dislike them so much? They're well respected, and he was a Protector."

Ezra shook his head. "They've fooled you. Just because you have a powerful position doesn't make you a good person and in my experience it's more likely to be the opposite. Alexander was happy to do whatever it took to justify his status. No concern for who he trampled on in the process. Take the latest project, the building of his precious observatory; it wasn't even his idea. He stole it from that Penrose." He chuckled to himself, as if remembering something amusing. "Now I come to think of it, they had a blazing row about it last week and Penrose threatened to kill him. A man after my own heart!" and he smirked again.

"But that can't be true," she said, more to herself than to him.

"Huh?" he said.

"Theo Penrose. He acted as if he didn't know the Professor's name was on the plans."

"Well, he did, and that's a fact."

Quill grabbed the sleeve of his tunic, rattled his arm. "Did you report this to the guard? When they questioned you, please tell me you told them."

He pulled away. "Get your mitts off me. No, I didn't. Why should I care? It's nothing to do with me."

"You have to go back, with me, and explain it to them." She was frantic. The Master was in real trouble.

"I'm not going anywhere except to look for my Val. She's missing but no-one will listen to me. Why should I help the guard? They won't help the likes of me, or you, for that matter. Face reality, we're nobody and we have to take care of ourselves." And with that stark statement ringing in Quill's ears, Ezra spun on his heels and tramped away.

Quill charged up-and-down, carving a deep rut in the roadway, clenching and unclenching fists, muttering and moaning under her breath. The nerve of that man. What was his problem? How could someone be so bitter and twisted? Unconvinced that what he said was true, the situation looked more and more bleak. If only she had persuaded the miserable old Defecto to repeat the story about Penrose to the Guard.

Time evaporated again. Still, what was the point of hoping to change something that had already been and gone? Quill needed to focus on the here and now. What were the options? What should come next?

The speed of Quill's pacing slowed and, concentrating on the soles of her feet pressed against the road, she homed in, sensing a multitude of stone chips jutting into the bottom of her moccasins. Like being stabbed by miniature knives. But strangely, it felt pleasant. Grounded in reality, the tiny pulses of pain doused the lingering embers of outrage and rescued the power of rational thought.

The state of affairs at first looked clearer. It had been a waste of energy struggling to convince Ezra he should help the Master. So now would be a suitable moment to find an alternative solution. If only that were as straightforward as it sounded. But with a mind which resembled the Master's study, the grey matter so chaotically disordered that it was impossible to tidy up without the lot collapsing, she was at a loss. Imagining being buried under the pile provoked a growing tightness in her rib cage, dizziness and confusion. Claustrophobic, Quill scrambled, squeezing her forehead, trying to restore stability, but over-thinking just increased the confusion.

As she was about to concede defeat, a new possibility presented itself. Perhaps making sense of the case was unnecessary? Just persuade the guard that there were possibilities other than the Master. Why hadn't she considered it before? Could it honestly be that straightforward? There could only be one way to find out, and standing around speculating wasn't going to achieve anything. She would make them listen, one way or another, regardless of whether they liked it.

Chapter Twenty-Nine

A fine mist of drizzle moistened the atmosphere as Quill arrived in the legal district. With each new footstep, thighs and calves and ankles whinged and complained. A growing cacophony, lamenting the hardship of the miles covered.

This district was the only one on the original map that remained unexplored. Fortunately, there had been no reason to visit personally and, until then, neither had the Master. Quill wondered how to track down Guard HQ, but needn't have worried. From the Science District a distinctive building in the distance, a smaller version of the library on stilts, was impossible to miss. It conjured a hazy memory of the Master recounting that the architect had modelled the newer building on the pentagonal construction of the old. Later he'd perched it on top of cement legs, a sentinel in the centre of Law and Order. It was the ultimate compliment to the designer of the Great Library, a man whose name she couldn't recall and who had long since turned to dust.

As Quill drew closer, the construction filled more and more of the horizon and declared itself as nothing better than a poor imitation. A concrete sham jutting into the skyline like a pustular boil in a district otherwise packed with sleek, opaque glass-fronted office blocks. Was the unattractive design a deliberate attempt to remind the occupants of the dangers of celebrating the aesthetic? It was impossible to get away from the fact that it made a strong, visual statement.

Nevertheless, arriving at last, wobbly legged like a newborn lamb, at the front of the headquarters, Quill let out a huge gasp of relief. What amused her less were the significant number of enormous steps which had to be climbed up to the double doors guarding the entrance. A trembling feverishness returned and pangs of hunger and exhaustion sapped what little strength remained.

Collapsed in a heap on the bottom step, Quill took a few minutes' rest to catch her breath and then face whatever obstacles lay ahead. Head in hands, she heard approaching footsteps. Moving was simply not an option in her current physical state, she decided. With plenty of room, whoever it was could steer around her. As the footsteps got nearer, she picked up a waft of sweetness, cherry blossom and honey, followed closely by the quiet, high-pitched mutterings of at least two people, deep in conversation. A grin formed as she guessed from the perfumed air and nature of the voices that a pair of women advanced toward her. Maybe she was better at this investigating business than she had given herself credit for.

Reality hit hard the moment the people passed by. Quill glanced up and saw the small, rotund frame of a man and the whisper of a glimpse of womanly curves on his far side. The lengthy, wispy brown ponytail snaking down the man's back was instantly recognisable as was the understandable confusion caused by the high-pitched tone. It was Mr. Penrose.

How was this possible? Yet again, the guard was releasing a prime suspect. Now was the moment to act, so forcing herself up from the ground, she called out to him, "Mr. Penrose, excuse me, Mr. Penrose."

Theo Penrose did a double-take, stopping in mid-conversation, the reaction to hearing his name etched in a stiff, fake smile. "Can I help you?" he squeaked.

"Oh, I hope so."

"Who are you?" he asked, looking Quill up and down and dry-washing his hands in response to her dishevelled appearance.

"I don't know if you recognise me. We met at Professor Hawkin's lab yesterday. I'm Quill, I work for Master Wittgenstein." With each fresh nugget of information she hoped he would remember, but he continued to look at her blankly until the very last mention of the Master's name.

"I see," he responded, squinting hard through his enormous round spectacles. In any other circumstances, his remark would have been comical. "I don't think I should speak to you," he added, and he turned and walked away.

"Please, don't go," she begged, trotting after him like a lost child. Quill reached out, touching his arm, and said, "What did you tell them? Have you seen him?" She regretted making physical contact almost immediately. His size clearly belied his strength, and before she could register what had happened, he sent her sailing through the air. Landing in a crumpled mess on the pavement, she narrowly avoided striking the nearest step with her forehead.

"Never touch me again," Penrose screeched. The duo loomed over her like demented apparitions. "Released? They didn't hold me captive! My civic duty is complete, a waste of time if you ask me, but I answered their preposterous questions. I've done nothing illegal and anyway, as soon as my wife explained we were together all evening and all night, they didn't really have much choice."

The woman was Mrs. Penrose then, and she was Theo's alibi. How very convenient. The smell of perfume was overwhelming now that she cowered directly beneath them, and the sweetness had made way for a cheap, acrid undertone. They were an odd couple. Not that a great deal of Mrs. Penrose was visible as she squatted on the tarmac in their shadows. A lustrous head of jet black hair descended into an overgrown, bushy fringe through which peeped a faint glimmer of violet eyes and garish, sunflower yellow drop earrings. Mrs. Penrose towered over her husband, though that could doubtless apply to just about all the adult population of Scolaris.

"Come away Theo. You've said too much already," the honeyed voice of the woman urged. And then, just like Ezra, they had gone, and left her to pick herself up and check for broken bones. Fortunately, nothing appeared to be damaged, other than pride. The brown tunic clung like a second skin, soaking up the pool of water collecting at the base of the steps like a dishcloth. And both wrists throbbed, scraped and bruised where she had saved herself from being knocked unconscious. A surface graze along the edge of the left hand, below the little finger smarted and on closer inspection it was full of particles of grit and mud. Quill rinsed it in the puddle, wincing now that her senses had woken up again.

Bruised, battered and in pain, she imagined crawling away like a wounded animal, waiting for the whole awful saga to be over. Who could blame her? If only it was an option, but self-preservation wasn't the only consideration when more than just her future was at stake. Whatever the Master had got involved in, he desperately needed help, whether or not he wanted it.

Chapter Thirty

The buzz of voices cut off, the sudden silence deafening, as ten pairs of eyes scrutinised every move Quill made as she entered the principal office of the City Guard. Instinct urged her to hide the facial deformity, the habit entrenched and unshakeable, but, standing there alone and exposed in the doorway, every part of her froze.

Curls of discoloured paper hung off the interior walls like surrendered convicts. A distinct stomach-churning smell of greasy meat and sweat clogged and strangled her airways. The whole place smelt as if it could do with fumigating. Every guard had quit working to stare. Whether it was the customary shock of seeing her marked face or they were not used to meeting a young woman in their workplace, especially not a Defecto girl, was unclear.

"Please, I need to speak to the Chief," Quill said to the nearest guard, who answered with a snort of laughter.

"Get back to work," came the gruff voice of the Chief, cutting through the school yard mentality, and the guards obeyed at once, returning to their paperwork. "Don't know what you want girl, but you'd best come to my office."

The guardsman's use of the word 'girl' grated on her nerves once again, but she followed, avoiding the stares, glares, and pointed mutterings of the men.

The Chief's room looked just as she'd imagined. The man slid into a huge swivel chair, which creaked and groaned, protesting at the weight of him. His desk was even bigger than the Masters' and he settled his hands on the desktop, as if comforting an old friend. Though looking at it made her wonder if the man had any friends. The work table cried out for love and attention. Its top and rear bore deep scratches and dents, but in contrast, the sides provided a hint of former glory. Their high shine finishes the colour of succulent red cherries.

A picture gallery on the wall behind the desk displayed a row of distinguished-looking men, all in the recognisable blue uniform. A glance from the Chief to the wall and back again confirmed the family resemblance. Commonplace in Scolaris; occupations were passed down from one family member to the next—sons followed fathers who followed grandfathers who followed great-grandfathers, ad infinitum. Quill remembered her own father, Master Wittgenstein's Defecto before her. Where was he? A twinge of pain accompanied the familiar unanswered question and, inadvertently, Quill reached for the mark on her face.

As Quill's gaze left the pictures of distant relatives, an unusual object, pride of place on top of a battered metal filing cabinet in the far corner, drew her attention. A large, triangular-shaped piece of rock. In the main it was a dark metallic grey, but also contained flecks of red and brown. At the apex of each corner, in perfect symmetry, a fossilised ammonite. Each was so perfectly formed, their shells organised into distinctive chambers arranged in a spiral. It was incredible to think that this was a petrified replica, a perfect specimen of an animal that had lived in the sea at least sixty million years ago. Like many things, Quill had seen pictures of them in books but had never seen the real thing. She longed to touch them and struggled to imagine why the Chief would be interested in such an object, or how he even possessed such a thing.

Suddenly, it occurred that her own thoughts had preoccupied her for far too long and, looking up, she realised the Chief was staring straight at her. The hard expression on his face proved he would have preferred to be anywhere other than sitting with her.

The old guard raised an eyebrow. And, removing his middle finger tips from his lips, leaned backward in the revolving chair, saying, "If you've quite finished inspecting my room perhaps you could tell me what you're doing here?"

Quill fought the urge to run, crossing restless legs under the chair. Natural curiosity had distracted her once again, and the last thing she wanted to do was to irritate the man. Face to face with the grizzled specimen, she found herself strangely tongue-tied, afraid to ask about the Master and expecting to learn the worst. Steeling herself for bad news, she hoped instead for a pleasant surprise. So, taking a sharp inward gulp of air, Quill began, "When will you release Master Wittgenstein, please?" she said, hands curled into tight fists. Apart from the intriguing fossil, nothing of any interest about the man piqued her curiosity. To be frank, he projected the appearance of a typical boorish bloke, confirmed by the gallery of forefathers. She doubted he could recognise the truth if it sat up and hit him in the face.

"I'm not at liberty to discuss an ongoing case and even if I were, I certainly wouldn't discuss it with you," he replied, businesslike and to the point.

And there it was again, the superiority complex, and a dash of chauvinism thrown in for good measure. Quill's jaw throbbed from clenching, imagining what it would be like to throw the man over the desktop and punch him right between the eyes. A thought from which she derived a sizable measure of satisfaction.

"It's simple. I just need to talk to him for a few moments. As you well know, he's a very respected member of The Protectorate and I'm sure that they would want him to be afforded special privileges," Quill said, hoping that the not-so-subtle reference to his superior status might just do the trick.

"I'm completely aware of his position, but this situation is unprecedented. We've never had to investigate a murder case, never mind a murder committed by a Protector. Don't presume to tell me how to do my job."

"Are you doing your job? From what I've seen, you've paid more attention to releasing suspects than you have trying to establish the facts." The frustrations and feelings of inadequacy which had plagued her over the previous thirty-six hours were boiling over, and the attempt to stay calm and subservient unravelled.

"I'm going to pretend that I didn't hear any of that. You're not helping him with such an outrageous outburst. Now if you don't mind, you've taken up more than enough of my day and I have to return to my duties." And with that the Chief stood up and moved toward the door, signalling that, in his opinion, the discussion was over.

"But I haven't finished! I spoke to Ezra earlier today, and he told me that Theo Penrose had threatened to kill the Professor just a few days before the murder. That means Mr Penrose already knew the Professor had stolen his work. And as for Ezra, he said he wished he'd killed him because he hated him. I just don't understand why you let them both go? Either of them could be the killer."

For the first time, an odd look of surprise crept over the Chief's features. Left eye twitching, as if registering these details all of a sudden and wondering how he'd not understood them until now. But, no sooner had she thought she saw a moment of self-doubt, than it vanished, replaced by the familiar air of puffed up self-importance.

With a hand pressed hard into the curve of her spine, the Chief continued ushering her out of the room. Unable to keep any traction on the dusty wooden floor, she could not offer any resistance.

"Is everything okay?" The polite, mellow tones of the Deputy were soothing compared to the Chief's roughness. She recognised his voice before realising that he was even there, and wondered how much of the conversation he had witnessed. "Please, Chief, I can see how busy you are. Allow me to show this young lady out."

The Chief grunted and waved his arms at them, dismissing them from his presence.

"It's Quill, isn't it?" the Deputy asked as he walked her to the exit. "Don't mind him, his bark is worse than his bite but he genuinely is very good at his work." She couldn't be sure if he was attempting to convince her or himself. "Sorry, but I couldn't help overhearing your conversation. Master Wittgenstein is fine and being well looked after. We can't release him at this point because there remain several questions he has been unable or unwilling to answer."

Deputy Red was the first person, other than Kai, who had spoken to her like one human being to another. With no pretext or giving of orders. It was a welcome change. "Look, the Chief's right, you can't talk to someone in custody but I'll let him know you were here, okay? And as for the rest," his speech turned to a whisper, and he glanced around and said, "I'm looking into it."

Chapter Thirty-One

Red couldn't shake the suspicion that the entire investigation had been flawed from the start. The Chief's methods were at best unorthodox, at worst inept and tainted by bigotry. First, the widow had steered him into a single-minded decision that Ezra was the guilty party, even though the man claimed to have an alibi. And despite verifying ninety-five per cent of the cover story, the Chief had still been loathe to release the poor man. But now, he fixated on the idea that Master Wittgenstein was a murderer without giving a thought to how damaging that might be for Scolaris. It was bad enough that the city which boasted a record of zero criminal activity had now seen a murder. But to suggest the killer hailed from within The Protectorate, the expression 'political suicide' came to mind. On top of that he couldn't stop recalling the young Defecto woman's words—Quill, an unusual name for a singular young woman, he reflected. Theo Penrose was distasteful to put it mildly. He had observed first-hand the man's intention to step straight into the dead man's shoes.

That was a motive for murder, unlike the unproven allegations of petty theft in Ezra's case. And, as for Wittgenstein, what plausible reason would he have to kill anyone? The whole scenario sounded illogical in his opinion as did jumping to any conclusions before the forensics report was complete.

Motionless, mulling over the facts, the blur of a drab raincoat and the unmistakable rumble of booted footsteps disturbed Red as the boss strode past, evidently on his way out. "Hey, sunshine. Wakey, wakey, get up, we're on the move," urged the Chief.

Feeling flustered and confused, Red grabbed his blue jacket and followed, adding, "Wait—what's up? Where are we going?"

"Jackson's just called in a tip-off!"

"What?—Who?—Where?" Red replied, trotting after the boss, down the stairs and out of HQ.

"No time to talk, we're meeting with a patrol unit in twenty minutes, so just follow me."

And the two men disappeared into the night.

Chapter Thirty-Two

The citrus tang of lemon beeswax polish and lavender infused bed-linen was an enduring source of calm and comfort. An ordinary pine bedstead with stars carved into the headboard, a throwback to childhood, squeezed tight against a narrow tallboy complete with three drawers. It wasn't much, but it was Quill's sanctuary, a place of safety and security. Sat on the patterned rug, back against the bed, its woollen fibres were downy, furry like dandelion fluff. Legs stretched and toes pointed, she could just about touch the opposite wall. It served as a daily reminder of the years' passing. As a little girl, she longed to rest her feet against the warmth of the wood panelling. But at that precise moment, she would have given anything to go back to the days when her tiny skinny lower extremities didn't even reach to the edge of the mat. Return to an era when life was simple. Reading books with her father and serving the Master.

The road home from Guard HQ had been long and lonely. Reflecting on the last couple of days had left her morose and despairing. She had utterly failed to piece together a puzzle that seemed to grow in size and complexity with every new discovery. More importantly, she had failed to serve and protect the Master, and with that, her existence in that very room was under threat.

Scattered all around her were the endless sheets of paper on which she had scribbled her notes. The single page started the previous night had multiplied tenfold. In her hurry to unload all the thoughts and observations that were crowding her brain, they looked very much like a small child's scribblings. She had been sitting there, staring at the scrawl, hoping that the answer would jump out, but to no avail. She had even forgotten her intense hunger despite the persistent growling stomach. Eat, a voice instructed. But she honestly didn't know how to summon the energy to get up off the floor. Even the thought of a walk across the library was too much to bear, or perhaps it was the idea of the Master's rooms lying empty, wondering if he would ever return.

The thud of heavy boots in the library startled Quill out of her lethargy. She hurried to the door and, opening it a sliver, glimpsed with one eye, her pulse rate climbing, panic-stricken, a contingent of at least five guardsmen and bringing up the rear the tan coat of the Chief.

"Search everything," he ordered.

Wide-eyed, white sclera swallowing green iris, clinging to the door-frame, the genuine horror of the situation struck. The shirt. They were going to find it!

Chapter Thirty-Three

Quill needed a plan, and fast. The consequences of them finding the Professor's blood-stained shirt didn't bear thinking about. She couldn't afford to be implicated. If they took her into custody, how would she continue her investigation? They had been heading toward the Master's rooms. If she assumed that's where they were going to begin the search, that might just give her a few minutes to move the incriminating evidence. Where should she put it without getting caught in the process?

Harried, grabbing the not-so-subtle orange sack from under the bed, she still had precious seconds and the presence of mind to tuck her notes under the rug. They were for the most part illegible to anybody other than her and she doubted whether they could consider their contents criminal, but didn't want to take the risk.

Glimpsing herself in the mirror, Quill desperately stuffed the bag under the front of her tunic. The resulting bulge made it look as if she'd piled on the pounds overnight, but that was still less conspicuous than the neon orange. Tentatively creeping out into the library, her first thought was to get as far away as possible. But as she approached the north-eastern corner, she saw that the double doors were ajar and the sound of male voices drifted toward her. Thwarted, silently cursing the bad luck, there were guards at the entrance barring the escape route.

Despite a desperate desire to flee, Quill soon decided trying the other exits would be pointless. In all likelihood they were being guarded too, and the longer she spent roaming inside, the more likely they would catch her with the compromising bag. Harassed, she groped inside her mind for an alternative solution to the problem. There had to be a hiding place right here, but where? The more she searched around, the less she saw. The books on shelves in endless rows all merged into a blur.

Just as she was about to surrender to the anguish, a flash of inspiration sparked like a lit match in a cave. Off to the right of the doors she darted, checking as she went that the guards outside weren't looking in. A few metres from the doorway, tucked against the solid stone outer wall, at the far end of a bookshelf was a plain wooden coat stand. It reminded her of a timber door, much like the entrance to her bedroom. Only attached to its top edge were six turned hooks. Quill had grown used to seeing it heavy with the coats of scholars, but the building had been eerily quiet since the discovery of the Professor's body. The feature she had in mind was a hinged-lidded compartment fixed to the stand's middle, and it thrilled her to discover it wasn't just a figment of her imagination. The creak of its hinges echoed like an alarm within the vast place as she lifted the lid. Frozen, rooted to the spot, she held her breath, waiting to be discovered, but no-one came. Pristine pairs of white cotton gloves filled the space, compulsory wearing for anyone handling the items preserved in that magnificent collection of knowledge. It was her job to replenish the box with fresh gloves at the start of each new day. And something, call it fate, admonished her as she hadn't done it that morning. She wedged the conspicuous sack into the slot left by the absent gloves and laid them back over the top of it.

Alerted again by pounding boot steps, the approaching guards had finished in the Master's chambers and were marching back in her direction. To avoid it giving her position away, Quill eased the top down and ran towards the bedroom, hugging the stone-walled perimeter. And with immense relief, she made it back inside the door moments before the patrol hammered to be let in.

The room search was swift and brutal. Quill's bed flipped upside down, bedclothes dumped in a heap in the doorway's corner, followed by the contents of the drawers; brown tunics and underwear, the icing on a haphazard looking cake. The discovery of books under the bed led to raised eyebrows, sniggering and an exchange of incredulous looks. Steered, for the most part, by a towering guard with a pimply complexion. Quill clamped her mouth shut, deciding it was best not to correct their mocking recommendation to find publications with more pictures.

When they took the Lilith-bird box, all resolve dissolved. Begging them to be careful, she fought hard to stem the tears that welled and threatened to overflow. The pleas had no effect, as utter contempt and disdain took hold of them. After ceremoniously tipping out her meagre possessions onto the rug, trampling back and forth over them, they threw the box against the back wall. It struck the wooden surface with a thud as the lid came clean off its hinges.

"No!" she cried out, seizing the two pieces, cradling them like an injured bird with a broken wing. They ignored Quill's distress, meeting it instead with further laughter and derision. Grabbing a discarded pillow, she hurled it at the nearest vandal and screamed, "Get out, get out. You've no right, no right to touch my things."

"Men, time to go, there's nothing here of any interest," the Chief's statement cut across her outburst. How long had the man been standing in the door? From the rolling eyes and dismissive head shake, Quill guessed he had watched the whole thing, allowing it to happen. The sights and sounds of the squad of guardsmen tramping away in unison, leaving the destruction behind them, relieved a moment of pure hatred.

The old guard hesitated in the entrance, as if weighing up the idea of adding to her misery. As if by magic, the warm tones of the Deputy's voice broke the silence. Where had he been? "Chief, I've got something!" Red hurtled through the door and, hanging from his left hand, was a bright orange rubbish sack.

The search had replaced citrus, clean smells and soft, comforting textures with testosterone and destruction.

Shoulders dragging, arms limp, head bent low, Quill yielded as the Deputy pulled out the familiar blood-stained shirt from inside the sack. If anyone doubted who it belonged to, those reservations wouldn't last long. The initials A.H. embroidered in close red stitching on the top pocket proved ownership beyond any question. The expression of triumph on the Chief's face would haunt her forever, followed closely by a stark announcement, "We've got him! Whoever called in with that tip-off deserves a medal."

"Tip-off? What tip-off?" Quill blurted out without thinking.

The Chief glared. "Not that it's any of your business, but we received an anonymous call that led us to suspect there might still be evidence to find here. It seems they were right."

History repeated itself as she fought a growing urge to wipe the self-satisfied grin permanently from his face.

"Don't you see that's a little suspicious?" Quill asked, trying to cast doubt on the wisdom of relying on information from an unspecified source. Who would have known about the shirt? Think jerk who?

"Doesn't really matter, does it? We've found the Prof's shirt covered in blood hidden in this building. A great day's work!" The Chief preened, chin jutting in and out like a peacock, and the smug man slapped the Deputy's back with an open palm.

"Hmm, don't you feel we should wait until we have it analysed?" the Deputy whispered, an uneasy look about his body language and fidgeting with the gold buttons of his jacket, clearly discomfited by this display of affection.

It was the Deputy's turn to receive the full force of the Chief's glare and the earlier moment's male bonding vanished with the older man's growling response, "Don't question me, sunshine."

"It was me. I hid the bag. It's nothing to do with Master Wit. The Hawkin's lawyer, Ms Ginsburg, that's her name I think, she had it, the orange sack. And when I saw her throwing it in the silo outside the Hawkin's apartment I grew suspicious. So I followed her and discovered the shirt. I got scared, so I brought it back here and hid it." Numb, drained and defeated, Quill offered up a confession, accepting that life as she knew it was over. Retreating inside herself, she waited for them to seize her.

The deep, throaty roar that followed was totally unexpected. "Ha ha, nice try, girl. What a story! That would've made an entertaining addition to those books under your bed. Shame you can't read them." And then, signalling to the Deputy, he added, "Let's head back, we've got enough to charge him now and then we can look forward to the trial. They won't hang about, The Protectorate. My orders are that as soon as we have the culprit, they'll only need three days to prepare for the hearing and then justice will be swift and merciless." And the sound of uncontrolled laughter echoed in her ears long after the Chief had left, with the Deputy trailing in his wake.

Chapter Thirty-Four

Three days to save the Master. What had she done? What breed of useless moron bungled the making of a confession? No wonder everyone she cared for left. How Quill had ever believed that she could solve a murder was suddenly beyond comprehension. A short crawl back to the bedroom to hide should have been an attractive proposition, but she couldn't face looking at it, its contents strewn around like discarded rubbish. Stood in the deserted library, forehead against a bookshelf, her nose filled with the sweet aroma of apple and vanilla seeping from the aging pages of the books that lined the shelf. Usually, it soothed and comforted, a smell so readily recognisable, but in that moment nothing could take away the self-loathing and despair.

An inrush of cool air encircling the ankles was an alert that somebody had entered the library. It had to be the Chief, a change of heart, returning to drag her into custody after all. Why care? It would be a relief. Glancing sideways, struggling to move, she was wrong.

"What are you doing here? How did you even get here?" asked Quill, stumbling toward the visitor, grasping an arm, leading him towards the safety of the outer wall.

"I managed just fine, thanks," Kai replied, finger-tipping a route down the surface and onto the cold tiled floor. A gnarled, warped stick waved in the air, just missed connecting with her chin and he added, "I used my wooden friend here. She gets me from A to B."

"She?" Quill asked, sitting beside him.

"Yeah, all my best friends are women."

Despite the joke, his boyish charm and sense of humour failed to pierce the thick shroud of doom and gloom clogging the atmosphere.

The bitter draught blowing in from under the doorway submitted to the warmth radiating out from his body. Without thinking, Quill lay her head on his shoulder-blade and gave in to the frustration and fear that she had unsuccessfully tried to conquer. Warm, brackish tears flowed down cheeks in rivulets, collecting on mass at the base of her neck, silent sobs. Whether Kai knew she was crying, he did not say. He was a rock, which was precisely what she needed.

After what seemed an age, the tears dried up. Had she dozed off, leaning on him for comfort?

"Hey, sleepyhead. Good to see you," Kai whispered, confirming the answer.

The rising flush of hot cheeks amplified the self-consciousness, and Quill mumbled, "Err, yeah, sorry about that. I don't know what happened there."

"Don't worry about it. I quite enjoyed it," he said, staring directly at her. It was inconceivable that those golden eyes didn't work as they should. What did he see? It felt too awkward to ask. Automatically Quill's hand rose to cover the mark but with lightning reflexes he grasped those fingers and in hushed tones said, "Don't, you don't need to do that. Come here, you're worn out, rest a bit more and then I'll explain why I came."

Relieved, she nodded and returned to the comfort of his shoulder.

Quill and Kai sat on the bed, finishing the supper of bread and cheese cobbled together from the supplies in the kitchen. With Kai's support, she had found the strength to tackle the destruction in the bedroom, and all was back as it should be. Kai's fury at the guard's tyranny simmered like thick broth on a stove.

"That was great, thanks," he said, passing an empty plate. "It's getting late. Suppose I should get on and say what I came here to tell you. Old Jed said she'd cover for me but I don't want to take advantage."

"Of course. What is it?"

"Jed's the reason I'm here. She's still got family in the Defecto Quarters, cousins as far as I know. Apparently, there's talk that Defectos have been going missing. People feel scared, especially now with this murder. Everyone's saying those events must be connected," said Kai.

"Ezra's younger sister, Val, he called her, he kept saying that she was missing. He was heading towards the Engineering District when I talked to him earlier, going to search for her. I wonder if he found her?"

"Maybe," Kai shrugged, "maybe not. Friends and relatives reported them missing but the City Guard isn't interested. No one cares, they're just Defectos. Nothing changes."

"This is all very interesting, but I'm not sure how this helps me or the Master? Agreed the guard is a tad lacking on the people skills' front but I still can't accept that if people were genuinely going missing they wouldn't investigate. That would be foolish. This is Scolaris, the city where 'Knowledge is King', things like that just don't happen here."

Kai scratched his jaw, expressionless apart from a single raised eyebrow, and stuttered, "Do you mean murder?"

There was no answer to that.

"Are you serious?" Kai shot up from the bed, jabbing the stick in the air. "I can't believe you just said that. Do you actually think that's true? You really don't get it, do you? Has it not occurred to you that this endless search for knowledge is dangerous? Nothing is how it looks. We ignore whole sections of society. Treat them as invisible and disposable. And as for the rest, they fixate on position and power and don't care who they trample on to get there."

"But we can't condemn an entire society based on one crime. You've only got to look in the library to know every amazing thing we've accomplished."

"What? You mean a collection of dusty old books that most people will never get to touch, let alone be able to read?"

"It's easy to learn to read. I could teach you, if you wanted," Quill said, without considering the consequences.

"I can't see the words," he whispered, "but that doesn't mean I'm ignorant. My mother taught me about the world and everything in it, before she died. I do okay." The tight eyes and set jaw betrayed his anger, and it provoked an equal response.

"Did you tell the guard where to find the shirt?" she blurted.

"What?"

"To be honest, it's been bothering me since this afternoon. How did they know the shirt was here? The only person I told was you."

Kai stood tall, legs spread wide, ribs thrust out. Expecting an explosion, what happened instead was worse. With measured, calm, disdain he said, "Unbelievable. I don't deserve to be asked that question. One of us is blind but, guess what? It's not me."

Chapter Thirty-Five

"Right, Wittgenstein, it's time to get serious," the Chief said in his usual growl.

"That's Master Wittgenstein to you, Chief, and I can assure you I've been taking this whole matter seriously, as I hope have you."

Red observed the two men sparring with interest. He sat beside the Chief across the table from the renowned Custodian of the Great Library. They conducted the interview in the barren room set aside for the purpose in the basement, next to the cells. The airless space sat empty save for a table and the three spindle-backed wooden chairs they occupied. A bare bulb attached to a frayed cord hanging from the ceiling was the only source of light. And even then, that barely lit a tiny circular zone in the middle of the table, the rest of the dismal square box languished in darkness.

"Okay, now we've got the pleasantries out of the way, let's get down to business. We know you did it so now is the moment to own up," said the Chief, drumming his fingertips on the tabletop. It was hard not to admire the man's conviction that this interview was just a formality. Unfortunately, Red found it impossible to ignore the gigantic hole running right through the centre of their case, a hole in the shape of a single word. Why? What plausible reason could this studious old man have to kill the Professor? He knew the Chief didn't care about such an inconsequential detail, but to be honest, this realisation added to the growing discomfort. He wished he could be anywhere else other than in that place. If only he could steer the Chief toward actual evidence gathering rather than this farce, without stoking his temper. But so far he'd failed.

"I'm uncertain what you're asking me. Can you repeat the question?" the ancient man asked, every inch of him wrinkled and hunched, all of his eighty plus years of life on display.

"So that's how you're going to play it, is it? Let me spell it out for you. Rather conveniently, you discovered Professor Hawkin's body at your library. His appointment book tells us that the pair of you met the day before, and we know they discovered your diary in his laboratory. And you don't seem very keen to answer our questions about that meeting."

The scholar listened with interest to the Chief's summary. Motionless, not a flicker of recognition or emotion registered on his face.

"Is there a question in there? I'm still not sure."

The Chief balled a hand into a fist and Red stiffened, holding his breath, waiting for the eruption. But instead, the boss flexed his fingers, rubbing the palms on his trousers before saying, "Oh don't you worry, there are questions. We're just getting to them. Let's start with the easiest so we don't tax your old brain too much."

Red crossed and uncrossed his legs under the seat, examining a black stain on the stone floor, wondering if it was mould. Though he hadn't missed the suspect's raised eyebrow, responding to the insult. Nevertheless, the wise man said nothing, settling himself as much as possible into the rickety wooden chair.

"Here we go then. We asked you this before but your answer wasn't true. So try again. Why did you have an appointment to meet with Hawkin on the day of the murder?"

The Master sighed, scratching the long white hair behind his ears. "I don't remember a meeting. There is nothing more to say."

"Nothing more to say. What about your dirty boots? There was a muddy trail of footprints in Hawkin's lab and the boots you'd tried to clean look to be a match."

"What can I tell you? Boots get muddy and then people clean them. I expect if you looked hard enough you'd turn up quite a collection of grubby pairs across the city. As much as I enjoy your company, I am very busy and would like to go home now."

"No doubt you would, but you're not going anywhere. You're lying. We found a shirt belonging to the Professor hidden in the library, covered in his blood. If you didn't kill him, what was it doing there?"

Why was he saying the blood belonged to Hawkin when they were still waiting on forensics? Red chewed the innards of a cheek, restless limbs fidgeting on the hard and unyielding seat.

"The library is a public building, hundreds of scholars visit every day. I didn't murder Alexander, and I do not know why someone hid his shirt there. I assume you're planning to interview everybody who has access to the building?"

The head guard ran two fingers around the inside of his collar, stretching his neck from side to side. Sweat formed a damp curtain on his forehead as the sharp-witted old fellow succeeded in calling his methods into question. A jarring ring of metal scraping on stone echoed in the tiny space as Red's boss pushed the chair away from under him. With both hands on the counter, he fixed the accused with a probing glare. "How I plan to run my investigation is none of your business. Now stop wasting our time and confess, otherwise you might learn some details about my preferred method of interrogation that you'll wish you hadn't."

Red fought to keep the shock from showing on his features, instinct turning his upper body towards the door, pretending to hear a noise. The sound of his pulse grew loud in his head and a sudden metallic tang registered before he realised that he'd bitten his lip and drawn blood. He couldn't be positive about what the boss meant, but the threat was self-evident. Pulling himself together, he returned to the conversation, where the shrunken demeanour of the suspect suggested the message had hit home. I can't let this continue, he told himself. Things have gone far enough. Red grasped the edge of the tabletop, knuckles white, his lips parted, preparing to register a protest. Before he had a chance to intervene, the Chief interrupted with a simple order, "Red, our guest clearly needs some more time to think. Take him back to the cells."

Stifling an enormous sigh of relief, Deputy Red led a grateful Master Wittgenstein toward the relative safety of the pitch dark pens in the lock-up.

Chapter Thirty-Six

The reception committee, standing shoulder to shoulder in the doorway, was not a good sign. After the day he'd suffered, the only thing Red wanted to do was fold himself into bed and hope his mind could switch off long enough to fall asleep. The hard, flinty expressions on his mother and father's faces left no doubt they had other ideas. Red's father jabbed a finger, directing toward the lounge and as usual, he obeyed.

The pastel-mint upholstered chairs stood to attention, dotted around the matching room like remote islands. Their unforgiving rigid backs and missing arms were an antidote to relaxing. The loud ticking of a wall clock syncopated against his heartbeat, off-beat, jarring as he waited for someone to speak.

"I don't appreciate having to hear reports of my son's disobedience while I'm at work. Your mother and I, brought you up better than that. It's tough enough tolerating your choice of career without you dishonouring the family name." The deep, authoritarian voice reverberated, encircling the room. A voice honed like a fine instrument over years of addressing a commercial courtroom. What's more, the proud man oozed self assurance from every pore, a ram-rod stature adding to the cloak of invincibility that Red admired growing up. Father was an exceptional orator which, coupled with a prodigious intellect, produced a fearsome adversary. "First thing tomorrow, you will apologise to the Chief and you will stop this nonsense about missing Defectos. Your duty is to follow orders, and you'd do well to remember this fact."

Reflecting on those last words, Red recognised the threatening undertone. As he looked from one parent to the other, their tight expressions were identical, implacable, exhibiting a steadfast unity. They weren't terrible parents; they weren't overtly cruel and had provided him with a comfortable existence. Even so, he couldn't recall ever being surrounded by the comforting warmth of their love. They were aloof, keeping themselves detached and above mere mortals, content to be respected through fear.

"Sir, I'm afraid I can't agree," he whispered in response. "The onus is upon all of us to uncover the truth."

"Nobody denies that, son. But there are standards and procedures that you must follow. A lack of experience is to be expected, and that's why you need to focus on following orders."

"We all lack experience. Nothing like this has ever happened before but the Chief isn't keeping an open mind."

Red's father rose and paced back and forth in front of the marble fireplace. He spoke as if presenting arguments to a judge. "Son, you must show more humility. It's not your place to judge your superiors. If you'd followed family tradition, I would have taught you these lessons from day one." The barbed comment took aim and fired straight at his heart.

Red muttered under his breath, "Is it any wonder I didn't?"

"I beg your pardon?" his father replied.

Red shook his head and hoped his observation had been inaudible.

"We have worked hard to establish our good standing in this district, and don't want our good name tarnished by your insubordination. Do I make myself clear?"

In return, Red got to his feet, like father, like son. "Crystal. But what I need to make clear is that the Chief is a bigoted old man who doesn't understand the meaning of the phrase, 'thorough investigation'. This case involves identifying who murdered the Professor, not just pinning a crime on any passer-by for an easy life."

A slight sway of the man's stocky legs was the only visible sign that Red might have said too much. The matriarch of the family, who had remained uncharacteristically silent until that point, joined the fray. She maintained the mask of quiet assurance that he had grown accustomed to by choosing to stay seated. "I don't believe that I have ever heard you raise your voice in this house, and I tell you plainly we will not tolerate it. The Protectorate charged the City Guard with upholding law and order in Scolaris, not embarking on this misplaced personal mission. We live in a safe and honest society and you cannot persuade me otherwise."

This should usually have been the signal to retreat. But buoyed by the rebuttal of his father's lecture, Red uncovered an inner resolve. Released from the grip of family pressure, his confidence overflowed like a swollen river. "Good and fair for who, Mother? For the privileged few? Tell that to the Defectos who live in hovels, on the fringes of the City, conveniently hidden from view. I'm not a child any longer. No doubt I'm a disappointment to you but this career is the choice I've made and you'll have to come to terms with it."

"And what you do from our house affects our reputation. If you have so little respect for this, then—then,"

"What, mother?" Red shouted.

The woman stood, taller than both men, body tense, eyes blackened with bitterness, and bristled, "You should go."

Chapter Thirty-Seven

The bedroom hid, cowering from the hollow silence, its warmth and comfort dragged out like a deflated old mattress. Quill languished inside, alone on the star spangled blanket, staring at the cracks in the ceiling, Kai's parting words on repeat. Usually, she filled her mind with pictures from the books she read, drawing them on the plaster with her imagination. They would come to life in front of her. Constellations, galaxies and black holes were her particular favourites, an obsession inherited from her father, but laying there that night her mind was blank and desolate.

Was he right? Was her view of the city misguided? The more she thought, the worse she felt. Perhaps having her head stuck in a book had left her naïve, dreaming of a world that didn't really exist. The last couple of days definitely opened her mind to the way people judged Defectos. She had always assumed that the odd looks she drew were because of the mark, but perhaps she'd been wrong about that too.

The universe shifted. Spinning in reverse, Quill studied it with a fresh pair of eyes, golden eyes that saw better than hers even though they were blind.

Despair and exhaustion had finally felled Quill in the early hours of the morning. Even the Lilith birdsong, followed by the six o'clock city wide call, failed to wake her.

Hunger had eventually broken through, dragging her from sleep. Quill endured the monotony of starting a new day, setting everything in order: the Master's rooms, the reading room and the main library. The normality of tidying, organising and cleaning was a welcome distraction from reality. When it was all finished she surveyed her work, a sense of satisfaction growing inside like a seedling, forcing self-pity out with the dirt.

Quill knew she couldn't avoid life forever, and finishing the chores had discovered a renewed sense of purpose. It had been a pointless exercise, trying to reason with people who considered she was subhuman, like the Chief and his cronies. But the Deputy behaved differently and, she decided, might be worth an approach.

As she'd trekked across to Law and Order through driving hail and skin-biting wind, she'd wondered if this was going to be another colossal waste of time. On several occasions she'd contemplated turning back, but Kai's words had driven her on. And there she stood, dripping wet, in the centre of a puddle of her own making, in front of Deputy Red.

"You look half frozen to death," he said, taking off his blue jacket and wrapping it around her shoulders.

Quill's teeth chattered as her entire body convulsed.

"Here, sit down," suggested Red, directing her to a chair in front of what she assumed was his desk. The photograph of a proud-looking man and woman suggested that she was right. The Deputy exhibited the perfect mix of the strong, stocky masculinity of the older fellow and the more delicate features of the woman.

"Your parents?" she asked, nodding toward the picture.

"Yes," he answered, turning the picture away.

"I can see the family resemblance. Must be nice."

Red nodded. "To be clear, I'm unhappy about what they did to your things. That shouldn't have happened," he said, changing the subject, cheeks flushed, gaze averted.

Red hadn't seemed very comfortable talking about his family, and she wondered what that was all about. Her eyes must have glazed over because he said, "Hey, are you okay. Do you need a doctor?"

Quill shook her head. "No, sorry, just thinking. I've been doing a lot of that over the last few days. So, I expect I'm wasting your time and mine, but I sensed I could talk to you. Unlike the Chief, the man hates me!"

"Hah, don't take it too personally. In my experience he doesn't like anyone much," said Red, glancing around to confirm they were still alone.

It had only just registered with her that, apart from the two of them, the office was empty. "Where is everyone?"

"Not sure. My guess is they had a late night, celebrating their success. Promised to hold the fort, so here I am. But

I'm expecting them any minute."

Quill recognised that was a subtle way of telling her to get on with it. "Defectos, they're scared. People are going missing and now this murder. They're convinced they're connected and angry that no-one is doing a single thing about the situation. I realise you're satisfied the Master killed Professor Hawkin. But why? And if we assume a connection to missing Defectos exists, it cannot have anything to do with him. He's a man of books and learning. What possible reason could he have to make Defectos vanish? For a start, he doesn't go very far, he's old, that's what I'm for. There are too many other possibilities you've ignored. The wife, she didn't seem upset that he was dead and she was cleaning him out of her life at top speed. Ezra, he told me he hated the Hawkins, and wished he'd killed them. And then there's Theo Penrose. He suspected the Professor had stolen his idea and if we accept anything Ezra has to say, Penrose threatened to kill the man just days before his death. Have you actually come up with one reason that would give Master Wit a motive for murder?"

Red paused, leaning back in his chair, and said, "No, not so far. The Chief is pretty happy that he'll secure a conviction without it, especially now we turned up the shirt." A moment's awkward silence passed between them as guilt resurfaced. Brooding, Quill strangled herself with an imaginary shirt, the pain a penance for stupidity.

"Okay, I shouldn't be saying this," Red continued, "but you have a point. The evidence against the Master is mostly circumstantial. I've been trying to find out what I can about the missing Defectos, even though the Chief ordered me not to, but it's proving impossible. There are no official records to go on that even corroborate the existence of these people. It's unbelievable really."

The unexpected groan of hinges interrupted their exchange, and they fell silent. Expecting to see the Chief and the rest of the guards, it surprised her when in fact the turned-out figure of Mrs Lucinda Hawkin appeared in the doorway. The widow wore a jade silk dress under a rich plum-coloured coat, all well protected from the hideous weather by an enormous green umbrella which she shook clean of icy raindrops onto the office floor. The colour of the umbrella was an exact match for the hue of the woman's frock, and Quill wondered whether one existed to compliment every outfit.

To overcome the initial shock of seeing such an important person standing inside the grubby interior, the Deputy stood to greet her. "Mrs Hawkin. How may I help you?" he asked.

The widow finished shaking the umbrella and leaned it up against the wall. A wrinkled nose and arms clamped to her sides were the woman's reaction to the place, and she didn't venture any further into the room. "I was hoping to speak to the Chief."

"Sorry, he's not here at the moment. Please, I'd be happy to assist you," declared Red.

"I suppose you'll have to do," the woman replied, "though now I'm here I can't help wondering if I'm overreacting."

"I'm sorry, I don't follow?"

"Yes, yes, I'm getting to it," she said, waving a hand at him. "Mr. Penrose, my late husband's assistant, he was due to meet me at the lab first thing this morning. We agreed to put our differences behind us and discuss continuing the Professor's work. But he didn't turn up, it's very unlike him. He is exceptionally studious—-brilliant, much like the Professor. To be frank, he would never miss an opportunity to discuss scientific work. I telephoned him at home but there's no answer. And I don't know why, but I get the feeling that something is wrong. I decided it would be better to report this in person. Wanted the Chief to treat it as a matter of utmost importance and, while here, I thought he could update me about the investigation."

Could it be true, Quill wondered? Theo Penrose missing? She frowned, recalling their physical altercation. The runt of a man had shown himself more than capable of inflicting physical injury, despite the small stature. Perhaps their conversation had touched a nerve. She knew he had access to the lab and, it seemed, a motive for killing. Maybe he'd decided that it was only a matter of time before the crime caught up with him. The more she thought about it, the more assured she became. It made sense, Theo Penrose was the murderer and his decision to disappear was all part of a plan to get away with it.

"I knew he was up to no good," Quill blurted out.

"Oh, I didn't see you there. Why are you here?" Mrs Hawkin snapped.

"She's lending a hand with some general enquiries," the Deputy interjected, glaring at Quill, a face that told her in no uncertain terms not to say another word.

"Hmm, all right, I see. Well, I expect I've done my duty and I'll have to leave the rest to you. Are there any developments regarding the Professor?" she added.

"I'm sorry, no. We are still waiting on chemical testing, though we're not expecting it to add any more details. Look, you did the right thing. Thanks for telling us about Penrose. I expect there's nothing to worry about, but I'll check it out. Are you able to get home?"

Mrs Hawkin nodded, a curt jerk of the chin, grabbed the brolly, and left. Quill still couldn't believe that this was a woman who'd lost her husband only two days earlier. Whether it resulted from a lifelong experience of putting on a good show or something more sinister was still up for debate.

No sooner had they heard the woman's footsteps descending the stairs outside than the Deputy was keying in a number written in neat script from the papers on his desk. Quill leaned in, hearing the beeps of the dialling sequence followed by the ringing tone. But it was the only sound they could hear, aside from the wind and the sleet driving against the windowpane. She held her breath, waiting, waiting to hear if anyone answered.

Red replaced the receiver after what seemed like ages of the monotonous, mocking ringtone. He frowned.

"We need to do something," she urged. "I told you he was a more likely suspect. I can't believe you let him go. Why else would he go missing unless he had something to hide?"

Red fixed her with a defiant stare, drawing her again to the dark depths of his eyes. "First of all, I didn't let him leave. That was down to the boss. Second, we know nothing, we don't have confirmation that he is missing. There could be any number of explanations."

"Well, there's only one way to find out," she said, grabbing the piece of paper out from under him.

"Hey, if you're wanting me to lose my job, you're going the right way about it. That's evidence, give it back. Now!" he demanded.

Like a scolded child with a bottom lip protruding beyond the top, Quill grunted and shoved the piece of script at his chest. Red's wide shoulders relaxed downward as he took it back. "Thank you. Look, you're correct, I need to discover whether anything untoward has happened to Penrose and take it from there."

"I'm coming too," she declared and before he had a second to register a protest, she added, "And nothing you can say or do will stop me!"

Chapter Thirty-Eight

The bottle green front door stood wide open, inviting anyone to enter. That was unusual. Even though the city was proud of its reputation as a place of safety and security, its residents valued their privacy and no-one was in the habit of leaving their front door ajar.

The Deputy had sprinted all the way to Reynard's Close, and Quill had struggled to keep up with him. On arrival, both panting and gasping for breath, they exchanged knowing glances as they took advantage of the open invitation and tiptoed into the house.

The house was more modest than the Hawkin's apartment, which was to be expected, but nevertheless its generous proportions were still vastly superior to her single room. As soon as they entered the hallway, it was obvious that something untoward had happened under that roof. Viewed straight through to the living room from the entranceway, the scene was reminiscent of the mess in the laboratory. Books strewn across the room with bundles of pages ripped out of their hearts, lamenting their destruction on the carpet. An upturned black velvet chaise longue had fought with a coffee table and smashed glass showed that the chaise had won.

"Touch nothing!" Red ordered, pointing a finger at her as he stepped over the broken glass and scraps of paper. To the right of the living room, the kitchen was a sea of calm in comparison. Other than dirty dishes in the sink and a collection of mismatched glass tumblers on the side containing various amounts of yellow liquor, everything appeared normal.

To continue the search, Quill followed him back to the hallway from which ascended a staircase. Hesitantly, they crept up the steps in perfect unison, stopping every couple of seconds to listen for any signs of life. At the top they reached a galleried landing, off of which were five white doors, every one of which yawned wide open, beckoning, inviting. All apart from one. The door at the far end was closed tight. They made their way along the landing, checking the open doors as they went, but everything looked normal in the three bedrooms and a bathroom.

The closed door was intriguing, begging to be investigated. Red grasped the silver door handle and slowly turned it anticlockwise. As she heard the faint click of the mechanism, Red raised his right index finger and touched the digit to his lips. Inside, the darkness snuffed out their visual senses, and the stark contrast to the brightness in the rest of the house rendered it almost impossible for their sight to adjust. They both stood in the doorway, waiting for senses to recalibrate.

A thin band of light crept into Quill's consciousness, directly in front of them and, as her sight adapted, she could see that it came from around the edge of the room's only window. A thick, black roller blind covered the glass, blocking out every light particle other than a tiny strip flanking the base and sides. Whatever this room was and whoever used it, they were serious about protecting it from prying eyes.

Impatient, having decided that she could now see perfectly well, Quill took a few steps further into the space, skin crawling as she felt something disintegrate underfoot. A crunching sound highlighted her obvious mistake, and the Deputy hissed, "What are you doing? Don't move another step until I've opened the blind." Edging his way around the area, he raised the shade. And they were both blinded for a few seconds as the light from outside flooded the room.

Gunmetal filing cabinets lined the far right wall and a small leather-topped desk took pride of place in the room's centre. Similar to the living area, this office was in disarray. The filing drawers were hanging open like the beaks of parent birds disgorging their contents. The office owner's chair was on its side, poking half in and half out of the leg space beneath the desk. Quill picked up the broken object under her right foot. A cracked glass frame displayed a smiling photograph of Theo Penrose, looking young and hopeful, shaking hands with Professor Hawkin. Both of them inside the lab. She held the image up for the Deputy to look at. "I'm assuming this room is Penrose's office. What do you think?"

Red nodded, a tight-lipped expression of grim determination on his face. Below the left-hand corner of the chestnut desk was a set of three large drawers. And trying the handle of the uppermost tray, the Deputy frowned. It was locked. Carefully lifting an array of papers and replacing them in sections, the two of them soon realised that if a key existed, they weren't going to find it. Underneath the last pile, Quill discovered a half-filled tumbler and a brass letter opener. The straw-coloured contents of the glass emitted a spicy, pungent odour of fresh ginger. Delicious warm sweetness, but with a faint note of lemon. Scrutinising the tool, she observed that one end was fortuitously sharp. She handed it to him and with remarkable dexterity he used the pointed end to force open the top drawer and with it the bottom two sprang open. The contents of the upper tray were unremarkable. The usual mundane collection of pencils sharpened to a stub, a multi-coloured web of elastic bands in a myriad of different widths and lengths and pens with no ink which someone should long since have thrown away. Not forgetting, a considerable pile of small waxed wrappers which the Deputy sifted through with the end of the letter opener in an effort not to contaminate the scene. "Wow, someone's got a sweet tooth!" he declared.

To access the two drawers underneath, Quill held on to the lower ones, preventing them from shutting by accident while Red closed the top. Incredulous, the pair stared, wide-eyed, looking into the middle drawer. The world spun as, disoriented, Quill choked, inadvertently holding her breath. Dropped to her knees, head thrust between trembling thighs, she tried to steady her breathing. She heard a heavy thud as the Deputy placed the astonishing find on the desktop. By the time she felt well enough to stand up, he was already leafing through the object, protecting it from contamination with a crumpled tissue.

The find was at least five inches thick, maroon leather covered, its pages edged in gold and it shone like a jewel. The spine had thick ribbed sections holding its hefty weight together. It was the most incredible book Quill had ever seen, and she had seen tens of thousands. The pages were wafer thin, and as Red held each one up for inspection, the light from the window shone through like a golden halo. Each of the innumerable pages was hand crafted. A pain-staking endeavour involving ornate calligraphy of every imaginable design graced the inside, supplemented with intricate drawings and embellishments. This was a book to lose yourself in, and she could sense the pages sucking her in with their power.

"I can't read this? What is this book?" he said and then looking uncomfortable added, "Um, sorry. That was insensitive."

"Typical. I can read thank you!" she complained, arms crossed, scowling. "Contrary to popular belief Defectos aren't stupid, we just don't get the same opportunities."

Red formed a triangle of fingers in front of his mouth and apologised, "I'm the stupid one, it's obvious you're not unintelligent. You've proved that by figuring out who could have killed the Professor. I'm sorry," he said, looking straight at her, holding her gaze. Her stomach somersaulted, and tiny arm hairs shot upright.

Quill tore away from his intense stare, rubbing her left arm, trying to dispel the awkwardness. Had something just happened between them? Ridiculous, pull yourself together, fool. Please, just say something, "It's like nothing I've ever seen," she said, reverting to safer ground—-the book. "I can't read the text either. It just looks like a series of jumbled letters, though—-I don't know, maybe these are words. Can you see, they're arranged as if they are words?" and as she pointed to the groups of letters he nodded. "One thing I am sure of," she said.

"What's that?"

"This publication is a forbidden text and shouldn't be here, in someone's home. These belong in the library, locked away."

"What do you mean? Isn't that a little extreme? I mean, it's just a book. Why does it need to be concealed?" he asked.

Quill paused, she'd never even thought to question why they kept specific books from the general public. That was just what the law dictated. Shoulders shrugging, she said, "I suppose I've never really thought about it that much. The Protectorate ruled hundreds of years ago to forbid a range of texts. They relate to subjects that celebrate form over substance, beauty and creativity above knowledge. They deemed them dangerous as they lead people away from society's common goal."

"Knowledge is King!" he declared in a mocking tone.

"It is, though," she countered in all seriousness.

"So you've never found enjoyment in anything just because of the way it looks, or sounds, or tastes?" he asked.

Quill chewed the collar of her tunic, turning left and right at the hips. This was a troublesome question to answer honestly, with him standing so close, "Erm, maybe, but that doesn't make it right. On the odd occasion that happens I try to fight it—much like the next person." What was this conversation?

"I've always thought the rule was stupid," Red said, unemotional, continuing to leaf through the pages. Glancing at her, he added, "I've shocked you, haven't I?"

She turned to gnawing fingers and concentrating on the ornate book, her voice cracked as she said, "No, not really."

Who was she kidding? He made her feel about twelve years old, and no doubt he could read the discomfort written across her face. "Wait, what's that?" Quill said, and she pointed at the book, directing him to go back a couple of pages. Wedged into the binding was a folded piece of paper. As he pulled the scrap out and opened it with the point of the paper knife, they could see that written in a spidery scrawl, altogether distinct from the book's contents, were two identical rectangles, arranged one above the other. In the top box, a number, a 3 or perhaps an 8; the smudged ink was barely legible. The bottom box was even stranger, as if someone had tried to imitate the banned text and failed miserably. It read 'TP 19264548'.

"What is this?" he asked.

"Honestly, I don't have a clue. This scrap of paper though, I'm sure it's modern. Not like the book," she said.

Red returned his attention to the central drawer and pulled out a pad of plain paper. To compare, he placed the pad next to the strange note. Side-by-side, they were the same in every way: the same cream colour, the same thickness, and both edged in silver. "Great deduction," Red said, smiling.

"If we could just work out what it meant," Quill said to herself. "Mm, it's a long shot, and it goes against every single one of the Master's rules but it makes sense that if this work is what I think it is, a censored text, then there might be clues to understanding the contents in other forbidden books. I should return to the library and see what I can uncover."

"What if you get caught?" he asked.

"Well, I don't know. Can't imagine it would be good. I'll have to make sure that I don't."

"I don't like the idea," he said. "That sounds dangerous to me. Let's just check the last drawer and I'll think about it."

As soon as Red opened the bottom tray, his countenance grew bright. From in front of the desk, she couldn't see what he was looking at. As he reached in grabbing it with a fresh tissue, whatever it was, the object was small. It remained hidden as his hand emerged and carefully placed it on the only empty square of desk that was left.

"I found one of these, hidden behind an old photograph, on a shelf, at Bill's place," the Deputy said.

"Who's Bill?" Quill asked, unable to take her eyes off the new find.

"One of the missing Defectos. I mean, people," he added, fussing with his jacket sleeve, "the only one I managed to track to an address."

"It looks just like the ones in Professor Hawkin's lab," she said.

"That's exactly what I thought about the one I found at Bill's. Sent it for analysis but forensics got nothing from it, it was empty."

"And the ones at the lab, they were all smashed and their contents spilled over the floor," Quill added. "But this one," and she crouched so that her view was level with the tiny vessel, "is intact. A perfect specimen, and it looks to me as if it still has its contents."

The liquid inside the vial shimmered, its luminescence magnified by the daylight from the window, and she reached out to take it.

"Here, use this," Red said, passing the crumpled tissue. Surprised that there were no orders not to touch it, she grasped the stopper between thumb and forefinger and eased it out, hearing the faintest of popping sounds as it came loose.

The sickly sweet scent assaulting her nose was instantly recognisable. It transported her straight back to the lab and to the disastrous day that had started this mess. "I don't know what this stuff is," she said, "but it was definitely in the lab. I recognise the smell." Something else was nagging at her, a faint memory, but much like the odour, it was difficult to pin down, floating away like clouds in the sky.

"I thought I recognised it, but I couldn't place it," he said.

"I expect most of the scent had evaporated by the time you got there."

He nodded, "Look, there," he pointed, "there's something on the bottom."

Quill replaced the stopper, carefully turned it upside down, and saw that he was correct. On the underside of the vial, a symbol picked out in black, inconspicuously embedded into the glass. She recognised it straight away, reminding her of a G, though it was more of a swirl, an exact miniature replica of the symbol carved onto the lid of her broken box.

She glanced up at Red and it surprised her to see a look of recognition on his face, as wide upturned lips signalled obvious excitement. "That swirl, that's what we found tattooed under the Professor's hairline, behind his ear."

Chapter Thirty-Nine

Weaving and bobbing, insides vibrating, re-energised, Quill raced back to the library, clutching a copy of the mysterious note. Red had reluctantly agreed that she should search for anything that might help them decipher it. In the intervening period, he planned to break the news to the Chief and do what needed to be done with the added crime scene. He confessed to apprehension at the prospect of the impending conversation with his boss. Revealing that the Chief was not a man who took kindly to his authority being challenged. It was going to be difficult to persuade him that his single-minded belief that Master Wit murdered the Professor might have been a mistake.

Quill smiled, recalling the earnest expression on Red's face, and the parting words urging caution. Absent-mindedly she tucked a perfect curl of hair behind her left ear and, in doing so, caught the raised rim of the brown mark. It was the first time she had thought of it all day, and it startled her. In all the while that she had been with Red, she hadn't felt self-conscious about it at all. Why was that?

Perhaps she was learning to accept it, embrace it, feeling comfortable in her own skin. Self-acceptance was a brand new emotion, but it might take a while to decide if that was a good thing or not.

The forbidden texts were shut away, isolated like a contagion from the books in the main library. Stood often at the fretwork of the wrought-iron gate, Quill had craved the chance to take a peek. Heavily padlocked, the gate barred all access to the intriguing room attached to the south-west wall of the main building. Despite strict instructions never to set foot inside, it seemed logical that the keys to the padlocks were somewhere on the Master's set. The iron ring was exactly where she expected, hanging from the hook behind the kitchen door.

Quill's mission, now that she stood before the gate, keyring in hand, was to work out which keys she needed. There were at least twenty of them, all different shapes and sizes. It was a struggle just to hold the iron circle up, and eager to gain entry before anyone found out, she fumbled with each key. She worked systematically, testing the keys in turn and then pushing them to the far side of the ring, using a fist as a placeholder. But it was so unwieldy that on more than one occasion she dropped the keys clanging onto the floor, and cursing under her breath had to start all over again. It took a full forty-five minutes of intense concentration, but finally, she heard the reassuring clunk of the last of the padlocks opening, and pushed open the barrier, entering a restricted world.

Chapter Forty

"Chief, it's Red. I'm at the Penrose's. I'm going to need an extra pair of hands."

The silent pause over the radio was tough to read but the Chief's eventual reply wasn't, "What the—? What did I tell you about interfering? My conversation with your father doesn't seem to have got through to you like I intended!"

"Hey, look, the widow reported him as a possible missing person. What choice did I have?" Red shot back, and pressed home the point. "In any case, this place is a mess. Maybe a break-in, I can't be sure. Whatever happened here, it was violent. We need to treat it as a crime scene and see if we can find Penrose because there's no sign of him."

The Chief's breathing was loud and ragged over the crackle of the transmission. But he eventually followed an enormous sigh with, "I'll send Jackson. Secure the area."

Red beamed and jabbed a fist into the air. "Already done, Sir!"

"And Red,"

"Yes, Chief?"

"There's something else. Forensics called. We're back to square-one on the body. The bookend didn't kill him—that came later."

Chapter Forty-One

Quill glanced behind, head jerking, checking she was alone but needn't have worried. The building remained silent and unoccupied. The earnest faces of the scholars who spent their days there in quiet study remained missing in action. Another painful reminder of normality. What was the Master doing?

Whilst she had often looked into the forbidden room, it had never once occurred to her she would one-day find herself within it. The rules were sacrosanct. Nobody, other than the Master, went inside to study. And even then, she'd never seen him going in there. Sweat dripped down her back like sap oozing from the bark of a tree. Heartbeat thrashing in her ears, she did not know what she might find. And despite what the Deputy thought, believed that there must be a solid reason to have kept these works under lock and key for all these years.

Quill scanned the shelves, summoning the courage to search. These books belonged to a different world. Bright colours, sumptuously covered in many types of materials:

leather, suede, brushed velvet and others that were unidentifiable. Just like the book in Penrose's office, many of them had silver or gold trimmed edges.

As she selected a burgundy, suede-backed tome, leafing through crisp, arid pages, the room's temperature soared. Every page contained paintings and sketches of the human form, both male and female. Quill had, of course, seen anatomical drawings and understood the workings of the human body, but these looked extraordinary. The sweeping lines of a perfectly curated torso and the intimate study of a young woman's fine features hypnotised her. Startled, slamming the work shut, she threw it back on the shelf.

The Protectorate knew best when it came to core values. The appreciation and creation of beauty for beauty's sake was dangerous. A principle she had always embraced, and the Master had impressed upon her that The Protectorate would punish anyone who thought otherwise.

A return to the search clarified, almost painfully, that she had no idea where to begin. The task was monumental. There were so many books it was conceivable that it might take weeks to scan them all. Quill thought of the Master's life of study and found a renewed sense of admiration for his tireless work. As she continued pulling books out, she discovered more and more depictions of beauty, and the more she looked, the more fascinated she became. It was intoxicating, thrilling, much like the rush of pleasure derived from studying the books about constellations and black-holes. A moment of clarity allowed her to acknowledge that it wasn't only the secret knowledge of the universe that attracted her, but because it was breathtaking, utterly exquisite. Did that make her wicked?

The further in she moved, the deeper Quill delved into the world depicted on the pages, a world that she didn't recognise or understand. Distracted irretrievably from the job at hand, the harder she tried to concentrate on looking for an answer to the mysterious note, the worse it became.

The light from outside faded, confirmation that time was not on her side. A lack of window drapes meant that turning on a lamp was not an option. The glow would act as a signpost in the murkiness of late afternoon, attracting unwanted attention. Confronted with no other alternative, she resigned herself to working more quickly if she was going to discover anything before it got too dark to continue. Unthinkable, the prospect of repeating the entire process the following day.

As she approached the end of the third shelf, closest to the expanse of windowpane, she spotted a lone black book stand. It was ordinary and functional, as were most things in the library, but it struck her as odd. They provided scholars with ample space to work. With room enough to sit five abreast, at the rear of each study table was an elevated plinth on which they could place their book of choice. It enabled them to examine it at the perfect angle whilst at the same time having space to take notes or write their own versions. She had never seen an individual book stand anywhere else in the vast building.

Headed toward it to carry out a closer inspection, she realised it wasn't empty. Reclined upon it was the smallest book Quill had ever seen. She suspected it would fit in her palm. Compared to the opulence of those all around her, this particular book was unremarkable, and she almost ignored it in favour of running back to the shelves. But something drew her to pick it up, hold the tiny work in her hand. Its black leather covering felt cool and supple in her left palm, and as she caressed it with her fingertips, she felt the channels of a circular indentation which she had not noticed in the deepening gloom. Eager for a clearer view, she took the work to the window, holding it up to what little light remained. And there she saw what her fingers could not decipher. A shape embossed in the centre of the front cover. Recognition struck like the clang of a bell, a symbol, and one that was becoming familiar. Its subtle addition to the black leather ensured that it hid in plain sight. A swirling G, surrounded by a circle.

A dry mouth forced her to lick her lips, attempting to drive more saliva to her tongue. Quill sensed the sound of the blood rushing around her body. Inner ears vibrating like the taut skin of a drum being struck. Could this innocuous book be the key?

Quill leafed through the pages in a hurry. They were amazing. Someone had handwritten the text in the minutest lettering imaginable. Designed with secrecy in mind, from its plain exterior to the indecipherable interior, the combination proved a worthy challenge to even the most curious of readers. The contents simply weren't legible to the naked eye. She needed a way of magnifying the content. Had she been in the central library, she would have known instantly where to look. Years of painstaking study took their toll on the eyesight of the library patrons and providing magnifying equipment was a necessity. But the last thing she wanted to do was to leave the text and return to the main building. What if someone saw her? It would be far easier if there were a magnifying glass here, but she couldn't remember having seen any.

With the book clutched to her breast like a mother comforting a child, she made a more general search of the restricted room. Just as she was about to admit defeat, hanging on the far side of the very last set of shelves was a single, solitary magnifying glass. It was at least double the size of those in the main library, and in place of a traditional wooden handle, its trim and hilt were bone. Ice-cold to the touch, carved into the macabre object, were eyes—eyes of all shapes and sizes staring out from all angles. Tendrils of fear crept through her skin and into her consciousness. "It's just a carving. Pull yourself together," she muttered, carrying the bizarre object and prized find back over to the diminishing light at the window.

Finally able to see the ant-like lettering, Quill was desperate to devour the contents of the book like a barren wasteland slakes its thirst on the first rain shower. A tight band of pain across the forehead intensified to an insistent throb as she battled with the text. Stops and starts, over and over, repositioning the glass to focus on the letters through gritted teeth. Whoever had been its author had spent hours creating each letter in varied sizes and at disparate angles to each other. A fastidious effort that must have taken months of work.

At first, it was the most infuriating exercise imaginable, hindered further by the shortage of light. But, after many minutes of perseverance, the distorted text abruptly unscrambled itself. A miracle. The realisation that she could read it was jaw dropping, though not nearly as incredible as the contents themselves.

The subject-matter was equal parts terrifying and mesmerising, but it was impossible to turn away. Set out in precise detail were all the subjects forbidden by The Protectorate. The full gamut of creative arts; Art and Sculpture, Music, Dance and the Dramatic Arts. Topics unheard of in Scolaris, those that valued the aesthetic, the antithesis of everything she had ever read or been told, that beauty and creativity had value.

In fact, the ideas led the reader further. It was a treatise. Much like acquiring knowledge enslaved the City of Scolaris, this intricate work deified beauty and creativity in any form.

Quill switched to the view through the expanse of window and gasped, arms flailing as she threw herself to the ground. Afraid to look up, she was stunned by the sight of a wizened, intelligent face, peering back at her through deep emerald eyes all framed by unkempt, white hair. The Master had caught her.

Before she'd had a chance to think of a plausible excuse for her disobedience, in the blink of an eye, the apparition disappeared. Perhaps it was a trick of the light or a sign of a guilty conscience. Only he would have answers to the million questions firing off in her head like bursts of solar light. If only she could speak to him.

Turning the final few pages absentmindedly and distracted by the Master's appearance, Quill came to a blank beige sheet nestled inside the black cover. She reached the end just as the last fragment of daylight shrank from the glass panes, a last breath of life swallowed by the cavernous jaws of the night.

In the dying of those last seconds of daylight, she noticed a shadow. No, a mark, something on the back of the last page. Flipped over, it wasn't blank at all. Astounded, blinking in disbelief, fingertips tracing its outline again and again, a symbol, the same symbol etched on the cold, pale skin of the Professor's corpse. And underneath, one miniscule but perfectly formed word, 'Meraki'.

Chapter Forty-Two

A million thoughts raced through Quill's brain as she careered through the darkened library, leaving the restricted room and its treasures to the silence.

A solution to the coded note had not presented itself. But what she discovered was more troubling than anyone might have imagined. What was Meraki? Whatever it might be, somehow it linked to the tattoo on the Professor's body and to the mysterious secrets of beauty and creativity hidden in the pages of the unassuming book. The object she'd returned to its resting place in the locked room.

Thoughts battled for attention. Snippets of knowledge dangled like tantalising threads. The symbol related to some dark and forbidden unknown. If she could just unravel what that was, maybe she could follow the whisker thin skeins to the spider's lair.

Events of the last few days had started with the discovery of the Professor's corpse. He lay at the centre of everything. The discoveries in the book did nothing to dispel that theory. Acknowledging that corpses can only reveal so much, she recognised she had no choice other than to speak to the next best thing. Though describing Mrs Hawkin as such without doubt stretched the truth to its limits.

Quill steeled herself for a confrontation as she reached the front door of the apartment. The time for tact and diplomacy was over. The Master faced an imminent trial, and she refused to think about the consequences if they found him guilty. Doubtless, the widow knew a lot more than she was saying. For a start, she had given different accounts of her movements the evening before the murder. She realised the idea that a wife would be oblivious to her husband's work and interests sounded utterly incredulous. More importantly, she thought, how would she not know he had a tattoo?

The front entrance of 1 Courtyard Place swung open easily on its hinges as her fist connected firmly with it, and loud, high-pitched voices assaulted her ears. Something was happening inside, and it was not a polite gathering of old friends.

"No wonder he couldn't stand the sight of you anymore. You're just a bitter and twisted old drunk."

"How dare you? There's no accounting for taste. I can't imagine what my husband saw in you. You're nothing but a—a desperate, pretentious floozy."

The haughty tone of Mrs Hawkin's raised voice reached Quill's ears, the sound unmistakable as she entered the living room. Confirming suspicions as to the source of the other female tone, she caught sight of the young, svelte figure of Ms Ginsburg, the Hawkin's family lawyer. Eyes bulging, stifling a gasp, Quill stared at the pair, incredulous, their almost identical pin-striped dress suits twisted at unnatural angles. Red faces and matching sheens of sweat created make-up land-slips as, oblivious to her arrival, the slanging match continued unabated.

"You're a vision of misery, tired and ragged around the edges. At least I have a brain and a purpose. Exactly what do you contribute? I don't think liquid lunches count."

"Insult me all you like, but I was his wife and you'll never be anything more than his sordid secret. I could end your career in an instant. One word in the right ear and you'd be finished."

"Are you threatening me? Don't forget shameful secrets apply not only to me. There's the small matter of your intoxicating habit."

Hatred hung in the air between the women like noxious gas. Quill knew she shouldn't be eavesdropping, but they rooted her to the spot, hypnotised by the vicious exchange.

"You might have been his wife, but he didn't love you." Ms Ginsburg's stark statement was like a punch to the head, felling Lucinda Hawkin onto the low-slung sofa. The state of the two women left no doubt that there had been a physical altercation.

It appeared, though, as if Ms Ginsburg's ultimate taunt had dealt the older woman a deadly blow, one from which she seemed temporarily unable to recover.

The silence that followed was excruciating. "What do you want from me?" Mrs Hawkin's dead voice at last broke the silence. It lacked its usual haughtiness as the woman diminished. Before the lawyer had an opportunity to answer, the widow rose, reborn, striding toward Quill, fists clenched, "How long have you been standing there, girl?"

Panic took hold, strangling Quill in its grip and, to make matters worse, out of the corner of a damp eye the steely eyed, pursed-lipped lawyer closed in. Cornered by the pincer move, paralysed, the enmity between the two women resurfaced, but at that moment it was redirected and she was the unfortunate target.

"Please, I'm sorry. I wasn't snooping," said Quill, curling into a ball, anticipating an attack. "The front door was open, and I noticed raised voices. To be honest, bearing in mind the last few days, I got scared and wanted to check that you were okay," she pleaded.

The widow grabbed her by the arm, skin pinched in the firm grasp. The woman had recovered much of her strength and smirked, apparently buoyed by the ability to inflict pain on another human being. Tightening the grip further, she hissed, "Don't lie to me, girl. What did you overhear?"

Quill glanced up at the young lawyer, her wide-eyed wordless plea for help eventually answered. "Let her go, you're hurting her," Ms Ginsburg finally said, all at once grasping what was happening. She pulled Mrs Hawkin away and stood with her arms crossed across her body, staring out into the garden. "No-one is going to hurt you but you need to tell us what you overheard," the lawyer said, emotionless now, but insistent.

"Okay, I heard everything," Quill stammered, casting her gaze down to the tiles beneath her feet.

"Go on," said Ms Ginsburg.

"Mrs Hawkin drinks too much and you and the Professor were—" she couldn't say anymore, it was too uncomfortable. Though she suddenly remembered sharing the inside of a lab cupboard hiding spot with a stiletto heeled shoe, and reckoned she had just identified its owner.

"Perfect, okay, you picked up all of it," the lawyer whispered into the floor and then added, "Coffee, I need coffee, preferably with a dash of something stronger."

"Yes, in a moment but—madam, there's something important that you don't know," Quill said, walking over to Mrs Hawkin who had slumped back onto the sofa. "You were correct. Mr. Penrose is missing, and it looks more and more likely that he was somehow involved in the Professor's death. I don't care what I overheard, I'm just trying to save my Master. I know you loved the Professor and I believe you want to understand what really happened to him."

"You're right, girl, I do," the widow acknowledged.

And Ms Ginsburg nodded and added, "And so do I."

"I hate to admit it, but you're right. I have grown rather too fond of a pomegranate martini of late. But can you blame me? Discovering your husband is having an affair with a woman half your age is reason enough." Mrs Hawkin's admission didn't exactly roll off the tongue, and she scowled at the lawyer throughout.

"So, on the evening of the Professor's death you said you hadn't felt well and went to bed early. But later, you told the Chief you'd been with a friend. Which is the truth?" asked Quill.

"Mm, I suppose neither really," she shrugged. "Don't honestly remember. True, I'd been drinking, but the next thing I recall was you, girl, pounding on the front door. I've been wracking my brain for an answer, but must've been out cold all night. The last thing I recall was Alexander fixing me a drink but then my mind, it's a blank."

"Like I said, she's a drunk," interjected the young lawyer.

"And whose fault is that?" the older woman snapped back. "I'll concede I need to curb my alcohol intake, but I'm sure I hadn't consumed too much that afternoon. To be perfectly frank, I just don't understand it."

"Why did you lie?" Quill asked.

"Simple, to protect my reputation. I couldn't admit I'd been out cold, inebriated."

Quill almost felt sorry for the woman. The marriage had clearly been a sham. But a need to paint a picture of perfection still drove her to apply a false veneer over her private life. Position and power came at a heavy cost.

"I'd love to ask how we know you're not lying now?" asked Ms Ginsburg, "but have to concede that you're telling the truth."

Mrs Hawkin's vacant stare and trembling hands registered the shock Quill suffered too, hearing this concession. "How very magnanimous of you. Don't expect me to be grateful, and how do you know anyway?" the older woman asked.

"I don't expect you'll think very highly of me, in the circumstances, but lawyers don't lie."

A low, gruff, masculine tone startled all three women and, in response, a trio of heads jerked around in perfect unison, as a voice said, "Who's been lying, sunshine?"

Chapter Forty-Three

The Chief of the Guard stood before them in his recognisable, if shabby and grease-stained beige overcoat. His eyes pinched together, and he reminded Quill of a well-fed rodent. She wondered if maybe he needed glasses.

Typical, just when things were getting interesting. Heat rose in Quill's chest in response to her carelessness. How could she have been so reckless again? Leaving the front door open might prove yet another costly mistake.

"Never mind, ladies," the guardsman said, deliberately inserting himself amongst them with his back resolutely facing in Quill's direction. "I'm sure it's not as important as the information I need to share with you, Mrs. Hawkin." He gestured with his right hand as if to usher the older woman away from the living room to explain his tasty tidbit in private. However, she stayed firmly rooted to the spot and replied, "This lady is Ms Ginsburg, the family lawyer. You can say whatever you have to say in her presence."

The Chief raised his eyebrows and paused but then added, "Please ladies, sit."

Quill squirmed, tugging the tunic tight to her waist, unable to process the absurd observation of polite niceties. Particularly as the odious man was inviting Mrs Hawkin to sit in her own house.

"Erm, there's no kind way to say this, Madam," he stated, clearing his throat, "but we've had the last reports from the forensics lab on your husband's body. I'm afraid that a blow to the skull didn't kill him after all."

"You're not making any sense, Chief. Someone hit him on the head with a bookend, correct?" asked the widow.

"Yes, but that isn't what killed him. The forensics lab has discovered a chemical in his bloodstream, it's the same substance found spilled all over the laboratory floor. So far they can't identify it but they have tested a small sample on a lab rat."

"And?"

"Let's just say it wasn't a happy ending for the rat. At first it simply appeared to be drunk."

A moment of understanding passed between the women as three pairs of eyes met.

"Did I miss something?" the Chief asked. But, Mrs Hawkin shook her head and responded, "No, please carry on."

"As I was saying, the rodent appeared to be tipsy, and they used the word 'euphoric'. Not that I understand that really," he said to himself, eyebrows knitted together, "but, within thirty minutes, it was dead."

Those last words hung in the air between them like a foul odour. The women exchanged confused glances, but no-one seemed willing to break the uneasy silence.

The sound of the Chief's stomach grumbling finally broke the awkwardness. And, as if suddenly woken from a dream, he continued, "Obviously forensics are still running tests on it, but I'm thinking we need to clear-up what the Professor was working on. Especially as Mr. Penrose seems to have disappeared. It's perfect that you're both here, together, I mean. Madam, Ms Ginsburg, so I can ask both of you. What was this chemical? What was the project he was carrying out?"

"I can't believe you break this disturbing news to me, Chief," Mrs Hawkin snapped. "And then expect me to answer questions I've already answered," she said, an ugly twist to her mouth. "The Professor was the most eminent cosmologist and chemist in all of Scolaris. Of course he would store chemicals in his lab, you ridiculous little man. As to what they were or what he was doing with them, I've absolutely no idea, as I've been at considerable pains to tell you, over and over again." At that point, the widow was breathing hard and red in the face.

Quill had particularly enjoyed the woman's sarcasm at the Chief's expense and waited with great anticipation to see how he would respond.

"I am sorry to offend you, but we are dealing with a murder case and we must investigate every detail. Ms Ginsburg, your name was on architect drawings, also found in the lab. Perhaps you know the answer?"

The lawyer paused and steadied her gaze, looking the guardsman directly in the eye. "You should know better, Chief. I cannot discuss it with you, because that would be a breach of my duty to preserve client confidentiality. But you know that, don't you?"

The Chief smiled, the thinnest of white-lipped smiles, and nodding imperceptibly, turned on his heels and left.

Chapter Forty-Four

"I suppose I should say thank you," said Lucinda Hawkin, after checking that the Chief had gone.

"No need, it's my job. Whatever our differences, I presume we agree we need to learn what happened to Alexander. I don't believe the Chief has the faintest clue what he's doing."

Quill wanted to offer some words of agreement about the Chief but decided not to push her luck. Nevertheless, she felt vindicated in her own low opinion of the man.

"Of course," continued the lawyer, "as the guardian and benefactor of the Professor's estate, I am at liberty to discuss his business affairs with you. In fact, that was the reason for my visit. There are papers that need signing," she added, gesturing towards a black briefcase at her feet.

"I'll sign the papers, but first I want you to tell me what you know."

Quill noticed that the atmosphere in the room had changed. The two women would never be friends, but they had discovered a common purpose to unite them.

"Are you certain you wouldn't prefer to discuss this somewhere more private?" asked the younger woman, glancing sideways at Quill.

Mrs Hawkin looked firmly at Quill, who had chosen to look busy by plumping sofa cushions with great gusto. "No no, continue, I guess she's earned the right to be here."

Fingers touching parted lips, Quill gaped. Maybe a heart was beating somewhere inside the proud woman after all.

"I'm unsure how much use the information I have is going to be. Alexander and Theo were working on several projects. What they all were exactly, I can't tell you because I don't have a clue. The one thing I do know about are the blueprints for an observatory."

"Those drawings in the lab, the ones the Chief mentioned, the designs with your name on?"

The lawyer nodded and continued. "I assume so. No-one has asked me to file a note of ownership on any other projects."

"Was that really Mr Penrose's work?" asked the older woman.

"Nothing ever gave me any reason to suspect that it might not be Alexander's idea. Everything appeared above board. He'd correctly drawn up the plans and specifications I lodged with The Scientific Advisory group for verification and proof of ownership. It wasn't until after we'd received approval that Mr Penrose visited my offices and alleged that Alexander had stolen his work. Even then, I didn't believe him. For a start, I saw no evidence to prove the allegation."

"Why do I get the feeling that you changed your mind?" Mrs Hawkin asked.

"I didn't, not really. I had no suspicions until the day before Alex died." The young woman paused, pacing up and down the length of the sofa, and went on in muted tones. "We met often, in the lab, mostly in the evening. Knew no-one would disturb us. He would leave the glass doors open for me. On the rare occasions that you came to the lab I could just slip outside into the garden, but mostly you stayed away, often because you were drunk."

Mrs Hawkin studied the floor, fixated, refusing to meet the gaze of the younger woman.

"When I arrived as usual, on that last evening, he wasn't there. There were a load of papers in a heap and to pass the time, I thought I'd be helpful and tidy. As I sorted, I found a set of old drawings of the observatory. Alexander didn't prepare them because I would have recognised his handwriting and Mr Penrose's name was at the top of the page. I wasn't sure what to do and I'm not proud of myself, but I took them. I have them locked tight in my safe."

Quill could contain herself no longer, having rearranged the cushions at least a dozen ways. "This confirms what Mr Penrose said. I've been trying to say this from the start. What reason would the Master have to kill the Professor? But Mr Penrose had an obvious motive. And now we've been told this chemical killed him, Penrose has to be the murderer. Who else would have known about it and what it could do?"

Lucinda Hawkin waved a dismissive hand and turned to the lawyer. "You had access to the lab, and you were here that night. You'd just discovered that Alexander used you to commit fraud," she said. "Now, that's a motive for murder!"

The young lawyer turned grey and wobbled unsteadily on her high heels, grasping for the support of the settee.

Sipping the water that Quill had fetched and taking deep breaths seemed to restore the young woman enough for her to continue. "Believe me when I say that I could never hurt Alexander. I'll admit I was suspicious about the plans and that's the reason I took them. But, again, they weren't definitive proof Theo was the rightful owner of the observatory. And as for suggesting that I would know anything about a toxic chemical, well, that's just absurd."

An invisible fingertip poked Quill repeatedly, vying for attention. But she just couldn't pinpoint what she needed to remember.

"Not forgetting, you had greater access to the laboratory than I did," added the lawyer. "And based on the lab rat's behaviour, it's obvious to me you'd been sampling this mysterious substance for a while. I lost count of the number of evenings we looked in on you passed out with a stupid grin on your face."

The earlier truce was well and truly over and the pair of women were back on their feet again, facing off like commanders in chief of their own one-woman armies. The shouting and hurling of abuse resumed.

Quill almost wished for the return of the Chief, powerless to intervene as the two women traded insults. To tune out the sound, which resembled an incessant buzz of flies, she surveyed her surroundings. How had she been so impressed by the place earlier? The apartment wasn't a home. It was a glossy veneer, and if you scratched the surface, you uncovered a hollow shell. It was something she needed to learn in the future. And then, through the clamour of the ruckus, an image took shape in her mind. And the words shot forth before she was even aware of them, "The shirt!"

"What shirt? What are you talking about, girl?" Mrs Hawkin shouted. "I demand to know what you mean."

Quill glanced at the young lawyer who was looking decidedly green and said, "The day I helped you sort through the Professor's clothes, I saw her," and she nodded towards the lawyer, "throwing a rubbish sack into the silo, the one in the courtyard just beyond the passageway. I went back later and took the bag back to the library. Inside it I discovered a shirt, a dirty brown stain down the back of it. It was the Professor's, had the initials 'A.H.' embroidered on it. When the guard searched the library, I had to hide it, but the Deputy discovered the bag and that's when they arrested the Master. I don't know how I'd forgotten about it." Quill's words came tumbling out all at once, together with a huge measure of guilt.

Mrs. Hawkin, hands on hips and a broad grin on her face for the first time in several hours, turned to her rival, "Try getting out of that noose Ms Kitty Ginsburg, if you dare."

The lawyer paced once more and chewed her immaculately manicured fingernails. After much deliberation, she followed frantic chomping and alternate glaring at Quill, with an unforeseen announcement, "It's mine."

"Don't be ridiculous. The girl's already said it had his monogram," replied Mrs Hawkin.

"Not the shirt, the blood. The blood is mine."

"That's very convenient. You expect me to just take your word for that? How would your blood be all over the back of his shirt?" asked the widow.

The young woman sighed. "Listen and I'll tell you. It happened that same evening. After I found the plans, I put them in my briefcase and waited for Alexander to arrive. When he finally turned up, he said he'd been cleaning up in the apartment because Ezra was off running some errands and you were drunk, again. Together we checked on you and you were comatose, on top of the bed, fully clothed. After, we, um," she could not continue, her cheeks flushed with embarrassment. "I mean, the glass doors were open as usual and it was chilly. Alexander gave me a shirt to put on. We held each other, it was a wonderful, crisp, spring night." She was lost in memories, Quill realised, a distant stare in moist eyes, teardrops forming in the corners.

Returning to reality, the lawyer swiped at those damp eyelids and continued, "We'd both drunk some red wine and in the excitement he spun me around and I lost my balance. I hit the back of my head on his telescope.

Couldn't believe how much it bled. See—here," she said, parting the blonde curls at the base of her scalp.

Mrs Hawkin peered intently down the length of her nose at the young woman's head and then, looking up, said, "There's a small gash under the hair. It looks recent. I guess she might be telling the truth. But, that still doesn't prove you didn't kill him," she added half-heartedly.

Kitty Ginsburg sighed. "I didn't murder him. I loved him and he loved me. After we recovered from the shock of me hitting my head, he swore he always wanted to be with me. He was going to leave you, and we were planning to start a new life together. It was a perfect evening, and it's all I have left, the memory. When I went home, I can assure you he was very much alive." The fragile woman crumpled then, and covered her face with the palms of her hands.

Mrs Hawkin scoffed. "It seems Alexander took us both for fools, my dear. He assumed I didn't realise about the two of you together, or he didn't care. He knew I wouldn't complain because I adored him before you learned the meaning of the concept. And as for you," she said, jabbing her finger at the younger woman, "he manipulated you so he could pass off Penrose's work as his own. Do you really suppose he would have risked his position and everything he had lied and cheated for? And for what, love? You may have the intellect required to be a lawyer, but it seems we have both been victims of his charade. Love blinkered us both and rendered us blind. Blind to the truth."

And from the tremors rippling through Kitty's body, Quill could see that finally everyone's blinkers were off.

Chapter Forty-Five

Night closed in tight, gripping and pressing bare skin, sucking the warmth out of every living thing and sending goose bumps hurtling along Quill's arms. Theo Penrose had access to the lab, access to the toxin and an obvious motive for murder. The fact that he had disappeared wasn't looking good for him, either. It was true there were still loose ends, and the frustration was debilitating, but progress was being made. However, to persuade the Chief that he had got the wrong man, she knew she needed to eliminate as many obstacles as possible.

Grasping the aquatic door-knocker, condensation dripped into her palm as if the finned creature wept at her touch. Tainted by uncertainty, she nevertheless pounded on the door, deciding to trust in her ability to say the right thing to whoever answered. A conviction that Doctor Cooper was one of those loose ends that needed binding spurred her on.

"What are you doing out by yourself on such a dark night?" asked a rich, mellow tone from the shadows of the entrance. Quill frowned. She had been expecting Kai, but as the owner of the voice stepped into the porch light, it was a relief to see the familiar, kind face of old Jed. "Terrible about your Master. Terrible business."

Quill smiled. The mature woman radiated kindness and comfort like a bear hug. "Thanks Jed. He didn't do it, I just don't believe it."

"Don't doubt it, Miss. Trouble is, there's folk who can't see the truth even if it's right in front of them."

"That's something I'm learning," Quill replied. "Sorry to call so late but I really need to speak to Doctor Cooper."

Jed took a step closer, examining her features, and asked, "Are you sick, Miss? There's me banging on about seeing the truth and there's you looking peaky and I don't notice."

"Err—yes? Yeah, I don't feel great," she said, seizing upon the opportunity presented to her.

"Why didn't you say? Come in, come in, out of the cold." And the kind old woman ushered her into the dark hallway and the hospitality of the Cooper residence.

As they moved through the hallway, Quill glimpsed the Doctor's private living room through an open doorway to the left. She wondered if the library key was still in its hiding place. The elderly woman moved briskly for her age, and keeping pace left no time to linger. There were three other rooms off the corridor, but their doors were closed, so she could not satisfy her curiosity any further. The hallway was dark and depressing, a stark contrast to the general warmth of the place. With a glance up, Quill could just make out crystal teardrops hanging from the ceiling. But for some unknown reason the light fittings were devoid of bulbs. She had never been into the main house, and the darkness was adding to the sense of disorientation. Focus returned to the hypnotic, side-to-side sway of old Jed's hips as the old lady effortlessly motored through the home.

Without warning, the woman took a ninety-degree turn to the right and vanished from view. The confusion was immediate, sending Quill walking straight into a wall. Eyesight adjusting to the darkness, gathering her wits, she could just pick out the dogleg to the right and hurried to catch up with her.

"Nearly there," said the old woman.

A minute later they arrived at a pair of glass panelled double doors which led out into the garden. And right behind the house stood the Doctor's clinic, shining like a beacon in the night.

"I'll leave you here, missy. The Doctor will see you're alright."

Quill shivered, stepping out into the dark, the warmth of the big house evaporating in an instant. The clinic and the principal residence were both white, but there the similarities ended. Sterile and perfectly proportioned, the clinic was a recent addition to the grounds. The building was a prefabricated construction, a cube with windows that they'd dropped into place in a single afternoon.

Automatic doors slid open with a breathless hiss, inviting visitors to step into the waiting area. Inside, cool, clean air circulated through purifiers which hummed a low, soothing note. As she stepped forward, a door to her right, Doctor Cooper's examination room, swung open.

"Hello, may I help you?"

It was Kai. This was awkward. The aftermath of the last encounter remained fresh in her memory. She recognised she had been hoping that they wouldn't bump into each other.

"Hello. I can hear you're there," he said again, foot tapping, sounding irritated.

Quill stepped towards him as he reached the curved white reception desk, navigating the way with his hands to take up position behind it. She exhaled, thankful for the barrier between them. "Kai, err, hi," she said. "It's me, Quill."

He paused, then said, "What do you want?" in a low voice, busying himself shuffling papers from one side of the counter to the other.

"I just need to talk to Doctor Cooper."

"Why? Are you ill?" he asked, still unwilling to look in her direction.

"No, I'm fine but,"

Before she could continue, he spoke over her. "Well then, I can't disturb him. Doctor's very particular, clinic hours are for patients only."

She strode towards the desk, fists clenched and shoulders hunched into the crevices behind her earlobes. "If you'll just let me finish, I could explain. Why are you being so difficult?" Quill said, placing both palms on the desktop.

Kai stared, golden eyes once again threatening to bewitch her, and she had to look away. "Difficult? I'm just doing my job. I tried to help you, even though it could cost me everything, but you seem to think you know everything. Haven't you solved the murder by now? Suppose you've come to tell us all how clever you are. The Protectorate will be so grateful they'll give Quill a medal. And then, you won't have to be a filthy Defecto any more."

Quill could almost taste his bitterness. Tongue sticking to the roof of her mouth, teeth like balls of cotton-wool. The memory of their disagreement flashed before her. And it was clear that he hadn't forgotten the harsh words spoken, either. She didn't have a spare minute to get into an argument and she didn't want to, anyway. "Stop, I don't want to argue. Master Wit's still being held prisoner. Please, I need to speak to the Doctor, just for a few minutes. I won't involve you in any way, you have my word."

Kai jerked. A dazed expression reflected that he expected a fight. Quill's measured response was a distinct departure from their earlier exchanges, but arguing was tiring and pointless. The sound of a door opening interrupted the standoff, and they both turned in unison.

The man in blue scrubs was immediately recognisable. Doctor Cooper approached the counter, deeply engrossed in a set of patient notes and clutching a dark, leafy green litre cup of thick smoothie from which he periodically slurped, eyes crossing and cheeks hollowing in response to the exertion required for each suck of the straw. Reaching the desk, he finally looked up from the papers. Pale and drawn, despite the seemingly healthy drink, the scrubs hung off his petite frame in folds. Were they the wrong size? Though he had never been a big man, Quill estimated he had lost at least two stones in weight since the last occasion she had come for the Master's herbs. The Doctor practised what he preached, believed in healthy living, good nutrition and exercise, but at that exact moment resembled a walking skeleton.

Quill's sharp intake of air prompted a glance her way. Their eyes met momentarily, but then the physician turned and headed straight back to the examination room. Sure that he had seen her, she called after him, "Doctor, doctor, I must talk to you." She followed behind and caught up to him just as he was about to close the door, ignoring her plea. His shoulders sagged and after a few awkward seconds he turned back to face her, examining his rubber shoes as if his life depended on it. "Quill, do you have an appointment? Hmm I don't think you have. Please, see my assistant," he said nodding towards Kai, "I'm sure he can book something in for you." And with that he continued into his room, closing the door behind him and signalling that their conversation was at an end.

"Is he ill?" she said to Kai. "He's lost weight, I'm sure of it."

"I'm not sure, maybe. Jed said the same thing this morning. He's definitely not his usual self."

"In what way?"

"I'm not certain exactly, more a feeling than anything concrete. Like, just then, with you, he wasn't very caring.

There aren't any other patients coming, and he knows that."

"Look, I realise this is a difficult situation and I shouldn't be asking, but I don't have anyone else who can help me. There isn't time to explain everything right now, but I need to see that key. I have to find out if it unlocks the reading room once and for all. And if so, I'll have to confront him with it, ask him why he has it hidden." She patted the pocket sewn into the tunic's bottom seam, checking for the original key. The cold, hard outline was comforting. Contented, she relaxed. It was still there.

Kai did not answer straight away, instead feeling his way behind the desk and on the floor. Stick in hand, he set off at speed towards the entrance. "Stay here," he commanded, "I won't be long."

Quill paced, gaze flitting between the entrance and the examination area. The fact that Kai had decided to lend a hand filled her with hope. Perhaps they could be friends after all and put their disagreement behind them.

No sooner had he headed off into the darkness to fetch the key than the hiss of the automatic door and the rhythmical tapping of his cane interrupted her thoughts. He was grinning, that hypnotic, fresh-faced smile that could melt a block of ice. Clutched between the thumb and forefinger of his right hand, he held a small brass key.

"I got it," he said, beaming, holding it aloft. And at that precise moment, Doctor Cooper emerged once more from his room. What little colour he had left in his cheeks drained away. His skin resembled wax paper and could not disguise the myriad of capillaries underneath the surface.

He covered the ground between himself and the boy in seconds and snatched the key from his grasp. "What the? What are you doing going through my private things? After everything I've done for you and this is how you repay me? A thief, I've invited a thief into my home."

"Please, I'm not a criminal. It's not how it looks. Let me explain," answered Kai, voice strangled, distraught.

"Be quiet. I don't wish to hear it. I want your things packed, and you gone by morning."

Kai's mouth opened and closed, searching for words that never came.

The enormity of the situation hit Quill like a storm surge, biting into the base of a cliff. She had dragged him into this perilous situation, and now she would have to find a means to steer him through it. She had done her best to stay on the periphery, a silent watcher absorbing information, relying on social invisibility. But that could not continue. If she remained in the shadows, her friend would pay the ultimate price. Kai had risked everything to assist, and she wasn't about to sit back and watch him thrown onto the streets.

"You can't do that," she said, raising her voice. "Kai wasn't stealing anything. He was trying to help me and Master Wittgenstein. You do remember the Master? One of your oldest and most respected patients? The one they've locked up, facing trial for murder?"

The Doctor backed away, shambling, "Quill, I, I didn't realise you were still here. Of course I'm aware of his predicament but I don't see what that has to do with any of this." And he waved the key around in the air ahead of them.

"I saw you, hiding that key, in your living room. I think it's a key to the reading room, where we found the Professor's body. What I want to know is why do you have a key and why were you hiding it?" Quill asked, anxious and exposed, nowhere left to hide. She was a Defecto and over the last few days she had learned what that truly meant. She had no right to ask questions, and her opinion held no value. Kai was right. Her life with the Master sheltered her from the truth, and she was now seeing reality. She waited, anticipating him to explode with indignation, but it never came. Instead, he perched himself on the edge of the welcome desk, running his fingers through a slick of black hair, kneading his temples as he did so.

Muttering under his breath, barely audible, he said, "I knew it would all come out. I should have known better."

Quill and Kai stepped closer and waited for him to continue. "You've got it wrong. All wrong, just wrong," he repeated, head in his hands, unwilling or unable to meet their gaze. "That's my key. I don't have one for the reading room. You're mistaken."

Chapter Forty-Six

Was that scenario possible? Could she be mistaken? If it wasn't a key to the reading room, why was he hiding it?

"I don't understand," Quill said, "it looks just like one. I saw you hiding it in that pot in your living room. If it's your key, why do you need to hide it?"

"Hide what?" The fresh voice startled them all. They had been so engrossed in the key's mystery that they hadn't noticed the hiss of the automatic door and the footfall of sturdy boots.

Deputy Red stood in the reception, hands on the hips of his blue uniform. Quill's sense of relief was immediate. She had confidence in him; she realised. If anyone could get to the truth, it was him.

"Apologies, I should've introduced myself. Deputy Red of the City Guard and you are?" he said to the doctor.

"Good evening. Doctor Cooper. Good to meet you. Now how can I help?"

"We're investigating the murder of Professor Hawkin. I assume you know that someone murdered him?"

Doctor Cooper nodded, top lip sweating beads.

"I came to ask you for some general information about the Hawkin family and your dealings with them, particularly in the six weeks or so preceding the murder. But, now I suspect I should ask you what you're hiding and why?"

The Doctor glared at Quill and looked around the room as if searching for an answer. "I don't know what you mean. I think you must have misheard the end of a private conversation."

Red cleared his throat and stepped closer to the medic. The difference in size between the two men was telling. Red's muscular physicality a striking contrast to the skeletal frame of the clinician. As he fixed the doctor with a steely glare, he demanded, "Quill, what has the doctor been hiding?"

Pulled deeper into the core of the investigation, dragged from the shadows, kicking and screaming like a toddler, Quill's usual preference to hide from life resurfaced. Threatening to undo all the boldness she had discovered over the last few days, a voice in her head urged her once more to run as far away as possible and only emerge from this nightmare when it was all over. Circumstance, it seemed, had other ideas. And, realising that she had nowhere left to shelter, she mustered all the courage she possessed and answered, "I was here, the evening after we found the Professor. Mrs Hawkin sent me for something to help her sleep. The Doctor sent a message with Kai here," and she turned and nodded in the young man's direction, "that he was too busy with patients to speak to me. But while I was waiting at the door, I saw him hiding something in a pot in the fireplace in the private living room. It's a key. Possibly a key to open the reading room," Quill said, blurting all the details out, relieved to get them off her chest.

Three pairs of expectant eyes now focused on the medic, who remained perched against the edge of the reception desk. All of a sudden his head dropped into his palms, trunk and shoulders heaving. The scene made uncomfortable viewing, but they waited patiently for him to speak. Slowly, the rise and fall of his body settled, and he took a deep breath, gathering his emotions. "I've been such a fool. Follow me," he said, rising from the desk and heading into his room.

The examination room was much like the rest of the clinic, sterile and impersonal. There were no personal effects on display, no family photographs or knick-knacks. The only object which punctuated the glaring white of the walls, floor and furniture was a spiny green cactus adorned with a solitary cerise bloom, tufted like a feather duster.

From a desk drawer, Doctor Cooper retrieved a red metal box built with strength and security in mind. With shaking hands, he attempted to insert the small key into the lock on the front of the box and, after several failed attempts, finally opened it. "Like I said to Quill, this key is mine. I don't own one for the reading room. Why would I?"

"Well, you certainly proved that, thank you. What I don't understand is why you needed to hide it?" asked the Deputy.

"I should have come forward at the outset, but I was afraid. Terrified that I'd be implicated in the murder. But, I had nothing to do with it, I swear. I felt pressured. Professor Hawkin was a powerful man, and I relied on his recommendation for my practice."

"Pressed into what exactly?" Red asked.

Doctor Cooper looked at them wide-eyed, the fear etched in the lines on his forehead and hanging in the folds of skin beneath his chin and over his emaciated frame. "The Professor didn't tell me what he was working on, said he needed to find volunteers for a medical trial. He asked for details of particular patients who might be suitable. I didn't want to do it—-I shouldn't have done it, it's not ethical. But, he made it clear that I didn't have a choice. The building of this clinic cost a fortune. The expense has almost crippled me financially, so I need a steady stream of sick clients to pay for it." Missing bulbs in the house and his careworn appearance suddenly fell into place as he paused to catch his breath before continuing. "Basically, he told me that if I didn't do as he asked, he would make sure that work would dry up. The whole situation frightened me, so I kept records of all the patients that I suggested. When I heard that he'd been murdered, I panicked. I didn't want anyone discovering what I'd done."

"I'm going to have to take those records and you'll need to come with me," said Red, an authoritative and unwaveringly business-like demeanour blossoming in front of Quill's eyes.

The doctor submitted with a nod and handed over the box. Red pulled out the patient record from the top of the pile and studied it. "One last thing before we go," he asked, "you said Professor Hawkin needed specific patients. What did you mean by that?"

The humbled man hesitated, shoulders slumped in defeat, and added, "It was odd, and he never explained it. Defectos, they were all Defectos."

Chapter Forty-Seven

Quill clung to a solitary crumb of hope. The hidden box of patient records was safely in the hands of the Deputy, as was Doctor Cooper. A furtive glance at the uppermost file disclosed a name—'Val' written in a spidery scrawl.

And yet, face up on the bed, pallid dead bodies flitted across the white-washed ceiling as Quill gripped the bedclothes. What had become of Ezra's sister and what had the Professor been up to? Nothing they had uncovered so far even hinted at the answer, but whatever it was, couldn't be good.

Every piece of additional information yielded nothing more than crippling confusion. On each occasion that Quill felt herself edging toward unpicking the tangle of details, a new knot popped up and she had to start all over again. Professor Hawkin had been the architect of a project involving Defectos, and at least one of them was missing. But she still could not think how or even if it related to his murder. Theo Penrose was still unaccounted for, and she was no nearer to decoding the note they'd found in his office. As for the secrets noted in the little black book which continued to whisper to her from the forbidden room, she chose not to share those. Something incredible lived and breathed in those miniature pages, something powerful and hypnotic. She fought the urge to return to it, to give herself once again to its magnetism. It frightened her how an object so small and innocuous could have such a potent effect. Like a drug, she was afraid that she might never be free of it.

The depths of night closed in on the city. She had never spent so many hours away from the library nor her own private haven, and she sank down into the blankets, creating a Quill-shaped cocoon. As her eyes shut, a crystal-clear image of her father greeted her, and her heart raced with excitement. He held out his hand, and she reached for him with her whole being. How could she have forgotten his face? Wispy brown curls framed intelligent, kind eyes and soft whiskers moved as one as his blood-red lips mouthed her name. He pulled away, blurring anew at the edges.

Quill battled against it, but her thoughts drifted, and behind sealed eyelids the familiar view of galaxies and black holes emerged, taking shape. She inhabited a world between dreams and consciousness, merely an observer floating among the stars, omniscient, all-knowing. As she slid toward the black hole, feeling its magnetic pull, she heard her father call her nickname. Searching for him, she looked back and caught the bright lights of a city. Scolaris, shrinking into insignificance below her. The pentagonal construct of the library dominated the skyline, surrounded by districts on all five sides. A city that didn't sleep shone in a blaze of light from every corner. The thirst for knowledge never dimmed.

Just as she was turning aside, dazzled and blinded by the glare, his sing-song voice cried out to her once more. And then she saw it, dark and in the shadows, at the far extremity of Law and Order. She had to shield her vision from the glare, to be certain. What was she seeing, and why did it seem familiar?

Jolted from the intense epiphany, Quill sat bolt upright. What she'd witnessed would never leave her. A domed building shrouded in darkness, part of the city and yet separated from it. And then the melodic call of a Lilith-bird on the ledge outside the window connected the disparate thoughts. She had seen this before, and now she knew where.

Chapter Forty-Eight

There it stood, silently watching from the folded and creased piece of old paper grabbed from her one and only treasured item, the Lilith-bird box. It could almost have been a replica of Professor Hawkin's observatory. Why hadn't she realised this before now? Was it possible that the project was for renovation and rejuvenation, disguised as something else? The goosebumps undulating down her neck pointed to the building being real and connected to the conundrum posed by the Professor's death. She just needed to work out how.

Quill couldn't shake the distinct image of her father's face, and the sound of his voice showing her the way. Looking at the leaflet with a different viewpoint, she straightened, animated and alert. An impressive octagonal base climbed up two storeys to meet the domed roof. Built with solid stone, at each apex stood a supporting cornerstone. And on each side were six windows, arranged in threes, each set above the other. Now that she thought about it, she remembered how, as a child, she'd imagined herself inside the dome. Stood in the centre, surrounded by sunlight streaming in from all sides, spinning round and around, eyes shut, giddy with excitement. Perpendicular to the octagonal end, the building continued. Rectangular and stretching away into the distance, so much so that it disappeared off the page. The project would never compete with the sheer scale of the library, but nothing quite like it existed in Scolaris.

The closer Quill looked at the image, the more additional details she noticed. Flecks of white and red in the stone walls, the tips of green and yellow leaves dangling over the edges of the paper. Details that she had paid no attention to before then. As she studied its intricacies, her breathing stalled.

This wasn't a leaflet at all. Unmasked, minute brush strokes discovered—it was a painting!

Here was yet more evidence of her failure to truly appreciate the world around her, as opposed to living a safe, vicarious existence in the pages of a book. And then, a further possibility emerged. If this was a painting, perhaps the artist had marked their work, and maybe that would tell its own story. Quill examined the artwork from this fresh perspective, but found no signature, nothing to point to the painter. Having almost admitted defeat, she turned onto the back. But to no avail, it was empty.

Disheartened, she folded the sheet back into the box, and in doing so removed her right thumb from the bottom right-hand corner. And there, where the thumb had been, sat a tiny black smudge. As she brought the blot closer, it reminded her of something she had seen recently. A detail just out of reach, a memory that she needed to recall. What was it?

Hands shaking with nervous anticipation, Quill held a magnifying glass up to the black smudge. Stood amongst the bookshelves in the early dawn, the eerie quiet strummed her eardrums. Shadows covered the ground, merging into black holes beneath her feet.

She was right, her memory had not failed her. The black mark wasn't a smudge. The magnifying glass translated everything that was invisible to the naked eye. Just like the little black book, a perfectly steady hand, perhaps the same hand, had made their microscopic mark.

Astounded and animated, she read the strange writing aloud; 'TP 19264548'. It was exactly the same as the coded note in Penrose's office.

With the magnifying glass hooked back onto the end of the study table, still clutching the painting, Quill circled, piecing everything together. The Professor's plan for a new observatory, or was it Penrose's project? Its uncanny resemblance to the building in the painting and to the place shown to her by her father. A vision, a dream, or a memory? She struggled to decide which. The forbidden text in Theo's drawer; coded message stashed inside. And now the same code on this painting, hidden in plain sight, altogether like the text of the black book. They all had to be connected, otherwise there were just too many coincidences.

Whatever had happened, it still seemed real, vivid, and tangible. Her father had pointed the way to the structure in the picture, she felt sure of it. The place waited at the outermost edge of the city, beyond Law and Order. But how was that possible? That district was the one area of Scolaris that she had never visited. Perhaps she was letting imagination overtake logic? Maybe it was just a dream, after all?

Exhausted, stiff and sore from head to toe, limbs trembled, willing her to sleep, at least until daybreak. Quill trudged back to the bedroom, dragging her reluctant body along too. In the haste to climb under the covers, she somehow kicked the box, flipping it over and sending its contents spilling onto the rug. Griping, she righted the prized casket, returning her meagre possessions into its care. The map of the city, painstakingly marked with each new place that she called on, was at the bottom of the pile. Eagle-eyed, she smiled, tracking the multitude of black crosses. But entirely bare, past the eyesore that was Guard HQ, sat the unmarked section.

Quill's mind erupted. Had that been the answer all this time? How could she have missed it? The code. It wasn't complicated in the slightest.

Chapter Forty-Nine

Skinny legs pumping like pistons, Quill wobbled uncomfortably on the Master's bicycle. He treated it like an old girlfriend. Even giving it a name, 'Doris'. The elderly scholar had given strict instructions never to touch, let alone ride her. But today, she was incredibly thankful that she'd ignored him and taught herself to ride over the course of many secret midnight excursions. She wasn't an expert cyclist, but she hoped to reach her destination without serious injury. With any luck, it could just add to the long list of evil deeds that the Master would never discover.

Quill's attempt to speak to Red before setting out had been unsuccessful. All she had managed to accomplish was awakening a very irate guardsman named Oliver. The poor man simply shouted in her ear that he expected the Deputy to be still asleep at home, just like every other civilised person. He, on the other hand, was on duty and didn't mind chewing her ear off about the inconvenience of it. She had dithered, not knowing what to do for the best, unhappy to leave a message with the oh-so-cheerful Oli. But in the end, seeing no other choice provided him with details of where she was heading. The sleep-deprived curmudgeon had reluctantly agreed to get the Deputy to meet her there as soon as possible.

Quill did not want to go alone, fearful, not only of what she might find, but of what would transpire if she was wrong. What would happen to the Master if she found nothing? Hesitant, she floundered like a hooked carp before wheeling out 'Doris' from the study and setting off on her journey of discovery.

The start of the trek had been difficult. Riding over the cobbled courtyard encircling the library had certainly woken her up, but she knew she would suffer with bruises later. But now, reaching the Legal District, the cobbles gave way to slick, tarmac streets and the road ahead smoothed out. The streets were empty as daylight approached, a crisp, chilly dawn expanding over the horizon, bringing with it a rain-washed, fragrant atmosphere. As she cycled into the wind, downy hairs stood on end and she relished the rush of air against skin and pedalled harder.

The map nestled in the tunic pocket. A safety net in case she got lost. But it wasn't truly necessary. She knew exactly where to go. The Code having unscrambled instantaneously, revealing its humble truth—it was just a grid-reference.

As she passed row upon row of high-rise office complexes, the road climbed, forcing her to pedal harder to keep moving. Quill was just wondering how much longer she could continue when she glimpsed the brow of the hill, relieved by an absence of anything other than blue sky beyond it. At the summit, she stopped for a few moments to catch her breath. Dazzled by the view, the rest of Law and Order stretched out below her. To the left she could just make out the margins of Science, plumes of coloured smoke belching unknown substances into the atmosphere. And, to the right, the dissonant shapes of the unique buildings of the architects.

The city was nothing short of miraculous, but she needed to keep going. Stood on the top pedal, she launched herself and old 'Doris' down the hillside. Hurtling along, the buildings all blurred into one and she grinned until her cheeks hurt, the exhilaration of the ride bubbling up and out of her like a wave.

With the slope conquered, the way ahead was flat and uninspiring, and she settled into a monotonous rhythm. Experience had taught her that the map was not exactly to scale, so it was impossible to estimate how long it was going to take to reach the city's edge.

After about an hour her calves burned, and she contemplated stopping for a rest. As she looked for an ideal place to get off, the office buildings were becoming noticeably scarce. Their business-like facades replaced with crude units; a hodgepodge of random materials recycled to make homes. She had reached the Defecto quarters, attached to Law and Order.

She must be getting close, she hoped, reminded that time was against the Master.

Quill continued cycling, forcing her body weight to bear down on the pedals, ignoring the creaking and whining of Doris beneath her. The tarmac roads turned to rutted and potholed dirt tracks which, in many places, were under several inches of rainwater. Evidence of the last few days of spring weather.

The contrast in living conditions was appalling. Seen for the first time, the blindfold of naivety disintegrated and she saw the city and what it represented in a new light.

Just ahead, off to the right-hand side, rose a mountainous stack of cardboard. It sagged in the centre, weighed down by the recent heavy rain. And then, out of nowhere, it lurched sideways.

Quill flinched, throwing herself and the bicycle off course, hurtling out-of-control straight toward an enormous pothole filled with stagnant, muddy water. With a pounding heart and weak knees, she whimpered, fighting to control the panic and the bike's trajectory. Just as she was convinced the dirty pool was about to engulf her, a welcome squeaking, screeching sound confirmed that she had, at last, successfully applied the brakes. Finally able to open her eyes, she was relieved to see that Doris had ground to a halt only millimetres before the track dropped over the edge of the murky lake.

After catching her breath, Quill turned back toward the corrugated mound and thought she could detect something underneath, sheltering from the cold. Closing in, she could just pick out the curve of a bald head, pitted and dimpled. The creak of Doris's wheels disturbed the outdoor sleeper, propelling her upward, jettisoning the cardboard shelter in its entirety. The figure was old, even older than the Master, mottled skin puckered and pinched tight over an angular, emaciated frame. When she spoke, she displayed a toothless mouth, but the voice penetrated the silence with its strength and authority. "Who are you? Why have you woken me?"

The shock of uncovering the woman rendered Quill speechless, struggling to articulate an answer.

"What a rude girl," announced the ancient woman, gathering the soggy cardboard remnants around her.

"Sorry, I didn't mean to wake you. I didn't know you were there," Quill blurted out, garnered into a response.

"Where else would I be, girly? I'm always here. Everyone knows this be my spot," she said with the assurance of someone who hadn't moved in decades.

"I didn't know that. I don't live here. Sorry—"

"But you're in the right get up," the toothless woman said, looking up and down at her brown tunic. "Where else would you live? There isn't anywhere else for the likes of us."

"Oh, I understand what you mean," said Quill. "I am a Defecto, but I don't work here. I work for Master Wittgenstein."

"Huh?" the woman replied, demonstrating that she had no clue who Quill was referring to.

"He's the Custodian of the library at the centre of the city. Where the city-dwellers store and study all the knowledge they've gathered. I'm his Defecto so I get to live there."

"Poor you," the old woman commiserated, "I can't think of anything worse, being cooped up inside four walls. The open air, that's where I belong. Freedom, you can't beat it. And who wants to be serving one of those rich types?"

"It's not like that, not with him. He's kind, and he looks after me. Even after my father deserted him, he kept me on. I owe him everything."

"I see. Maybe he's different from the rest. I've never met one of them like that. You're lucky, you should hold on to it."

"That's the trouble," Quill replied. "I thought nothing would ever change. Assumed we'd carry on day after day, reading and studying and writing, until one day he'd realise that I was capable of all those things too. But everything's changed and now I don't even know if I'll ever see him again."

All Quill's hopes and dreams and fears poured out in a torrent of words. In the presence of a stranger, she unburdened herself, clinging to the stiff, iron embrace of old Doris.

"Better?" asked the old woman.

Quill nodded, feeling lighter somehow. The pent-up emotion of the last few days released entirely.

"What I really want to know, being as you live with the rich folks, is what you're doing here?"

The bald woman's question jolted her back to reality. Taking the map out of her pocket and unfolding the sheet, she pointed to the rough location and said, "I'm looking for a building. Expect it should be relatively nearby. The place is rather distinctive." And Quill described in detail what she was searching for.

The ancient woman listened intently, filmy eyes widening at every word. When Quill had finished, the woman looked around her in all directions. "What d'ya want to go there for?" she whispered, furtive glances continuing to search for unwanted eavesdroppers.

"Look, I can't explain everything, it's much too complicated, but I hope there might be answers in the building that could prove useful."

The old lady turned from side to side in slow motion, scratching her skull where the hair should have been. "Really don't see how. No one goes there, no one, not ever," she confided, taking a sharp breath before continuing. "They abandoned it long ago, years before my birth even. My ma wouldn't tell me why, told me never to speak of the place, let alone go there. She just said it was forbidden, unnatural. She wasn't afraid of anything— except that. A few of the young-uns dared each other to get inside, but that's where that ended. Talk but no action."

"Take me there, please?" Quill pleaded.

The hairless woman shook her head vigorously, "Not me, you'll not catch me going." And then she sighed and her body slumped as if someone had sat on her, expelling all the air from within her lungs. "Follow this track until it ends, where it meets a thick bank of trees. Imagine that the route continues along the same path through the tree line. Eventually, you'll reach the place, The Pavilion, that's what she called it, my ma. Funny, I'd forgotten that, and it's just popped into my head." And she chuckled to herself as she returned to hibernation beneath the saturated layers of cardboard.

The Pavilion, TP, the initials from the coded note, now made sense. "One last thing," Quill called. "I'm expecting the Deputy of the City Guard to meet me there. His name is Red. Can you—?"

"Yes, yes. I expect nothing good's going to come of this but on you go, you're disturbing an old woman's beauty sleep."

Chapter Fifty

Quill fought through the thick bank of trees, hoping that the directions were reliable, particularly as the old woman had supposedly never been where she was headed. Much to her annoyance, riding the bicycle was no longer possible because the trunks squeezed tight, packed against each other like matches in a box. Their roots tangled above ground, fighting each other for sustenance. The treacherous terrain magnified tenfold by the all pervading murk, which hung like a shroud beneath the evergreen canopy.

Valiantly, she pressed onwards, grunting and groaning as she dragged the iron hindrance with her. No birds sang to greet the new day, and not even the wind penetrated the tree line. The silence was unnatural.

Without warning, the mass of trees spat her into a clearing, the silent shadows transforming all at once. The rising sun startled her with its brilliance, and she squinted and shielded her face, trying to dispel the kaleidoscope of bright spots that flashed across her vision. Looking down at her moccasin covered feet, she blinked hard, and as her sight returned, her gaze moved upwards and she breathed a sigh of relief. The place was real, and finally she had found it.

The Pavilion towered above her, an exact incarnation of the painting that nestled in her treasured box. The unrelenting march of time had taken its toll, but its carcass remained intact. Its sandstone walls worn and weathered, dry and cracked like sun-burnt skin, the original yellow now a muted beige. Most of the ground-floor window panes were missing, but those at the top had fared better.

She entered the clearing at the octagonal end and walked along its perimeter, running her fingertips around the stone walls in awe of its construction. It wasn't possible to see the domed roof from her position at the base of the walls, and she doubted whether it could have survived.

Quill continued circumnavigating the boundary wall, searching for a way into the building. Just as she began to doubt whether she would ever find a point of entry, she suddenly found herself on the opposite side of the octagon. From this vantage point, the building took in a panoramic view of the world beyond Scolaris. In silence, The Pavilion watched.

The clearing stretched away for miles in front of the dilapidated building before it again gave way to trees. Those trees continued almost as far as she could see, blurring finally to a jagged, glinting streak of contrast right at the edge of the horizon. Was that the sea?

Reading the books in the library, Quill knew life existed beyond the city, but they were just two-dimensional representations. She had never really considered the reality of an existence elsewhere. To look at it now, real and alive, close enough to touch, was exhilarating. How exciting would it be to experience first-hand the wonders of the places on the pages of those books?

Turning back to the building and to the immediate challenge, the rectangular section, perpendicular to the tower, stretched away to the left and into the distance beyond her field of vision. Straight ahead were four broad stone steps, flanked by cylindrical columns which supported a portico. Relieved to be leaving the bicycle at the bottom, she trotted up the steps, heading towards a pair of white solid-wood doors. It was hard to miss a muddy trail which preceded her, dotted with plump green blades of grass, all of which squelched underfoot.

Out of breath, arriving at the doors, she recognised they had not escaped the effects of weathering. What looked like pristine white slabs from a distance, sadly flaked and peeled. The evidence that humans had deserted the place was scant, and in reality, much to prove the contrary was true. The doors stood open, and the building enticed her to step over the threshold.

Darkness squeezed Quill's chest, devouring the air inside her lungs as she crept forward. Disoriented by the sudden plunge into blackness, she threw her arms out ahead, stumbling as nausea washed over the nervous moments. As her vision corrected itself, she saw with enormous relief that she stood in a small vestibule which could be crossed in four strides. Marching through the claustrophobic entranceway with confidence, it delivered her unharmed into the main building.

As soon as she stepped inside, the view transported her straight back to childhood. A look upward to the top showed, to her surprise, that the domed glass ceiling was mostly intact. The sun had not yet risen sufficiently to penetrate the tower's entirety, but beams of light were bouncing and refracting off the inner surfaces of the octagonal structure. The floor had at some point in the past been covered in tiles, arranged geometrically, white octagons bordered by ink-blue. Much of the flooring was missing or broken apart, leaving behind only islands of tiled perfection. In places, the reflected rays of the sun lit up those islets. Captivated, Quill hopped from one to the next, hunting for a refuge bathed in sunlight. Stood on one such spot, she turned her face up towards the glass roof, and imagining a night sky full of stars, spread out her arms and whirled like a gyroscope. Turning faster and faster, grinning with utter joy, rotating on and on, until she was unbearably dizzy and had to stop.

Once the world had righted itself she continued to island hop across the tower floor. The further forward she went, the less light reached her until, finally, she plunged back into the dark shadows. Sweat trickled down the back of her neck and travelled over her shoulder and onto her collarbone. Her breathing shortened, becoming erratic, and the bliss that she felt only seconds earlier vanished. As she inched closer to the opposite border of the tower, she could just make out the edges of something heaped on the floor. Its shape was irregular, which made it difficult to identify. The closer she crept, the more it reminded her of the piles of washing that she did for the Master. "It's definitely clothes, nothing to worry about", she whispered to herself.

To calm an out-of-control heart rate, Quill inhaled deeply, crouching down to scrutinise the heap. And as she reached for a handful of clothing, she jumped, flinching, and let out a strangled cry.

Recoiling in horror, Quill struggled to process the brittle, wiry texture against her palm, expecting instead something soft and malleable. Whatever she'd touched did not feel like the Master's clothes. What was it? Desperate for more daylight, she stepped across the unidentifiable mass and turned to face back toward the entranceway. The daylight from that side of the tower just penetrated the floor in front of her, the irregular heap no longer obscured in its entirety by the shadows. Quill's eyes fluttered, blinking, waiting for pupils to adjust, and as they did so they grew wide and her mouth fell slack.

The lump was Theo Penrose. Quill had been gripping his ponytail.

Someone had secured his hands and feet with coarse, orange rope. Quill feared Penrose might be dead and crouched on all fours to examine him more closely. Tentatively, she stretched out her right hand and poked a fingertip into his right shoulder. His tiny eyes remained firmly closed, and she was still none the wiser. She studied his chest, hoping to see the natural rise and fall of breathing, but struggled to catch any movement. "Mr Penrose. Can you hear me?" she implored, but he made no reply. As a last resort, she ventured to touch his face. The skin felt raw and damp. But then, much to her relief, she sensed a very delicate hum of warm air from his nostrils. The lab assistant was alive, though barely, and she couldn't guarantee for how long.

Quill searched around for something to revive him with, but found nothing. And then the true reality of the scene hit her. If he was the murderer, why was he here, tied up and left for dead? The carefully constructed web of clues leading to this man disintegrated in an instant and ran through her fingertips.

What had she missed, she asked herself, battling to understand what was in front of her? Quill drove her fingers through her hair, grasping large handfuls and pulling them at the roots. Longed to shout and scream, but knew it wouldn't do any good. Penrose needed help, she needed help. Where had the Deputy got to?

It couldn't wait, she decided. Leaving to fetch some backup was the right thing to do. Just as Quill garnered herself to head out, she suddenly thought she heard a noise. Frozen to the spot, she raised an ear, focusing all of her attention. Something was definitely making a sound behind her. The muffled noise was practically imperceptible, like the murmur of the wind. But Quill was sure she hadn't imagined it.

Turning towards the sound, she plunged again into the darkness cast by her own shadow. Hands outstretched for protection, she edged forwards. She had not gone more than a few steps when she noticed a faint crack of light, which gradually illuminated the edge of another door. Grasping it with her fingertips, it opened towards her and she stepped through, finding herself in another section of the tower. On this side, sunlight penetrated every surface, and the effect was joyous. It reminded her of scenes depicted in the little black book that had so entranced her. She imagined the melody of music and the rhythmical accompaniment of dancing feet.

A stone fountain sat in the centre of the space, drawing the eye toward it. The monolith stood grey and bleak and no water flowed from it. Propped against the far side slumped another human shape, and as Quill approached, the noise grew louder. A guttural rumble, reminiscent of a wounded animal, setting teeth and nerve and synapse on edge. What was that awful sound?

Drawn ever closer, Quill tiptoed towards the prone figure, intent on retaining the element of surprise. As more of the body came into focus, she detected soft curves and a head of black hair. Together with the distinctive aroma of something sweet and heady. Pleasant at first, but underneath a sickly, rotten undertone, like cheap perfume.

Closer still, the lustrous, black mane extended along the full length of its owner's back. The strands in Quill's mind reattached themselves, linking one to the other, tentatively adding a brand new suspect.

Chapter Fifty-One

The figure muttered and as Quill rounded upon them, threw back a head of thick black hair and chuckled. An onslaught of the cloying scent watered Quill's eyes and, lightheaded, she reached for the stability of the fountain, afraid that she might faint.

Convinced now that this was a woman, the head lolled forwards and backwards as she continued the muttering. "Stupid man… mouth shut…" was all that Quill could decipher as she waited for the swoon to pass.

At long last the giddiness subsided and Quill registered a pair of distinctive earrings which co-ordinated with sunflower yellow high-heeled shoes. Footwear which looked to be a match for the lone shoe which had shared her hiding place in Professor Hawkin's lab. Heart hammering in her chest like a woodpecker, crouched in front of the woman feeling beneath the curtain of hair, Quill took hold of her chin and lifted her head. Instantly, her suspicions confirmed, she found herself staring into the face of Mrs Penrose.

"Mrs Penrose. Are you okay? What's happened, what has he done to you?" she asked.

The woman's eyelids remained clamped tight, as if she were sleeping. Suddenly, those eyelids snapped open, and she fixed Quill with a determined stare. "Ivy Laburnum, that's my name. I'm not Mrs anything," the deranged woman said. "And as for him," she said, waving her left arm in the general direction of her husband, "he really wasn't capable of doing anything. Unless you count shouting his mouth off about his precious project. Still, I was right about one thing, making my darling spouse disappear made you believe he was a murderer," she snickered again, amused by her own cleverness.

So, it was true, Mrs Penrose had used her husband as the perfect cover for her crime. Shaking the woman, trying to rouse her from whatever she was under the influence of, she shouted, "I don't understand why. I get the Professor copied Theo's work, but murder? How? Why?"

"You truly are a clever one, aren't you, my darling? Much too clever for a Defecto." And then her head flopped again, and she hissed through her mane, "It was all worth it. I have it coursing through my veins."

"What are you talking about?" Quill begged, "Ivy—please—wake up."

Disconnected, drifting in and out of consciousness, Ivy's head continued to flop from side to side, as if attached to her torso with elastic. Quill shifted the woman's hair from the right side of her face, behind her back and across the left shoulder, trying desperately to increase her air intake. As she rearranged the last black strands from behind the woman's ear, a familiar symbol confronted her. It was the same small swirling G that the guard had found on Hawkin's body, and identical to that on the end page of the black book. "Ivy, Ivy wake up," she shouted, shaking the woman and dislodging the hair that she had only just moved.

"Huh?" the woman grunted, opening her eyelids a fraction, revealing a recognisable trace of violet around enormous black pupils.

Pointing to the distinctive tattoo, Quill asked, "What is this? What does it mean?"

An enigmatic smile appeared on the woman's full, crimson lips, and looking up towards the domed roof she said, "Now that is a long story, and I'm not sure there's time left to give it the attention it deserves. It was a shame, about the Professor. He perfected the serum as instructed, but his obsession with testing and retesting it became a problem. He thought no-one would notice missing Defectos, and at first nobody did. And then, who could forget his wandering eye? He was a handsome man," she declared, momentarily fixing her eyes on Quill. Her declaration was a challenge, and as if in recognition of that fact, she chuckled to herself and added, "Have I shocked you, my darling? What is living without an appreciation of beauty, devoid of the skills necessary to create beautiful things? Pah, what a waste of an existence. The Prof knew that at least, yes, he was a man of science, a disciple of knowledge but never at the expense of creativity. Though, I suppose in the end that was his downfall. I enjoyed his physique, and he enjoyed mine on and off for years. On that last night, I waited for Kitty to leave and then I joined him. We drank, it was easy enough to add a dose or two of his own serum to his wine, and then I led him in a merry dance to the library."

Quill reeled, unable to comprehend what she was hearing. The lurid account dismantled the essence of everything Scolaris stood for, all that she believed in, and a negative voice in her head would not shut up, repeating over and over, "No, this isn't true. Lies, all of it." But then, the sudden memory of three wine glasses in the lab made a mockery of her denials, and she forced herself to listen once again as the woman continued.

"Alex was high on life and followed willingly. He was eager to be appreciated, and once naked, enjoyed himself immensely," she added, giggling again before proceeding. "The chemical did the rest. He died a lucky man, joy written on his face, a mind opened to all the beauty in the Universe. Hitting him with the bookend? My idea. A flash of inspiration, you might say. I wanted to make certain that he was dead and that everything pointed to Wittgenstein."

Quill shook her head and stood up, flexing her legs at the knees to ease the cramp that was setting in to her muscles. "Why would you want to hurt the Master? What has he ever done to you?" she yelled.

"I should thank you, really," Ivy added, ignoring her pleas. "We bumped into each other right before I saw you find that shirt. Now that really made things interesting."

So that's who she'd collided with. Quill shuddered, remembering the accusations she'd made against Kai. But the important questions about framing the Master remained unanswered as Ivy floated into oblivion once again.

Quill drew back her right hand and slapped the older woman's cheek, anger spilling over, out of control. The woman's eyes flickered and then immediately glazed over, staring straight through Quill as if she was invisible.

"Open your eyes my darling and you will see."

"See what? What should I see?" Quill growled.

"The Master. Optimise the serum, they said, and then infiltrate The Protectorate. So close, so close to removing Wittgenstein and replacing him with one of our own. Theo, Theo, you ruined it all with your bruised pride," the woman said, and then drifted back into a semi-conscious state.

Agitated, rocking Ivy violently once more, Quill yelled, "Who are they?"

Ivy turned her high-cheek boned, sculpted countenance towards the sunlight streaming in through the domed ceiling. Violet eyes lit up, and she smiled, pointing towards the roof, seeing something that Quill could not. "Look, see there. So lovely," and she sighed, expelling with a soft rushing sound, every molecule of air in her lungs.

"Who are they?" repeated Quill.

"Meraki—you'll never find her," the unhinged woman hissed through pristine white teeth and slumped to the floor, an expression of ecstasy frozen on her features.

The chance to uncover the whole truth came to a fatal end.

Ivy lay dead.

Chapter Fifty-Two

"Quill? Quill, where are you?"

Red's confident voice punctuated the silence, making Quill flinch. She called back to him and he was soon by her side, examining the body of Mrs. Penrose. "She's gone," he declared and Quill nodded in sombre acquiescence. "Penrose, he's dead too. That smell," he added, nose pinched and sucking in lungfuls of air.

"She did it," Quill said.

"What?" he replied.

"Ivy, Mrs Penrose. I figured it out just before I found her. She confessed to murdering the Professor with his own drug, the one he's been testing on Defectos." Quill's stilted words hung in the atmosphere between them, and Red opened and closed his mouth as if to speak but didn't utter a word.

Turning back to the corpse, Red expertly searched Ivy's black wool coat. As he patted the woman down with deft gloved fingers, he extracted a set of keys and an empty glass vial from the front right pocket. Holding them up to the light, they could both see a brown leather fob embossed with the initials 'A. H.' and a black swirling G on the bottom of the hollow bottle.

"All right, it seems Mrs Penrose told you the truth. Now I need to search through the rest of the building. This has been rough. It might be best if you wait outside?" he suggested.

Quill rose to her feet, and despite his superior physicality she held his gaze, her chin raised and responded, "I've come this far, I have to see it to the end." And she set off, leaving him trailing in her wake.

Theo's body now bathed in light, the sun having risen high enough in the sky to penetrate both sides of the tower with its warmth. Daylight breathed life into every corner, but even its fiery touch could not revive the stricken man. Headed for the rectangular section of The Pavilion, Quill filled him in on everything she had discovered since their last encounter at Doctor Cooper's clinic. Everything except the contents of a little black book, Ivy's reference to 'Meraki' and an unknown female. Not that she didn't trust Red. In fact, she recognised it was quite the opposite. Unlike the Chief, the Deputy had kept an open mind and hadn't treated her like dirt. As they walked and talked through the deserted building, she realised she couldn't tell him all the details. With nothing concrete to divulge, it was impossible to explain what she'd found without sounding crazy.

They entered the wide nave of The Pavilion through a stone-clad archway which was intricately carved with flowers and ferns of every imaginable species. And dotted here and there, hundreds of perfect replicas of butterflies. The winged figures were so lifelike; she imagined animating them with a stroke from her fingertips and sending them off into flight. Red whistled through his teeth. "Wow. I've never seen anything like it."

A thin piece of wood which blocked the line of sight through to the far side covered the gap underneath the decorated arch. As Red pushed it with his knuckles, it fell away, and the hidden section of the building opened out before them.

Red's words of wonder for the stone-carving seemed hollow compared to the view that now greeted them. Had she somehow injected life into the carvings with her imagination? Neither of them spoke as they fumbled and juggled with the incomprehension of the scene they witnessed.

The smell was unbearable. Quill covered her nose and mouth as best she could with the sleeve of her tunic, but was fighting a losing battle as the odour penetrated the thin fabric with ease. Red coughed and spluttered, but they pressed on regardless.

Butterflies perched on every available surface like a bewitching plague, and the air filled with flashes of colour from the beating of delicate wings.

"Fascinating," Red said in hushed tones. "The word from forensics is that the Professor's laboratory was swimming in a toxin, understood to be derived from an unknown insect. I guess we may have just found it."

Quill crept closer to a large specimen, alighted on the frame of an unbroken window. She recognised the kaleidoscope of colours at once and said, "I've seen this before. One got caught in a spider's web in the library and so I rescued it, before we discovered the Professor."

Red added, "I suspect he must've been breeding them, to extract the toxin. I didn't understand what I was looking at before. He had a glass tank in the lab, nothing in it except sticks and dried husks of vegetable matter."

The disappointing memory of an empty aquarium flashed before her. And she knew he was right. It was difficult to imagine that such a creature could contain something so deadly.

Passed the halfway point, what had appeared to be the far end was in truth another crude erected wooden screen. A narrow opening cut into the centre of it was only just wide enough for one person to squeeze through sideways. Red ventured across first, but before he pushed the entire way through to the other side, he turned to her and extended his hand. "Here, let me help you," he said.

Quill's stomach flipped, and she bit her lip as she reached out to his fingertips. Despite the chill, the touch radiated warmth, and it was impossible to ignore the faint buzz of excitement. The moment, however, was fleeting.

Chapter Fifty-Three

Beyond the screen, the butterflies enjoyed the luxury of human perches. Six perfectly formed alabaster statues lay head to toe on metal trolleys. Just like the relief carved into the archway, she imagined rousing them from sleep with a touch of her fingers. Every face bore the same look of frozen ecstasy, the bodies preserved by the toxin, each draped in the remnants of a plain brown uniform.

Apart from their gender and age it was difficult to separate them, or so Quill thought at first as she went from one to the next. Red studied those figures sleeping on the opposite side, rending the hush with a whisper. "Bill," the only harrowing word to escape his lips as he pointed to a head of salt and pepper curls.

The last soul, however, stood out. As Quill stopped in front of the young girl laid out to rest, she smiled at the blood-red shoes and neatly plaited auburn hair tied with a matching red ribbon. The girl belonged on the pages of the black book. Quill's gaze travelled from the girl's feet to her head and settled on the delicate hollow at the base of a long neck. Here she saw that a red scar marked the maiden's skin. Poignantly, it resembled a teardrop. Edging closer, Quill traced around the edge of the red patch with one hand and her own marked cheek with the other, feeling the connection. Acknowledging the reflection of her own insecurities, remarkably those self-doubts were transformed. Quill stared into almond-shaped, cut-glass-blue eyes, striking in their family resemblance, interspersed with jet black flecks. The girl was perfect.

Val—beautiful, embracing her imperfections, but tragically gone forever.

Chapter Fifty-Four

It was hard to contemplate that only a week earlier Quill and Red had uncovered the bodies of Mr and Mrs Penrose and all six of the missing Defectos. Subjected to a lengthy grilling about the whole affair, the Chief jumped at the chance to adopt the first explanation. Relieved, the guardsman swallowed the story that Ivy Penrose and the Professor's romantic connection had turned sour when she discovered his infidelity with Kitty Ginsburg. She'd picked up the distinct impression that he was under enormous pressure from The Protectorate. Doubtless, exonerating the Master and brushing six dead Defectos under a very large ornamental carpet was a satisfying resolution to the problem. The Chief delighted in magnanimously claiming all the glory for himself. Citing nothing more than a desire to preserve Master Wittgenstein's health and well-being as an excuse for having held him captive for three days.

Quill had longed to batter the smug grin from the old guard's face as he delivered the Master back to the sanctuary of the library. However, Red had sent word to her that The Protectorate had offered his boss a generous retirement package and he'd gratefully accepted. The man would leave in a matter of weeks. That factor alone had enabled her to sit on her hands and thank him through gritted teeth for solving the case.

The hardest part to swallow was knowing that six Defectos and their families might never get the justice they deserved. True, it seemed that Alexander Hawkin was responsible for their deaths and he had paid with his life, but she would have to live with the guilt of knowing that some as yet unidentified individual might have orchestrated the entire plan.

Whilst mourning those who died, she also thought of the living casualties. The Protectorate reassigned Professor Hawkin's lab and Lucinda moved in with a distant cousin, her circumstances diminished.

Doctor Cooper lost a great deal. Stripped of his private practice and ordered to return to hospital duty, he was no longer a resident of Serenity Gardens. And that left Jed to keep an eye on the place while they awaited the appointment of a new physician.

Kitty Ginsburg fared rather better. Somehow managing to retain her legal practise despite the infidelity. Suspicion lingered that her physical attributes might have played a part, but no-one was ever likely to admit that.

The thought that Kai might lose a job and his home terrified her. But she needn't have worried. He found himself reallocated to the new Science District Protector, Professor Moore, and now lived in the Hawkin's old apartments. Quill suspected Red had played a hand in that too, but asked no questions, just satisfied that her friend was okay. Their disagreements sounded petty with the benefit of hindsight, and she was hopeful for the future of their friendship. Content knowing she could rely upon him to tell her the truth, no matter how painful.

The initial few days of liberty for the Master had seemed tough for him to deal with. At first Quill had questioned him about life as a prisoner, but he brushed it off in the usual brusque manner. For the first forty-eight hours he slept, but not peacefully, plagued by nightmares, shifting and muttering incessantly. Nevertheless, she soaked up every second, watching, appreciating each line and wrinkle.

On the third day, it surprised her to find him at work, poring over a manuscript as if he'd never been away. Quill watched, comforted, celebrating the normality of daily life. After consuming at least four servings of scrambled egg together with copious amounts of his favourite herbal tea, Master Wittgenstein called to her to join him in the kitchen. "There's something I've been meaning to show you," he said. "I think you've proved yourself."

As Quill peered around the cupboard sized room, at the small stove and an array of dirty pots and pans which sat waiting to be washed, she wondered what she was meant to be looking at.

As if reading her mind, he said, "Not the pots. Here, come here," and beckoning with one hand, with the other he drew back the edges of the blue and green tapestry which hung where it always had, floor to ceiling on the back wall. It was difficult to comprehend, but inching closer she realised that what looked like a solid wall, in fact, contained a stone door.

The old scholar stepped into the boots that had returned to him with his freedom. And planting a shoulder against the stone, pushing off with rubber coated feet, the hidden door swung outwards.

Chapter Fifty-Five

The coffee was thick and black, steaming hot and laden with sugar. A bitter aroma steamed Red's nostrils, comforting as he sipped and surveyed his new kingdom. The apartment looked modest compared to the luxury of his parent's house, but it was his. An occasional twinge of anxiety at the thought of being alone troubled him, but for the most part, he felt relaxed and happy finally to be free.

His belongings remained cocooned in the boxes which lay all around him in the living room, but Red was in no mad hurry. His father extended hearty congratulations on concluding the case, but since their disagreement, mother chose to stay absent. Neither of them offered any help with the move, nor did they say goodbye. It was a shame that things ended badly, but he hoped that, given time and space, they could learn to understand each other better.

Content to allow Chief Ross a moment of glory, the entire City Guard, him included, celebrated solving the murder with boundless enthusiasm. But much to Red's surprise, no sooner was that shindig over than they were marking the Chief's retirement. Red had expected a replacement boss indistinguishable from the old. A Jim Ross clone. But nothing could have prepared him for a bleary-eyed Chief naming him as successor.

To mark the passing of the mantle of law and order from the old guard to the new, they had presented him with that odd looking triangular stone that always sat on top of the Chief's filing cabinet. Red discovered this was a guard tradition, another procedure he'd missed along the way. The Chief's explanation for the strange custom was that the fossilised creatures served as a reminder of how far man had come, and more importantly what he might return to without the order that laws bring to society. For the sake of good manners, he'd gratefully accepted the object, whilst at the same time wondering where he could hide it. But now he'd grown accustomed to the hypnotic effect of the creatures' spirals and looked forward to installing it in the new office.

Red couldn't deny that he was still grappling with the idea of being in charge. At the outset he'd wondered if there'd been a mistake, or if the amount of whisky that the old man readily consumed had addled his brain. But the official letter bearing the seal of The Protectorate had arrived. The thick, cream envelope was the first piece of mail to reach his new address and he'd struggled to stop grinning since opening it, leaving his cheeks aching.

'Chief Red', the title had quite a ring to it.

Chapter Fifty-Six

No sooner had the dust settled than Gaia had gained access to the house in Reynard's Close. After all, the Penrose's didn't need it any longer. She knew it was not a permanent solution, but for now, it would have to do. The place was a mess, broken furniture a prominent feature, not that it mattered. She wasn't planning on inviting anyone for dinner.

It was a real disappointment that they failed to remove Master Wittgenstein from the equation. The tip-off had been a stroke of genius. A move that came to her within seconds of hearing Ivy's story about the Master's Defecto running off with the blood-stained shirt. The forfeiture of Ms Laburnum's life was a waste, but she'd known the risks and the mission would go on.

The pain of losing the girl, however, remained cruel and unrelenting. Thank goodness she possessed an antidote to suffering. Holding a glass vial above her eye-line, she enjoyed the look of the multi-coloured serum, sparkling and refracting in the shaft of light which pushed through the crack in the curtains.

Gaia pulled the stopper and took a small sip, straightaway feeling the slow burn spreading down towards her feet. Surrounded by the boxes transported from The Pavilion, she hadn't yet been able to count the supplies. But at a rough estimate, reckoned on there being about five thousand vials, each containing sufficient for three doses.

Gaia smiled, stretching out long, languid limbs across the entire length of the black velvet chaise. And then she returned to braiding the hair that dropped from her head to brush her ankles. Slick and soft, silver strands which shone like stars.

Fifteen thousand shots of liquid joy. Gaia chuckled. It was more than enough to get started.

Chapter Fifty-Seven

This had to be another vision. No other conclusion rang true as Quill's mind battled the confusion caused by the bizarre events of those last few moments. A second before, she stood within the precincts of the library. Admittedly, in the Master's private rooms, but nevertheless, still inside a public building. Yet now, fresh air tickled her face, and the distinctive aroma of mint intermingled with lavender proved beyond doubt they were outdoors.

Raised beds stretched away to the left, the deep brown soil punctuated with green sprigs of new life, and pairs of Lilith birds enjoyed the worms. A ten metre stone screen gripped the secret garden in a hard embrace, imitating the construction of the library in every detail. As a result, anyone on the far side would notice nothing unusual. Two stone walls merging seamlessly into one, an optical illusion protecting the hidden natural sanctuary from prying eyes.

"Come," he said, leading the way. "Let's sit for a while and enjoy the quiet." And they held tight to each other on a wrought-iron bench. As Quill sat, mesmerised by the surroundings, she couldn't help noticing clumps of mud collecting around the toe of his boots.

Doubtless reading her thoughts, the old man turned, saying, "I have to thank you, Quill. I owe you my life. Each Custodian passes the mystery of this garden to the next scholar who takes on the mantle. A secret I am sworn to take to the grave if necessary. The pursuit of knowledge is indeed a wondrous thing, but if there's one fundamental truth I have learned from my studies, it's that knowledge alone does not nourish the soul. The Protectorate turned society aside from physical attractions and the creative arts because of fears surrounding the power they hold. But as scholars, how can we do the same with such delights all around us? How foolish are we to believe that 'Knowledge is King' and in the same breath ignore a key part of what makes us human? Over these past weeks, I learned I can trust you to keep this secret. And you must never reveal it. The Protectorate offer certainty and order to ordinary people, and any single factor that threatened the status quo could signal the death of knowledge as society's purpose and a return to chaos."

Quill remained in stunned silence. Everything she considered she knew and understood to be true and good disintegrated, exploding like the death of a star, normality caught in the aftershock.

The opinions the Master articulated were dangerous, the sort that could get the smart man locked up all over again. Regardless, Quill was no longer so afraid. Their way of life would never be the same, and she was glad.

"What happened to my father?" Quill asked, tentatively testing a newfound courage.

A contortion of pain washed over the old man and she clutched his hand tighter, awaiting a reply. "I should have explained before, but it never felt like the right moment. And as the days and weeks passed, it got harder and harder and I fooled myself into believing that you'd forgotten. I was ashamed. Your father—Matthew's absence is my fault," he whispered.

"I don't understand. He left. How is that your responsibility?"

"He only went because I sent him, across the Chares sea to Asteria, to recover a forbidden text. I know he arrived safe, received messages by post to begin with, and then, nothing. I tried to lead you to the letters when they arrested me, didn't you find them?"

Quill shook her head, confused, and then all at once it fell into place, and her insides vibrated as the excitement bubbled out of her. "The clock, they're in the clock. I assumed the stress of the arrest overworked your mind, confused you, and couldn't figure out why you were telling me to wind a mechanism that doesn't need winding."

"Ah, yes, I see. No matter, they are safe and waiting to be read. I'm so sorry."

"I told myself he'd just disappeared, scared off by this deformity," she said, brushing her hand across the feather shaped mark. Why hadn't she just looked at the clock like he'd asked? All this while the letters just sat there, waiting for her to find them. A link to her father and yet another example of why making assumptions was a bad idea. She felt she'd come a long way in just a few days, but clearly she was still a work in progress.

"What have I done? He'd never leave you for such a dreadful reason. Your father's love is not so fickle. How will you ever forgive me?" The Master's plea interrupted her thoughts. His wrinkled face radiated the fear of a lonely old man and she reached up to swipe away the single teardrop which ran down his cheek.

"He's alive, I feel it, and that means he'll be back," Quill replied, for the first time convinced, "and after everything we've been through, I can't be angry. I'm sure you thought it was the best way to protect me. But from now on, no more secrets. Agreed?"

The elderly fellow's downcast expression slowly morphed into a smile, emerald eyes crinkling, adding to the lines acquired over a long and productive life. And giving a hesitant nod, he said, "I appear to have blinked and missed you becoming a young woman, Quill. There's no doubt you're ready."

"Ready for what?"

"To seek the truth. Equipped to think for yourself. Everything necessary for growth as a scholar. And before you ask, we will discuss The Meraki, but only when I decide and not before." And reaching into the pocket of the white robe, Master Wittgenstein, Custodian of the Great Library of Scolaris, pulled out a familiar little black book and placed it in Quill's lap.

Thank you so much for reading *The Death of Knowledge,* Book 1 in the Scolaris Mystery Series.

Would you like to discover more about Master Wittgenstein? Delve into his past? The truth might surprise you!

Sign up to my mailing list and I'll send *The Death of Hope,* Book 0.5, a prequel short mystery in the series, straight to your inbox.

Get the FREE eBook at loulovesbooks.com/hopebk1 and be the first to hear about new releases.

Coming soon...

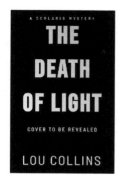

With the first crime in centuries solved, will the City of Scolaris return to peace and tranquillity? Or have the floodgates just opened?

Find The Death of Light, A Scolaris Mystery, Book 2, at loulovesbooks.com/dol

Enjoy the Story?

This book took 18 months of blood, sweat and tears to produce. Not to mention the preceding 40 plus years daydreaming about becoming an author. Apparently, that's the simple part!

To turn dreams into reality, I want to share the magic of stories with as many readers as possible. But, here's the problem—have you ever felt like finding your next great read is like looking for a single strand of hair in an ocean of DNA? Well, for a new author, multiply the size of that ocean by a bazillion (not sure that's actually a number?!), and that's the probability of readers finding my book (eek).

Before I lose all hope, if you enjoyed the story, you can help other readers to find the book by leaving a review on Amazon, Apple Books, Kobo, BookBub and Goodreads. Or anywhere else you can think of!

To make life easier, scan the QR code with your smartphone camera to be taken directly to the review page on Amazon:

Thank you so much for your review ♥

Also By Lou Collins

Acknowledgments

Huge thanks to my VIP reader team for their time and words of encouragement. I couldn't have done it without you ♥

Alison U, Debbie W, Harriet T, Liz W, Ruth N

About Lou Collins

Lou Collins is a wife and mother to two incredible teenagers and lives in the beautiful East of England. In her life B.C. (before children!) she practised as a solicitor, specialising in litigation. Her career satisfied her passion for words, for medical matters minus the gore and for winning arguments!

In a quest to find herself again, she has returned to her love of words, and writes mysteries for armchair sleuths who love devilish whodunnits. Lou draws inspiration from her legal background, and traditional mystery writers such as Agatha Christie and Sir Arthur Conan Doyle to pen fast-paced plots that keep you guessing until the very last word.

Don't miss out!

To learn more, find Lou online: loulovesbooks.com or connect in all the places: loulovesbooks.com/lets-connect

Printed in Great Britain
by Amazon